Acknowledgments

I am in the privileged position of being indebted. To col-
leagues and students at the Centre for Interdisciplinary
Aesthetic Studies and the Department of Comparative
Literature, both at Aarhus University, for inspiration,
patience and space; to the Faculty of the Humanities,
Aarhus University for buying me time; to Aarhus University
Research Foundation and to the Danish Research Council
for the Humanities for financial support; to Dr. Anne Varty,
University of London, for revising the English text. Finally,
my greatest debts are those to Birthe Kibsgaard, Centre for
Interdisciplinary Aesthetic Studies, Aarhus University: for
never-ending, generous and far too unselfish help and
support in the establishing of the English text and in the
handling of the manuscript at all phases of the project.
Thank you.

Aarhus, December 1991   *Morten Kyndrup*

Contents

SECOND DEVELOPMENT SECTION

STRETTA

REPRISE

CODA

Intro

Récit. Un jour vers midi du côté du parc Monceau, sur la plate-forme arrière d'un autobus à peu près complet de la ligne S (aujourd'hui 84), j'aperçus un personnage au cou fort long qui portait un feutre mou entouré d'un galon tressé au lieu de ruban. Cet individu interpella tout à coup son voisin en prétendant que celui-ci faisait exprès de lui marcher sur les pieds chaque fois qu'il montait ou descendait des voyageurs. Il abandonna d'ailleurs rapidement la discussion pour se jeter sur une place devenue libre.

Deux heures plus tard, je le revis devant la gare Saint-Lazare en grande conversation avec un ami qui lui conseillait de diminuer l'échancrure de son pardessus en en faisant remonter le bouton supérieur par quelque tailleur compétent.

0

Some Points of Departure

1. Material and Purpose. Many literary studies aim primarily to state something substantial about the *world*. It is far less common to study literature in order to lay bare what *literature* actually is, does, and is able to do.

The interest of this book is the latter. Since literature and art undeniably form a part of the world, it is not impossible, truly, that by doing so we shall make certain statements about the world as well. But since the world is equally undeniably constituted by phenomena other than literature, the statements here will in no way be able, nor intend, to claim any pretension of being exhaustive descriptions of, or theories about, the world at large. Our purpose is not to produce concealed or overt philosophy utilizing literary texts as a medium, the way it, unfortunately, very generally happens in something which calls itself literary criticism/literary science – and which for that reason often turns out to be both miserable criticism and miserable philosophy.

The object of this study is *the novel* as it has developed in Western Europe/USA in a period from the late eighteenth century to the late twentieth century – *and* the questions which a dealing with this realm of objects *as literature* immediately raises. That is *textual analysis, interpretation*. And *history*.

2. The Novel: Aesthetics, history, interpretation. This, of course, is already quite a bit. We shall allow ourselves to take as a point of departure that these phenomena and problems do *exist*; we shall not attempt to substantiate them empirically-genealogically or philosophically. The novel does exist as a rather well-defined genre. The aesthetic, comprehended here only in terms of a predication of kind (and consequently not in the allegedly strict sense of philosophical aesthetics) does exist at least as a fairly stable (but highly changeable) convention. History does exist in the supreme sense that time does, and that phenomena obviously change in time. This fact raises the particular problem of regarding objects and phenomena, which genetically belong to foreign (i.e. from the point of observation) historical contexts, i.e. *nows* which have now become *thens*. We assume that interpretation, analysis, does exist as a potentiality in the sense that given communicative discourses can be examined in order to lay bare their construction and their function. *That* these phenomena, transformations, and activities exist, is in other words a presupposition. What we shall attempt to examine is *how* they do so, which mutual influences, limitations and perspectives they produce: what they *do* and what they *can*. In the centre of our examination as a point of departure is literature. But since literature, art, history, interpretation are entangled with each other as mutually conditioning constructions, it will from time to time be difficult to decide just *what* actually the material of this examination is; novel, interpretation or history. Or the whole formation of meaning. What is figure, and what is ground?

In a traditional notion about "science" of the humanities this may be comprehended as a 'fallacy'. This inquiry will show other 'fallacies' like that. It embraces too much as regards both time and space, and, consequently, it is rather general; in its undisguised polemics against a series of existing paradigms and notions it is highly selective, and consequently does not always offer sufficient coverage; it is not always sure to carefully disguise its opinions as inferences; and it even contradicts itself at certain points. To this should be added the fact that in a supreme sense this book insists on speaking from a position, which it is at the same time its purpose to claim does not exist and cannot exist. It has been forced to choose between silence and this paradoxical speech. It has chosen the latter, modelling itself in a certain structure in order to make visible its own problems of revocation. But it has, as a part of this construction, not totally renounced the former.

These 'fallacies' form part of the book's deliberate, and in our opinion, considering the purpose of the inquiry, *necessary* construction. This is not mentioned here in order to secure ourselves against objections to these dispositions; on the contrary we aim to elucidate the strategy of the inquiry in order to make it even more accessible to criticism. From the start, as a point of departure.

3. Structure. We have chosen to structure the whole inquiry in an overarching form drawn from *music*. This obviously does not turn the many ponderous words of this book into music, unfortunately, one might say. The musical form has been chosen in order to dispatch a series of certain signals about the construction, the intention and the self-acknowledgment of the inquiry. Above all the musical form exposes the decisive emphasis on *course*. Music does not exist (in the capacity of *that* music) outside its concrete course. Something similar applies to the examination performed by this book. It acknowledges itself as something which must *necessarily* be performed by means of several tempi, by means of several alternative elaborations of the same themes. But also as something which, *qua* its own movement, consequently *alters itself*; as something which – just like music – above all *is* its own movement. That is: this book is not modelled on the basis of a certain comprehension, it does not consist of an abstractable "statement" which then in turn has been dressed in a sequentially disposed, verbal-lingual clothing, just because the verbal language actually necessarily unfolds itself in a sequential dimension, as course. On the contrary, it is one of the basic purposes of this inquiry to show that a "statement" like that does not exist. This discourse is itself a rhetorical construction, and what it shows or does not show, penetrates or overlooks, it does *in the capacity of* rhetorical construction. When for example it *reiterates* certain statements at certain different positions within its course, it does so because (it imagines that) the signification of the statements respectively do change as a function of the context's own progressing construction of itself. The fact that it does not, for instance, as is usual in 'scientific' discourses, to any high extent support its points of view by references and explicit markings of positions in relation to the present tradition of this field, similarly is not exclusively due to the author's ignorance; it is due to an intention of permitting the discourse's construction of arguments and inferences to make *itself* probable, of making these themselves shape and defend their positions within the rhetorical construction, rather than ascribing them legitimisation by referring to the present inertia of tradition. Just as a certain motif within music has to justify its own presence and development *within* the proper musical context itself. References are consequently only utilized to the extent they have appeared to be of interest to further studies.

Comprehended like that the movement of the book looks as follows: This *Intro* marks some points of departure as regards the book's own structure. The *Exposition* will subsequently isolate the themes and instruments of the examinations; partly through an exemplary dialogue with five selected strategies for the reading of literary texts, partly through a presentation of the mode of reading and of the concepts and figures employed here; this concludes in a formulation of a series of assertions. The *First Development Section*, will then in one register, based on the philosophy of history, and, one after the other and in a chronological sequence, read five different novels from the period, from Diderot to Calvino. After this laying bare of the *Entwicklungsgeschichte*, the *Second Development Section* will show, through a reading of six other novels from Paul Auster to Jane Austen, and a re-reading of Diderot, one after the other, but now in reversed chronological order, how the result of this historical development now decisively influences the reading of what was already present. In a *Stretta* the readings of the two development sections will subsequently be 'close-ordered', *enggeführt*, in their apparent contradictory paradoxality. The *Reprise* will step back a little to condense some perspectives of the examination's movements, as regards textual analysis, the novel, the aesthetic, and other art forms (the latter through an excursus of film analysis). The finishing *Coda* will finally discuss interpretation as regards its more general conditions, *inter alia* within cultural studies in a broader sense, and the circular movement of the examination will be closed.

The whole examination, consequently, is above all a *movement*. Not just a travelling through an enormous amount of material, but also explicitly a movement of the relative position, from which this material is surveyed; this alteration of the point of observation is continuously produced by the examination itself. That is, a mutually producing movable interplay between material and point of observation is constructed. This interplay constitutes the "*doing*" of this examination. The total statement of the examination is constituted by this movement, by this "doing".

Just as it is the case in music, this examination considers itself obliged to create its signification by means of differences and variations within and towards itself, by means of its own construction. Just as in music, its signification then, its 'meaning' as a whole, is tied to these intrinsic differentiations, is linked with the concrete course, is a function of the movement itself. And just as music it proceeds, turning every apparent point of conclusion into yet another point of departure.

Exposition

Alors. Alors l'autobus est arrivé. Alors j'ai monté dedans. Alors j'ai vu un citoyen qui m'ai saisi l'oeil. Alors j'ai vu son long cou et j'ai vu la tresse qu'il y avait autour de son chapeau. Alors il s'est mis à pester contre son voisin qui lui marchait alors sur les pieds. Alors, il est allé s'asseoir.

Alors, plus tard, je l'ai revu Cour de Rome. Alors il était avec un copain. Alors, il lui disait, le copain: tu devrais faire mettre un autre bouton à ton pardessus. Alors.

1.0

Introduction

Another Point of Departure

At issue: Novel, literature, history, analysis. Concepts which are so extensive and whose signification is so over-coded that in order to be able to even discuss them it may be necessary to pretend to start all over again.

In fact we obviously do *not* start all over again: as regards lingual constructions this would mean to remain in, literally, non-sense. However, one can pretend to start all over again. For example by choosing to regard the existing tradition as an un-obvious and accidental *proposal* for a solution to the problems in question. In other words, by tentatively disregarding the performativity of any tradition within the formation of meaning.

More precisely, we shall try to let the examination be advised and inspired by some of the experiences, suc-cessful as well as less successful, made by the very tra-dition of serious treatment of literature in our part of the world. But preferably without an automatic repetition of the thought tracks whose limitations it is a main intention of this book to expose. The performative force of any present tradition makes it necessary to outline explicitly the con-tours of the immediate landscape as the point of departure from which to suggest another. The clear admission should evidently be added that this critical examination too is a product of this tradition. Nothing comes from nothing.

Without intending to undermine the pretended impartiality of the examination by making introductory confessions we shall first point out some of the instruments which will be used. A point of departure is the notion that any exchange of meaning takes place by means of *signs*: generally *aliquid stat pro aliquo*, or with already Peirce's inclusion of the context "something which stands to somebody for something in some respect or capacity."[1] Corresponding to thought tracks of this type, concrete exchanges of meaning have been described by means of generalized *models* which both catch this "something" (the sign) standing for "something else", regulated by some sort of convention (the code), and place this sign into an exchange which in its simplest form must include a sender and a receiver. Models of this type have been discussed most extensively by Roman Jakobson,[2] but are moreover applied to a number of different contexts and traditions from Bühler's simple analysis of communication to Lyotard's advanced discussions of the sentence.

Here too that kind of *modus operandi* will be applied, at first in simple forms in the discussion of the present traditions. This immediately indicates that this work considers its own basic method as semiotic. It will become clear, however, that this does not imply – and definitely not *a*

---

[1] Collected Papers, II, 228. See the survey in Eco 1984, pp. 14ff.

[2] Among other things in his generalized model of the levels of the lingual expression corresponding to the basic differentiations of the communication model, for instance Jakobson 1960. We shall return to this specific theory.

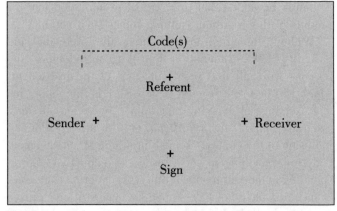

Fig.1. A general model of communication.

priori – accordance with every representative of that tradition which characterizes itself as semiotic. But back to the landscape.

What is Literature?

Literature is a proper name, you might say, rewriting the French theorist of aesthetics Thierry de Duve.[3] He applies the definition to art as such, and writes, incidentally, in *l'imparfait* in order, as it is stated, to emphasize the construction as historical and linked with Modernity, *die Moderne*. In a similar way you might with the Russian formalists state that literature is occurrences in possession of

---

[3] Cf. de Duve 1989, part one *L'art était un nom propre*, De Duve refers among others to Kripke's notions of proper names as "rigid designators", i.e. names which designate the same object in any possible world, see Kripke, 1972, p. 269.

literarity (originally "literaturnost"). But in this way, of course, you just move the problem. If there is a problem.

It is not difficult to state that literature *exists* inasmuch as something called literature over the last couple of centuries in our part of the world has continually been and is still produced, distributed, consumed and criticized. In great quantities, and under the general consensus that *this* is literature. As opposed to everything else which is not literature. But where is the limit? And what sets this limit?

This question is implicitly dealt with by any discussion on literature. Explicitly too, it has played quite a role within the history of the dealing with literature. It is almost possible to single out an independent kind of discourse under the name of "what-is-literature" or "what-is-art".[4]

In this kind of discourse many of the offers seem to place themselves along a main axis which as its extreme poles has the conception of literature as an exclusively *structural* and a *functional identity* respectively.[5] To the structural identity are linked the notions that in various ways literature, by means of its construction as meaning, possesses properties different from the properties of every other similar object; the literary in terms of quality is linked with the literary *object*. In favour of this notion you

---

[4] Cf. Hans Hauge's similar "what-is-history" in his discussion of Hayden White in Hauge 1991.

[5] The designations are due to Todorov (1987) although he does not himself opt in favour of the mutually exclusive position presented here. The distinction is related to (but not completely identical with) Genette's distinction between *constitutivist* and *conditional* conceptions, which we shall use later on, in section 4, as a basis for discussion. To the present, introductory isolation Todorov's distinction, however, is more appropriate.

might for instance count the formalists' above-mentioned "literarity" which they claimed to be able to define and describe.[6] Following this we have also mentioned the model by Roman Jakobson which also considers *the poetical* as one out of six levels or strata present in any lingual statement; literature is at issue when and if this poetical stratum prevails[7]. You might of course count up many more examples of that kind of conception within traditional aesthetic sciences, not to forget within philosophy from Adorno to Heidegger. But moreover a variant may be found in a modern literary semiotician like Robert Scholes who argues in favour of the conception that you are dealing with "literature" when a *duplicity* of one or several of the strata of Jakobson's scheme is at hand[8].

On this side "literature" is thus defined by a kind of intrinsic quality. The other end of the axis, conversely, is made up by the point of view that literature is *nothing* in itself. That only through the confrontation with certain horizons of expectation, through concrete interpretative communities, does the lingual expression become literature. Consequently "literature" is a definition *outside* the object, something which it is supplied with from the outside. This

---

[6] For a survey see the classical monography by Victor Ehrlich (1981), or concretely for instance Šklovskij, 1971.

[7] Jakobson 1960. The other levels are the emotive and the conative, concerning sender and receiver respectively, and the referential, the phatic and the metalingual concerning respectively the referred to, the contact and the code. The poetical concerns the expression itself, i.e. the "expression-ness" of the utterance in question.

[8] Scholes, 1982. The conception develops into almost a systematization of genres (see the scheme, op.cit. p. 31).

notion of course appears immediately counterintuitive, given the fact that the general division into literature and non-literature, by everyday consciousness takes place without any kind of problem and seemingly on the basis of the object; a poem is not the same as a fried sausage. As asserted by Stanley Fish among others, part of the intention obviously has been to challenge deeply rooted conceptions of the opposite camp[9]. But also the so-called deconstructive criticism in the USA (de Man and others) and its avowed philosophical ideal in France, Jacques Derrida, have maintained that the poetic text does not in itself contain distinguished properties of construction. It is the reading which – potentially – makes it literary.[10]

A rigid set up like this makes it evident that none of these extreme positions are reasonable. The notion that the special character of the literary is exclusively linked with the object, with 'structure', is contradicted not only by the fact that literature's elements of construction (tropes, narration, fictionality &c.) all of them form part also of other lingual occurrences. The evident *historical* alteration of what is considered as "literature" supports this contradiction as well.[11] On the other hand it is not difficult to

---

[9] See for instance Fish, 1980.

[10] This radical denial of any intrinsic quality of the texts (of course implying decisive consequences for *what* it is possible to say about them, cf. below) has even motivated the formation of the nickname *Dertyfish* (i.e. *Der*rida, R*orty*, *Fish*) for this position, see Molino, 1989, pp. 9ff).

[11] And if an immediate comparison to pictorial art is permitted, the very relativity of this borderline's position has been convincingly illuminated exactly by the so-called historical movements of avantgarde

demonstrate concretely that (certain) literary constructions by means of their 'literarity' immediately seem to be able to do something which no other lingual construction is able to[12] ("literarity" here understood as broadly linked with text-code/field-receiver).

The either/or-setting of the problems confirmed by this axis consequently appears to be false. Literature is a both/and within this register; not understood as an in-between position or even a mediation between the radical extreme positions of the axis. No, literature seems to be heterogeneously constituted, at one and the same time structurally and functionally determined, by performing a mutual, reiterated engendering of the respective elements of this determinateness. Semiotically it seems obvious that some instance 'between' the concrete literary work and the world is at stake here: "literature" as a code, or rather as a system of codes. "Literature" as the (conventional) rule which assigns exactly this expression to "literature". This code is not placed 'outside' the expression in any sense but the one in which any communicative act only has signification by means of the *relation* between sign and code. In the conception of a more sociological outlook the institutionalized code has been called merely *the institution of*

---

of the 20th century; one may once again point to Duchamp's *pissotière*: art or non-art as a matter of context. The above-mentioned Thierry de Duve (op.cit., 1989) in his essay *Kant (d')après Duchamp* takes the pissotière as the basis of his discussion of what "the aesthetics of Modernity" actually are.

[12] We have sketched this out in *Dinesen versus Postmodernism* (Kyndrup 1992). But for that matter the present book as a whole is supposed to elicit support for this notion.

literature (or – *the institution of art*).[13] The German historian and theorist of literature Peter Bürger has defined the institution as the 'instance' which decides whether discourses about art are 'legitime', i.e. adequate or not[14]. The designation, however is not decisive. Decisive is, on the contrary, the overall assertion of an instance *between* single work and world, an instance which as a code of meaning defines and regulates both production and reception of art/literature. This code has no concrete 'topos' (although for instance the literary system as a whole obviously also expresses itself as visible installations). This code is, what might be called an 'optical' feature of the formation of meaning, i.e. it is a feature of *the object as meaning*. This makes the code *historical* as a category, i.e. makes it something which emerged as a part of and which is included in a complicated system of other codes of meaning; all in all codes like these are the precondition of any intelligible exchange of meaning as a whole. And *the code changes* under the influence of both displacements within the object which it 'signifies' (literature) and alterations within the supreme system of codes of which the code forms a part.

This construction evidently has a lot of consequences, *inter alia* as regards the overall concept of "history" and "interpretation". We shall return to these later. For the moment we shall just note that the outlined construction

---

[13] See for instance Bürger, 1974 and 1979 and Sanders 1981. See also the introduction of Bürger's conceptions in Kyndrup, 1986, pp. 68-83.

[14] Bürger, 1983, p. 91: "Man kann die herrschende Institution Kunst auffassen als diejenige Instanz, die legitime Diskurse über Kunst von solchen unterscheidet, die nicht-legitim sind".

does not hold any elements which limit it to literature: if at all adequate, it seems to be applicable to art as such.

What is 'Literary Criticism'?

Readings of literature by more or less 'professional' readers are called literary criticism. Or literary understanding, literary analysis, literary science, literary history, literary interpretation, literary intermediation ... the list of conceptualizations is as long as the often mutually contradictory definitions of what is what. It is, consequently, only as a temporary, supreme conceptualization in a crude sense that we have used the Anglo-Saxon designation "literary criticism" as a headline.

The paradox of the fact that the academic, pedagogical and journalistic activity *round* art keeps many more people busy (who are furthermore mostly much better paid!) than does the exercising of artistic activity itself – despite the fact that the latter as the cause of the former must be said to be absolutely primary, has often been emphasized. And especially with regard to literature it has quite incisively been remarked that what pretends to be academic dealing with literature, in fact generally deals with anything but literature.[15]

Both the large force and the diversity of interests have very good reasons; reasons concerning the fact that art and literature and its intermediation hold certain positions, play certain roles within the formation of meaning as a whole within our kind of society, roles which go beyond their own immediate construction of meaning. Art and in particular

---

[15] Paul de Man *The Resistance to Theory* (de Man, 1986), p. 26.

literature have historically acted *inter alia* as vehicles to parts of the construction of "the public" and to general formation within the educational system (the national literatures). This in itself of course does not imply any 'abuse'. It is, however, absolutely necessary to include these functional relationships when evaluating and analyzing the present thinking about reading of literature: the contexts of utilization necessarily become a part of the very meaning-construction "literature".

Generally, the single methods do not show any overt recognition of the way in which their concrete appearances are linked with their positions and functions – including particularly which *limitations* their specific approaches more or less necessarily activate. Conversely, the history of institutional dealing with literature demonstrates a unanimous tendency towards the fact that single methods 'rule' within certain periods and within certain contexts, and that these often in a tremendously explicit exclusion of other methods understand themselves as *exhaustive* of the literature they are dealing with.[16]

This state of *fight* has its reasons as well, connected to the above-mentioned special positions and functions of the dealing with literature, and to more supreme changes of ideological and scientific paradigms. Still this state of things seems at best meaningless to many historians of theory. At worst it seems to obstruct the achievement of appropriate insight, because it hinders dialogue between the differing approaches or methods, a dialogue which

---

[16] For a thorough discussion of the regimes of methods within the modern American academic context see Jonathan Culler's essay *Literary Criticism and the American University*, in Culler, 1988.

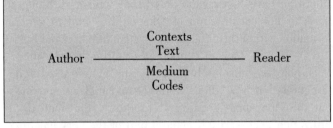

Fig. 2. Scholes' model according to Jakobson.

–viewing the problem from just a little distance – appears as undoubtedly fruitful. Only very few, however, argue directly in favour of *pluralism* within the critical approach. A significant example is Northrop Frye's already classic *Anatomy of Criticism*. Frye deals with four types of literary criticism: historical, ethical, archetypal, and rhetorical criticism. His book, as it is said, "...attacks no methods of criticism [...] what it attacks is the barriers between the methods".[17]

Frye's typology is rather crude, but his discussion of the types is extensive. A more fine-meshed typology is outlined by Robert Scholes, assuming that it is possible simply to segregate the schools of criticism according to Jakobson's six strata of communication, as mentioned above (fig. 2).

---

[17] Frye, 1973, p. 341. The book concludes with an optimism according to which the development almost automatically will turn into the (to Frye) right direction. The events since 1957 (when *Anatomy of Criticism* originally was published) have not been able to fully confirm this assumption.

Another example of pluralism as a conscious method is Wayne C. Booth's *Critical Understanding. The Powers and Limits of Pluralism* (1979).

Exposition

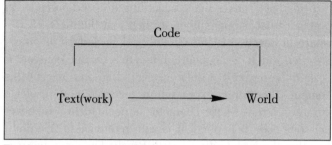

Fig. 3.

Consequently, to the instance of "author", the author-oriented schools should match (intentional criticism, psychoanalytical (author)oriented criticism & c.), to the instance of "the reader" should match the reader oriented (aesthetics of reception, sociology of literature), to the instance of "text" for instance New Criticism, to "codes" structuralist and formalist, and so on.[18]

It is true that Scholes' model is capable of sorting out roughly which *relations* of the literary work are in the centre of attention of the respective methods.[19] The problem is that it does not really catch the problem of which *kind* of semiotic operation these methods conduct within their respective fields of interest.

Any analysis, description, interpretation &c. of a literary text may be regarded as fundamentally a sort of re-writing of something specific and concrete ("literature") into something more general (common meaning, "the world"). This

[18] Scholes, 1982, pp. 7ff.

[19] Scholes' model crudely matches the model of *interests of relation* which we have once suggested (see Kyndrup 1980, pp. 27ff). The critique below will thus also include this one.

"writing back" takes place according to a certain code. In practice what happens is most often that the piece of literature in question is immediately acknowledged as an *expression*, which consequently refers to a certain 'content': it is then the purpose of the analysis to find and present this content. The literary expression is regarded as a *sign* for a certain referent whose character is decided by whichever concrete code is applied. It is with reference to this problem that the New Critic Cleanth Brooks has made the reasonable remark that precisely the compulsion of "communication theory" is a main problem to text reading.[20]

This outline does not permit a further discussion of the *reasons* why a "referential fallacy" of this kind has been so predominant within the understanding of the literature of Modernity. Of course the referential fallacy is connected with the above-mentioned positioning and instrumental utilization of literature; but its predominance has its basis also in the existence of more supreme codes of meaning generation (as for example the one which Jameson designates the 'depth'-model[21]). Whereas then the mechanism, crudely regarded, remains constant, the concrete codes change. Psychoanalytic-oriented analysis of literature reads the work as expression of mental states and processes within

---

[20] See for instance the chapter *What does Poetry Communicate* in Brooks, 1971. We shall return to Brooks in detail below in chapter 1.1.3.

[21] See Fredric Jameson, 1984. Jameson notices the almost compulsory inscription by Modernity of the world of phenomena into a figure of reflection according to which the real, the substance, the truth is hidden by/under/within appearances (*Schein/Wesen*, latent/manifest, form/content &c.).

the psyche (whether in general or for instance of the author) of the kind which it regards as important. Historical-materialist criticism finds in the work an expression of the basic historical relations it considers to be prevalent within its space of emergence. The structuralist recognizes certain structural configurations in the work, either of the kind which he has pointed out to be general to for instance any narration or perhaps in the position of arche-structures of the civilization in question. The New Critic is able to demonstrate that the apparently unintelligible modernist poem is in effect an expression of the highest imaginable adequacy to this or that paradox within reality. And finally different kinds of understanding of literature as part of *Geistesgeschichte* are able to conceptualize the works as the expressions of these or those constructions of that history. And, one might add, deconstructive criticism is able to show that the presupposition about the *unity* of the single work which is an implicit part of almost every method within Modernity is constitutionally untenable; the analyses by deconstruction may consequently to some extent remain at the same level as the ones they criticize, *qua* their being tied to the very emphatic underlining that the texts show ('are expressive of') this untenability.

Within this supreme sign/referent-community an additional couple of rough differentiations may be established. One according to which *side* of the model (cf. fig. 4) the methods direct themselves: towards the aesthetics of production (to the left), or what is finally becoming more common, towards the aesthetics of reception (to the right). The axes may also be sorted out according to their interest as regards the literary work. These interests may be pre-

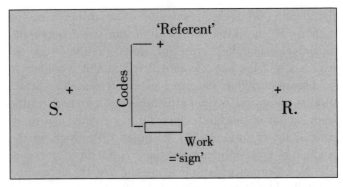

Fig. 4

dominantly *ontological*, i.e. directed towards an analysis of
the status of the literary work *within* reality. They may be
predominantly *cognitive*, i.e. directed towards the cognitive
utterance of the works *about* the reality. And finally they
may be predominantly *pragmatical/rhetorical*, i.e. directed
at first primarily towards the works *as* living realities, as
constructions of meaning, as "doings".

It is not difficult to realize that for instance the directions of interest within the latter differentiation are in no
way mutually exclusive; in fact they may follow one another
or be juxtaposed in the concrete analysis. This is actually
what they are going to be, in the concrete readings of literature later on in this book. The almost unprecedentedly
crude generalizations we have made here as an introduction, do not aim to ridicule schools and traditions whose
merits are indubitable. Our particular underlining of the
extension of the referential fallacy does not intend to insist
that literature could not or should not be read as "sign",
implying "reference". We have tried, as a point of departure, to draw critical attention to the fact that the opera-

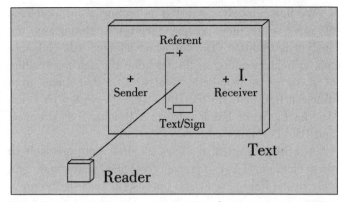

Fig. 5. The text's implicit position of interpretant (I) is part of the text itself – and thus different from the 'factual' reader instance.

tions of decoding have traditionally been made from a point of view, as if the position of the analysis were the same as that or those positions of interpretant held by the literature in question within its own construction of meaning. What we are going to argue later on is not, then, that the works are not allowed to, or not able to mean anything. We shall argue, on the contrary, that what they might mean or what you might choose to let them mean, they must in all circumstances 'mean' as *a rhetorical whole* (which, obviously, is not necessarily 'whole'). This notion is roughly outlined by the perspective of fig. 5. We shall return to this.

The Course of the Exposition

The main purpose of this first section is to introduce the points of view and methods which are used by this book, in order, as a prelude to the development sections, to make it possible to formulate some preliminary theses.

We have already suggested an outline of the problems of analysis as they present themselves throughout the analytical tradition. The following chapter will elaborate this critical reception of the tradition through the reading of a series of concrete theoretical contributions from different traditions, in the shape of texts written by Erich Auerbach, Georg Lukács, Cleanth Brooks, A.J. Greimas, and Paul de Man.

After these critical readings we shall more precisely in three chapters (1.2-1.4) present tools and terminology. Not only in the field of analysis, but also as regards the problematics of history and aesthetics. The exposition will terminate in a preliminary wording of the hypotheses concerning the item examined (1.5).

1.1
Critical Readings

1.1.1 'Interpretations of the Real' (Auerbach)

As our first example we shall present Erich Auerbach's already almost classic study *Mimesis*, subtitled *Dargestellte Wirklichkeit in der abendländischen Literatur*, 1946.[1] It is true that this work explicitly does not give any manifesto for its literary criticism, and thus does not have any pre-dominating pretension about *completeness* when dealing with the analyzed works. On the contrary, Auerbach expli-citly reduces his object down to '...die Interpretation des Wirklichen durch literarische Darstellung oder "Nachah-mung"'[2] Still, on the other hand, no critical consciousness is obviously singled out according to the systematic ex-clusions of certain dimensions of the texts which charac-terizes the analyses. Our reason for choosing Auerbach here is that these exclusions are arche-typical within traditional readings of literature. Our aim is not to denounce his work altogether. It does not in fact deserve that either: *Mimesis* is within its special point of view an extremely sharp, deeply read and inspiring study which actually deserves its

---

[1] Bern, 1946. References below apply to this original edition.

[2] Op.cit. p. 494.

good reputation. It is, on the other hand, above all usually commended for its concrete *analyses*. And it is precisely in the analyses that certain closures, as we shall see, become highly obvious. In accordance with our purpose and the structure of the book itself we shall just pick out one of Auerbach's chapters.[3] The 12th and last chapter but two, *Im Hôtel de La Mole*, discusses three extracts by Stendhal, Balzac and Flaubert, respectively, to illustrate the development within 19th-century French realism.

Auerbach's analyses of the three extracts aim explicitly to throw light on a movement of development within what is called "modern serious realism". As regards the extract from *Le Rouge et le Noir* (1830) Auerbach convincingly demonstrates that the presented conflict is intelligible only on the basis of a thorough knowledge of the situation in France at the time of restoration. Obviously he is perfectly right about that. What is more interesting in this connection, however, is Auerbach's astonishing blindness as regards the levels of the *enunciation* of the quoted extracts. He writes:

> Der Abbé wird hier als vrai parvenu bezeichnet, der die Ehre, bei einem großen Herrn zu speisen, hoch zu schätzen weiß und Juliens Äußerungen daher mißbilligt; zur Begründung der Mißbilligung hätte Stendhal auch Anführen können, daß die kritiklose Unterwerfung unter das Böse dieser Welt, im vollen

---

[3] On a previous occasion we have dealt with Auerbach's work (Kyndrup and Stæhr 1982, vol. 1, esp. pp. 83-90) and parts of the debate over it. *Mimesis* itself is constructed as a series of concrete readings of small extracts of texts from a literature 'presenting reality' from Antiquity to 20th century. The book has been translated into several languages.

Bewußtsein, das es böse ist, eine für strenge Jansenisten typische Haltung ist; und der Abbé Pirard ist Jansenist. [p. 402]

What is interesting in Auerbach's opinion is only *what* the abbot is presented as, not by whom, i.e. at which level of the enunciation of the text. It does appear from the subjunctive construction a little further on that Auerbach *schlicht und einfach* regards "Stendhal" as the sender of the text. Physically he certainly is, being its author, but by equalizing these instances Auerbach excludes himself from even considering the *narrative* construction of the literary text in question. In fact this construction positions the narrator of the text in such a way that it/he commands a certain level of *insight* (and is subject to certain limitations) in relation to what is narrated; an insight and a construction which decisively determine the meaning of the text as realized through the act of reading, because the narrative insight of the text into what it narrates is also, actually, the reader's channel for apprehension of the narrated. Auerbach, in the ensuing discussion, continues this complete identification of the text's levels of insight and blockings with those of the author: with the support of a sketch of Stendhal's life history it is argued that his realism (= his work) is a product of his fight for self-affirmation (412). Indeed, on the basis of the author's biography, Auerbach is even able to consider it probable that Stendhal has 'over-exposed' certain perspectives (of the 'presented reality', 406-07).

What is important in this context is to realize the actual perspective through which Auerbach reads the text, or which axiological code, said or unsaid, is used. The metaphorical register of the sequences of evaluation in

Auerbach may give a clue. It is argued – positively – that certain conditions "...auf eine so genaue und reale Weise" are woven into the action (403), and that Stendhal's works are "...enger, wesentlicher, bewußter und konkreter" linked with the state of things during this period compared with Rousseau and Goethe (404). An extensive number of parallel examples might be advanced. Closeness, and substantiality are consistently valorized as positive, linked with the concrete and the real, whereas distance, superficiality, nonauthenticity – as for instance ascribed to the merging of styles in Romanticism, represented by Hugo, are valorized as negative.

These axes of value are supported by the reading of Balzac. Balzac's writings are ascribed "weit mehr Wirklichkeitsnähe" (415), and the analysis of the extract[4] exposes above all the *accordance* between person and environment, the "Stileinheit" (417) of environment which prevails spontaneously and without motivation. Compared to that of his predecessors, Balzac's realism is furthermore designated as 'far more deeply' linked with its time (428) and the form common to Stendhal-Balzac, the combination of seriousness and everydayness is characterized as

> ...weit entscheidender, echter, wichtiger als die der Gruppe Victor Hugos, die das Sublime mit dem Grotesque vereinen wollte (427).[5]

---

[4] From *Le Père Goriot* (1834) which we shall discuss extensively in Chapter 2.2 below.

[5] It may be a part of this picture that Auerbach's hypothesis of modern, 'serious' realism (and consequently implicitly altogether which part literature is able to play within Modernity) is the very statement of

Perhaps Auerbach's method of analysis is to be most clearly elucidated by his discussion of a scene from Flaubert's *Madame Bovary* (1857)[6]. This novel's very special construction of enunciation is characterized as follows (once again based on a concrete quotation):

> Zwar ist durchaus nicht Flauberts, sondern allein Emmas Existenz in diesen Worten; Flaubert tut nichts als das Material, das sie bietet, in seiner vollen Subjektivität sprachreif zu machen (430),

and a little later

> Es sind zwar in der Tat einige paradigmatische Anlässe von Emmas Widerwillen [i.e. against the husband], aber sie sind sehr planvoll vom Schriftsteller, nicht im Affekt von Emma so zusammengestellt worden (430-31)

> Wir hören zwar den Schriftsteller sprechen; aber er äußert keine Meinung und kommentiert nicht. Seine Rolle beschränkt sich darauf, die Vorgänge auszuwählen und sie in Sprache um-

---

its ability to exceed the classic separation of levels of style which for instance in Renaissance were obligatory. In Auerbach's opinion a serious realism like that exists throughout history when it is possible. This is the transhistorical conceptualization which makes Wellek accuse Auerbach of confusing two mutually incompatible concepts of realism throughout his analyses. See René Wellek: Auerbach's Special Realism, in *The Kenyon Review* vol. XVI, No. 2, 1954. Cf. also Kyndrup and Stæhr, op.cit. 1982.

What is interesting here, however, is rather the level and the kind of Auerbach's rhetoric than the literary-historical stringency of his concepts. More decisive, more genuine, more authentic, more important in terms of which criterion? Further below.

[6] Which we are also to discuss below, in the Second Development Section, Ch. 3.5.

zusetzen; und zwar geschieht dies, in der Überzeugung, daß ein jeder Vorgang, wenn es gelingt, ihn rein und vollständig auszudrücken, sich selbst und die an ihm beteiligten Menschen vollkommen interpretiere; weit besser und vollständiger, als irgendeine noch dazugefügte Meinung oder Beurteilung es tun könnte. Auf dieser Überzeugung, also auf einem tiefen Vertrauen in die Wahrheit der verantwortungsvoll, redlich und sorgfältig verwendeten Sprache, beruht Flauberts Kunstübung. (432)

Although Auerbach here of course explicitly comments upon a certain *stylistic* construction he does not seem far from having the opinion that reality almost 'itself' speaks 'the truth'. He claims to be able to make a distinction (in the mid-quotation) between what the author does, and what the author's person of fiction, Emma, does: *she* is the one delivering the material (first quotation). The description *is* its own interpretation, if sufficiently "clean" and "complete". Opinions and judgments are 'added to' the clean description, and above all disturbing the truth of it. Flaubert meets these demands, much more so than his two predecessors; with Flaubert's realism Romanticism is consequently definitely *conquered* (437), as Flaubert's project is to 'force language into giving the truth about the objects of his regarding' (436).

And it seems that this project, one might add, is Auerbach's as well. At any rate judging from the implicit valorisations, and obviously because the preconditions and consequences, in short whatever is problematic about Flaubert's project, is not even hinted at. The basic notion seems to be that reality, the world (W. in fig. 1) is transformed into a text (T.) by an author (A.). But A. may hold different positions within this transformation: the clearer A. positions

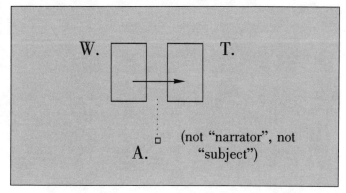

Fig. 1. The instance A. (here "author") is ideally totally outside the transformation

himself (by removing himself into the transformation, 'upwards' in fig. 1), the more artificial T. becomes, and the less W. and T 'resemble' each other. And conversely: the less artificial the discourse T. appears to be, the greater is its similarity with the world (i.e. the more "realistic" is the text). In Auerbach, consequently, we meet an absolute presupposition about the implicit *well-ordered* character of the world (the language). For *if* one had presupposed the world in itself to be contingent, and if one had still been dealing with an 'ordered' text, then this relation would have turned out to have the opposite character (i.e. the text being absolutely untrue). An elaboration like that from contingency into intelligible structure would then have to be assumed to imply the maximum artificiality in terms of 'added elaboration'. Whether or not this 'objective' artificiality would then appear as such would be a matter of convention, of institutional framing. On the basis of this you might consequently just as rightly claim that the seemingly absence of the narrator in Flaubert's narrative

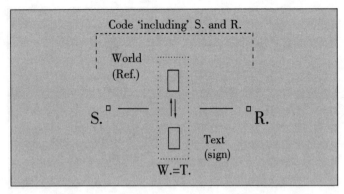

Fig. 2. Auerbach's construction of code in the general model of communication.

expresses an accordingly *greater* extent of narrative organization – which according to Auerbach's own value axes should then be regarded as 'subjective' and consequently (in Auerbach's own sense) as 'non-authentic' (and Auerbach does not even operate with a "narrator", but still talks directly about the corporeal author).

In terms of the model of communication it becomes the function of the code of operation to make a critical comparison of the text as a "sign" to the world as its "referent"; the axiology of the code will then have as its basis the extent of resemblance (a high degree of resemblance being most positive). Indeed, the code also even tries to integrate the instances of sender and receiver by regarding a *dissolution* of them as such as the optimum. As W. (= world as object) and T. (fig. 2) merge, the instance of the sender is, as mentioned, drawn 'into' the discourse; the same thing happens to the receiver as the work is assumed to merge with the world (as referent).

Consequently, what Auerbach does *not* consider in the

method and perspective of these readings[7] is the character of the lingual expression as *communicative construction* which apart from what may be operatively distinguishable as a "statement" at any rate also unfolds an *enunciation*; a system of sending and receiving (and thus statement-organising) instances also *within* the text. Consequently, the apparent non-artificial self-organisation of Flaubert's text is due neither to reality nor to Emma, but on the contrary to Flaubert's radical artificiality. The character of this construction might easily be described and analyzed. That is to say, not just how it *appears* (very well outlined by Auerbach), but how it actually constructs this appearance (which Auerbach ignores).

To this should finally be added Auerbach's renunciation of the discussion on what might be called the "subject-/object-relation of enunciation" or, put in another way, the specific character of the text's relation to, including its knowledge about, its own utterance. We shall return to these problems.

1.1.2 The Call for Objective Subjectivity (Lukács)

The next example is also in German and it is drawn from the Hungarian theorist of aesthetics and literature *Georg Lukács*. The radical orientation towards literature's relation with the reality which it immediately presents or represents is common to Lukács and Auerbach. Their concrete notions of this relation are, however, almost diametrically opposed:

---

[7] Once again underlining that the critique applies only to certain concrete exclusions within certain concrete readings; it does not claim to express qualified attitude to Auerbach's project as a whole.

Auerbach wants the author (i.e. the narrator) totally *out* of the narrated, and thus regards Flaubert's novels as the most developed prose fiction of the 19th century, whereas Lukács wants the same instance to organize the material visibly and overtly – and consequently regards Flaubert's work as a *déroute* of realism. And both, so to say, speak on behalf of reality.

Ever since 1915 when Georg Lukács, at the age of thirty, got in touch with the Labour movement he was, as a theorist of aesthetics and literature a declared *materialist* and politically, a Marxist. But even within this framework the oscillations of his theories are considerable (not to mention the distance to his pre-marxist works, e.g. *Die Theorie des Romans* of 1914-15). The discussion here of Lukács' paper *Erzählen oder Beschreiben* of 1935-36[8] in no way pretends – just as the Auerbach example above – to extend its conclusions to the work of Lukács as a whole. Our only purpose is to show a specific way of reading a

---

[8] Published in the Moscow (German language) periodical *Internationale Literatur*, 1936. Lukács himself was exiled in Moscow during these years, and the context of emergence – on the eve of Stalin's excesses of purge – is beyond any doubt very important to the concrete wording of the text. This applies particularly to its polemical context formed by the so-called debate about expressionism with among others Brecht (who chose to keep rather a low profile for strategic reasons). A couple of years later Lukács himself was by the way very close to being removed; only his international fame seems to have saved him, so that he 'only' lost his official positions.

This historical context as a whole, however, is without importance *here* where we do not discuss the *why* of the Lukács text, but its elaboration regarded as an exemplary piece of literary analysis.

The quotations below refer to the edition printed in *Essays über Realismus*, in *Werke*, vol. 4, Berlin 1971 (Lukács 1971).

concrete piece of work, particularly in order to make visible *the type* of some of its concrete closures – and hesitating openings.

Lukács' extensive paper argues in favour of a typological bipartition of epic literature, using the 19th century as the primary realm of examples, but in principle claiming universal validity. The labels are – as stated in the title of the paper – "narrating" and "describing", respectively.

With support in examples from texts, and quotations from authors, Lukács argues in favour of the absolute divergence of the two types. *Description* is in the 19th century primarily found in Flaubert and Zola (with tracks up to the 20th century represented by Joyce and Dos Passos among others). "Description" is based on 'observation' of the *outer* attributes of reality, says Lukács. It thus has a fundamentally 'accidental' character. The accidental stage of a given scene remains indeed accidental and outward; only by being turned into an ironical symbol it may become even just 'partly' justified as art. This happens to some extent in Flaubert. But in Zola it all goes wrong:

> ...Wenn aber bei Zola das Symbol eine soziale Monumentalität erhalten soll, wenn es die Aufgabe hat, einer an sich bedeutungslosen Episode den Stempel großer sozialer Bedeutung aufzudrücken, so wird die Sphäre der echten Kunst verlassen. *Die Metapher wird zur Wirchlichkeit aufgebauscht.* Ein zufälliger Zug, eine zufällige Ähnlichkeit, eine zufällige Stimmung, ein zufälliges Zusammentreffen soll unmittelbar Ausdruck großer gesellschaftlicher Zusammenhänge sein. Beispiele ließen sich aus jedem Roman Zolas massenhaft anführen [202, italics added]

A mode of generating like that, it is said, is fundamentally *false*: it keeps the reader in a state of completely detached observation, deprived of 'real epic coherence' (205) in a levelled universe constructed on the basis of 'false objectivity'.

Against this we have the 'real epic art', as found in Scott, Stendhal, Balzac and Tol'stoj – and further on in Gor'kij and Andersen Nexø, among others. There is nothing 'incidental' about 'necessity'. The details of Balzac are, as opposed to those of Zola, necessary because the description here is not a purpose in itself: Balzac's description is

> ...nichts weiter als eine breite Fundamentierung für das entscheidende neue Element: für die Einbeziehung des Dramatischen in den Aufbau des Romans [204]

The presentation does not aim at making the reader observe the outer forms of appearance of the presented; no, here the relation takes the shape of an *experience* of the presented in its *intrinsic* truth, its *why*. As worded supremely:

> Die epische Kunst – und selbstverständlich auch die Kunst des Romans – besteht in der Entdeckung der jeweils zeitgemäßen und bezeichnenden, menschlich-bedeutsamen Züge der gesellschaftlichen Praxis, Der Mensch will sein eigenes deutlicheres, gesteigertes Spiegelbild, das Spiegelbild seiner gesellschaftlichen Praxis in der epischen Poesie erhalten. Die Kunst des Epikers besteht gerade in der richtigen Verteilung der Gewichte, in der rechten Betonung des Wesentlichen. Er wirkt desto hinreißender und allgemeiner, je mehr bei ihm dieses Wesentliche, der Mensch und seine gesellschaftliche Praxis, nicht als ausgeklügeltes Kunstprodukt, als Ergebnis einer Virtuosität erscheint, sondern als etwas naturhaft Gewachsenes, als etwas nicht Erfundenes, sondern bloß Entdecktes. [212-13]

Lukács also suggests that certain elements within the epic

construction correspond to the two main types. The narration is, it is said, generally constructed by means of an omniscient narrator who has an also temporal distance to his material (making the necessary selection possible). This omniscience makes the reader 'confident' and thus allows him to experience. As opposed to this, the "description" is oriented towards the *contemporary*, towards an immensity of different, casual elements, thus also often intermediated as observed from differing points of view and perspectives. This draws the reader out of the universe of the narrated. As mentioned Lukács emphasizes that this apparent objectivity of description is *false* (as for instance the description of single individuals' subjective moods exclusively structured by chronology is characterized as 'false subjectivity'): "description" is grounded upon a "fundamentally false notion of reality", upon a "clearly subjective prejudice" [208], that is to say the one by which the curves of meaning, the peaks, are engendered as something added, being a product of art. Against this we have the narrating realism's 'unprejudiced correct, deep and extensive poetical reflection' [209]: the peaks are here based on the object ('reality') – not on the construction of meaning. In accordance with the basic notions of this thinking Lukács emphasizes that the emergence of the 'descriptive' and consequently false methods are not casual either. Description is a product of the development of capitalism, leading humanity to a 'lower' level. It is even said that '...the poetic level of life is declining – but literature is overemphasizing this decline' [213]. As a support of the objectivity of this development a parallel development within the visual arts is drawn as an example:

...es ist keineswegs zufällig, daß zur selben Zeit, in der die beschreibend malerischen Bestrebungen des Naturalismus die Menschen der Literatur zu Bestandteilen von Stilleben erniedrigten, auch die Malerei ihre Fähigkeit des erhöhten sinnlichen Ausdrucks verlor. Die Porträts von Cézanne sind ebenso bloße Stilleben, verglichen mit der menschlich-seelischen Totalität der Porträts von Tizian oder Rembrandt, wie die Menschen Goncourts oder Zolas im Vergleich zu Balzac oder Tolstoi. [224-225]

The seeming truth is indeed false. And "truth" is, according to Lukács, a condition of art *sine qva non*.

In Lukács we obviously deal with an extremely significant example of the so-called *depth* model which is so characteristic to the coding of meaning within Modernity from Hegel's philosophy to Freud's psychoanalysis. The surface, the seeming, the appearances must be *expressive* of underlying contents, substances, incentives. Being in their turn 'objective', constant, thus contrasting the fickle subjectivity of expressions.

In order to be good literature, a text must, for Lukács, demonstrate primarily a fundamental *congruence as to content* with the reality. And this above all means: it must reconstruct the special relationship between the *Schein* of the world of senses, its seeming, its immediate appearance, and the *Wesen* of reality, its genuine nature. Furthermore, this reconstruction is to perform a kind of intensification, a kind of clarification of the nature of this basic state of things (including these relations). Lukács constantly talks about the *revelation* ("Entdeckung") of phenomena: an "objective" truth is at hand, and this is the one into which the works, notwithstanding the contingency of the sensory world, must produce insight. *Cognition* thus becomes the

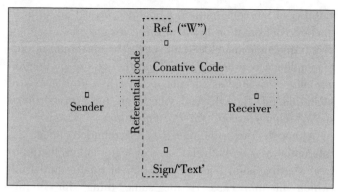

Fig. 3. The starting point of the implication cannot be located as it is double-sided. An appropriate (cognitive) effect will always be due to a 'correct' reflection, and a correct reflection in turn will also have an appropriate effect. Consequently, truth is *unable* to be inappropriate, and the appropriate *is* true. This short-circuit construction results (among many other things) in a peculiar relationship between literature, politics of literature and theory of literature in the part of the world with a Communist outlook since the 1930s. It does, however, also here force Lukács to taking enunciation into consideration, at least by way of suggestion, cf. below.

actual purpose of the novel. And this cognition is naturally assumed to be given to the recipient(s) of the work. This actually implies a peculiar transformation of codes. *The criterion* for any evaluation of the quality of the work (S) will be the extent of its accordance with the nature of the world, W. The work is unambiguously generated by its referential dimension, by its positions of sign and reference. But still the cognitive *effect* of the work is its basic *raison d'être*. What happens is in fact a kind of projection of an intentionality of action linked to aesthetics of reception into the register of aesthetics of production. Fortunately (for the stability of the construction) a contrast, or just an (un)productive confrontation between these axes seems to be out of the question in Lukács' universe: the maximum of correspondence between W and T on the axis of production *automatically* implies the maximum effect on the axis of reception (cf. fig. 3). And vice versa on a proportional scale.[9] *Keine Hexerei. Nur Präsupposition.*

Although the cognitive level, grounded upon the referential axis, is both the basis of legitimation, the practical starting point and the criterion of quality and truth (which in this case is the same thing) for literary production, it is interesting to notice the way in which Lukács nevertheless includes the rhetorical construction of the works, their *enunciation*, into his theory. He does so only peripherally, but still significantly compared to so many others (Auerbach, for instance). In the seemingly immediate aporia Lukács underlines what he calls the role of the "author" in relation to the presented world.[10] It is

---

[9] Precisely this exclusion has been characteristic of above all Soviet (and related Eastern European) theories of literature: it has constantly insisted on regarding the changing strategies of literary politics (the axis of recipient outlook) as determined by 'objective' mechanisms of reflection (the referential axis). Even the most far-fetched beautifications thus have had to – and been able to – be referred to the objective nature of reality. This has indeed caused some rather grotesque constructions along the road, cf. the famous 'metaphor of building' from the discussions 1932-34 (see Kyndrup & Stæhr, 1982, Lunačarskij's metaphor of building is quoted in vol. 1, p. 27 after Ivanov, 1975).

[10] Of course technically speaking it is the *narrator* of the text who is at issue. Lukács emphasizes this text-analytically primitive character of his construction by also generally paralleling competence and insight in the "narrator" instance of the text with competence and insight of the authors of the novels in flesh and blood, for instance the way these

emphasized that the engendering of *objective* truth must take place through an extremely rigid and clear organization of 'real' material by means of the author(/narrator) instance. And conversely that the 'let-material-speak-itself' which in Auerbach above was made the ideal of a reality-representing narrative discourse, deteriorates into "false objectivity", into mere lie and thus miserable art. Lukács consequently is able to agree with Flaubert when the latter (about his *L'education sentimentale*) says that it is "too true".[11] The only difference is that to Lukács this characteristic is negative, whereas to Flaubert – with a certain

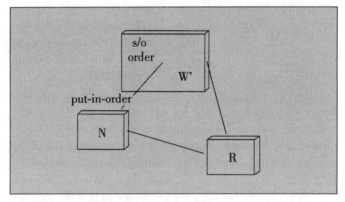

Fig. 4. The existing 'order' of the presented world (W') is only realized in the work qua the narrator's (N) *ordering it* qua the presentation of it; *this* put-in-order/order movement thus appears to the real reader, in casu Lukács, as an exemplary subject/object-relation.

---

insights or lack of insights appear from non-fictional writings or simply biographical facts of the authors.

[11] Quoted by Lukács op.cit. 1971, p. 207f.

appropriate regret for the unfortunate aesthetic consequences of this necessary truthfulness – it is basically
positive.

Lukács reasonably realizes that if his prescriptive notion
of a certain *order* within the presented 'world' of the work,
within the enounced, within what may metaphorically be
called the horizontal level of the work, if this notion is to
be maintained it must necessarily be matched by a notion
of a *putting-in-order* within the presentation of the work,
within its enunciation, within its vertical level (cf. fig. 4).
As the enounced statement, the world, to Lukács is not *in
reality* contingent, though it may *appear* as such, exactly
the *relation between (contingent) appearance and (ordered)
contents of substance* becomes the obligatory main purpose
of any work, based on the cognitive primary ambition.
Obviously this elicits great possibilities for the legitimation
of anything: the inherent tautological linkings make it
possible to substitute the conventional code in question
(here Marxism-Leninism) by any other code structurally
congruent with it.[12] This problem which necessarily is a
part of any thorough conception which claims privilege as
to truth and insight *objectively*, cannot, naturally, be solved
by Lukács. What he can do, however, is to take care of a
certain symmetry between the instances so that the framing
does not collapse immediately because of inescapable
inherent aporiae. And this is what he does. He argues in
favour of structural congruence between the elaborations of

---

[12] And potentially most supreme codes will be: "history", cf. "socialist
realism" in Eastern Europe and China throughout the twentieth century,
has by means of this register been able to make anything "truthful", and
consequently great art.

the subject/object-relation respectively at all levels. The double determinateness (cf. once again fig. 4), which is the condition of the presented subject of the horizontal level of the work, between on the one hand submission to an 'objective' order, and on the other hand the possession of certain ('ordering') possibilities in relation to this order (that is to the extent that they are making order in accordance with the objective historical forces of alteration) – this double determinateness is *repeated* within the relation between author/narrator and the world of the work in the vertical dimension of the work, in the enunciation. You can finally see the structure repeated in the stipulation of the reader's relationship to this narrative construction as a whole (R in the figure), the latter instance implicitly represented also by the discourse of criticism itself.

Things are straight, then, or more precisely: the relation between order and ordering is straight. Just as the protagonist controls his world, the enunciation controls the enounced and the reader controls the utterance overall. The work, consequently, is told the way the world ('objectively') is told.

Lukács' way of thinking thus to some extent includes the rhetorical construction of the work, includes a certain view of the work as a sign, seen as a whole, and not only within a derivation of reference called "statement". It is true that this happens in the most simple way imaginable, the enounced enunciation's instances ("narrator(s)", "implied reader") are merely identified with the ones of the virtual, real enunciation (author, real reader). This narrows possibilities of complexity in the analysis; and as a consequence of this the prescriptive aesthetic mounting of a norm points out one definite historical, concretely functioning aesthetic construction as the transhistorically aesthetic optimum. And this, as a matter of fact, is what makes the conception cut off above all its potential attention to precisely the aesthetic as a problem. The emphatic underlining of a definite sign-referent-code *in spite of* the appearances, actually might have been supposed to bring the issue of the *historical* character and movements of alteration of that kind of supreme codes, institutions, framings up for discussion. Not least to an optics understanding itself as basically historical-materialist, would the ensuing inclusion of a reflection of the historical conditions of possibilities and extensions have been natural, and should at any rate as a principle be within reach.

This, though, was not the case here. But, after all: Lukács does demonstrate, as mentioned above, a certain attention to the relationship between the enounced and (the enounced) enunciation.[13]

1.1.3 Close Reading of the Told World (Cleanth Brooks)

In both Auerbach and Lukács the perspective of *historical alteration* of literature was highly present within, indeed

---

[13] Which, considering *Die Theorie des Romans* (Lukács 1920) and its focusing on the problematics of subject is no great wonder at this level. What may, however, indeed be the source of some wondering, against the background of the same frame of reference, is the transhistorical apotheosis of a certain form of novel, and the all in all absent sensitivity towards the historical character and thus historically sensitive strengths and limitations of the constructions of meaning: in *Die Theorie des Romans* a sensitivity like that actually is the determining basis for the definition of the novel as being exactly that aesthetic construction of performing the specific, 'impossible' subject relation of modern bourgeois reality.

almost governing the conception. In Auerbach historical alteration was to be understood as a genuine development towards the implicit ideal, the latter incorporated as 'pure' representation of reality in literature, understood as the disappearance of the author. And this probably seems to imply the disappearance of enunciation. The Lukács essay was perfectly in accordance with this in its ontological presuppositions (the possibility of total representation) as well as in its cognitive intention of movement. But in Lukács the notion about historical alteration is formulated by means of a so-called 'golden-age' construction: the development has culminated at a certain peak, from which it has now declined. The purpose, then, is now a restoration, a return to this historically ideal form which has been left/lost. Lukács suggestingly includes the constructions of enunciation positively into his considerations (i.e. as something different from their ideal absence with which Auerbach operates). This, however, explicitly happens in order to support the emphatic underlining of the cognitive function of literature within a universe of meaning distinguishable into what is objectively true and what is objectively false. In order to match the fundamental, potential, cognitive (and consequently pragmatical) control of the world which it ascribes to the human subject within "reality", the text must necessarily be able to *know itself*, i.e. intrinsically include a dimension, an insight, sovereign as regards the narrated. This sketches out an extra dimension above and beyond the basic notion of a possible bi-unique isomorphy between the worlds of the work and of the reality, respectively.

In accordance with one of the basic doctrines in New Criticism a perspectivization of that kind, into a logic of alteration within a register of philosophy of history, is completely absent in the paper by *Cleanth Brooks*, one of the main figures of this school, which we shall read below. *The Criticism of Fiction: The Role of Close Analysis* is a lecture of 1959, printed in the collection of essays entitled *A Shaping Joy* (1971).[14] The title already states the generality of the intention: What should be thought about the analysis of prose fiction? Is it possible, with profit, to transfer the so-called close reading, primarily developed with lyrical poetry and programmatically practised upon this, to prose fiction?

From the starting point of the essay Brooks already makes it clear that in his opinion a transfer like that is possible, and profitable as well: he sees no fundamental differences between the reading of poetry and the reading of prose. This he sets himself the task of illustrating by means of the reading of three prose texts by Faulkner, Joyce and Mark Twain.

Brooks starts out from what he regards as two basic types of misreadings of prose: one of them is 'losing the intrinsic meaning' by overemphasizing the historical background; the other is 'disintegrating' the text into completely improbable symbols. In other words, Brooks mounts what is meant to look like an axis with two counterpoles: one overemphasizing the extrinsic relations of the text, and the other over-emphasizing its intrinsic ones. It is, however, not hard to realize that both types focus the *referential* functions of the text; also what Brooks calls "symbol mongering" (an irresponsible blowing up of details without

---

[14] The following quotations refer to the original edition, Lnd. 1971.

genuine relation to the wholeness of the text, performing
'...a grotesque parody of anything like an adequate "close
reading"' (144)) – also this variant, judging from Brooks'
own examples, aims at making the single elements of the
text *represent* above all certain states of things.

With these 'typical' failures as a starting point, however,
Brooks argues in favour of a middle course in order to start
from what he calls "old-fashioned questions": what is going
on in this story, what is it about &c., &c. It becomes clear
that Brooks' notion of close reading seems above all to
apply to the revelation of movements and motives within
the narrated space. For instance he embarks on a scrupu-
lous discussion of the text's presentation of how the son
refuses to avenge the assassination of the father in
Faulkner's *An Odor of Verbena*. The quotation below clearly
states the field of interest:

> Yet in refusing to avenge his father by shooting the assassin, it
> can be argued that Bayard is actually following his father's
> example. Two months earlier his father had told him: ".... I shall
> do a little moral housecleaning. I am tired of killing men, no
> matter what the necessity or end." In any case, Bayard evidently
> loved his father: the intense scene in which he views his father's
> dead body is sufficient testimony to that. If the scene also
> testifies to Bayard's candid admission to himself that his father
> has been fiercely intolerant and ruthless in his life, that fact but
> stresses the complexity of his relation to his father. His decision
> to refuse to kill his father's assassin stems not at all from any
> rejection of his father, but rather from a love for, and
> understanding of, him. [147]

Note that the penetration and the entire analytical interest
apply to the question of what is the 'right' understanding of
what is happening to the figures of the fiction: Bayard loves

his father and does so and so because of that and that. The
constructed world of the work is treated and discussed as
if it were a real world. It is true that Brooks points out the
way certain passages may

> show the way in which Faulkner focuses our attention

which might indicate an attention concerning the construction as construction. But the continuation goes

> upon the basic issues or illuminates the conflicting impulses in
> Bayard's mind or dramatizes for us the state of Bayard's
> heightened sensibility [148]

The 'focusing', the 'illumination', the 'dramatization' applies
to 'something', seemingly *being* there a priori. Brooks seems
to regard the role of the author – and consequently his
artistry – in his *intermediation* of a world actually already
present. The fact that this 'world' exists only in and as that
fictional construction for which "the author" is generally
responsible, and within which his narrating is incorporated
as a certain construction of narration, a certain (enunciated)
enunciation, which in its turn determines the conditions of
possibility of reading and consequently finally 'the meaning' – Brooks' 'close reading' of Faulkner's text seems to
ignore all this completely.

Brooks' discussion of the two other literary texts does
not change this picture very much. In Joyce's *Clay* the
attention is drawn towards what kind of person the protagonist Maria actually is, what she "really wants" [150], as
it is put. Even when Brooks – correctly – points out that
we, the readers, know something which the protagonist
Maria does not know, the considerations terminate in an

animation, a personification of the fictional persons:

> Maria makes no bid for our sympathy, and *is unaware* that she is a figure of pathos, but in the context that Joyce has established the final incident is one of intense pathos [152; italics added]

Besides the personification it is the word *but* which shows that Brooks regards the figure of Maria and the "context" of Joyce as *different* levels.

In the discussion of *Huckleberry Finn* Brooks succeeds – in connection with pointing out that a certain detail in Huck's behaviour would hardly appear in real life – in demonstrating that

> *Mark Twain* is arranging matters so that Mrs Judith Loftus, with whom Huck is talking, will be able to score her point [153; italics added]

Once again the mere pointing out demonstrates that the author (the narrator) through the optics of Brooks apparently deals with something already present; who ever should actually have arranged matters in a novel by Mark Twain?

It is for that matter in the Twain analysis that Brooks comes closest to a discussion of the importance of the construction of enunciation. The analysis underlines the importance of the fact that the point of view of the novel is placed with the figure of Huck Finn, who is 'primitive', unprejudiced, incorrupt, and consequently in Brooks' opinion a very competent observer. A discussion of *the relation* between the perspectives by the implicit narrator of the text and its explicit narrator (Huck) – and the importance of this relation to the meaning of the text – is actually not far to seek here. But this discussion is not brought up. Even as for Huck's role as the bearer of point of view Brooks' interest concerns the psychological structure of his character rather than its effect within the interplay between the different instances of the construction of enunciation. Brooks actually succeeds in interpreting Huck as narratingly superior to Twain. In connection with the discussion of the Grangerford episode it is put:

> ...Emmeline, as mediated through Huck's vision of her, manages to be something more than ridiculous. Perhaps Mark Twain here has outwitted himself [156]

And later on, in the conclusion, Brooks even manages to call Huck the real, "born artist":

> Small wonder that Huck Finn embodies the finest imaginative qualities of his creator. Indeed, Huck as an artistic intelligence actually surpasses his creator, for some of the traits of Samuel Clemens get in the way of the artist – his bitterness, his rage against man's follies, his verbosity, his preconceptions and prejudices concerning science, religion, and politics [164; as is well-known Clemens is Mark Twain's real name]

On the basis of Brooks' own notions one might say that *either* 'Clemens' and his "unartistic" notions *are not* present in the work. In that case the application of them to the factual author of the book is wrong and at best irrelevant (inclusion of biographical matter alien to the text within the close reading). *Or* these notions are present as a narrator's level *behind* Huck's immediate level. In that case exactly the clash, the interplay between the levels of narrating should be of interest to the analysis. But Brooks' remarks on that matter are confined to the qualitative differentiations mentioned. And in conclusion, to propose a metaphor for the hardly comprehensible fact that an author "...is deliberately delimiting himself to the perceptions and intelligence and language of an almost illiterate boy" [164]: Huck is a *lens* or (since a lens precisely is complicated) rather such a thing as the snow glasses of the Eskimos which force the eye to perceive only through a very small opening. This delimitation – in the case of Twain successfully excluding 'abstractions, generalizations, and prejudices' – becomes the force of the novel, in Brooks' opinion.

He is, indeed, obviously right about that, although he does not catch the *interplay* mentioned between the points of view as that which creates the dynamics and consequently the strength. To Brooks the world of the work, i.e. the world about which it is speaking, seems to be closed around and within itself. Furthermore it is a decisive condition of his statements that *coherence* prevails within this world (for example 146, 148): coherence is simply a condition for artistic quality.

In conclusion Brooks' way of thinking appears as highly reductive and at some points immediately self-contradictory. On the one hand the world of the prose work is taken highly seriously as a *world* (S=W', Fig. 5). Truly it demonstrates certain decisive outward and structural resemblances with the real world, but these are above all presupposed: the world of the work as a *statement about* the real world or as a *representation of* this is not the focus of interest. No, it is all about the world of the fiction itself: how figures are acting and why, all of it treated and conceptualized as if 'real' persons and events were dealt with, and all of it mounted into a basic notion of the world

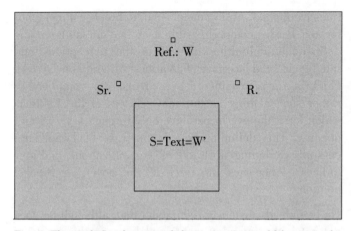

Fig. 5. The work S enlarges and thus as a new world becomes the object of analysis. Every other relation is just understood, and is ignored by the analysis itself.

of the works as exactly (necessarily) intrinsically *coherent.*

The doctrine of autonomy of New Criticism in other words here seems to have been turned into a parody of itself. Because what is left altogether of scanty attention concerning the "craft" of fiction is written directly into the non-explicitated basic notion about the world of the work as a model world; the character of this world as a construction – and consequently how meaning is dependent on the concrete appearance of this construction – is not discussed. What is here conceptualized as 'intrinsic' is so, exclusively because of a certain 'mimetic' basic understanding, which for that matter far more is latently 'extrinsic': we do not get even a scanty exposure of relations and structures 'inside' the texts.

The fact that Brooks' readings according to their own narrow preconditions appear to be penetrating does not solve their problem (and let us remember the readings' self-understanding, self-acknowledgement as exemplary to any analysis of prose fiction): they do *not* discuss texts' dependence as regards meaning, on their concrete context. They do *not* take into consideration the way in which the texts are playing into, and in their meaning are influenced by the conventional institutionalization of "literature" (not least decisive in the Joyce text). Ultimately, as stated, they are *not* interested in the historical changes, neither concerning the contextual systems of the texts (which are part of the determination of their "meaning") nor more immediately the way in which these changes manifest themselves as mutual differences between the analyzed texts.

All in all Brooks' 'exemplary' readings show *closures* towards almost any level and relation of meaning of the prose works regarded *as literature*; including not least the level which they were supposed to develop according to their own self-understanding: the 'inner' one. Cleanth Brooks' "close analysis" is thus not "close" at all: not close to the texts as texts, at any rate. And not at all close to the texts as literary texts, which is rather surprising.

1.1.4 Analysis as Endless Catalogue (Greimas)

The next example resembles Brooks' way of thinking by the absence of the dimension of history and the pretension to regard the text as an independent text. But in this case the latter pretension is fulfilled.

Semiotics is a very widely ramified theoretical tradition and in spite of courageous efforts in terms of both substance and organization to merge it into one discipline, or even into a specific science, intrinsic divergences still appear to be so decisive that it is far more satisfactory to talk about just a community of points of view. But semiotics in a developed sense is still young and maybe a lot of the divergences of today will later appear to have been necessary children's diseases. Quite some work is devoted to the matter, at any rate.[15]

A.J. Greimas is considered to be one of the pioneers of modern semiotics, among other things by virtue of his dictionary of theoretical concepts, today an indispensable standard work for any semiotical discourse.[16] Still his theoretical achievement is in no way undisputed within semiotics (but that kind of contribution can hardly be found). A number of traits in his method as presented in the lecture *The Love-Life of the Hippopotamus: A Seminar with A.J. Greimas* (1976)[17] do however appear to illustrate both strengths and weaknesses in at least great parts of the heterogenous semiotic tradition in formation. This said, we shall underline that here as well as in the previous chapters we only draw conclusions which apply to the concretely discussed text. The work of Greimas holds in itself diverging tendencies which it is not, however, appropriate

---

[15] For a historical outline of the development of semiotics see Marshall Blonsky's informative essay *Introduction: The Agony of Semiotics: Reassessing the Discipline*, in *On Signs*, 1985, from which also the Greimas text discussed below is taken.

[16] A. J. Greimas and J. Courtés: *Semiotique. Dictionnaire raisonné de la théorie du langage*, Paris 1979. This work has been translated into a number of languages, including English.

[17] A.J. Greimas: *The Love-Life of the Hippopotamus: A Seminar with A.J. Greimas*, in *On Signs. A Semiotics Reader*, ed. by Marshall Blonsky, London, 1985.

to thematize for our purpose; something similar could obviously to an even higher degree be said about the 'tradition' as a whole.[18]

Greimas' paper is a transcription of a lecture given in the USA in 1976, and it has kept its oral form. We must assume, however, that the author has authorized the wording; if not, this of course further intensifies the reservation regarding the representativeness of the text. The analytic activity of the lecture as a whole is directed against an ultra-short prose text by James Thurber, *The Lover and his Lass*, which we have reprinted *in extenso* below[19].

---

[18] Among other things, a number of points in Umberto Eco will be included later in this main section. There is no need to make a secret of the fact that we basically consider our own method to be "semiotic". However, as will be stated also already in the present chapter, this does not imply that this conception is not critical towards certain exclusions within parts of the present semiotic tradition.

[19] From *Further Tales for Our Time*, London 1956. *In extenso* the text is as follows:

> An arrogant grey parrot and his arrogant mate listened, one African afternoon, in disdain and derision, to the lovemaking of a lover and his lass, who happened to be hippopotamuses.
>
> "He calls her snooky-ookums," said Mrs Grey. "Can you believe that?"
>
> "No," said Grey. "I don't see how any male in his right mind could entertain affection for a female that has no more charm than a capsized bathtub."
>
> "Capsized bathtub, indeed!" exclaimed Mrs Grey. "Both of them have the appeal of a coastwise fruit steamer with a cargo of waterlogged basketballs."
>
> But it was spring, and the lover and his lass were young, and they were oblivious of the scornful comments of their sharp-tongued neighbors, and they continued to bump each other around in the water, happily pushing and pulling, backing and

Greimas' discussion of the text primarily decomposes it into a number of 'segments' or constituents along different semiotic axes, suggested by the author. *Decomposition*, Greimas designates the process, referring to the fact that "analysis" originally means the decomposition of something into its constituents.

Greimas starts out with the narrated space which is temporally and spatially divided into three segments

---

filling, and snorting and snaffling. The tender things they said to each other during the monolithic give-and-take of their courtship sounded as lyric to them as flowers in bud or green things opening. To the Grays, however, the bumbling romp of the lover and his lass was hard to comprehend and even harder to tolerate, and for a time, they thought of calling the ABI, or African Bureau of Investigation, on the ground that monolithic lovemaking by enormous creatures who should have become decent fossils long ago was probably a threat to the security of the jungle. But they decided instead to phone their friends and neighbors and gossip about the shameless pair, and describe them in mocking and monstrous metaphors involving skidding buses on icy streets and overtuned moving-vans.

Later that evening, the hippopotamus and the hippopotama were surprised and shocked to hear the Grays exchanging terms of endearment.

"Listen to those squawks," ruffled the male hippopotamus.

"What in the world can they see in each other?" gurbled the female hippopotamus.

"I would as soon live with a pair of unoiled garden shears," said her inamoratus.

They called up their friends and neighbors and discussed the incredible fact that a male grey parrot and a female grey parrot could possibly have any sex appeal. It was long after midnight before the hippopotamuses stopped criticizing the Grays and fell asleep, and the Grays stopped maligning the hippopotamuses and retired to their beds.

MORAL: laugh and the world laughs with you, love and you love alone.

(temporally "afternoon", "evening", "after midnight", spatially the room of the hippopotamuses, the room of the parrots and a common one). All of it at the immediate level of the enounced of the text. Subsequently a differentiation of the *subjects* of the text is made. Here there is first of all a distinction between "discursive" and "narrative subjects" and secondly between "pragmatical" and "cognitive subjects". It is underlined that these differentiations are possible because the subjects are "syntactical constructions" and do not correspond to persons in the room of the text (who in their turn are able to shift between for instance pragmatical and cognitive positions, cf. in this text between loving and acknowledging somebody else doing so).[20]

The "knowledge" of the cognitive position is now further divided, at first into 'common' knowledge, which in turn may be transitive (apply to others) or reflexive (apply to oneself), and "meta-knowledge" (i.e. knowledge about knowledge) and finally "making-know".

All these differentiations are applied continuously to the instances of the analyzed text, while it is underlined that in all circumstances it is a *must* to semiotics first of all to reveal and discuss grammar and syntax and only *after that* to deal with semantics. This means to examine the existence of the axes and their concrete graduations, their 'intrinsic' functions within the analyzed discoursive room of

---

[20] Greimas points out (p. 345) that he uses "pragmatical" in the meaning of the French tradition, i.e. plainly as a synonym to "évènementiel" – as opposed to the American tradition which relates the concept to a certain philosophical tradition. Also in the present book this concept is generally used in this immediate meaning as in Greimas.

meaning *before* discussing their 'meaning' within and not least 'out of' that room.

This process of differentiation as a whole concludes with the statement that the text actually redoubles its own narrative programme in a series (within which the differentiations of positions, subject positions, etc. are mutually symmetrical), in a narrative model well-known from the folktales. This programme may be repeated *ad infinitum* and, as it is put with a reference to Jakobson, we are dealing with a 'projection of the paradigmatical into the syntagmatical'. This reading of the text Greimas calls the first one; it may be concluded as something like

> ...we can know ourselves so long as we ignore what others think of us [359]

It is based on the very *pattern* of the text and it emphasizes and gives priority to the proclaimed potential replacement of hippopotamuses by parrots, donkeys or field mice in the symmetrical, repetitive structure.

But up against this 'very simple truth' you may also read the text at a level two in Greimas' opinion. This happens if you furthermore consider the respective levels of hippopotamuses and parrots actually not to be completely identical. One is up, the other is down, and this axis seems to structure another two systems of oppositions. A classic culture/nature-dichotomy whose nature-pole is linked with the hippopotamuses (and which, it is said, in its turn is homologous with life-death) and closely connected with that, is a corresponding 'social' dichotomy. Whereas the hippopotamuses are down and linked with the nature-pole, the parrots are up, and besides the cultural position they hold a certain social position (marked in different ways within the text: "The Grays" (a married couple) as opposed to the free love of the hippopotamuses, their *talking* love as opposed to carnal love, &c). The parrots in other words hold a sort of bourgeois position of power and it is indeed symptomatic that they speak the "language of power", seriously considering to call the ABI ("African Bureau of Investigation") in order, by means of power and by the legitimacy of those in power, to have this promiscuous beastliness of the hippopotamuses stopped. According to *this* reading the apparent symmetry between the two parts of the text is false: false because an axiological axis is implemented, according to which the hippopotamuses are 'right' and the parrots 'wrong'. The couples' behaviours are at least not equally ridiculous. This reading is then linked with the inclusion of what is called the *uttering* of the text.

In continuation of this there is, in Greimas' opinion, a third possible reading. He does not really touch on enunciation (uttering) until only briefly at the very end of his paper, discussing it both as a principle and as related to the analyzed text. It is emphasized that enunciation is always implicit and thus part of the *intrinsic* determinateness of the text – and that the enunciation and the enunciated, uttering and uttered, do not work at the same level. Concretely in this context a third reading of the text is suggested, as "irony" ("a word I do not like very much because I do not know its definition"): this reading would lead to the experience that

> ...the text capsizes, and the result of the final signification of the text is derision. In other words, both couples are derisory and the whole thing is meaningless. Irony negates the signification that is posited. [365]

And there Greimas' discourse ceases abruptly. Perhaps rather in a sort of ... irony, at any rate as regards the suggested third reading. It is in fact hard to imagine that this meaninglessness, this negation, is not also to be understood as precisely a "qualified nothing" in the sense that *the final result* "nothing" intrinsically must hold the shadows of both first and second reading in a unified complex of meaning. A meaning, whose precise inner construction above all is to be characterized by exactly the *indeterminateness* which is, it goes without saying, the mark of irony, at any rate of possible irony. But Greimas simply leaves this, and that is, actually, perhaps rather symptomatic.

All in all a number of 'average' weaknesses and strengths of semiotic analysis of literature appear rather clearly in Greimas' exemplary reading.[21] To begin with weaknesses, the mania for conceptual cataloguing is conspicuous; the distinctions and their sub-distinctions are almost always binary either/or-constructions which from time to time leave the impression that the *process of naming* becomes its own

---

[21] "Average" still in the sense that certain branches of the tradition seem to be specifically harassed by the weaknesses whereas other ones are enjoying the strengths, as regards both cf. below. A genuine systematization of the branches of the tradition is not appropriate here, but schematically often a "hard" and a "soft" semiotic approach, respectively, are mentioned; the distinction does not least apply to the conception of the ontological status of the semiotic models (the "hard" one regards the models as objective structures, the "soft" one regards them as instruments of understanding implied by means of the situation of objectivation). In terms of this distinction Greimas ought rather to belong to the "hard" semiotics, whereas for instance Umberto Eco is "soft" (cf. already Eco's critical discussion of the models in *La Struttura Assente* (from 1968)).

purpose. Concepts and differentiations fill the air, differentiations which cannot themselves be regarded as incorrect, but whose function, on the other hand, is not always quite evident. The latter is obviously due to another important weakness of Greimas' reading. The *recollection* of what has been presented by the work of decomposition of the semiotic differentiation, which Greimas himself in the paper underlines as important (cf. p. 349), never really takes place. The extent of the 'reconstitution', which in fact happens, apparently has no sensible proportion to the extent of the previous differentiation. The three readings (cf. above) appear as rather disconnected, as different possible levels of a process of synthesis, and particularly the fact that their mutual relations and thus the whole 'multi-tracked' statement of the text are not subject to any attempt at discussion, seems against the background of the minute differentiation of concept to be a distorted organization of the analytical effort. In addition comes the fact that what may appear as a forced application of certain levels of texts to preconceived *models*, primarily in the form of the so-called "semiotic square" (the butterfly model),[22] often takes place. An example of this is the so-called "square of veridiction" (360) which does not evidently give any information about the analyzed text and which at the same time overtly renounces any causing of its own construction.

---

[22] "The actant model" (which in its roughest shape fundamentally thought it possible to inscribe all texts of fiction into a certain pattern with support in among others Propp's examinations of folktales) Greimas on the contrary here declares to have given up ("I realized that it was a much more complicated matter", 346). Instead a differentiation in actantial and thematical roles takes place which is then to merge (but precisely also continuously to be spread and replaced) in "actors" (347).

Within the reading of texts, finally the *course*, the *sequence* is peculiarly absent in the formation of syntheses. It is true that "segmentations" in the shape of simple temporal and spatial movements within the narrated room are registered, but the very consequences to the meaning, which the sequential dimension of unfolding of the mounting of these segmentations brings along are completely ignored. The fact that "meaning" as related to texts is necessarily 'processual' in its own architecture does not appear. "Meaning", on the contrary, seems to be the extract left in the process of a retrospective rationalizing-away of the unfolding of the text's dimension of sequence. This concretely becomes a problem in the discussion of the self-commenting structure of repetition of the text here analyzed, a structure which exactly only gradually (and even then just partly) emerges to view.

A number of rather marked strengths are, however, also present in Greimas' reading, especially when compared to many other traditions. An especially important gain is the basic method: The text is regarded and discussed as a system, as a construction, which *in itself* establishes and carries out some operations as regards meaning which then *altogether* are supposed to 'mean' something. This thorough revelation of what Greimas calls the "grammar and syntax" of the text *before* the discussions of the semantic "statement" of the macrostructure is a decisive gain, theoretically and methodically, which virtually legitimates the gymnastics of concepts in so far as this one establishes a polemical counter-position to a traditional type of decoding which utilizes semantical/referential connections even in the starting-point, and when dealing with single parts of the text very often *a priori* excludes the possibility of revealing the constructions, which actually *constitute* meaning. The differentiation of concepts itself deserves to be emphasized as something generally positive: although the schematical binarity may appear problematic, a great number of important differentiations are established which are extremely fruitful to textual analysis. This for instance markedly applies to the distinctions between cognitive and pragmatical modalizations.

Finally Greimas pays full attention to the importance of *uttering* within the signification of the text (strictly speaking we are dealing with "uttered uttering", obviously). It is clearly emphasized that enunciation is an *instance of the text*; Greimas explicitly warns against taking the opportunity of reinstalling "...the author and biography and all that..." which it took twenty years to get rid of (361). Although the dimension of enunciation within this reading is not very fruitfully included in the analysis (because the three readings, as mentioned, are not discussed in their mutual connections) the pointing out of it is extremely important.

If you look at the exterior relations of the text, Greimas' exclusions, on the other hand, seem more unambiguous. It is for instance stated programmatically:

> Either we are content with the indications of the text and we say: 'Outside the text, no salvation!', or we bring in psychology and psychoanalysis and history and sociology *and we no longer have semiotics*: there is a great deal of intelligence, genius, but no longer any coherent analysis. [361, italics added]

In that way Greimas happens to exclude the more supreme frame conditions of the signification, its 'framing'. And especially for instance the historical alteration of the codes

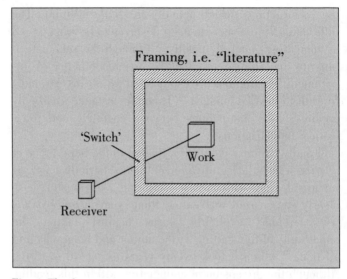

Fig. 6. The frame acts as a "filter" or a "relay": The "meaning" of the work cannot be abstracted without considering this level, forming a part of the sender-receiver-linkage.

and the very continuum of fields of meaning, present in a given room, necessarily *join* the game, become a part of the meaning of any text. Not least important in this case is the framing of the text as "literature". This framing is determining, *a priori* and on the basis of the meaning which the single elements have and are given, respectively and altogether. The reason for the absolute impossibility of ignoring these framing codes, is the obvious fact that meaning in any circumstances is actualized only with a receiver who in turn necessarily will have to utilize codes like these in order to abduct the signs. Considerations about macrostructures like these, also in relation to the singular manifestations, are thus not to be placed *outside*

Exposition

semiotics; if the statements are valid *within* the text, they are also valid around it. Semiosis is unlimited, rhizomatical, as it has been characterized methaporically;[23] Peirce already underlines, as may be well-known, the infinite character of endless displacing of the formation of meaning.

This 'built-in relativity' does not make the formation of meaning unacknowledgable, nor impossible to discuss in local extracts such as a literary text. The relatedness of the local to other levels cannot be suppressed completely in the analysis the way Greimas does it here. The claimed universality of the structures and consequently their reappearance in every micro-universe does not in itself guarantee this linkage. An *inside/outside* is absent. This does not affect what is well-deserved and analytically necessary in Greimas' thorough work of differentiation. On the other hand it does indeed become decisive for what the result of this process might be said to *mean*. Here the either/or-thinking should at least be supplemented with a type of complexity in which differences also, to some apparently paradoxically, are able to deliver meaning both/and.

1.1.5 The Definite Inevitability of Indefiniteness (de Man)

An emphatic argument in favour of precisely a both/and like that, we find in Paul de Man's essay *Semiology and Rhetoric*[24], which has been read as one of the central

---

[23] Cf. Deleuze/Guattari 1976. This designation is discussed further for instance in Eco 1984, pp. 81ff.

[24] Originally in *Diacritics* 3, 1973. Here and below we quote from the version printed in *Textual Strategies. Perspectives in Post-Structuralist*

manifestos of so-called deconstructive criticism. In this essay Paul de Man explicitly settles with both New Criticism and especially semiotic literary science, both based on versions roughly matching the texts by Cleanth Brooks and Greimas discussed here.

De Man starts from the tendency, which he at that time detects in American literary criticism, to see New Criticism as a phenomenon over and done with: after the technically perfect work with the intensional, formal structure of the texts it is now possible to see how "...critics cry out for the fresh air of referential meaning" (123). What is searched for, de Man states, is a kind of *reconciliation* of the internal/external- opposition which structured the discussion all the way through:

> Behind the assurance that valid interpretation is possible, behind the recent interest in writing and reading as potentially effective speech acts, stands a highly respectable moral imperative that strives to reconcile the internal, formal, private structures of literary language with their external, referential, and public effects. [122]

As to this it is, however, de Man's point that neither extreme positions nor mediating reconciliations along this axis in fact change anything at all. Twentieth-century formalism (including presumably New Criticism) has just turned the values of this axis upside down. The external, the form, is now turned into the essential, the internal, and the referential meaning, the 'substance', the content, has been turned into something external. An inversion like that, however, changes nothing in itself. To de Man this very oscillation

---

Criticism, ed. and with an Introduction by Josué V. Harari, London 1980.

and dreaming about reconciliation demonstrate the limitations of that way of thinking, demonstrate that the binary division of the axis is impossible in itself: to the ones who accept this polarization it is consequently bound to reproduce itself over and over again. The *direction* of the values is without significance: the problem is the internal/external metaphor of the very structure of conceptualization. And metaphors, it is stated, last longer than facts.

From the discussion of New Criticism and the prevailing metaphor within American debate of literary theory, de Man directs his attention towards French semiotics. Here, it is stated, a process of theoretical qualification based on linguistics has been carried through according to which

> ...the entire question of meaning can be bracketed, thus freeing critical discourse from the debilitating burden of paraphrase [124]

This is, in de Man's opinion, fruitful. French semiotics has:

> ...demonstrated that the perception of the literary dimensions of language is largely obscured if one submits uncritically to the authority of reference

> ...exploded the myth of semantic correspondence between sign and referent, the wishful hope of having it both ways, of being, to paraphrase Marx, a formalist critic in the morning and a communal moralist in the afternoon, of serving both the technique of form and the substance of meaning [ibid.]

So far, so good. The problem is, however, in de Man's opinion, that by mapping literary texts by means of application of the *grammatical* structures of linguistics, semiotics in fact identifies these with the *rhetorical* structures of the text as if there were no differences at all. Rhetoric, it is stated, becomes a sheer extension of the grammatical models, becomes a specific sub-division of the joint syntactical relations. And this combination of grammar and rhetoric is treated for instance in Genette (to whom, for that matter, "the most perceptive work to come out of this school" is ascribed)

> ...descriptively and nondialectically without suggesting the possibility of logical tensions [125]

As opposed to this de Man argues that "meaning" cannot be understood as independent of rhetoric, which, in turn, can neither be reduced to grammar nor even be included in a polarized axis, into a binary construction with this. Consequently, no kind of parallelism or isomorphism with the above internal/external axis is possible. As for general theory de Man refers to Kenneth Burke ("deflection") and to the 'founder' of semiotics, Peirce (the transformation of the position of interpretant into new sign in an endless chain process). By means of the reading of three concrete text-examples he then illustrates his point of view. He shows that one and the same grammatical structure may have different meanings which are only decidable by instances *outside* the text (i.e. by code, context, lingual norms). And perhaps these meanings may furthermore – as demonstrated in a poem by Yeats – be unable to even co-exist; they are in fact contradictory and mutually exclude each other. No choice can be made between them. The grammar, consequently, may be "rhetorized" into differing 'directions' of meaning. But conversely also rhetoric may be 'grammatized'. de Man sketches out this in his reading of a text by Proust through the revelation of a kind of intrinsic contradiction, as it is stated,

> ...this doubly metonymic structure is found in a text that also contains highly seductive and successful metaphors [...] and that explicitly asserts the superiority of metaphor over metonymy in terms of metaphysical categories [136]

The acknowledgment of a contradiction like that does not, however, terminate with any kind of "negative certainty". As a parallel to the undecidability of the examples dealing with the grammatical rhetorization, the rhetorical grammatization is bound to remain in what is called "the same state of suspended ignorance" (140). That is because it is impossible to answer the question of the rhetorical mode of the text unambiguously. About the Proust-example it is stated,

> Individual metaphors, such as the chiaroscuro effect or the butterfly, are shown to be subordinate figures in a general clause whose syntax is metonymic; from this point of view, it seems that the rhetoric is superseded by a grammar that deconstructs it. But this metonymic clause has as its subject a voice whose relationship to this clause is again metaphorical. The narrator who tells us about the impossibility of metaphor is himself or itself, a metaphor, the metaphor of a grammatical syntagm whose meaning is the denial of metaphor stated, by antiphrasis, as its priority. And this subject-metaphor is, in its turn, open to the kind of deconstruction to the second degree, the rhetorical deconstruction of psycholinguistics, in which the more advanced investigations of literature are presently engaged, against considerable resistance. [140]

De Man underlines that he is unable to illuminate generally the complicated question about the relationship between the epistemology of grammar and rhetoric respectively; he is only able to illustrate the problems concretely by means of examples. Still he makes a clear programmatic generalization. As regards the Proust-example it is claimed – with proper variations as to method and paradigms – that "...the whole of literature would respond in similar fashion" (138). And making it do that is overtly proclaimed to be the purpose of literary criticism in the years to come.

To this generalization can be added a number of statements on literature and deconstruction in general. Already early in the essay (i.e. before the discussion of the literary examples) de Man maintains that

> ...I would not hesitate to equate the rhetorical, figural potentiality of language with literature itself [129-130]

This later becomes 'to recognize the existence of the deconstructive moment as constitutive of all literary language' and to the laying down that this deconstruction is linked not with the generating of meaning through reading, but 'objectively' a property of the text itself:

> The reading is not "our" reading, since it uses only the linguistic elements provided by the text itself; the distinction between author and reader is one of the false distinctions that the deconstruction makes evident. *The deconstruction is not something we have added to the text; it constituted the text in the first place.* A literary text simultaneously asserts and denies the authority of its own rhetorical mode... [138-39; italics added]

Deconstruction is made an immanent property of particularly literature while at the same time the non-specificity of literature also in a general register is emphasized: poetic writing, truly, is the most advanced "modé of deconstruction", but, it is stated, it only distinguishes itself from other discourses, for instance that of criticism, by its economy of articulation, not by its type. This point of view is repeated emphatically in the last, programmatic sentence of the essay which states the difference between literature and criticism as "delusive" (140).

Compared to the other theoretical texts which we have discussed in this chapter de Man's essay differs decisively by including the *rhetoric* of the literary texts. Although the concept is universalized through its use it evidently remains linked with the 'saidness' of the texts, with their (enunciated) enunciation, their uttering. This is made explicit in connection with the text by Proust in which it is stated, among other things:

> But even if we free ourselves of all false questions of intent and rightfully reduce the narrator to the status of a mere grammatical pronoun, without which the deconstructive narrative could not come into being, this subject remains endowed with a function that is not grammatical but rhetorical, in that it gives voice, so to speak, to a grammatical syntagm. The term "voice", even when used in a grammatical terminology, as when we speak of the passive or interrogative voice, is, of course, a metaphor interfering by analogy the intent of the subject from the structure of the predicate [139]

Here de Man is dealing with the delicate problem about the texts' *knowledge* about themselves. Not by fixating certain constructions as Lukács does, and not by inscribing, like Greimas (or Genette) the problem of enunciation as a subdivision under and consequently structured by general grammar. But precisely as a delicate, conflicting, by definition ambiguous, relationship in which the toldness and the told are wrapped up in a mutual, sensitive dependence which any ("theoretical", "critical") development will necessarily have to try to consider, though without ever being able to avoid influencing it, changing it. And this precisely because it concerns the said-ness.

Apparently it is this inescapable transformation through which the undecidability is necessarily transferred to the critical discourse, to the text about the text, which makes de Man claim that literary texts as regards types are identical with those of literary criticism, indeed, in fact with any text. And furthermore, as stated, this makes him emphatically claim that deconstruction is a property of *the texts* rather than of the reading.[25]

In this matter de Man seems to overlook the role of the conventional codes *outside* the single signs or texts, which are necessarily always parts of the formation of meaning. It is true that one written discourse at the level of 'objective' signs in general will probably be indistinguishable from the other, but this level of signs is exactly in any sense detached from meaning, and consequently completely irrelevant to the discussion on what these discourses 'transport' or 'constitute' communicatively. Because only through the codes' maintaining of the relations between the signs and certain (imaginations about) referents, is "meaning" engendered. This applies to primary linkings of the very language in question; even at this point, however, we deal with a conventional code which for instance changes historically and furthermore is to be differentiated socially and geographically. This emphatically applies also to

---

[25] At this decisive point de Man is completely in accordance with his primary, continental philosophical source of inspiration, Jacques Derrida.

sophisticated particular codes such as "literature"; this is the – conventional – code which 'engenders' literary meaning, including the "non-meaning", which Paul de Man pleads in favour of. To maintain that literature does not exist as a specific kind of written lingual discourse is consequently a statement which immediately denies itself by even being made. And obviously it does not support the claim that it is possible to read non-literary texts "as literature": the fact that texts change their meaning according to the framing within which they are positioned, is not just a trivial experience of everyday language; it can also be proved experimentally for instance by deliberately passing texts off as something different from what they are.[26]

Considering this exclusion of "literarity", of the conventional "institution of literature" in the capacity of a historically changeable, co-meaning relay to the formation

---

[26] If for instance you make a class of students analyze a miserable amateur poem, passing it off as written by this or that world literary celebrity, you can be rather sure to have read out the most sublime profundities; something similar happens if you pass off extracts of nonfiction as fiction. This state of things, and that kind of concrete experiment are of course what make Stanley Fish (i.e. 1980) think that texts themselves mean nothing and that only the "interpretative community" decides the meaning. Against the background of a simple sign/referent/code-model it seems evident that Fish goes to the opposite extreme: the convention concerns precisely a relation in which also sign plays a role. The very demonstration, into a field in which the ignoring of the code is very common, of the fact that a similar ignoring of the sign has absurd consequences, may of course have a valuable effect as provocation. But that does not make the latter more adequate. See also Robert Scholes' critical discussion of Fish in *Textual Power* (Scholes 1985), espec. pp. 149ff.

of literary meaning,[27] it is no great wonder that de Man has to keep demonstratively silent about the historical changes of meaning. An inclusion of this would in fact support parts of his main purpose. And more than that, it would be able to suggest a consciousness concerning *from where* the deconstruction which a Paul de Man commits with the texts (or: from where the deconstruction, which the texts commit with themselves, intermediated by a Paul de Man) is made. As appears from the quoted passages, especially concerning the objective generality of deconstruction, it is undeniable that in Paul de Man a certain absoluteness of the opinions is emerging instead, which – as they are positioned within a rhetorical discourse – are very close to the sheer contradiction of their statement.[28] If exactly undecidability becomes the – thus decided – absolute referent which the texts 'express' automatically (because language is "like that") and which it consequently becomes the purpose of literary science to find and demonstrate in any text, then you are very close to a tautological movement unable to supply the reading of texts with anything but a (truly often needed) reactivation and elaboration of the terminological instrumentarium of rhetoric.

If, however, as stated, you switch from this 'universal' undecidability into thinking the demonstrated collision of the texts with themselves as situated within certain critically analyzable framings, then the gains of deconstruction on the other hand become highly obvious. But of course

---

[27] See fig. 6 in the above discussion of Greimas.

[28] Which of course they were also supposed to do. Though probably not in this immediate sense.

they become considerably more complicated to deal with, because in that case it is no longer the mere existence of this collision (as opposed to the unifying reading by tradition), but also the concrete physiology of that collision which moves into the realm of interest. The impressive critical penetration which de Man so successfully and pertinently lets loose both on New Criticism's and the tradition's "internal/external-syndrome" and on the uniform grammatization of the rhetoric of literature by hard semiotics, this penetrability he might have used with great advantage on the aporiae of his own discourse.

1.1.6 Instead of Conclusion

The texts, by five widely different theorists, discussed above, are obviously not even close to *representing* the joint theory of literature or the methodology of literary analysis. As stated, this was not the intention either. The purpose was only to make visible certain levels and dimensions, particularly through the demonstration of blindnesses towards them, which are central to the purpose of this book. The fact that for instance an important school of literary criticism such as the one of psychoanalytical outlook does not act as an example here, is due to the fact that its exclusions (at any rate in this context) appear to be so evident that the demonstration of them would hardly in itself contribute to the isolation of the problems which it is our aim to discuss. On the other hand we might of course have chosen theorists whose notions are closer to the viewpoints of this book: in addition to areas of semiotics, approaches and points of view of modern hermeneutics might for instance have been included. But in that case as well, the need for elucidation has been given priority over the paying of due credits.

We shall not try to summarize the substance of the Odyssey from Auerbach's classical history-of-thought method, over Lukács' normatively historical-materialist one, Brooks' pretendedly close reading, Greimas' equilibristic of segmentation and to de Man's, from Europe inspired and later on back to Europe glamorously re-imported, deconstructive method. For our purpose we have made quite a point of demonstrating especially the respective closures, but hopefully it also appears that each and every one of the five texts holds decisive qualities which any literary analysis might profit from. But, exactly, at different levels. Still it must be obvious that the theoretical perspective of this book is more closely related to some than to others of those mentioned here.

In the centre of interest have constantly been, stated or unstated, the texts' tacklings of the problem of *referentiality*. It should, consequently, be clear that Auerbach, Lukács, and Brooks each in his own way, may be said to be subject to the "referential fallacy", while on the other hand Greimas and de Man seem to carry through the confrontation with this fallacy so radically that referentiality altogether, including in the capacity of necessary framing, engendering meaning, has been thought completely over and out.

In the following chapters we shall against this background attempt to outline how it is possible to elaborate on the necessary openings in the form of concepts, metaphorizations, and practical-analytical modes of approach in preparation of the series of readings of novels which is the *Schwerpunkt* of this book.

1.2

Inside/Outside:
The Semiotic Field

In the introductory chapter (1.0) we have touched on the classical inside/outside-problematics of literary analysis, among others through Todorov's contrasting of the structural and functional determinateness of the work. The exemplified expositions (1.1) have further demonstrated this problem as one which at any rate seemingly moves along in the shape of closures, exclusions, in one 'end' or the other: the *contrast*ing in a complementary axis model seems empirically to be almost inevitable, although this contrasting is very often solely implicit within the points of view. This means that the literary-historical context of the engendering of this problem, and its history of theory appear to be obvious, potential areas of research which we, however, shall have to leave here.[1]

For the moment we shall instead try to arrive at the heart of the problem. Or *hearts*, because on just a little bit closer examination we are obviously dealing with an interwoven set of problems. The distinguishing between inside/outside, intrinsic/extrinsic, intension/extension, and

---

[1] But which at any rate indirectly are to be illuminated by the development sections below.

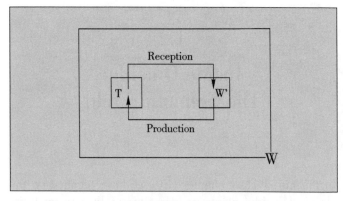

Fig. 1. The functional relations are of course mutually displaced in time. Further about this in 1.3 below.

(even) more crudely "form/content" applies to the determinateness of the literary work, often more or less implicitly *both* designating its (ontological) *status* and the level of its (privileged) *meaning*. But at any rate as central points to the method of the analysis and consequently decisive for its results.

Let us once again regard a simple model (fig. 1). In the relation of the text T, with the world W' an external determination at two substantially different levels is involved. One is placed *before* the text and deals with a question of how the text qua its strictly material process of production originates *in* the world (from W' to T in the figure). The second is placed *after* the text and deals with its 'reinstallation' in the world in the form of its meaning; a process which in principle can only take place through a reception of it (from T to W' in the figure). This whole distinction is, as suggested in the figure, metaphorical and merely operative: both T and W' in this interchange are of course parts of the 'greater' world (W). The text consequently originates in the world, and is delivered back to the world by means of these concretely functional, external relations. To this it should be added that it probably says something *about* the world *in* these relations.

But the text is also something 'in itself': being a concrete, lingual construction it is made up of a number of axiological, actantial, narrative, &c structures, including a certain rhetorical mode, the enunciated enunciation, its 'uttering'.

Now it is obvious that these aspects may be given different priorities (and within different registers of interest of cognition which we also discussed in 1.0). One may be interested in the text's worldview and/or its function within the world, utilizing the world or the text respectively as the privileged correlate (for instance Auerbach, Lukács, Brooks) without any particular considerations as to the inward construction of the text, or even its whole (since single elements, for instance attitudes, characters, &c, may be assumed to 'mean' directly without considering the work as a whole). Conversely, you may (like Greimas and de Man) concentrate on counting up differentiations, perhaps including emphatical inconsistencies, within the inward structure of the text.

It is not difficult to realize that this contrasting is strictly untenable. The text is a crowd of signs, and each of these signs only means something when conceptualized in its specific context of conventional codes of the language in question. Both Greimas and de Man necessarily have to utilize codes like these in order even to make the inferences which they are making. This, however, has nothing to do particularly with the text as *literature*, and it does not solve the problem about whether this literarity is linked with a specific 'inward' organization of the signs, or with a plainly 'outward' placing of the signs in the world. Or whether it does not exist at all, as for instance de Man claims.

As already suggested we shall here argue in favour of answering this question with a roaring "both-and" (or "neither-nor", which is the same thing). The fact that a conventional code must be a part of the game in order even to engender meaning does not only apply to the level of signs (as is the case of any everyday exchange of meaning); it applies also to the level of text.

The existence of a code like that cannot be strictly proved, but it can be made probable rather convincingly. Since a notion about literature actually exists, which according to its own self-understanding is fundamentally stable throughout centuries, and since a whole system of physical institutions, jobs, propositions of taste &c. match this notion – and since this literature is continuously produced and consumed and bought and sold and reviewed and taught and discussed – it is difficult to claim that a code of "literature" like that does not exist. This is the one which Peter Bürger and others[2] call the *institution* of literature (resp. the institution of art), and which is also designated by Bürger as a "framing condition" (*Rahmenbe-dingung*). We are in fact dealing with what is in a semiotical sense called "framing". With a notion about "literature" acting as semiological code to the single literary work in such a way that the work gets its specific

---

[2] Cf. notes 13 and 14 in chapter 1.0 above.

Exposition

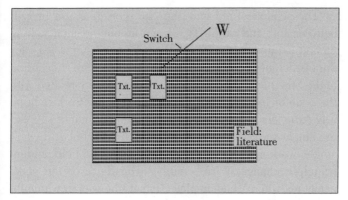

Fig. 2.

"meaning" through this code (whether regarded from the productional or from the receptional side). The code, the institution, the framing are consequently related to the single text, regarded as a sign, as for instance the reference code of a national language is related to the single everyday sign. This 'framing' consequently is a part of the formation of meaning, in each and every case. In several ways: it may be seen as a 'filter', as optics, as a relay, as the point of 'exchanging' meaning into the room called literature. The very best metaphor may be the notion of literature as a "field". *Inter alia* because this metaphor may then be elaborated further in the concept of "field strength", which within physics designates exactly a state of not immediately visible, but highly perceptible and differentiated determination of objects of the field. In fig. 2 we try to outline the notion of work/text[3] and field.

---

[3] Roland Barthes' distinction between "work" and "text" is not utilized here: although it has been productive in order to demonstrate some

The semiotic field may thus be seen as a sort of gate between text and world. This has a number of far-reaching theoretical and methodological consequences, not least for the inside/outside-discussion sketched out here. According to this, the meaning of the work is very closely related with the code or the field; but the meaning of the work is in no way *reducible* to this code or this field. You might say that the single work is (co)created by the field – but still every single work respectively will influence the field and in principle change it irreversibly.[4] The field, or the code, exists no 'where', has no place, is not (the way in which for instance the signs of the text are, strictly physically) localizable, isolatable or for that matter 'removable'. The field is manifested through everything concerning literature, including the works themselves, but the field itself 'only' exists as a semiotic function. This, however, does not in fact make the field a merely subjective phenomenon. It has, for instance, its mode of existence in common with the re-ference codes of the single lingual signs – but on closer examination it is also rather evident that differentiated societies like ours, also are overall divided into such institutionalized fields of meaning, from religion to politics, from fashion to law. This includes fields supplied with sub-

---

important empirical theoretical differences of levels it is hardly functionally utilizable in this context. See for instance Barthes, 1977, pp. 155-164.

[4] The concept about "horizon of expectation" by means of which Hans Robert Jauss within the hermeneutic tradition tries to formulate a new receptional-aesthetic paradigm of literary history in replacement of the traditional productional-aesthetic one (Jauss 1975) is related to the metaphorics of concepts here and may be held within this.

fields through which the single phenomena become what they are. The institution, the framing or the field of "art" or "literature" (the latter substantially obviously a sub-part of the first), consequently, is no more an "illusion" or less "objective" than language as a whole. All codes are dissimulated, in this sense.

Practically-methodologically, applying to the inside/outside-discussion, this means that the single work is only properly analyzable through the field – and conversely that the field can only be examined 'through' the works which constitute it and which constantly change it. The "extensional meaning"[5] of the work, its 'statement about the world' is thus only understandable through the field's framing of this statement. This of course does not imply that the common reader's reception then necessarily could or should take the field into consideration *explicitly*. The assertion is that the field and its code systems more or less *implicitly* are included into that movement of abduction creating meaning, which in all circumstances takes place in any concrete reception.

It might on the other hand be asserted that precisely criticism and the 'scientific' dealing with literature seem to have shown specifically distinct tendencies to ignore the relay effect of the field in the concrete examinations. There are, as stated, good reasons for this, which may be illustrated historically. This we shall not do directly at the

---

[5] Umberto Eco (1979) operates with an extended scheme of differentiating between the intensional and the extensional level (p. 14). There, however, the codes seem to play a minor role compared to the differentiation (as opposed to here, where they are considered as supremely framing).

moment. It should, however, be noted, that for instance the "referential fallacy" seems to hold an almost axiomatic position within the field, at least within the understanding of literature by criticism. Something similar may be said about the "unifying fallacy", i.e. the notion of the supreme coherence or self-referential accordance of any literary work (which has often even been made a prohibitive criterion of quality, for instance by New Criticism and classical hermeneutics). Evidently, the existence of that kind of institutionalized "fallacies" within the field is performative in the sense that these fallacies also influence the *production* of works. Because of that, the tenacity of certain phantasms within a construction, relatively fragile, such as literature, actually is not hard to understand. It is harder to understand when theoretical attacks against certain elements of the field strength are exclusively directed against the texts. A current example is the deconstructive criticism (cf. the discussion of de Man above). It demonstrates – correctly – the attempt of unification within the text as an impossible Sisyphean project considering the inevitable contingency of any significance. But as it does not regard this attempt of unification as a consequence of the literary field strength, it also misses the specific potentials of meaning, held by that kind of invaginated covering through this concrete framing. Instead it is concluded that precisely *this* covering is an inevitable characteristic of *any* lingual utterance – and criticism itself is satisfied with demonstrating repeatedly the (compared to the axiom) trivial fact *that* this covering is taking place. The message is, you might say, correct, but the address is wrong, or at least partly wrong.

In conclusion: all in all it is untenable to privilege one of the instances "inside" or "outside", intrinsic or extrinsic meaning without considering them 'signified' through that relay or that code which 'makes' them "literature". No meaning is thinkable or even cognizable without its context; literary meaning in particular is to be acknowledged through its contextual determinateness *as literature*. This, especially, implies that the literary text in principle has to be acknowledged as a *whole*; only then may the determination of the field be taken into consideration.

To keep the record straight: this did not decide the 'place' of textual meaning. But we have argued in favour of an instance – "the field" – making palpable that place of "exchange" of the inward and outward determinatenesses of the work, a place which otherwise seems to cause tremendous difficulties and to lead to decisive theoretical and methodological misunderstandings. This did not 'solve' the problem. An additional link – but a distinctive one – has been introduced into the infinite system of codes and thus references which forms the condition of the formation of meaning. The fact that every meaning engenders by referring to a context which in turn refers to a context &c., &c.[6] does not, however, entail that nothing signifies anything. It does not entail either that everything signifies "the same". Exchange of meaning in fact does take place under these conditions: the 'local' positions of the contexts as related to each other do form rather stable rooms of meaning which at any rate temporarily are seemingly able to function with an extent of unambiguity not to be rejected

---

[6] Jonathan Culler has made a very precise pun on this problem: "Meaning is context-bound – but context is boundless", see Culler 1983, p. 128.

as non-sense. But the very temporariness is to be emphasized, because the codes and the contexts change, among
other things influenced by the single works, but also by any
other imaginable factor of the overall system of which they
are a part. Since the field is precisely not (only) an *intrinsic*
part of the single work and consequently does not immediately 'move along', the taking into consideration of the
historical change becomes an inevitable condition even to
reflect literary meaning, i.e. analyze literature. We shall
look at this in the following chapter.

1.3

Now, Now, And Then:
The Historical Character of the Field

Even the singular referential codes which regulate the signification of signs within for instance everyday language, are subject to historical change. This may be immediately demonstrated by studying the etymology of concrete expressions, or in practice by reading texts from another historical time. 'Identical' signs simply mean something different because the implicit code – "implicit" because it cannot be read from the sign itself – is different. A similar phenomenon may be observed in fashion, in considerably smaller cadences of time. One and the same 'sign' (for instance a certain dress length or hair colour) changes its "meaning" concurrently with changes of the code (i.e. the fashion). If, on the contrary, you want to achieve the 'similar' meaning (for instance to signal a certain social or intellectual position) you do exactly have to *change* signs in accordance with the ('outside' the signal itself) dissimulated code.

It seems obvious that if any lingual, single code is subject to a temporal change like that, then this must, at any rate at least to the same extent, apply to more complex systems of codes or fields, which in their turn among other things are *made up of* codes like these, concerning single expressions. It must, consequently, also apply to the field of "literature". So far the notion is simple and immediately conceivable. As we shall see, however, it is, in its consequences for the dealing with literature, more complicated.

The connection between "history" and the simple fact that phenomena change in time is not plain and simple. Within historical science critics of traditional paradigms (as for instance Hayden White) have pointed out that the notion about changing phenomena in change 'themselves' constituting history, is probably completely wrong. It is rather the retrospectively organizing "emplotment" by the historical *point of view*, which makes it possible to create "history" from the unsurveyable contingency of single events.[1]

Following among others J.T. Frazer,[2] Paul Ricoeur has pointed out the fact that it is necessary to operate with at least two distinctly different kinds of "time". One is the supreme 'objective' time, the 'scientific' time. It may – metaphorically – be said to consist of 'points of time' each and everyone 'equal' or alike, but on the other hand only connected through their outer 'succession'. As opposed to this there is the "subjective time": *it* in turn is always characterized by one "now" which has on the one side a past and on the other side a future. "History", Ricoeur

---

[1] See Hayden White, 1982, and 1987. Hayden White and other critics of the traditional concepts of history are thoroughly discussed in: *Findes historien – virkelig*, a special issue of the Danish history periodical, *Den jyske historiker* 50, 1990.

[2] *The Genesis and Evolution of Time* (1982).

thinks, may be regarded as an attempt to connect these two fundamental kinds of time.[3]

The complication of this, if only to general history, is not hard to recognize. Because the attempt to transplant historical "nows" into the olympic succession of events within objective time, which is in fact what "history" may be said to do, actually always happens on the basis of one and only one now, i.e. that of the historian. If this state of problems is transferred into the realm of literature it becomes further complicated. Because the very artefacts studied (historicized) appear in an outward sense to have been handed down as 'intact', i.e. as identical with their own previous reality; the signs as such have not changed. The problem is, cf. above, that *what is changed is the field through which the texts in question 'get' – and once did get – their meaning*. Consequently, a complex performance with a number of more or less indeterminable performers is on stage. Since an analogous (but always *qua* the displacement of time, changed) field exists in the 'situation of presence' (F1 in fig. 1) the work T2 also has a meaning directly in F1. This meaning will necessarily be different from the 'original' meaning in the F2-situation. It will not, however, be more 'right' or 'wrong'. You may of course by means of sources &c., try to *reconstruct* the original meaning (T2 in F2), but it will never be anything except precisely an approximate reconstruction, among other things ruled also by the conventions about the historical changes of literature which exist 'now' in F1. Although you may operatively try

---

[3] See Ricoeur's reflections in *Temps et Récit*, Paris 1983-85. What is at issue here is for instance discussed in Ricoeur 1988, pp. 215-221, or in Ricoeur 1991, pp. 343ff.

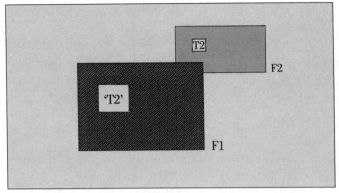

Fig. 1. T2 in F1 does not have a meaning identical to T2 in F2 although T2 itself remains the 'same'. But also this is stated from a position somewhere, which in turn is unable to escape its own determinateness, say F3.

to disconnect the forces of influence of the field (F1) from which is viewed, this very point of view will always already as a starting point have become a part of what is viewed. And furthermore, the *result* of this attempted comprehension will always be a "born member" of this field, so that the statement about history which is now produced, simultaneously is only conceivable concretely as a part of this field (F1), and in principle changes it irrevocably.

Since literature of 'the past' is in fact consumed not only by historians of literature but also by readers and – to make it even more complicated – by authors (who are in their turn able to reproduce the influence within *their* production) this relationship between literature and history becomes an exorbitantly delicate and twisted problem for the analysis of literature.

Delicate, indeed. But not insoluble or impossible to elaborate although the major part of the tradition of literary theory, including its allegedly most advanced, present part (i.e. the examples in 1.1) might suggest that. At the fundamental level discussed here we shall propose *four statements about the relation between analysis of literature and history*, four statements which in one way or another must be included or respected if you want to accept the – very general – semiotic preconditions presented here. The statements are:

1. Any analysis of literature must on the one hand understand explicitly that the framing condition or the field of "literature" changes historically, and that concrete texts consequently are not immediately transferable (as "identical") across history. But the analysis of literature must on the other hand also understand that this transference of meaning within the concrete text cannot be revealed completely. This wording marks that the taking into consideration of the 'objective' change of meaning is indispensable, but also that the reconstruction of 'original' meaning can only, for good reasons, be approximate. An approximation like that, by the way, does not even have to take place. The interest of acknowledgment may be exactly the collision between a text which originates in one time and the field of another time. In that case, however, it is indispensable to make this difference explicit, provided that we are still discussing a literary science with certain obligations to the factual state of things. This indispensability may be generalized in the following words:

2. Any analysis of literature must take into consideration the concrete, historically determined field of "literature" from which it itself regards what is analyzed. The concurrently valid codes will obviously often appear to be invisible. It is not, however, that attempts to map and include them in concrete studies are completely impossible. As a result no historical studies will ever 'just' be able to thematize objects from other historical contexts; they will always also have to thematize that context of their own, that field which has always already influenced or which simply constitutes their horizon of understanding, including their methodology.

As a consequence of the observations in chapter 1.2 above it furthermore appears that

3. Historical change of literature understood as the change of its meaning-constituting 'fields' can*not* be placed on one or the other side within a distinction of 'intensional' and 'extensional' determinateness of literature. This statement has already been argued in general above. "The field" and consequently the concrete historical convention of "literature" determine just as much 'intensional' codes of for instance consistence, rhetorical differentiation of levels (cf. the chapter below) or the existence and the significance of certain constructional elements as it – obviously immediately more visible *as* something historically determined – determines certain thematical concentrations, including certain attitudes within these.

Finally a not less evident but traditionally maybe even more overlooked consequence of a just minor inclusion of the problem of history into history of literature would be that

4. Historical change of "literature" may take place in two fundamentally different modes (and in combinations of these modes): on the one hand as changes of the field. On

the other hand as changes of the work/works. Decisive changes within the field of "literature" necessarily alter *also the already existing works* by changing the system of codes which supply their 'bare' sign with meaning. New works, as we have seen, always influence the field; the engendering of quantitatively and qualitatively weighty new works alters the field substantially, and thus throws 'new' meaning backwards as well. Since "history" is a product of that historically concrete field, in which it is engendered, it is no great wonder that it constantly changes in the shape of new backward-going reorganizations. More surprising is the fact that these "histories" often seem to have wanted to privilege themselves as *the* "history" – thus mistaking themselves for the 'objective' (but in this sense incomprehensible, cf. point 1), great history, or more correctly, "the temporal succession of events", here as an infinite series of concrete relations between text(s) and field.

An extensive number of examples from the history of literature and theory may be stated in support of what has here been worded about the problem of literature and its historical change. Of current interest might be the implications of the so-called postmodern alteration of paradigm: if the postmodern, as it has been formulated by among others Jean-François Lyotard, is a kind of recognition of Modernity within Modernity, it is not difficult to realize that this change alters also Modernity itself 'historically'. Concretely, especially modernist art, which to a very high extent consists of emphatical *absence*, is extremely 'sensitive' to the change of meaning which originates in an altered framing, including above all transformations of the notion of this art's notion about itself.[4] The fact that a kind of 'reverse-going' postmodernism can emerge at all, capable of threatening art history with a total historical de-differentiation by turning everything into one and the same, is in itself no great wonder seen in this light. On the other hand a total de-differentiation like that is not scientifically tenable unless you reject the existence of any historical change at all (which will lead you to a *contradictio in adjectio*). The tracks of the fields of genesis will necessarily be inherent to the texts and consequently – concerning this example, but a similar state of problems may be refound in any situation of paradigmatic transformation on a large or a small scale – *various* kinds of "postmodernism" must flourish if everything is "postmodernism"[5] Or maybe more precisely, at one and the same time there is both a complete 'similarity' and a complete 'difference', i.e. in the capacity of different features of the mode of existence of this very construction of meaning. We shall, however, return to *that*: the illumination of this complex of problems through a concrete literary historical examination is, as mentioned above, one of the main purposes of this book.

Before turning to the wording and later the development of this examination we shall, however, discuss yet another distinction which will become important to the study.

---

[4] Cf. the discussion of Eco's reflections on "open" and "closed" works respectively, to which we shall return in chapter 1.4 below, and later.

[5] See my article "Det venstre æg sidder mellem stolene med lukkede øjne – det smiler" in *Vinduet* 2, Oslo 1987, in which I discuss this distinction preliminarily and suggest the concepts of respectively a postmodernism based on "transformation of reference" and "genetical" postmodernism.

1.4

Optics and Horizon:
The Toldness of the Told World

A literary text is not only first of all framed by the semiotic field of "literature", in which it is always already included, and it is not only, secondly, in this dimension subject to transformations which the historical changes of the field are always already about to perform. But moreover, the text is thirdly subject to *its own framing* in the sense that it is placed in a certain position of tension between what it is 'telling' on the one hand, and its 'toldness' on the other.[1] Or put in another way, between its 'enounced' (uttered), *énoncé*, and its enunciation (utterance), *énonciation*. It is important to emphasize that by "enunciation" here and overall we have in mind "enounced enunciation", i.e. the 'frozen', objectified enunciation in the construction of the text. This enounced enunciation will of course then in practice once again always operate in concrete contexts of enunciation.

The distinction between enounced and enunciation, said and saidness, can of course ultimately only be merely

---

[1] This obviously does not mean that it only applies to *narrative* texts. It applies to all texts. But it is by far most immediately visible in narrative texts.

operative. Obviously it is not possible to separate these levels completely: any enunciation will always be linked with the enunciated, and conversely any enunciated with its enunciation. But within the analysis, enunciated and enunciation may be discussed separately with certain advantages. Although extensive parts of the tradition of literary theory have for good reasons[2] ignored the dimension of enunciation and consequently the interplay, the latter half of the twentieth century – for not less good reasons – sees an increasing number of theories about the analysis of literature which include this aspect.[3]

It is not our purpose to establish a thorough discussion of or a dialogue with this growing tradition. A short marking of its cornerstones might however be relevant, also in order to suggest that, to which the approach of present

---

[2] Reasons which as mentioned above, are linked with the supreme institutionalization of literature within Modernity as the ex-pression of certain substances (through an attempt to hide the aspect of construction of the product itself and which aspect of construction is in all circumstances acknowledged by literary criticism as something secondary).

[3] This is obviously caused by the new – in the works emphatically underlined – attention by literature itself on precisely form and character of construction. The retardation of the development of theory compared to the fact that classical modernism already places this problem on the agenda, has several reasons, also connected with the overall character and function of the institution; but besides that, the *inversion* of the form-content-relation which happens in the first place (for example within the radical conceptions of historical avantgarde) implies that the new at first, in the capacity of *system*, remains congruent to the old, and consequently conceptualizable within the categories of this. We shall return to these problems in the historical development sections.

work is more or less indebted.[4] Perhaps, before everybody else, should be mentioned Wayne C. Booth and his monograph of 1961 *The Rhetoric of Fiction*. Booth settles systematically with the traditional notions about certain 'natural' or 'correct' constructions; constructions which have – implicit or explicit – dominated the field. Booth shows that "rhetoric" is always present and always influences meaning; in a large number of examples he furthermore discusses the consequences of different types of positions of what he calls "author".[5] From a totally different tradition (but characteristically overtly admitting his debt to Booth[6]) might be mentioned the studies by Gérard Genette especially in *Figures III* and in *Nouveau discours du récit*.[7] Genette's work is classically structuralist in the sense that he is above all engaged on finding, naming and systematizing differentiations within his realm of objects. Despite a certain tendency to 'oversystematize' by means of typological schemes his distinctions between *focalisations*

---

[4] Without of course making these responsible for the constructions presented and applied here.

[5] This designation, unfortunately, is inopportune, although it has the advantage that it emphasizes the character of the enunciation as a *choice* of construction. The problem is that it merges the extratextual instance "author" with the intratextual one; "supreme implicit narrator or instance of narration" is thus better (although it may here be important to distinguish in relation to implicit narrators who may be a part of the narrative construction further 'down', cf. below). "Author's person" has also been suggested (Nøjgaard 1977).

[6] An acknowledgment reciprocated by Booth, cf. Booth 1983.

[7] 1972 and 1983 respectively; the latter is simply made as a commentary on the former.

and *voix* of the narrative construction are highly valuable, although he is not himself too interested in the hermeneutical consequences of these constructions. From semiotics should be mentioned above all Umberto Eco, whose – changing – ideas about the problems and interrelations of so-called "open" and "closed" texts have contributed to the elicitation of how texts' way of leading their readers into their room of meaning *qua* the narrative construction, also determine the mode of the meaning of texts.[8] Finally of course the whole so-called deconstructive criticism should be mentioned; we have already touched it above in the exemplifying discussion. Notwithstanding the possibility of discussing the *degree* of emphasis on rhetoric (cf. the tendency to universalize it) compared to factual, 'normal' (aesthetical) exchange of meaning, there is no doubt that deconstruction has strengthened the attentiveness of the saidness of the said decisively.

So of course have also in a supreme sense the critical hermeneutics from Heidegger and onwards; more recently within the French tradition for instance to Lyotard. And later on back to among others Kant: but here we are facing the all-embracing historical 'mechanisms of projection', which we discussed above in 1.3.

---

[8] Above all in *The Role of the Reader*, 1979, where there is an 'inversion' of his reflections on consequences of the open work compared to *Opera aperta*, 1962; whereas originally he emphasizes that the open work *opens* the room to interpretation, his latest considerations regard this problem as more complicated. The closed text actually metaphorically may represent the whole spectre of meaning, whereas the open rather forces the reader into the frames of a definite indefinibility. See for instance Eco, 1979, pp.8ff.

In order to describe and maintain this differentiation between enounced and enunciation in the textual analysis we shall here introduce our own metaphors. We shall emphasize the fact that they are indeed precisely metaphors. They attempt to inscribe some aspects, in practice connected, i.e. inseparable, as independent figures of a space. Figures, which may then be pictured and used to visualize (illustrate) differences. The spatial metaphors suggested here[9] have within pedagogical and scientific practice shown their ability to fulfil needs of clarification; but they are indeed not a *necessary* (or 'correct') picturing of reality (of the world) and consequently not the only possible (or just most adequate) metaphorical picturing either. This is said realizing the tendency of any such metaphors to 'naturalize' themselves.

But to the point: in this operative distinction we choose to designate the "enounced" of the text, the room of fiction which it unfolds as its *horizontal dimension* (W in fig. 1). This 'horizontal' dimension thus symbolizes the 'world' of a text, as often spontaneously discussed in novels of realistic type of style. The enunciation of the texts then constitute their *vertical dimension*. This includes the instances of the narrative construction situated *between* the reader and the world of the text. "Between" in the sense that the narrated universe in all circumstances is narrated: truly, in the case of parts of the construction, perhaps seemingly by persons *within* the horizontal level – but always *also* already determined by implicit or explicit

---

[9] And which has related versions here and there; originally we have suggested them in Kyndrup 1980b.

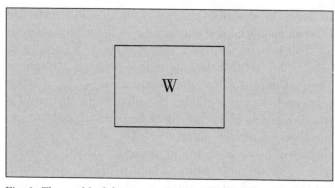

Fig. 1. The world of the text in the dimension of the paper levels with the surrounding world: horizontally.

instances *outside* this level (cf. as a minimum the implicit instance of narrating dealt with above).

In fig. 2 we have attempted to outline this construction 'up against' the reader. Besides the presented, horizontal world (here W') a minimum model might then include the implicit (or implied) narrator and further 'up' the (implicit) reader of the text. Obviously this instance of the reader (still the one placed *inherently in* the text, which should not be mistaken for the so-called real reader of the text[10]) besides the connection 'through' the narrative construction, to some extent possesses an insight of the whole dimension of verticality, i.e. of the construction as such. This, however, of course performs yet another 'picture' of the world (W' in fig. 2), a picture (meeting the real reader, but which in turn consequently hurls new implicit instances of reader up 'in front') of how the implicit 'frozen' reader of the text

[10] A solid survey of the distinctions within the system of reader's instances is given in Link, 1976.

is taken into the work's world. And that picture of course is concretely different from the one outlined by the horizontal dimension.

If it is possible at all to 'generalize' these pictures by ascribing them this or that character of being ('mimetically') representative, a possibility of an interplay *between* the two levels emerges. If the horizontal 'world' is regarded as a statement 'about' the world (being a "model world"), most often explicitly formulated, then the vertical 'world' may similarly be regarded as a statement like that, although generally implicitly.

These pictures can, as mentioned above, never concretely be brought into the position of an immediate 'symmetrical' comparison because their dimensions of unfolding are so different. But by means of 'translation' you may very well generalize their statements into a kind of

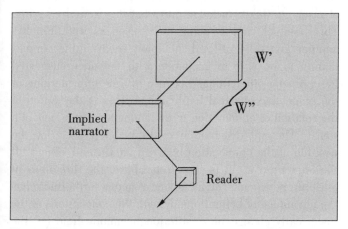

Fig. 2. The horizontal world W' of the text is *in the text* seen through a certain construction: its "vertical world" (up from the paper).

compatibility. You may for instance compare their supreme statements of the different levels of the subject/object-relation respectively. This is, *inter alia*, what we are going to in the development sections below.

Now the separation into these dimensions makes it possible to carry out a kind of re-linking, which permits a discussion of the *relation* between the world of enunciation of the text and the world of the enunciated of the text, as for instance *contradictory*. Using the register of enunciation/enunciated you may now designate this re-linked multi-dimensionality by using the term the *"saying"* of the text.

But of course it is also possible to connect with other terminological registers. The relation between the vertical and the horizontal dimensions of the work may be regarded as an expression of the work's *knowledge about itself* as a construction, respectively its ability and intention in terms of inserting this knowledge into what it is actually saying. This point of view is going to be used as well. Finally, another generally utilized metaphor seems rather immediately to be able to cooperate with the ones suggested here, among other things because of a certain merging of the respective physical implications. This is the notion of the relation of enunciation to the enunciated as a *view* of a world. The apt designation *optics* is often used for the position of the enunciation between viewer and 'object'. If the object/the world is seen from above, the directions at least are pertinent. The metaphor of optics furthermore has the advantage of being linkable with the conceptions of the historically changeable institutional/semiotic field (cf. the chapters above), which may be comprehended as further "optics" like that (potential creator of aberration). The same register of metaphors may then re-occur.

It is of course necessary to be aware of the fact that this is very thin ice. We are dealing with something which was a merely operative differentiation, which was then translated into certain physical-spatial metaphors, and which then in turn on the basis of a 'casual' physical congruence of the metaphors in between, is re-translated into other metaphorical registers, whose topographic implications then perhaps form the background of more or less far-reaching hypotheses and conclusions. These separations may, furthermore, in the present unexemplified presentation seen immediately not specifically intelligible nor useful. However, we are not going to discuss them further here: the very extensive use of them in the development sections will beyond any doubt make them clear.

1.5

The Assertions

Now we shall regard this relation between horizontal (enounced) and vertical (enounced enunciation) dimensions in a number of narrating literary works from the eighteenth to the twentieth century. In particular we shall examine and compare the types of the subject/object-relations which are exemplarily outlined within the vertical and horizontal dimensions of the works respectively. The term "subject/object-relations" does not fix problematics to the specific tradition of subject philosophy although the merging of on the one hand this tradition's emphatic mounting of these instances and later their demounting in the deconstruction of the tradition, and on the other hand the character of these instances of being, as regards theme and construction, the *Schwerpunkt* of the works in question, are obviously not coincidences. It is, indeed, caused by the central position within the very construction of the space of signification of Modernity, which this problematics holds. Here, however, we shall deal with the specific elaboration and transformation of these problematics within a series of concrete literary works. In order to be able to establish the extent of compatibility between these relations which we aim at here, we shall comprehend the relation more supremely and schematically as a positioning of individual/surrounding as regards especially general (symbolical and real) *exchange*, including particularly forms and relations of control, and within the register of cognition as knowledge, insight, acknowledgment.

Now our basic assertion is that the qualitative dimensioning of this relationship, above all conceptualized as the intrinsic (in)congruency of the works in this respect, possesses a considerable power of explanation or effect of illustration which is able to submit fruitful insights into

1. the constructions and potentials of unfolding respectively of the single works, their 'doing' and their 'abilities' in general, i.e. **analysis;** and in this connection of course especially the abilities of the **novel;**

2. the character of historical processes of change within art (here: literature) of Modernity up to now, i.e. **history;**

3. the concrete construction and the potentials of function within that "field" which as a frame constitute the precondition of the elicitation of the works, and within which their meaning is engendered, i.e. **literarity,** and connected to that in a further sense **the aesthetic.**

More concretely we shall assert that throughout the historical change of literature over this period certain 'conventionalized' types of works are developed, (types in general but thus also in particular concerning the relation between the 'pictures' respectively of the S/O-relation by enunciation and the presented world). We assert that the types of these works are in this respect reconstructible and can be revealed by analysis, thus showing a historical course of development, and consequently inscribable into a figure of reflection within philosophy of history. At one and the same time caused by and influencing these historical changes in the shape of the literary works' knowledge about themselves, the *field* of "literature" is changed, which among other things means the change of the semiotic codes which at a given time both in production and reception decide literary meaning (including its status, position &c.).

This particularly implies that the concrete field of "literature" which today frames and consequently decides the production, distribution and reception of literature on the one hand is acknowledgeable as a (for the time being) *result* of the historical process of development thus described. This notion, however, must be subject to its own statement, and consequently it will have to reflect the fact of itself being placed in (and consequently to some extent determined by) this field. In particular it will have to realize that a 'scientific' literary historical view of literature's processes of change indeed has this historical "field of result" as its very precondition, no matter whether intended or not. But as a consequence of this, any change within the present 'resulting' field must also necessarily change "history", or more precisely: must always already have changed it.

This 'redoubled' determinateness of the works in their construction and total statement may of course – the way it for instance happens here – be *asserted*. Our aim below will be to *show* this complex determinateness by *doing* it, (re)constructing it through a redoubled playing through of a certain historical sequence (from the late eighteenth century up to now) and in a certain literary genre (the novel):

In the first development we shall regard 'from below' a number of works from the period, i.e. attempt to comprehend history in a history-philosophical perspective of 'accumulation' or development. Tentatively we shall in other words attempt to look upon the works from the point of view of the fields 'themselves' in order, through a process up till today, to establish an understanding of the present literary field, its historical preconditions and determinations.

On the basis of this we shall in the second development regard the same period 'from above'; watch the way in which the historically 'produced' perspective alters the positions once held and the results once revealed. Not in the shape of contradictions or verifications at identical levels, but by means of a sort of complex parallel version, as precisely a making visible constructions of enunciation which as more or less unspoken *framings* are able to en-capsulate utterances and thus supply the same signs with other significative directions; directions which from then on, they do 'have'. Here the different works are so to speak supposed to be regarded from one and the same field (that is from the present which is the "result" so far of history).

Consequently we shall read off this consecutivity of fields by means of two different cuts. A point – or, if you like a basic assertion – is that these different cuts cannot be brought into one formula, or just into any community of level, through mediation, combination or something like that. Both movements have to be *done* as parts of the ana-lysis, both movements are compulsory. Only in this asym-metrical and fundamentally self-deconstructing system of mobile perspectives is it possible to 're-veal', lay bare, a text's complex system of blindnesses and insights, its knowledge about itself, about its creator, about its reader, and about its own world, and that of its reader, subsidiary. And, in a double sense, the perspective of this knowledge.

It is – as opposed to other positions which at first sight seem to base themselves upon some similar basic notion – not the intention with the demonstration of the fragility and mutual interdependence of these points of view to argue that they should deny the validity of each other and thus turn any insight *as regards* the field into illusion, triviality, or perhaps just make it so subjectively dependent on presuppositions that it would never be able to go beyond itself. On the contrary it is the assertion that through the demonstration of character and extension of this dependence on presupposition, and through the including of the relationship between the vertical and the horizontal dimensions of the text which has generally in literary history been underexposed, these two cuts will be able to contribute substantially to literary science as concerns analysis, history, and "literature", especially the novel.

First
Development Section

Métaphoriquement. Au centre du jour, jeté dans le tas des sardines voyageuses d'un coléoptère à l'abdomen blanchâtre, un poulet au grand cou déplumé harangua soudain l'une, paisible, d'entre elles et son langage se déploya dans les airs, humide d'une protestation. Puis, attiré par un vide, l'oisillon s'y précipita.

Dans un morne désert urbain, je les revis le jour même se faisant moucher l'arrogance pour un quelconque bouton.

2.1

Eighteenth Century:
Two Traditions?

Denis Diderot: *Jacques le Fataliste*
Johann W.v.Goethe: *Die Leiden des Jungen Werthers*

Introduction

Above all, the 18th century is the century of births. Essentially the whole complicated system of institutions, semiotic framings, "fields" (cf. 1.2) was formed in this period – in other words: the entire organization of meaning which we call "Modernity", or *die Moderne*, in a wider term. The extent and impact of this organisation has been so enormous, and so entangled in the basic preconditions of 'Modern' thinking, that only now, when it seems to be crumbling or at least changing its mode of existence, can it fully emerge to view.

Of course it is impossible here to lay bare the overall construction of Modernity. We shall just note certain figures. To keep the record straight, however, it should be stated that the entire installation of Modernity is closely linked with the social upheavals which are a characteristic feature of the period: the bourgeois revolutions, the formation of bourgeois national states in Europe, the entire economic reorganization which later on was to be called industrialism or Capitalism. That is: Modernity as a "space of meaning" is not just a notion without any material foundation. It is founded in and corresponds to certain overall types of social organization which had never been seen before.

The subject-feeling as we know it (and which we are often cheerfully projecting back all over the history we 'know') is shaped with and within Modernity. By the Modern subject-feeling or subject/object-relation[1] is meant, above all, the fact that the subject is fundamentally thrown back upon itself in what is historically a new way (ultimately connected with the "freedom" given to the individuals by the new social organization of economics). Thus subjectivity is objectified, and psychology – or rather *feeling*, the way we know it – emerges. Generally speaking: in its object-relation the subject is in principle being kept in a painful contradiction as it is not possible to be simultaneously the absolute centre of the world, and an 'objective' part of that world. The equilibrium of the S/O-exchange, which becomes an implicit and explicit ideal, can only be obtained momentarily. In practice the individual subject must *either* reduce the objective world to objects of value for it(self) *or* realize that it is being objectified itself, and thus 'disappears' as a subject. In both cases the balance is disturbed. One might hazard that Modern man's entire psychopathology is a series of variations of this simple construction. But, of course, to be convincing this would call for a more detailed discussion. However, it seems notoriously right that Modern art – not least evident in literature – has continued, emphatically, to circle around precisely this

---

[1] "S/O-relation" for short.

subject/object-problem. As mentioned above, it is one of the theses of this book that this interest is also visible in art's way of being art, in the very construction of "art", and that this "vertical" S/O-relation (art's positioning of its implicit recipient) creates certain historical types of figurations with the horizontal (thematic) S/O-relationships. And that these patterns of figurations or relations seem to throw light on the overall functional potential of art as well.

But let us return to the births given by Modernity. Apart from the Modern subject, the 18th century also gives birth to *aesthetics*. Not only to the concept itself (which is Baumgarten's idea and which later on Kant gives a place in his philosophical systematics), but actually to the *phenomenon* as well, the way we know it: the art-aesthetic is now being institutionalized in the position of relative autonomy, which throughout Modernity becomes art's unbearable straitjacket and simultaneously the condition of its possibility for unlimited freedom. Here the instances of "audience", "criticism", "artists" and physical institutions[2] to match are being created, instances which are to be dominant for several hundred years, with only a few supreme changes.

And finally, *the novel* as well is developed here. Of course epic genres have been known earlier, but generally they have been considered as 'low' forms of art. The development of the modern novel during 18th century is so remarkable that Ian Watt has called his classical study on

---

[2] As it is described by Hauser (n.d.) in its historical process, more systematically particularly with regard to the entire structure of "public opinion", including the position and role of the literary public in Habermas (1976), and finally in the development of the concept "Institution Kunst" in a broad sense (cf. 1.2) in Bürger (1974 and 1979).

the development of the novel during the 18th century *The Rise of the Novel*.[3] The novel simply seems to become the aesthetic archetype of Modernity. It does so for some very specific reasons to which we shall return.[4]

On the face of it, the 18th century seems to be a period of contrasts. Are these births intrinsically connected with each other? Do not the efforts which result in, for instance, the encyclopedists' rationalistic project of Enlightenment, form a direct contradiction of for instance, a Rousseau's criticism of culture and civilization, or to the extreme subjectivism of Romanticism and the cult of nature?

Yes, and no. These contrasts are undeniable. However, the simultaneous emergence of that kind of supreme contrast is semiotically very consecutive. Radical rationality also brings about a radical rejection of rationality. The cult of culture implies the rejection of culture in the fixation on the fantasm about the 'natural' (without thereby deciding which came first, the chicken or the egg). The overall pattern of contrasts is thus expressive of the fact that what is born or mounted are *axes*, registers of meaning, above all in the nature of implementing supreme organization, directions, a sort of *vectorization* of the space of meaning. What is new is not, consequently, the poles themselves, but

---

[3] Watt 1985. Cf. also Hans Hauge's interesting discussion on the relation between "novel" and "romance" (Hauge 1989b). Or Robert Scholes' useful semiotical systematization of the epic genres, in Scholes, 1987.

[4] These are generally supposed to be seen in the development sections. But the question of the abilities of the novel will be treated separately in the *Reprise* section 5.2. I have also outlined the problems (in general terms) in Kyndrup 1989.

the way they are connected: the way in which they mutually form each other as contrasts along axes thus being defined.

As to the *novel* it is not – at any rate not immediately – quite so simple. In all circumstances the birth of the novel appears to be a twin delivery – actually two-egg twins. The difference between Richardson and Fielding, between Goethe and Diderot seems to be immense. Are they also just counterpoles of the same axis, extreme cases of the constructive possibilities of the genre – or are we actually dealing with a sort of double being, only linked by external features? We shall attempt to supply an answer to these questions in the following readings of Diderot and Goethe.

Denis Diderot: *Jacques le Fataliste*

Around the Novel

A very strange novel. A novel which over several centuries was considered by literary history to be artistically imperfect. But which at the same time could be used as a prize example of various – very different – literary forms. And recently it is even beginning to be admired.[5]

---

[5] Concerning the former issue it is typical of the treatment of the work in the great standard literary histories of Modernity. In his *Handbuch der Literaturwissenschaft* Fritz Neubert calls it "no novel" and "typical to the philosophical century" (which is no literary praise! Cf. Neubert 1924-26, 391). Concerning the latter issue Diderot and his novel were considered to be a main figure/main piece of work in the *realistic* tradition of world literature (in the Soviet "one-stream-conception", cf. Kyndrup and Stæhr, 1982, esp. vol. II pp. 72ff). Rainer Warning, 1975, takes the novel as an example of an especially open and reader-oriented piece of

Jacques le Fataliste et son Maître was written between 1771 (when a first version is mentioned) and 1773 (when Diderot seems to bring a final version along on his thanksgiving journey to Katarina II and St. Petersburg[6]). In 1the beginning just a few copies are in circulation among Diderot's friends. Later (1778-80) it is published as a feuilleton in Grimm's *Correspondance Littéraire* (15 parts) in a somewhat inaccurate version. In 1780 Goethe is known to have read it and to have been very pleased with it. Schiller translates the Mme de la Pommeraye story[7] into German in 1785, and in 1792 the whole piece of work is published in German. It is not until 1796, 12 years after Diderot's death, that it is published in full in France.

Though Diderot actually had to earn his living as a 'free' intellectual for a long period of his life (above all as a translator of and later on an author of encyclopediae) after his father had broken financially with him, *Jacques le Fataliste* was never written for the free market as such. On the face of it, it is rather an *étude*, a discussion – or maybe even, as was subsequently argued, an anti-novel: written by

---

work to which the method of "Rezeptionsästhetik" is very applicable. Finally, Jean-Claude Bonnet, the French Diderot expert, claims that Diderot's novelistic art is an immediate basis for not only Borges' writings, but also for Luis Buñuel's films (Bonnet 1984, pp. 29-30). Anyway, precisely *Jacques le Fataliste* tempted Milan Kundera to make a dramatic adaptation which has been widely performed. And Kundera considers the novel to be the finest novel of the 18th century (with *Tristram Shandy*) (Kundera, 1986b, p. 22).

[6] As may be known, it was Katharina II who, by buying Diderot's library from him and hiring him as a librarian, paying him 50 years' salary in advance, enabled him to live fairly reasonably from 1765.

[7] Cf. below.

a man who was convinced that the faster he wrote the better the result; who admired Sterne, which is not so strange; but who also admired Richardson, which may seem strange when we contemplate the aesthetic construction of *Jacques le Fataliste*[8] Could there be any relationship at all between Richardson's sticky, moralizing, artistically clumsy (to put it mildly), and endless epistolary novels on the one hand – and what has been called one of world literature's two most complicated novels, on the other?[9]

The Text

> Comment s'étaient-ils rencontrés? Par hasard, comme tout le monde. Comment s'áppelaient-ils? Que vous importe?

This is how the text begins.[10] The narrator repeats a question from the assumed reader which he then answers, partly by hinting that such questions are senseless, partly by impertinently querying what it has to do with the reader. This sets the tone.

Addresses to the reader and, generally, the explicit narrator's objectifying relation to what is being narrated, are dominant and continuous dimensions of the text. Its vertical

---

[8] Cf. Diderot's *Éloge de Richardson*, 1762 (for instance in Diderot, 1968). Further below.

[9] For instance by Ernst Sander, 1972, p. 346. Ibid. the construction and development of the novel is called "almost madly artificial".

[10] The edition referred to here and in the following is the *Livre de Poche* edition (403), postface de Jacques Proust, Paris, 1972.

dimension is thus emphasized demonstratively (cf. fig. 1 below).

The novel has several different narrated levels. The main level (II in the figure), which is the one immediately told by the explicit narrator, consists of the story about the journey from somewhere to somewhere by the manservant Jacques and his unnamed master. That account, with its episodic character, and with the master/servant constellation, gives clear references to the picaresque narrative tradition (*Lazarillo de Tormes, Simplicissimus, Don Quijote*). However, no big thing is happening at this level. Apart from an almost suffixed epic tension towards the end (to which we shall return later) the plot is a circular one, forming above all the frame of a series of stories; told by Jacques, by his master, by a landlady. By means of these there are references back to a number of different events (which we, for convenience, have combined into one 'vertical' level, III in the figure). They are of more or less importance, but among those quantitatively and qualitatively essential should be noted (1) Jacques' love story, which is a continuous one, in the end (maybe) merging into level II; (2) the long story about Mme. de la Pommeraye (about sixty pages) told by the landlady in the "Grand Cerf", which as its only relation to level II has the fact that one of its protagonists happens to spend the night there at the same time as Jacques and his master; (3) the story of Jacques' captain who is said to be the one from whom Jacques' fatalistic outlook derives, and which is above all about an infinite number of duels with a colleague whom he hates and loves; (4) the master's lovestory in which he is systematically and emphatically taken in; and finally (5) the story told by Marquis des Arcis

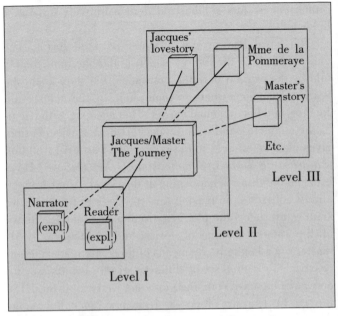

Fig. 1. The three primary levels in the narrative. 'Up' against the actual reader there are of course also implicit narrator and reader.

(who appeared in the Pommeraye case), about Hudson, the clever, but unimpededly randy abbot.

Every single story is narrated 'personally' in relation to II, which in its turn is (essentially) authorially narrated from level I. This is one of the most important foundations of the verticality of the text. Above all this implies a destabilization of the reliability of the narrators, both absolutely (narrated narrators) and relatively (as it is almost impossible to decide how to weight the statement of a given, narrated episode at level III, according to itself, and levels II and I respectively).

First Development Section

Throughout the novel the limits between the levels have different characteristics. Between I and II there is a differing status of fictionality, as II (and thus III) are "fiction" in the universe of I. On the other hand, II and III belong to the same level of fiction, and the distinction is thus only temporal (if III is to be told personally from II the events at III must have happened before the ones at II).

However, certain inconsistencies appear in this separation of the fictional levels. On the one hand, the status of fiction of level II is made clear by the narrator's demonstrative power to do what he likes with the characters. For example the narrator is happy to admit that in the middle of certain episodes he simply invents convenient details (like Jacques' spending the night with the police officer in Conches, p. 32). And the narrator has to admit that he has been unable to write the very shrewdly formulated letters from Mme de la Pommeraye which are mentioned: that would be beyond his talent, he admits (269-70). Later on, however, the narrator gets the idea that there are two "versions" of the story about a given (and in the context completely unimportant) situation. This suggests that what is told has in fact happened, and has not been invented – or anyway that it exists 'objectively' as the present story, i.e. as something which differs from the immediate ideas of the narrator. On the other hand, the reader is generously left to choose whichever version he might prefer – when having rested his head, as it is said (179).

Demonstrative, formal discrepancies are also to be found in the relations between levels II and III. Let us take, for instance, the scene in which, having just seen a funeral procession, probably his old captain's, Jacques recounts the following about him:

Le lendemain, dès la pointe du jour, mon capitaine, après avoir embrassé plusieurs fois son camarade, s'en sépara pour ne plus le revoir. A peine fut-il arrivé dans son pays, qu'il mourut. (68-69)

In answer to his master's question about how he knows this, Jacques refers to the funeral procession which just passed them. But it is obvious that the story about the captain has taken place a long time before that. Thus the levels are being mixed, are being 'pressed' together temporally into an impossible construction. This is also manifest in the grammar.[11] After this episode the narrator answers the reader that the story about Jacques' captain has not been invented; he himself has heard it from one M. de Saint-Étienne. It all concludes with a warning to the reader not to take "le vrai pour le faux, le faux pour le vrai" (70).

Here the convergence between the vertical levels which takes place towards the end of the novel is already suggested. It is true that the 'genuine' conclusion is just Jacques' going to prison for the rest of his life. But the last one of the 'optional' conclusions added after that, makes level II and most of level III merge into each other completely: Jacques gets his Denise, is perhaps – perhaps not – made a cuckold, &c., &c.

But also levels I and II approach each other. At one time the narrator suddenly proclaims that everything he has told comes from Jacques (thus postulated to belong to the

---

[11] French distinguishes grammatically between the aspects of a narrative (especially for example fictional) past, the "passé simple", and an immediately reporting one, "passé composé".

same level of fiction as the narrator, 196). And in the end, all the levels merge both in terms of insight and in terms of time; the narrator says that 'someone wanted to convince him of Jacques' status as a cuckold' (316) and the reader is encouraged to go to the prison to have the story from Jacques himself (a story which logically cannot exist if Jacques is in prison) (311). The latter not only implies a shift in the narrator's hitherto 'olympic' *point-de-vue* with its temporal *vision-par-derrière*. There is also a transformation of the narrator's status of being 'authorial': the instance is, so to speak, being personalized. Theoretically, the effect might be an authentification by virtue of the convergence towards a 'real' level of fiction. Far more likely, however, the breaks and inconsistencies towards the reader manifest themselves as a further fictionalization, thus creating a distance by undermining the narrator's (delimited) authority. By all means: The picture is flickering, and the implicit narrator of the text (behind the explicit one) becomes a *Spielverderber*, spoiling any idea about even just relative order in the fictional construction. Thus this instance emphasizes itself and its ability; this is important to the entire utterance of the novel.

Horizontally: The Thematics of the Enunciated

But first of all – tentatively separated – the thematics as carried forward by the levels of fiction themselves.

The focus is on Jacques' so-called fatalism: as everything has been written "là-haut" in advance, there is no use in trying to *affect* what is to happen, for instance by acting, intriguing, &c. It is not worth it.

That is why Jacques is not afraid when he and his

master have to spend the night in a sinister place with forty bandits; if it has been written that he is going to be killed, he will be, and if not, he will not. There is no reason to hurry just because you are being followed; it has already been decided somewhere else whether you are going to be caught up or not.

It is obvious that a consistent response to this attitude would mean Jacques' complete and thorough passivity, a totally subjective indolence towards his surroundings as a whole. But Jacques is not consistent. Not in the least (which his master points out repeatedly). True enough, he does not hurry when perhaps pursued by the robbers – but still he barricades their room to delay the robbers as much as possible. He loosens his master's saddle to prove to him his principles (that one acts without wanting to) – but still he hurries to dismount his horse in order to save his master when he falls; in the subsequent dispute Jacques explains the fact that his master is not badly injured like this:

> Il était écrit là-haut *et* dans ma prévoyance que cela n'árriverait pas (310, italics added).

Unfailingly, Jacques arranges the arguments so that they turn out to be most convenient for himself. The point of his philosophy thus seems to achieve the maximum *freedom* of the subject: As it is not possible, after all, to arrange the world in overall accordance with one's own wishes – and not even very sensible to trust one's own perception of the world, one might just as well try to satisfy one's immediate needs.

This is what the stories at level III express in different ways. Briefly, the long Pommeraye story goes like this: in order to revenge herself, a rejected mistress manages to make her faithless lover (who is a marquis, that is a very high nobleman) fall in love with and marry someone whom he thinks is a poor, but religious and fine young woman. In fact, however, she is an ordinary prostitute. The revenge is that his family and position are inexpiably disgraced by such a relationship. The staging of the intrigue, continuing for almost a year, takes enormous resources: changes of identity, involvement of all kinds of instances, &c., &c. The revenge succeeds as the marquis is trapped into marrying the *grisette*. But it also fails, even doubly: The marquis selects his choice of fate and in so doing, he realizes that he is actually still in love with the girl. On her part she has been changed by the situation and by putting on her act of innocence. To cut a long story short: the prostitute *becomes* a *marquise*. The staging of the revenge falls back on the revenger herself. The issue of the story is that on the one hand it is actually *possible* to create such a fraud, possible to lure another person into making such completely wrong – and precalculated – abductions; on the other hand the intrigue, however, might result in something completely different. The one who was originally being rejected has actually had to surrender *her* freedom by engaging in a revenge which was to secure the emergence of a reality, unbearable to the guilty person. Because he chooses to take on the unbearable reality, the revenge fails and the orchestrator is doubly deceived; the postman always rings twice, and however much calculation and staging, you always run the risk that he will ring once again. And so the stage turns into a reversal of itself.

The master's love story displays something similar, but in another register. Here the intrigue, staged by the chevalier, is so obvious that the master should have seen through it right from the beginning and many times during its unfolding (which Jacques does not miss any chance to tell him). In the Pommeraye story the intrigue was very canny and actually impenetrable to the victim, but eventually it failed after all. Here we find, by contrast, a most inelegant and penetrable intrigue which actually succeeds because of the victim's unlimited credulity. Only for a generous sum does the master narrowly escape marrying the *grisette* when she is pregnant by the chevalier. This result, consequently, is not what one might expect either; in this case an unwisely arranged – and thus in principle unpredictable – intrigue actually succeeds.

Several of the smaller narrated episodes have similar statements. One of the most important ones is the Hudson case about an abbot, who is very good at his job, but also a hopeless fornicator; symbolically his house has two exits: one leading to the abbey, the other to the town. His religious superiors try to make him responsible for his fornication, not because of this, but because of the order he has managed to institute into the abbey. Spies are sent out to trap him. Having been actually trapped, however, he succeeds in trapping the spies, thus saving himself. One plot is being surpassed by another plot – which then eventually can be surpassed by yet another one. And so on.

Appearances of the world, in other words, cannot be trusted; everywhere intrigues are being staged, succeeding or failing. There is no common reason 'behind' the signifiers, no arch-code securing the subject's access to any privileged arch-referent. The subject is left to itself, to the play which it produces and by which it is involuntarily produced.

This statement is also illustrated by the important second theme in the work/novel on *exchange*. First of all this is exposed in the relation between Jacques and his Master. Although Jacques is evidently the protagonist of the novel, and in almost every way better off than his master (which does not say very much), the master/servant-relationship is not merely being *reversed*. In fact, such a complete reversal (like for instance the one in *Don Quijote*) turns into a confirmation rather than a critique of the divine hierarchical order. In *Jacques le Fataliste* the master and the servant are mutually dependent on each other, and their roles or their identities are created only through their mutual interchange. That one is master and the other servant is accidental and unimportant. What is decisive is that they are different from each other, defined by a mutual difference, this being the condition of their coming-into-character or identity. In complementary, mutual dependence.

Secondly, the story about Jacques' captain and his friend who love and hate each other, focuses on the same problem. They cannot do without each other – yet have to duel with one another every week. They languish in discouragement and nothingness when they do not have the mutual interchange to create their own identity. By being radically alike and radically different they are tied up with one another in a relationship which can only mean dying together.

To summarize: The subject is free in the sense of no longer being part of a supreme order to which it must adapt. On the other hand it has (therefore) nothing absolute to refer to in its surrounding world. Every concrete discourse, interchange, or feeling establishes its own truth,

being subjectively unmanageable. Attempts to control discourses in a superior sense result in constraint and general
ridiculousness. Freedom means realizing these premises:
Neither as a subject wanting to shape the objective world
definitively, nor as an 'object' definitively letting oneself be
arranged by systems which are precisely just relative, random, always (just) part of this or that exchange.

Vertically: The Thematics of the Enunciation

On the face of it, these thematics are multiplied by the
enunciation. The narrative subject, it is true, demonstrates
its unlimited power over the elicitation of the story by
constantly interrupting, digressing, mocking the reader's
expectations. On the other hand, as has been shown, there
are also a number of shifts in the constructions of fiction,
like for instance obvious inconsistencies and thus absence
of 'power' in the explicit narrator. This does not imply any
contradiction of the critique of projectuality, formulated in
horizontal thematics. However, such a contradiction appears
when you take the implicit narrator into consideration. This
instance actually stages the uncertainty of the enunciation
as a whole (multiplied in the enunciated) – an uncertainty
for which the novel is pleading very clearly.

That this problem of self-referential inconsistency is not
precarious (at least hardly in Diderot's contemporary
context) is above all due to the fact that the implicit
narrator really *is* hidden. The explicit narrator's importunate and constant appearances, also in direct meta-
textual addresses to the reader, imperceptibly cover the
instance which is actually creating its voice and thus has
it under control. When for instance the narrator refers to

this or that contemporary writer (Sterne and Richardson for instance, the former directly – and rightly so – mentioned as an ideal) this strengthens the reader's feeling of a clear difference between the levels of fiction, I and II-III, respectively.

Even though the mockeries and the teasing may elicit a certain distance between the explicit reader on the one hand and the model or implicit reader on the other hand, also here it is the relative, potential closeness between the instances that makes them merge into each other. This probably prevents the emergence of distance in yet another dimension towards the real reader, at least the contemporary one.

The making-distance, however, as such, at the vertical level is exceedingly clear. The reader is not allowed to 'forget' that what is told is a constructed narrative, nor to forget his own role as the reader of an extremely artificial creation. The construction of a frame story also contributes to this (telling about someone telling), when considering the obvious and emphasized tendential unreliability of all the narrators. The narrated world is consequently not being immediately subjectivized into experience of the reader's own. The reader's experience overtly applies to the *narration* of a world, or rather a system of worlds. And that is indeed something else.

In total: The 'Saying' of the Novel

Altogether thus, there is a beautiful consistency between the thematizations of the subject/object-relation at the horizontal and vertical levels of the novel, respectively, in the statements of the stories and the enunciation of their constructions. The novel offers itself to the reader as an (aesthetic) object, in the same way, fundamentally, as the objective world offers itself to the subjects acting within the fictions, i.e. as something which cannot be explained by any spontaneous abduction, or as something which might very well differ completely from what seemingly could be unambiguously deduced from all the signs. That is, among other things, because the signs may have been put there, may have been manipulated, precisely in order to cause this or that spontaneous abduction as part of a greater, systematic distortion. But even though that kind of sign-producing project is possible, no projectualizing subject can be sure that they will lead to the desired result. In that sense the world of objects is ungovernable, unpredictable, and random. And only for that very reason do subjectivity and freedom become even possible.

Exit

Of course this scanning of the anatomy of subjectivity must be seen in the light of the historical context. The Great Order itself is at that time, immediately before the French Revolution, on the eve of melting away: the idea of the supreme, hierarchical relatedness of objects, as ideally expressed in the absolutist system, is breaking down. That is why the playing with reality in *Jacques le Fataliste* is more far-reaching than the novel's ridicule at the thematic level of morality, order in general, and religious order in particular; by being itself possible as a form the novel infringes this order directly. It does so simply by existing, and even more so by existing as something which itself has been produced by a subject. Thus the subject is so sovereign that it is able to stage and objectify the limits of its own sovereignty. And this is – at that time – indeed an unheard-of triumph for the subject.[12]

Jacques le Fataliste is neither in this, nor in its artificial form, however, unique in its time: it is closely related to Sterne's *Tristram Shandy* (1760-67),[13] to Fielding's *Tom Jones* (1748) and, to take a Scandinavian example, to Johs. Ewald's prose fragment *Levnet og Meeninger* (begun in 1774).[14]

Jacques le Fataliste thematizes itself as art, emphasizes its own artificiality. It is not an "organic" work of art in the sense which was later seen as the ideal in particular of narrative literature. Far more than a narrative it is a meta-narrative; it tells more by the way it tells than by the statement of what it is saying; it is not "mimetically" oriented in the sense that it pretends to fully represent the real world qua its own fictive world. But perhaps it is mimetic in the sense that it draws a picture of preconditions and

---

[12] Just in case, out of respect for the impatient reader: of course this is also something else within another historical context. For instance it is an unsolvable paradox or a radical criticism of sense. We shall return to this issue in the second development section (on *Jacques le Fataliste*: see esp. 3.6).

[13] Which it also says directly, for instance p. 313. In addition to this several concrete episodes in *Jacques le Fataliste* are direct or hidden quotations from *Tristram Shandy* (for instance the talk about knee wounds).

[14] Of course Diderot did not know the last one, just as Ewald cannot possibly have read Diderot's novel. But still there are striking likenesses, especially concerning theme/attitude, but also concerning aesthetics. The fact of the matter is that Sterne is the ideal for both of them. As to Ewald see Peer E. Sørensen 1989.

limits to subjectivity in general and thus to the conditions of cognition and existence – *qua its construction*.

Apart from that, it is completely without "self-expression". It does not refer to any finite identity with a given need for expression: described in a Jakobsonian register it is characterized by attraction to the metalinguistic and the phatic strata of language, whilst the dominant axis between the emotive and referential, ideal-typically becoming the foundation both within production and reception of art and literature in Modernity, is absent.[15]

Of course this is also the reason why Diderot's novel, with the exceptions of its closest contemporaries, for almost two hundred years, was not considered to be anything peculiar, especially not in capacity of a novel. A bunch of rather incoherent philosophical speculations, well OK. But a novel, no way.

Jacques le Fataliste is far too transparent at every level, in its thematics and in its mode of function. What is of obvious interest to the novel is the subject as construction. *Jacques le Fataliste* is thrilled with its own constructive ability; indeed it may be this very ability, into which it wants to communicate its insight. In the light of the following tradition which for a period of time was to dominate the narrative prose and which thoroughly tries to *hide* its own constructive character, its own *Kunstmittel*, it is small wonder that Diderot's novel turns out as bad, incoherent and vulgar. Strange, and above all: dull.

---

[15] Roman Jakobson's model on strata of the linguistic message comprises the emotive (concerning the sender), the phatic (concerning contact), the referential, the poetic, the metalinguistic and finally the conative (concerning the receiver) stratum. See Jakobson 1960.

Johann Wolfgang v. Goethe: *Die Leiden des jungen Werthers*

Around the Novel

The publication of the novel in 1774 was terribly embarrassing to the persons who served as models for its protagonists: Charlotte Buff and her husband Johann Christian Kestner in Wetzlar. But this was not the only striking effect of the novel; a wave of suicides is said to have swept Europe concurrently with the translation and publication of the novel in various countries.[16] The fictional character, Werther, did not only set a fashion in suicides; also his favourite clothes – blue on yellow – were diligently imitated. You would find these dandified *bourgeois* everywhere, wasting away with unrequited love, contemptuously turning their backs on the rationality of material world, which dictated sexual restraint, accumulation, anality and career.

For those who actually fulfilled their contemplated suicide the matter certainly had definite consequences. For everyone else (including Goethe himself, who later on became quite a different man, serious and with a sense of earthly life) it soon passed, fortunately. And the latter group was, as development has proved, after all largest.

But how is it that a literary piece of work can be so embarrassing to real, living persons? And what is it in the

---

[16] The size of the wave is not known, and the phenomenon has probably been exaggerated – now almost through tradition – in the various histories of literature. However, notoriously, one Christel von Lassberg committed suicide by drowning, actually carrying *Werther* at the time (cf. Rothmann 1987, p. 151). The novel was translated into French in 1775, English in 1779, Italian in 1781.

thematics and the construction of the work which creates such an immediate and uniform impact in a Europe, which was at that time – unlike today – not subject to any synchronizing coordination by mass media?

Anyway: The novel was a success and it was a scandal. What made it scandalous was evidently above all its unconcealed positive attitude towards suicide as a legitimate choice for anyone not satisfied with his life. As is well-known, suicide is damned by the Christian Church. But apart from that, in the novel the suicide, Werther, is endowed with a number of allusions to Christ (the expressions in his goodbye letter to Lotte, the time of death, etc.). In the opinion of the Church the combination of suicide and Christ made the novel almost blasphemous. Add to this the fact that the book in reality turned out to appear not only to be spiritually seductive but also to have direct, fatal consequences, and it is small wonder that it was forbidden in many places. Thus for instance in Copenhagen in 1776.

Werther's character of being a "key novel", *Schlüsselroman*, was known only to a narrow circle of contemporaries, so this cannot have been important for its impact. However, the fact that it was a *Schlüsselroman* had consequences for the outer life of the novel. Goethe, it must be mentioned, was markedly uninterested in hiding this circumstance. Not only does he retain the name of Lotte and a whole number of the real Lotte's outer family circumstances; he even sends her a copy of the book (which he has 'kissed a hundred times') and asks her to comment on it. Which she does not do. Kestner, her husband, in turn sends several angry letters demanding alterations in order to make the models unrecognizable. Goethe meets these demands to a certain extent, but at last he has to point out the disproportion between Kestner's personal demands and the success of the novel throughout Europe. It must be, Goethe writes, a modest sacrifice for such an immense, emotional effect on so many people.[17]

However that may be, Goethe did make some corrections. The second edition from 1787 was somewhat revised, especially towards the end of the novel. Albert (= Kestner) was made less jealous, more sovereignly noble, which tends to remove Werther's passion from the sphere of reality. Also in other respects the description of Werther renders him further insane. This makes the novel more suitable for the drawing-room, all things considered. The more mad, i.e. the more unusual a person who has to choose suicide, the smaller the general impact or model character of the solution. Many years later, as is well known, the novel seemed somewhat awkward even to the ageing Goethe himself, and to a certain extent directly dangerous. Still it was and has remained his greatest popular success.

The Text

Formally the novel is constructed as a collection of documents which are to elucidate the events which in the last couple of years of Werther's life finally lead him to suicide. The explicit sender of the material is the so-called publisher (*Herausgeber*), who is anonymous, pretendedly neutral, and who collects the documentation with the special purpose of showing – as exactly as possible – what happened.

---

[17] The concrete information on the creation and the history of reception history of the text is above all the work of Rothmann, 1987, and the epilogues in Goethe 1984 and Goethe n.d.

The publisher's criterion is truth, his reference is reality. Almost throughout the novel he lets Werther speak for himself in a great number of letters, above all to Wilhelm, his friend (but also to Lotte). Towards the end (and also after Werther's death, which Werther obviously cannot describe himself) the publisher takes over more and more, becoming the actual narrator, however still claiming to do so on the basis of posthumous documents, evidence, etc.

Basically the epistolary novel as a genre has its strength in the illumination of 'authentic' subjectivity. The construction of 'personal' narrating either objectifies the narrator or makes him immediately accessible to the reader's identification. At the same time the constant shifts of narrating moment in the epistolary novel, makes it possible to mediate between the Scylla and Charybdis of the extremes of temporal perspective: pure *vision-avec* may make it difficult to establish any (also cognitive) distance from what is narrated, whilst pure *vision-par-derrière* necessarily objectifies an instance outside what is narrated and thus removes this into a somewhat distanced position. Apart from that, the epistolary novel has the evident advantage – at least for novels which want to appear realistic – of solving the formal problem of artificiality of the medium. A novel is a collection of words, a text which, truly, may pretend to represent the world or a world. In all circumstances this is at least artificial. An epistolary novel, however, might actually – because of the fact that it utilizes an identical medium, the written word – consist of authentic documents. And something which naturally exists in writing is most naturally expressed in – writing. The success of the epistolary novel proves these facts, especially until modern bourgeois literature institutionalizes its own authentic naturalness.[18]

In *Die Leiden des jungen Werthers* the epistolary novel has been modified, since there are, apart from the traditional comments from the publisher towards the end, passages which are distinctly narrated by the publisher (and these have certain 'authorial' illogicality compared with the pretended retrospective reconstruction of actual events). But in spite of that, the novel appears above all as a collection of documents, as something which refers to concrete, actual events – or to events which might at least just as well have been actual. Formally, then, the novel is told according to the outline in fig. 2. Every bit of information passes through the publisher's 'neutrally' arranging instance, and in a certain sense also through the designated recipients of Werther's letters, above all Wilhelm, his friend. Immediately above the axis of events we have Werther himself as the actual narrator and interpreter of the events (with the above exception). As the structure appears here schematically, it might actually indicate an objectification of the narrating instance, i.e. Werther, and thus of his actions. However, this is by no means the case. The modifying elements, compared to the pure genre, in this case all work towards the same end:

---

[18] Cf. for instance the first best-seller in world literature, Richardson's *Pamela* (1741), which is also an epistolary novel. As a contrast one could remember how the narrator in *Jacques le Fataliste* who, precisely where he has a chance of proving a little authenticity by depicting some letters, mentioned in the fiction, explicitly refrains from doing so. His reason is even that he is not sufficiently talented to re-make these (very elaborated) letters. See for instance op.cit. p. 269ff, and besides our reading above.

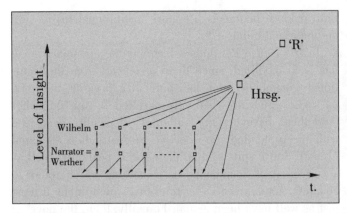

Fig. 2. The formal, narrative construction of the novel in a system of time/insight.

towards a reinforcement of the conceptual reader's direct identification with the characters of fiction. This can be seen for instance in the aspects of insight and time in the narrative structure. The majority of events are, as mentioned, told in the first person, 'personally' with the impact of authenticity implied by this. At the same time the voice of the publisher – and thus not least his direct narrative interventions – guarantee a certain authorial authority [sic!] which prevents a fundamental problematization of the reliability of the Werther instance, but without at the same time appearing as an alternative (because of the vast redundancy of the universe of values, cf. below). In the same way it can be noted how the mechanism of identification in the relative *vision-avec* of the letters (or anyway their constantly shifted *vision-par-derrière*), combined with the *vision-par-derrière* of the superior narrative instance, create an epic effect of a space which is at one

First Development Section

and the same time very alive, relevant, present – and objective, authentic.

The structure is very efficient (which in this case is unanimously confirmed by the history of reception). Even in preparation for the controversy of the novel and to an eventual confrontation with censorship the structure is quite clever. The novel *has* an instance, the one of the narrator, which in a completely outer sense, anyway, is distancing Werther, the madman. But as we have seen, this formal modification of Werther's subjectivity in fact has rather the opposite effect, i.e. it is reinforcing, by throwing this subjectivity into relief, by transporting it into reality, by 'authorizing' it, making it authentic. Literary censorship has always been a damned difficult business.

Although *Werther* may therefore appear immediately quite vertical, this verticality never has serious consequences within the novel's mode of function as an actual thematization of the problems of enunciation. Though the reader's insight (fig. 3) passes formally through a confrontation with, respectively, the instances of the publisher, the recipients of the letters, and finally the characters of Werther and his immediate co-actors, this passage is more or less only apparent. After all, these instances belong to one and the same level of fiction; moreover, everything is done in each case to make this level of fiction appear identical with the reader's real level; i.e. as "reality". An abstract sort of vertical distance always exists, of course, by virtue of the very reading situation. But at that level we are rather dealing with a reader oppositioning the entire, unbroken level of fiction (the detour, across the publisher and the recipients above, is active as an optimalization of the identifying *Einfühlung* with the character of Werther and

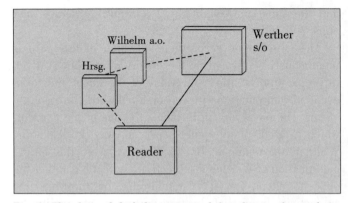

Fig. 3. The dot-and-dash line turning left indicates the reader's formal direction; in reality the direction is seen as leading straight from reader to Werther.

his experiences). The enforced, intricate way around, which is the *actual* vertical subject/object-connection, remains basically dissimulated. Part of the argumentation in favour of this will be evident below from the examination of the novel's universe of values. Moreover, yet another subtlety in the novel's use of the traditionally distance-making vertical instances for perfecting the mechanism of identification will be revealed; namely, the fact that the external (modifying) instances are drawn towards the negative side of the novel's very unambiguous system of values.

Horizontally: Thematics of the Enunciated

The narrative plot is easy to grasp: A young man of absolutely good and bourgeois family (but without the inherited privileges of nobility) takes a break in his intended official career (for various, somewhat obscure reasons). He has artistic gifts, he draws and paints, and he is passionately interested in literature. His idols are Klopstock and Ossian. Werther is highly, positively interested in nature, in what is natural, but also – and not least – in his own feelings in experiencing this nature.

He lives alone in a foreign town where he meets Lotte, with whom he falls in love. She is, however, engaged to another man, and after the return of Albert, her fiancé, Werther finds the situation so unbearable that he leaves the town and resumes his career. Now, however, the contrasts between his own ideals and feelings and the rules and conventions of society become glaringly clear to him. In society things do not happen in proper relation to personal abilities, and do not have any relation to criteria dealing with concrete matters. On the contrary everything is decided by convention, by the positions within the hierarchy held by the players of the proper game. As the result of an episode in which Werther causes a scandal because he stays at a party which only nobility, according to convention, is supposed to attend, he takes his leave and goes back to Lotte's town. In the meantime Lotte and Albert have got married, and Werther's position as a potential suitor of Lotte is consequently even more impossible. The situation comes to a head, and it becomes obvious that Werther cannot even remain a platonic suitor. He now has to make a choice: he can choose life, but that would have to be a life without the woman he loves and consequently a life, in a certain sense remaining empty forever. And, furthermore, this life would after all seem to be a life without himself. For in the narrowminded rationalistic, social reality of his contemporaries there is no room for his subjectivity, for his ideals and ideas. If Werther is to live, he then has to deny everything which is important and real and meaningful to him. His alternative is death by his own hand. Suicide: refrain from poorly compromising any relationship to one's surroundings. Suicide: carrying through – completely and unconditionally – one's subjectivity, which is the same thing as denying, wiping out the object world facing the subject. Or, consequently, wiping out the subject facing the object world: suicide.

Werther chooses suicide, and this is an obvious choice on the basis of the system of values established by the novel. It can be outlined as in table 1.

The attitude of the novel is unambiguously positive towards the left side and negative towards the right side. Werther himself as a character is described as completely

the individual's needs	society's needs
will	must/ought
nature	culture
realization of passions/instincts	self control
emotion	sensibility
value norm defined by individual	value norm defined by system
freedom	restriction
(Lotte)	(Albert)
+	−
death?	life?

Table 1. The system of values in the novel's world.

First Development Section

governed by the values and properties of the left side. Werther and the novel now bring into the system the choice, the dichotomy, "death" opposite "life", as concordant with the other dichotomizations. As it is not possible in real life to realize the positive values of the left side, the possibility of life is being linked to the values of the right side. Thus the choice is between a positive and beautiful death; or a life necessarily becoming flat and negative. In this situation the choice is actually one between treachery or death. And treachery towards one's own actions and feelings is an action which is very, very far from the figure of Werther.

This system of values is of course a crude reconstruction. Actually it is established slowly and gradually throughout the novel. But towards the end it has become so strongly and redundantly expressed that the result of Werther's choice is evident. Both the above narrative structure and Werther's own anticipations right from the beginning of the novel contribute to this.

Described like this, the thematics of the *enuncié* can be formulated at various levels. The fact that a freedom-loving subject, positively valorized, is deprived of the possibility of unfolding itself in its contemporary society, can of course immediately be held against this society. Thus *Werther* is easily read as a concrete criticism of the conditions in Germany at that time. The free scope at the disposal of the bourgeois subject actually *was* rather limited because of a vast number of privileges exclusively for the nobility and for certain powerful official classes. This, obviously, because at that time Germany still consisted of a great number of small states and principalities each developing its own system of privileges. In fact *Werther* has been[19] read as a "progressive" criticism of these conditions which held back any modern development in Germany at that time. In the same register, albeit not so concrete, the novel can be seen as a somewhat more general criticism of civilization in the spirit of Rousseau: culture spoils the individual's possibilities of a natural unfolding, and only a civilization which gives priority to natural, subjective needs over the constricting conventions of culture, will be able to solve the basic conflict between the individual and society.

Each of these scannings of thematics is possible, yet not sufficiently thoroughgoing and thus not satisfactory. For there are points supporting a far more radical formulation of the thematics. In fact, the most essential significance of the suicide is not a protest against concrete social conditions of the individual. No, the novel describes the subject-/object-relation as *impossible as such*, as something which cannot exist, cannot work, cannot do. This conflict is described as being so to speak endogenous to the human subject. In so far as the subject is constituted as a "subject", that is to say, has been furnished with a will directed against its surroundings, then this subject will necessarily be unbearably constricted by the objective world. Not only, initially, by tedious rules and conventions, but also in any circumstances by the very built-in contradictions performed by the inevitable clash with the will of other subjects. This is to say: if there is only one real subject in the world, then there is no room for others.

Many traits of the novel support this interpretation of

---

[19] Above all in the tradition of historical materialism/marxism, cf. for instance *Deutschsprachige Literatur im Überblick*, 1973, pp. 59-60.

the conflict as being constitutional, necessary, existential. For instance it can be noted that Werther seems to be facing the same problems everywhere, only in different versions (in his bourgeois life, his former and possible incipient love affairs hinted of, &c., &c.). Werther even hunts out the conflict which is to be the immediate, apparent cause of his suicide: He returns to Lotte, even though he has already once left her. More or less deliberately he aggravates the situation, making it completely insoluble (Albert's growing suspicion, Lotte's rejection). It can also be pointed out that there is no immediate indication of any emotional reciprocity between him and Lotte. True, Lotte is bound by a promise given at her mother's deathbed, but to her no contradiction seems to exist between her love for Albert and her close relation to Werther (not until the end, as Werther deliberately forces a precarious situation). Werther as a matter of fact clashes with other wills, which, from their own viewpoint, have as much right to their stance as he has to his own. In other words, the clash is an objective one, inevitable, irreversible: the only way out indeed is a way completely out.

It is then the statement of the novel that actually suicide is the only realization of the subject, which is not smirched with compromise and half-hearted pragmatism. The subject as such is an impossibility: it cannot live and therefore it must die.

Vertically: The Thematics of Enunciation

Of course it was this radical understanding of the impossible possibility of the subjective which made the statement of the novel so dangerous and controversial. But in this there is also a paradox compared to the way in which the *enunciation* of the novel thematizes the subject/object-relation.

As mentioned above, the apparently unfolded verticability of the novel is actually almost only pretended. The instances belong to the same level of fiction, and above all their presence serves to maximize the effect of the problems and attitudes of the enunciated 'world'. Enunciation, consequently, is in no way self-thematizing in terms of making itself the object of a discussion. On the contrary, the dimension of enunciation tries as far as possible to hide behind the allegedly documentary nature of the collection of texts. The novel's type of *Rezeptionsvorlage* is unambiguously and consistently *identification*. The figure of Werther is a central-perspective figure of identification.

Thus the pragmaticality of the text itself is not included by the radical rejection of a general possibility of the subject/object-relation which is claimed by the novel's statement. Symbolically, this difference is redoubled by the fact that in his intoxication by nature the figure of Werther from the very start rejects exactly books:

> Du fragst ob du mir meine Bücher schicken sollst? – Lieber, ich bitte Dich um Gottes willen, lass mir sie vom Halse! Ich will nicht mehr geleitet, ermuntert, angefeuert sein, braust dieses Herz doch genug aus sich selbst; ich brauch Wiegengesang, und den habe ich in seiner Fülle in meinem Homer. (8)[20]

Just as this book must advise against the use of books, so

---

[20] The page numbers refer to the Reclam edition (67 [2]), Goethe 1984. This is based on the revised (and enlarged) edition of 1787.

First Development Section

the world of the novel unproblematically installs itself in a position of being the object of the conceptual reader subject, notwithstanding its own statement that relations like that cannot be carried into effect. For several reasons, of course, it is not possible to parallelize and consequently it is by no means possible to talk about any logical contradiction. But as far as the enunciation is concerned it is worth noticing the way in which it makes the enunciated world accessible as an object to the reader of the novel; it effectively implies a merging of subject/object of the very kind which it is trying to prove impossible, in its own statement about its fictional world.

Summing up

This indeed marks – if not a contradiction, then at least a distinctive incongruity. An incongruity which in spite of its distinctiveness nevertheless is to become a constitutive feature of Modern literature.[21]

Die Leiden des Jungen Werthers is a serious work of literature, being thus in the process of formation; above all it takes itself seriously. It makes the fundamental, existential problem of the subject the focus of attention, and in so

---

[21] But at the same time in a certain sense also because of this incongruity. In this it is also possible to read the contradictory ambivalence in the institutionalization and framing of modern literature. Further on this below, esp. in 2.2. As matrix of rejection for the serious literature serves the idealtypical, 'congruent' bourgeois novel which, however, declines into literature of entertainment, almost before distinguishing itself as anything but precisely a pattern. See our analysis (however there in another context) of this type in chap. 3.6 below, where we shall discuss Jane Austen's *Pride and Prejudice*.

doing, it strongly emphasizes the fact that any self-experienced and self-defined need of the subject should, necessarily, in terms of value, hold priority over, for instance, the social rules and conventions laid down by the world of objects. It might be put like this: what *Werther* actually pinpoints is the subject/object-relation itself *as* an opposition. As – literally – a life-and-death struggle. But also a number of other pairs of those contrasts which are to become arch-fantasms, standard equipment with the architecture of the consciousness of Modernity, are being formulated in this novel. For good reasons these dichotomies can be seen as variations on the subject/object-relation – emotion versus sense, ideality versus reality, inside versus outside, freedom versus compulsion, nature versus culture. We find them all in *Werther*, appearing within a roughly redundant, rigid universe of values. It might be pertinent to recall the fact that within these kinds of dichotomies the poles are engendering each other and consequently do presuppose each other, mutually. Werther's foaming showdown with the principle of reason, with the principle of reality, with culture as a whole, thus at the same time implies an immense emphasis on precisely these principles. We shall return to this below when dealing with the 18th century as a whole. But already compared to Goethe's life it is obvious that for instance his sense of *feeling* walks arm-in-arm with his sense of that rationality, which at one and the same time engenders and is engendered by emotionality.

Werther's aesthetic construction, its mode of function, is just as exemplary. It may be worth emphasizing that in any case such a strategy of *identification* in terms of receptional aesthetics only works when and if it somehow hits an existing problem within the reader. A novel like *Werther* cannot make up a sense of subjectivity like that of Werther's figure of fiction, unless the basic characteristics of this sense already exist. On the other hand, if they exist – as they did and have continuously remained, that is why *Werther* became what you might call a classic – then the novel will contribute to a sort of authorization of what has been thematized. "Truth" always supports itself.

Conclusion

The above analyses have laid bare a number of obvious differences between the two novels – about thematic priority and as aesthetic constructions.

Both horizontally and vertically *Jacques le Fataliste* is broken, discontinuous, clumsy. Through a number of different stories it demonstrates how individuals' ambitions for a pre-calculated control of their surroundings are necessarily disappointed and consequently ridiculous, superfluous. The novel immediately repeats this qua its construction. The entire mounting of the hierarchy of fiction is demonstratively in contravention of any reality-resemblance. Even the reader's dependence on projectuality is being thematized and actively and overtly ridiculed. The novel's mode of function is *distance*, the objectification of persons and events in what is thematized.

Thus there is an immediate *congruity* between the horizontal S/O-function and the novel's vertical construction of its potential subject of reception. Within both dimensions the impossibility of the relation in capacity of any kind of calculated balance is demonstrated: things are necessarily to be taken as they come, you may perhaps decode or improve a little here and there as opportunity offers. Ingeniousness, however, does not pay whether any single attempt succeeds on the face of it, or not.

In one sense this also applies to the novel itself, to the genre, to the construction. The demonstrative heterogeneity of the levels of fiction, the overt thematization of the instances of narrators and readers, all work as a questioning of – and consequently after all as an emphatic outlining of the frame which classifies the novel as – "art" ("literature"). *Jacques le Fataliste* is *problematizing* this framing and this, of course, is the reason why its position in terms of genre (and consequently also in terms of "quality") has been so uncertain for some time.

Werther differs in almost every particular. It is true that thematically it terminates with an attitude which shows the impossibility of carrying into effect every balanced S/O-relation. But the premises are totally different: here the fantasm about the ideal unfolding of the individual's authentic emotions has priority over anything else, so much so that the individual would rather renounce its physical existence than compromise in any way. Thematically, the course of events of the novel is completely consistent compared to its narrative universe; as it is not possible to live, one must die.

In its construction, however, *Werther* introduces itself as 'authentic' material, as something referring to real events. No attempts are being made to break and/or objectify the novel's character as an artificial construction. On the contrary, *identification* is suggested everywhere as the mode of function, identification with Werther's, the protagonist's, central-perspective experience of his surroundings.

A kind of *incongruity* can consequently be noticed, an

incongruity between, on the one hand, the thematic focusing of the novel on a constitutional, individual disruption which generally makes life unlivable because these ideals are unrealizable in the secular world – and on the other hand, the functional openness, accessibility, of the novel as an object for the receiving subject. *With* the novel *against* the world, one might say.

Qua its reality-imitating efficiency, qua its ambition about unreflected enroling of the reader into the problems of the thematized world (where reflections then of course can be made) *Werther* above all *dissimulates* the framing. It does a great – and successful – job in hiding its own artificiality, its *Kunstmittel*. In reality *Werther* of course is neither more nor less constructed – and thus artificial – than *Jacques*.

But as types of novels *Werther* and *Jacques* differ very much in their very constructions – and neither of them are isolated phenomena within their contexts. As a type of novel *Werther* is related to works by for instance Defoe and Richardson, and *Jacques* is fundamentally connected with works by Fielding and Sterne, among others.[22]

The question is which *type* of difference we are dealing with – whether it can be understood as a kind of semiotic complementarity, as an axis which actually, on a supreme view, ties rather than separates. Diderot's enthusiasm for Richardson (in the latter's fight with Fielding, as well) and Goethe's enthusiasm for Diderot, might point in this direction.

But the answer must be a complex one of both-and. The

---

[22] Cf. the analogous distinctions in Watt (1985).

supreme likenesses are evident: the interest in the potentials and limitations of the new human subject is common – as is the interest in constructions, in the sense that the great writer's subjectivity in each case stages the excesses, although Diderot's staging comprises a heterogeneous 'scene'. In an imagined, contemporary, mutual light the resemblances of the novels thus may seem striking – since the observation of the pathetic ridicule of individual projectuality must be closely related to the observation of its pathetic seriousness.

By contrast, in the light of what happens later on, the differences between the novels may just as well be emphasized. For the differences, mainly in their relations to their respective framings as "art", make them *capable* in different ways. Not so much compared to their contemporarity in which this construction of "art" is only on the eve of being explored and engendered as a field, but compared to a posterity, in which precisely this field character becomes a decisive turning point, the two types have quite different potentials of effect. And thus of 'meaning'.

So we *are* dealing with two "traditions" – but within something which can be united as one (new) genre: the novel. In the near future the two traditions would not be in balance, however. The literature which seemed to be immediately mimetic, and 'true to reality' and thus elaborating itself as dissimulating its own constructional framings – that type was to be absolutely dominant within the new institution of literature. Which, in its turn, was consequently being shaped by that.

2.2

Nineteenth Century: The Heteromorphism Becomes Institutional

Honoré de Balzac: *Le Père Goriot*

Introduction. The Novel

There is no great distance in time between the novels by Diderot and Goethe discussed in the previous chapter and the 1830s when Balzac has success with his great novels. Nor in terms of type does a comparison with *Werther* reveal remarkable differences.

The reason why we, nevertheless devote a chapter of close analysis to a Balzac novel, is precisely because it seems to be sketching out a literary form which is very typical of Modernity, even its archetypical form. This holds at a number of different levels. It applies *thematically*, the novel forming the exemplary performance of the conflict between individual and surroundings which later on is to be more or less standard equipment in prose literature of ideal-typical Modernity. It applies to *genre* in a narrow sense, the novel forming the development of a modern novel of central ("one-point") perspective which no longer needs constructional systems of support (for instance in the form of 'real' letters, reports) to face up to its own diction.

And more broadly, it applies to genre, style and philosophy, the novel forming the establishment of the phantasm on *realism*: the *vraisemblance* which already in the framing of meaning by the literary field turns the 'autonomous', artificial constructions into even extremely privileged statements *about* the society whose human conditions they are, from now on, supposed to depict or reflect. And finally, closely connected with this, it applies because this type of literature forms a decisive contribution to the supreme historical, semiotic framing: to the field or the institution of "literature", respectively "art".

This, then, is the construction which – usually just implicitly – becomes the point of departure for a very great number of the seditious movements which literature is later on to form, in terms of construction, from the late nineteenth century. And, incidentally, the basic construction itself, and its variations, also continue to thrive into the present, in so-called literature of entertainment amongst other areas.

In the mid-1830s Balzac's huge system of novels, *La Comédie Humaine* is really taking shape. The relation between this great shape and the single works is extremely interesting at a very fundamental level. Unfortunately, the rich variety of details and persons also gives rise to extensive 'critical' studies, leading to statements like: 'Rastignac appears in 25 novels', and 'The Duchess of Langeais was not able to participate in that very party in 1820, because (in another novel) she had already taken the veil the year before'.[1]

---

[1] Cf. for instance *L'Année balzacienne 1961*, here cf. Riegert 1973, pp.

Of course there are significant alterations of emphasis among the novels of *La Comédie Humaine*. In our context, however, these alterations seem to be of minor interest. Here *the text* and its construction of and by its framing are at issue.

Le Père Goriot is considered as one of the main works of *La Comédie Humaine* and is still one of Balzac's best-known and most-read novels. Like almost any of Balzac's great novels it was written over a very short period of time concurrently with a number of other works and with tremendous urgency. Balzac does not seem to have commenced the novel until September 1834, and the first part is published (as a feuilleton) in *Revue de Paris* on December 14, the same year. The work is finished on January 26, 1835, and published as a book on March 2 (in 1200 copies). The audience is enthusiastic, but the reviews are rather guarded. Above all Balzac is accused of "exaggeration", not least in the final parts of the work:

> Le principal défaut de M. de Balzac est l'exagération. Le premier trait de l'auteur est vrai, il est pur, mais il charge ensuite tellement que la figure grimace. La première description est satisfaisante; continuée ainsi elle resterait irréprochable, mais il la fatigue et l'épuise. L'abus de tout, du bien comme du mal, est ce qui caractérise M. de Balzac... Ainsi *Le père Goriot*, bien pris dans sa première partie, plein d'intérêt quoiqu'un peu lent, spirituel et incisif, décline quand le drama arrive".[2]

---

52 and 53. Some of the factual information below on *Le père Goriot* originates from this as well.

[2] *Le constitutionel* (the most important bourgeois-liberal voice), March 23, 1835. Cf. Riegert 1973, p. 10.

Reasonable or not this criticism reveals the implicit horizon of expectation of the critics: "Truth" and "reality" as immediate correlations of evaluation have already won the character of axioms.

The World of the Novel

The "reality" performed by the novel is clear and stable in terms of values, that is to say, presented with such emphatical redundancy as to exclude any ambiguity. The universe may be outlined as follows

stability	changeability
family feeling	egoism
depth	superficiality
actions governed by values	actions governed by purpose
morality	(pragmatism, non-morality)
honesty	dishonesty
truth	lie
suppression of needs	fulfilment of needs

On the left are represented the old, the original and – unambiguously in the evaluation of the novel – the *good*. The right side, on the contrary, contains the values connected with the new, the growing civilization, the modern society. Appearing on stage now, with a solid background in the traditional values of the left side, connected with the country, is Eugène Rastignac, a young student. Good, young, handsome, of noble birth and – poor. Poverty becomes decisive for Rastignac's movement and thus for the construction of the novel. At Madame Vauquer's

First Development Section

pension, where we find Rastignac in the beginning, poverty rules. Not that Rastignac or anyone else among the boarders are suffering directly; but scarcity, shabbiness, the stale smell of human and material small-mindedness is already from the beginning of the novel (pp. 7-32) presented with an extremely distinct focusing on its repulsive, indeed insufferably abominable, aspect.

Generally, the boarders represent the values of the right side. This applies especially to Vautrin, alias Collin, a professional criminal, a recurrent figure in *La Comédie Humaine* who tempts the innocent, poor young men from the provinces by this or that Faustian pact. The two Goriot daughters and high society in general are also placed here. The exception is the genuinely unhappy Madame de Beauséant (who is actually descended from the really old distinguished nobility). On the left side we find the innocent Rastignac at his starting point. This includes his family back in Southern France. And his friend Bianchon, a medical student, and finally, of course, old Goriot.

In short, Rastignac's problem is as follows: Since society, the world, is ruled according to the principles of the right side, you will be hopelessly lost, if you choose to insist on the principles of the left side. Should you already happen to have plenty of money you may live with the values of the left side (though necessarily be prepared to be cheated properly like old Goriot). In any other case the only choice is to live according to the socially correct principle and accept an inconvenient, poverty-stricken life – and even then you must prepare to give room for free interpretations of the commandments of morality, unless you want to deprive yourself of the possibility of only a modest career (cf. Vautrin's description, p. 97). The alternative is a convenient, exciting, adventurous life, which abandons any values but those linked with the question of what is best in obtaining one's own immediate purposes. As Vautrin puts it:

> Si j'ai encore un conseil à vous donner, mon ange, c'est de ne pas plus tenir à vos opinions qu'à vos paroles. Quand on vous les demandera, vendez-les. Un homme qui se vante de ne jamais changer d'opinion est un homme qui se charge d'aller toujours en ligne droite, un niais qui croit à l'infaillibilité. Il n'y a pas de principes, il n'y a que des événements; il n'y a pas de lois, il n'y a que des circonstances; l'homme supérieur épouse les événements et les circonstances pour les conduire. (104)

The novel acts out Rastignac's choice between these possibilities. Or more precisely: his inevitable shift from left to right. Inevitable because these (on the right side) *are* the values of society, substantially. Inevitable because the novel at the same time demonstrates how people, insisting on the original values, are being stripped and thrown out (Mme de Beauséant and above all old Goriot).

Concretely, the choice is spelled out by means of the deal which the tempter tries to make with Rastignac. Curiously enough, the assassination of the rich heir in a staged duel is hardly a crime in the eyes of the law. But it is certainly "wrong", and Rastignac duly withdraws, tries in vain to warn the victim, &c., &c. But even without Vautrin's clear-cut offer the problem would have been the same: whether to preserve your integrity, your ideas about good and evil, your respect for other people and for that reason be punished by society, and allotted a miserable, lousy, grey, dreary life – or to snap your fingers at values overall, and instead stake pragmatically on *circumstances*

First Development Section

(cf. the above quotation) and thus try to obtain the delights available.

Rastignac wavers, of course. He is particularly shocked by the sovereignly cruel way in which the Goriot daughters treat their father: they gradually extort all his money from him, leave him to die in solitude. The students have to borrow money for his funeral. But in spite of this, Rastignac looks on the whole story as a sort of textbook of amorality. The novel becomes a sort of novel of (de)formation, about Rastignac's "negative" socialization, or, if you like, his moral *déroute* – which takes place at the same time as his social success. More schematically, what is at issue is the exposure of a totally stable space of values. Something is good, and something is bad. Unfortunately, the good is *out of date* and therefore has awkward consequences, while the bad pays off and thus leads to comparatively pleasant conditions. What we are dealing with, then, is a society in which the good ones cry and the bad ones laugh. But also a society, which actually offers individuals a choice. The subject has the *possibility* of moving – and (as a principle) the possibility of not moving. In other words man is able to control his own life. But the price is to *accept* being controlled, accept being subject (:object) to the conditions, currents, values which are in fact ruling in the society in question. The choice in which the possible is wrong and the right is impossible, or anyway prohibitively unpleasant, is to some extent similar to the one of classical tragedy. The opposition between ideal and reality. Or schematically, in the subject/object-relation: if the subject is forced to invest itself completely into and within the premises of the surroundings in order to create a precalculated effect to its own advantage, the price will be the dissolution in terms of values of the integrity of that subject, understood as a differing (because only then we are dealing with integrity) from the highways of values of the surroundings. For good reasons, it is impossible to throw oneself out and stay inside as well. But of course it is possible – the way Rastignac does it at the end of the novel – to give legitimation to the choice of right-side pragmatism by referring to the necessity of making war against a society so evidently suppressing all good values. This, however, does not alter anything, unless the war is won. And there is no danger of that.[3]

The general attitude to society which in the novel appears in the shape of a world sketched out like this, is highly critical. The individual's choice is at the most one between plague and cholera, between a life becoming miserable, because you have to sell yourself to your surroundings to such an extent as to dissolve into them – and a life becoming (or remaining) miserable because the price of preserving the right ideals is not only poverty and lack of comfort, but also the world's disdain and perhaps even ostracism. Was it not *necessary* for the reviews (liberal and conservative) to think that Balzac was exaggerating with a novel like *Le Père Goriot*?

---

[3] Strictly speaking, one might choose not to regard the final sentence of the novel ("Et pour premier acte du défi qu'il portait à la société, Rastignac alla dîner chez Mme de Nucingen", 256) as being ironical. Elsewhere in *La Comédie Humaine* the figure of Rastignac, however, leaves no doubt as to how the novel regards his motives.

Well, it probably was – on the premises according to which they had to think. Because on the other hand the reviews would hardly have had to distance themselves from the novel's rough presentation of the individuals' crippled possibilities of being, had they not been bound by their own framed attitude of reception on the immediate relevance to the reality, of the statements of the novel. If, in other words, they had been able to take into consideration the structure of enunciation and the mode of function of the text.

Formally, the text is constructed with an "authorial", omniscient narrator, pointing out its own almost olympic level partly through the use of both flashbacks and flashforwards and furthermore by emphasizing a demonstratively knowing, commonly generalizing meta-level, to which and from which the concrete events are from time to time linked or fetched. Explicitly, however, no difference is being pointed out between the narrator's levels of fictionality and those of the narrated. The text is already from the start directly commenting upon itself, and also in advance taking into consideration the accusations of exaggeration:

> Après avoir lu les secrètes infortunes du père Goriot, vous dînerez avec appétit en mettant votre insensibilité sur le compte du l'auteur, en le taxant d'exagération, en l'accusant de poésie, Ah! sachez-le: ce drame n'est ni une fiction, ni un roman. *All is true*, il est si véritable, que chacun peut en reconnaître les éléments chez soi, dans son coeur peut-être (8, Balzac's italics).

Likewise no differences are suggested either at the level of fictionality or the level of insight, nor between the explicit narrator's voice and the supreme, implied narrator. In other words, the visible narrator appears as "identical with" Balzac, the author; comments, attitudes, interests of movement are altogether demonstratively situated at one and the same level of reality, directly pointing towards that concrete reality of society, which the novel is written out of, which it is treating and which it is functioning into. With the exception of the above passage of self-commentary which indeed appears as an exorcising dissociation from the notion of any difference between fiction and reality, the novel *knows* neither more nor less than its own world. The statement, the enounced, regards the enunciation as belonging to its own level, i.e. acknowledges enunciation as holding a naturally subordinate position, as merely lingual bearer and intermediating construction, compared to the transmitted substance of content. The enunciation does not create a world, it just hands it over. This postulation on the convergence of levels is demonstratively intoned already from the start of the novel through the use of the present tense in the description of the pension (after 5-6 pages there is a shift into *l'imparfait* and from there gradually into the situational narrative *passé simple*).

Though the novel, then, from the very beginning effectively emphasizes the sovereignty of the narrator, and though old Goriot is both the title figure and (which can be read out of Balzac's notes and letters around the time of creation) the intended thematically fixed point, it is, after all, Rastignac, who is in the centre. Not only as has been shown because he is the person who actually moves in the universe of values (and thus concretely has to *choose* in the field of force) but also narratively. During the major part of the novel (and increasingly as it proceeds) the narrative

172

perspective follows Rastignac. Partly, technically speaking, as "inner focalization" with him and "outward focalization" with the other persons, i.e. Rastignac acts as focalizer, partly by concretely physically following him. The mounting of Rastignac as central perspective is gradually emphasized to such an extent that the breaks which occur at the situational level appear as almost clumsy (for instance the old lady's conversation with the police spy, an episode which is intended to anticipate Vautrin's arrest, pp. 148ff). Apparently, however, the novel is conscious of the problem, because on other occasions it uses rather subtle arrangements when it needs to describe a scene in which Rastignac does not appear, at the same time having to preserve his one-point perspective. The best example is the long scene in which Rastignac, without their knowing it, happens to witness the meeting of the daughters with old Goriot at the pension (pp. 202ff). Of course the consequence is that the reader watches this scene through the eyes of Rastignac, immediately emphasizing what it does to him.

All things considered, the mode of function of the novel is clearly based on *identification*, on the fact that the reader subjectifies the world of the text into a personal experience. Among the characters the positive identification is precisely with Rastignac. Technically, this follows from the whole mounting of him as a central perspective, and as to substance he is the person *choosing*, the only one *moving* in relation to the system of values, and thus he naturally becomes the centre of energy of the novel. And consequently the one attracting energy.

The identification with Rastignac implies that his dilemma is in fact transmitted to the reader, is turned into

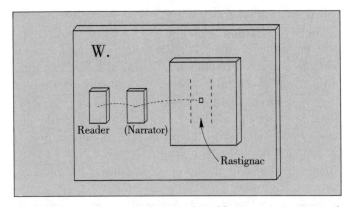

Fig. 1. Reader, narrator and narrated world appear as instances of the same world.

the reader's own dilemma. This happens in an immediate sense, since, evidently, it is a condition for this transmission that values and attitudes are implicitly shared by the reader and the novel. But the transmission of the dilemma also takes place in a different sense: all the fascinating features, all the attractions of the novel (certainly a part of the reader's assumed basis, but indeed also a part of the way in which the novel itself evaluates the universes) are linked to the right side. Rastignac, somehow, will necessarily *have to* choose a life on the right side to preserve/meet the reader's demands for fascination. Consequently, in the sequence of events the reader will have to 'want' Rastignac to choose the bad things – and is thus placing herself in a position of ambivalence, parallel to that of Rastignac when *he* is choosing the bad things: well aware of what it is, but in payment for something else, whose attraction he cannot resist though he knows he probably ought to.

First Development Section

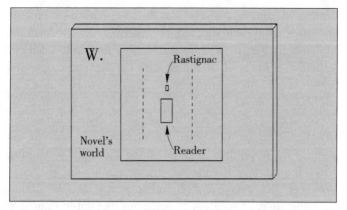

Fig. 2. The reader simply becomes a *part* of the field of tension of which Rastignac is also a part.

All in all the enunciating construction of the novel tries to remain hidden as a very construction. True, the reader knows that this fiction is born by the narrator: but its world of fiction appears as *identical* with that of the reader just as the narrator's does. The 'vertical' differences are transformed into mere quantities of space and/or time. The result is one horizontal dimension into which the reader is inscribed as well (figs. 1-2). Inscribed as a part of a continuum of a world in which certain qualitative differentiations of insight may occur (for instance narrators, values), but in which no possibilities of other worlds are being pointed out, i.e. no other potential registers of "quality".

The "Saying" of the Novel

In short, the world, then, is coherent and incoherent at one and the same time, according to the saying of the novel.

Unless of course, one chooses to accept its own explicit premises. But actually, while asserting at its level of statement that it is impossible for the individual to establish a mode of exchange with the surrounding world which is not either corrupt or leading to an unbearable way of life, the novel, in its construction of enunciation, is incorporating the possibility of such an exchange by offering itself as an immediate experience, as *world*, as object. The novel thus 'says' one thing and 'does' something else. It produces a coherent argumentation for the non-coherence of everything. In other words, the inevitable disintegration or splitting is not more inevitable than that it is not in force concerning "meaning" itself. Thus a figure of heteromorphism is emphasized in the relation between the figures, outlined by the enunciated and the enunciation of the novel, respectively. The arch-phantasm of a dynamic well-balanced subject/object-relation of Modernity is thematically being denied while at the same time confirmed qua enunciation. Or: the reader can do with literature what she cannot do with the world (and literature is able to incorporate the latter in an extremely recognizable and truthful way, using the former as its prior condition). This is, in short, the recipe for the ideal-typical literature of Modernity, the way it is being framed in this period.

Back to Balzac, *Le Père Goriot* presents another young, innocent man who is domesticated in a dirty home – a process repeatedly pictured in *La Comédie Humaine*. It should be obvious that as a type of construction this novel is very close to Goethe's *Werther*. This might at first glance seem more radical, thematically as well as formally: the rejection qua suicide of the being forced into compromise, the immediate authenticity of the epistolary form. On a closer look, however, Balzac's construction is in fact a "product development" at both levels. Thematically because the merciless presentation of the *actualized* costs of the compromise somehow are harder to shake off than the heroic suicide committed by a somewhat highly strung person, an act which must above all have had the character of a substituting experience (with certain exceptions, as mentioned above). And formally, because the absence of outer documentation of authenticity in connection with the text's claim of congruence of fictional levels actually makes the 'real' authority of the discourse much more convincing: now it is based on an implied prior condition which consequently can no longer, not even involuntarily, be turned into being the subject of discussion at the level of the text itself.

Outlook

This novel form basically dominates throughout the 19th century as the most important and most popular literary genre. The tradition from Diderot, immediately rooted in Sterne and Fielding, among others, of a vertical, frame-thematizing novel is pushed into a marginal position for the time being.

However, considered formally, the characteristic features of this winning tradition are not only those of the realistic style. Actually, these characteristic features also comprise the thematic orientation towards the subject/object-relation, the formulation of its impossibility as a condition (which implies a severe critique of society or civilization, implicitly or explicitly) and in terms of the aesthetics of reception also the transmission of this condition by a construction organized by a central perspective and oriented against identification. Certainly, the nice realism, which as to theme and attitude, pleads the *possibility* of the ideal s/o-balance of Modernity, formally resembles and of course has contributed to the development of the genre (the tradition from Defoe and Richardson, Jane Austen's novels around the turn of the century[4]). As Modernity is developing this 'prize realism', which indeed thematizes fundamental and recognizable problems and contradictions of the modern experience of life, but which is characterized by the fact that it sketches out these conflicts only *roughly* and often pretends that they are solvable through mediation or displacement, this prize realism degenerates into popular literature on the edge of the field of genuine art. Here it has been living since then – and, it should be added, living quite well, considering that this type comprises the paramount part of aggregate literary consumption in terms of quantity. In terms of quality, however, the former type dominates. From Balzac to Stendhal, Flaubert and Zola, from Charlotte Brontë to Dickens, in the great Russian realists Tol'stoj, Dostoevskij, and Turgenev, and in the epic tradition, which towards the end of the century develops in Scandinavia with among others Ibsen, Strindberg, J.P. Jacobsen and Henrik Pontoppidan.

This tradition the heteromorphism has demonstrated, between the figure of enunciation and the figure of statement/enunciated, as one of its general features. It is in fact co-constitutive of the whole setting of the framing of the ideal-typical literature of Modernity, of the rules of the

---

[4] We shall return to Jane Austen's realism in chapter 3.6 below.

institution or the powers in the field, which as one of its predominant properties has the attempt to hide its own character of "field" set by framing, by rules.

Thus a number of controversial and paradoxical circumstances are turned into natural premises which only much later are to be exposed and criticized as conventions which produce meaning. At the technical level this applies to the very development of an 'established' system of stylistic methods of producing this natural *vraisemblance* which of course is anything but natural.[5] It implies the whole notion of the author's general privilege of insight, and in relation to this, the phantasm about the cognitive orientation of the literary work of art and its pretended privilege of cognition. The literary work – and with that, to a great extent, art as such – becomes a highly peculiar, but totally natural, heterogeneous folding together of outside and inside. Here it is possible to confront the impossible – in such a way that it is possible to live on with it. Here, offered at one and the same time are emotion, adventure, identification together with substitutive experience, constituting a *serious* demonstration of radical criticism of society. This last functions above all as a *valve of compression*; it becomes a field of compensation, which precisely because of its separateness by definition remains undangerous and thus to some extent un-serious. In the same way as literature is 'doing' what it claims impossible to do,

---

[5] We shall return to this problem more generally in 5.4, where we shall try to clarify the problem by discussing comparatively another art form, the film, which seems even more "natural", but as a matter of fact is not.

it is being framed so radically, so thoroughly and exceptionlessly that its very framedness becomes invisible. The framing is becoming invisible: both as an outside conventionalizer and as an inside organizer of the constructions.

2.3

The Congruence of Modernism:
Consecutive Non-Coherence

Virginia Woolf: *To the Lighthouse*

Introduction

If the purpose here had been to write a chronicle of the development of fiction during the 19th century, the picture of a gradual and extremely complicated process would have emerged. Above all a process in which fundamental paradigms of narrative literature would paradoxically have seemed at one and the same time to be confirmed and to be undermined.

The confirmation is an immediate property of the subtle elaboration of the abilities and intentions of prose to apprehend and describe the world precisely at a phenomenological level. Not just the state of the material world, but also psychological patterns of reaction, that is to say their visible manifestations. Simultaneously an (at least seeming) withdrawal of explicit narrative instances privileged in terms of insight is taking place (cf. Flaubert). Priorities are increasingly seen as inherent to the material 'itself': the vertical dimensions of the texts, i.e. their form, their construction, is being dissimulated as far as possible. This appears both technically through the construction of the individual text – and 'aesthetically' in the way in which the framing conditions are controlling the focus of the attitudes of reception.

However, this gradual, seeming withdrawal of the narrator's interventions at the same time implies a threatening undermining of the paradigmatic claims for immediate truth and representation. For the more a 'clean' phenomenological description pretends to 'stand alone', the more fragile it becomes, and the more vulnerable to a critique, which claims it to be absolutely unable to satisfy the demands of cognition, of truth, of authenticity, with reference to which the description is exactly trying to make itself objective. And when this insufficiency emerges it is bound to happen – as proved by the history of literature – rather suddenly as an astonishingly absolute and irreversible insight.[1]

Parallel to this 'main process' in which writing, through its eagerness to be transparent, gradually and to some

---

[1] In his *Theorie der Avantgarde* this is the process which Peter Bürger (Bürger 1974 and 1979, see also my reformulations in Kyndrup 1986, esp. chapt. 5, pp. 68ff) sees as the *final fulfilment* by the works of the demands of the institution – of the framing conditions, *Rahmenbedingungen* – for autonomy, that is to say separateness from "praxis of life", to such a degree as to finally make these demands visible to the works themselves, and thus making them the possible object of criticism. Following "aestheticism" historical avantgarde projects are thus emerging, which try to lead art 'back' to life praxis.

As will appear Bürger's historical understanding obviously has much in common in terms of structure with the ones sketched out here, which is neither coincidental nor unintended. If you are going into details, Bürger's prioritizing of *intrinsic* dynamics of development of the institution in his explanation of the process, is probably too exaggerated; a lot of other elements in the change of society and thinking obviously play along. See also chapters 1.3 and 4.2.

First Development Section

extent unintentionally becomes visible as writing, and the vertical is thus becoming visible as verticality, other paths are being taken. Including paths which later on will appear as short cuts. In one register, in which the problems of presentation are included in thematics, we may mention Edgar Allan Poe. In another, a more explicitly philosophically directed one, efforts like those of Kierkegaard and Nietzsche.

However, the development of a chronicle *is not* our purpose, and consequently we shall not touch on the history in between with its extensive processes and complicated causal structures: a discussion of those would take us far beyond our scope. Instead we shall continue our discussions of singular (historically) different types of construction of literary fiction. And here we are able to demonstrate that in the early 20th century something happens which, also compared to the character of the process of the alteration of the novel since Balzac, is actually marking a difference. What happens is, so to speak, a scratching *break*, an assertion of a discontinuity, of an emphatic difference in the construction of the novel. But still a difference, which is actually a consistent continuation of some of the most fundamental intentions, in the ideal-typical bourgeois realist novel. You might push it to extremes by saying that in order to be able to finally fulfil its own substantial intentions, the novel has to break down its formal framework. This is happening with names like – among many others – Joyce, Proust, Musil and Virginia Woolf.

Virginia Woolf: To the Lighthouse

The novel was published in 1927; the author of the novel was 27 years old at that time and had already produced extensive works of literature and literary criticism. It was only with *To the Lighthouse*, however, that she had her breakthrough with a greater audience, and her breakthrough as an artist, in fact. Anyway, *To the Lighthouse* is almost unanimously considered to be Woolf's most brilliant novel. In fact, some even consider it possible to reduce her lasting contribution to literature to this very novel.[2] Anyway, this novel has been given a position as one of the few 'modern classics' of this century: it has been translated into a great number of languages, and it is still being read, also, obviously, because of the effect this status of a classic has in the educational system at all levels.

On the face of it, the novel appears peculiar, above all because its tempo of narration is demonstratively diverse. *To the Lighthouse* has three parts. The first part, *The Window*, has an extent of about 100 pages,[3] but in terms of narrated time it embraces no more than a couple of hours. The second part, *Time Passes*, however, manages a dozen years in 15 pages. While the third part, *The Lighthouse*, once again spends more than 50 pages on half a morning.

Furthermore, almost nothing happens in terms of outer events within the two main parts with their slow tempo of

---

[2] For instance Bradbrook, 1976, p. 275.

[3] The numbers here and page numbers below refer to the Grafton Books edition (1978, 1988 repr.).

First Development Section

narration. In the first part there is a discussion about whether to go the lighthouse the following day or not, some small conflicts develop, people dine and are reconciled. In the second part, on the contrary, there are a lot of outer events, but they are reported as marginal notes, often literally by being put in brackets. This for instance applies to the death of the absolute protagonist, Mrs Ramsay (120). In the third part, then, what happens is merely that the trip to the lighthouse takes place, eventually, and that Miss Briscoe, the artist, finishes the painting which she commenced ten years earlier – she draws the line she was not able to draw then.

In other words, this *plot* is not a traditional, epically suspense-building one, in which the outer events *narrated*, in themselves construct and respectively release the suspense. However, this does not mean that the novel does not generate conflict and suspense at the horizontal level during its development. It certainly does. But in a peculiar way. First of all, it does so by magnifying events and psychological states of things which should not 'normally' be considered as remarkable, into matters of life or death for the persons concerned. But the suspense is not least an attribute of the very specific vertical construction of the novel. As a matter of fact, this specific horizontal focusing would be rather unlikely without this very vertical construction. Having stated this we shall at once – for operative reasons – separate the dimensions of the text from each other: or try to reflect the level of the enounced world separately. Of course afterwards returning to the construction of enunciation. And later on especially to the mutual play and 'the totality'.

Horizontally: The Thematics of the Novel

Despite the stagnation of outer events, quite a bit happens at the thematic level of the novel, as mentioned. It happens along several different axes of meaning, not immediately organizable into an orderly, stable hierarchy of meanings. But still, through the bearers of value among the fictional persons, a transmission is created, sufficiently redundant to outline a certain connection between the thematical main axes.

In the foreground we have *symbolic exchange* as theme. By symbolic exchange is meant here the phenomenon that the balance of power among human beings is controlled through the participants' positions as *givers*, respectively *receivers* (in the widest psychological sense) within the interpersonal relations. As it has been described all the way back to the old *potlatch* traditions on the material level,[4] the symbolic giver is in the position of power, a power which can only be challenged by a higher bid from the counterpart. But in any case: any relation bears the character of such an exchange. And any, intended or un-intended breakup of this exchange will make everything harden, cease.

Mrs Ramsay holds a central position within this thematics – as everywhere, dead or alive. She is the great giver, in fact she is unable to deal with people and situations unless she herself can act as a giver (and thus a

---

[4] For instance in anthropology in Marcel Mauss. From here Jean Baudrillard takes up the phenomenon (for instance Baudrillard, 1976), giving it the extended 'psycho-social' meaning. See for instance the fine introduction in Gunder Hansen 1981-82 (1981) pp. 25ff.

First Development Section

ruler) in relation to them. Thus she is an extremely complex person in her relationship with herself as well as with other people. On one hand, she is really giving herself (and not in a vulgar, calculating sense). To anybody: if not to somebody from the family or to the dozens of guests staying overnight, then to poor or ill people from the village. But still giving, above all, to Mr Ramsay, her complement, and so much so that it simply empties her of life, making her die 'before time':

> Mrs Ramsay had given. Giving, giving, giving, she had died – and had left all this (140)

as it is put through the optics of Lily Briscoe, the painter. Still, or in fact: as a consequence of her giving, her beneficence, Mrs Ramsay, however, is extremely dominating, indeed a lover of power. This makes most of the persons' relationships with her ambiguous; at one and the same time admiring and dissociating. Most clearly dissociating is the poet, Augustus Carmichael (who in other ways as well holds a special position, cf. below). This is embarrassing for Mrs Ramsay:

> What was obvious to her was that the poor man was unhappy, came to them every year as an escape; and *yet* every year, she felt the same thing, he did not trust her. She said, 'I am going to the town. Shall I get you stamps, paper, tobacco?' and she felt him wince. He did not trust her. (41, italics added).

The "yet" emphasized is the key-note to Mrs Ramsay's way of thinking: even though Carmichael accepts something (the invitation) she still does not obtain power over him. And in trying to give him more she is rejected. Carmichael insists on staying outside the exchange which Mrs Ramsay represents and governs. She is so active in doing so that she sincerely tries to get as many as possible of her fellow human beings *married* (:inscribed into a kind of institutionalized exchange similar to her own). She succeeds with Paul and Minta, and she is trying hard, but in vain, with Lily and Bankes.

Generally, the persons are divided into givers and receivers (as basic types – the continuing exchange is of course based on the fact that everybody takes up different positions in turn). The axis of giver/receiver is to some extent isomorphous with another important differentiation: the opposition (the difference) between female and male. But only to some extent. It is demonstrated that the position of the giver is typical for the female. But also that certain women refuse to take up this position. Lily, torn apart in a painful compoundedness of being unable to and not wanting to (141ff). And Minta in her marriage with Paul, until she is able go 'give' him a mistress.

Furthermore, the female is characterized by something which mediates (as opposed to the conflict-seeking of the male), by something circular (as opposed to the linear, cf. Mr Ramsay's exemplary notion of a linear gradation of human intelligence from A to Z, 35ff), by an insistence on singular actions and events, on singularities (as opposed to universality, the inscription of the singular into a general substance), and in consequence of this by an insistence on subjective truth (as opposed to objective truth) and especially on subjective time (as opposed to objective time).

But these values are also exchanged, and they are not unambiguously connected to concrete representatives of physical gender (cf. again Carmichael and Lily Briscoe). At

First Development Section

the level of thematics, this is a very substantial part of the feminist potentials of the novel, which have so often been emphasized.

A rough, schematic juxtaposition of the main thematic axes in terms of the tendencies of transformations would be the following:

power	powerlessness
giver	receiver
authenticity	in-authenticity
'fullness'	emptiness
winner	loser
the female	the male
the mediating	the conflict-seeking
the circular	the linear
singularity	universality
expression/expression	expression/contents
individual truth	objective truth
subjective time	objective time

Apart from the fact that this juxtaposition should, as mentioned before, be regarded with reservations as the axes do not cover each other completely, it only represents part of the whole picture of the field of exchange.

First of all a complicated axiology is being inserted. At one level it is evident that the values of the left side are the positive ones, the ones with which the novel (among other things represented by its enunciation and its implicit narrator, cf. below) is primarily linked up. But at the same time, during the epic sequence of events these are linked with *death*, just as the right side is linked with *life*: Mrs Ramsay, the arch-representative of the left side, dies (leaving an empty space of explosive decompression with everybody, especially of course with her husband). Death also befalls one of her daughters, Prue, physically and psychologically the one who is most like her. In this it is reasonable to see a statement saying that you die from this unreserved giving, from this extravagant exercise of power. By contrast, the representatives of the right side, with Mr Ramsay in the centre, are truly *living*. But the price to pay for *that* life is represented by the negative values of the right side. Already qua his position of powerlessness Ramsay is described as almost pathetic, and his linearly dimensioned preoccupation with his own "success" or "failure" is described as almost ridiculously puerile. Men's conversations on "truth" are exposed as directly stupid; every move seems to have only the purpose of serving these men's own self-un-confident testing of their position along the line, which they are by no means able to look beyond. And thus unable to give reasonable proportions to the rest of the world.

Secondly, this – thus axiologically blurred – picture is complicated by the fact that even at the level of fiction of the text itself a position *outside* the polarized field of exchange is established: the position of Lily Briscoe and August Carmichael. They are *artists* (he is a poet, she is a painter) and characteristically, as mentioned, it is not unambiguously decidable whether the position outside is deliberate and thus sovereign, or forced and thus perhaps negatively conditioned as a compensation. Carmichael and Briscoe are both privileged in having insight. But besides this they are left outside, excluded from social exchange, in any sense. Lily Briscoe is *also* an anaemic, old maid, shy of contact; Carmichael is *also* a trembling old man with

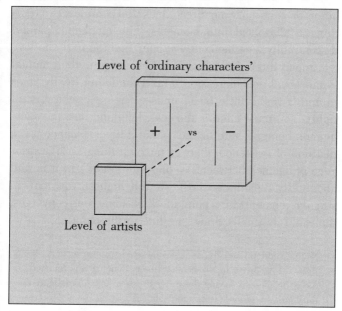

Level of 'ordinary characters'

Level of artists

Fig. 1. A position totally outside the system of values is established: that of the artist.

yellow stains in his beard. It is true that Carmichael is successful (though unexpectedly), but Lily is clearly aware that her painting is nothing special (according to herself her works are bound to end "in the attics"). In other words: though this third position indeed adds an extra dimension to the interpretation of the novel's space of polarizations of exchange (cf. fig. 1) it does not clarify the ambiguous value system of the novel. The choice seems to be between dying from living, living from being dead – or be left completely outside life, neither dead nor alive, being an "artist".

This is the general statement of the novel: there is no

order, no continuity, no directedness, no confidence. Everything is dissolved into moments, into emphatic, painful discontinuity; one moment you hate, and the next you love (cf. in part three, James' hatred of his father in their mutual symmetrical decompression – until the father finally gives in and 'gives' a little bit of praise. Then everything is all right). You must admire and fear, hate and love the same human being. There is no possibility of balance as a platform of existence, there is no such thing as "the razor edge of balance between two opposite forces" (as it is said about Lily's painting, 178). At the highest you may in singular moments hit a point in which something converges, the way Lily finally draws the line in the painting:

> With a sudden intensity, as if she saw it clear for a second, she drew a line there, in the centre. It was done; it was finished. Yes, she thought, laying down her brush in extreme fatigue, *I have had my vision.* (192, italics added)

This is the end of the novel. Decisive is of course the grammatical tense of the last sentence: the perfect tense. We are not dealing with an accumulated triumph, with a successful apprehension of a project. No, something singular has happened somewhere in the great time. It may happen again, and it may not.

The novel's thematic elaboration of the S/O-relationship consequently turns out to be one long demonstration of the impossibility of attaining and maintaining balance, controlled equilibrium. Some people take up too much space and are stifling from emptiness. Or they do not take up enough space and are stifling from inferiority. Or they may leave themselves outside as observers: having given up hitting they at least do not risk missing. They may suddenly have a 'vision' and thus hit. But the common, unchangeable condition is one flashing moment of balance opposed to the totally dominating (in quantity) weary and stifling tasks of daily life.

Truth is thus a phenomenon which you may meet subjectively in some situation of exchange and in that case as an expression. No great truth or meaning underlies the expressions, which in their turn, then, are not able to be either authentic or the opposite. Concrete expressions and exchanges 'are' what they are: they are not representatives.

Vertically: The Statement of Enunciation

The novel's mode of narration is extremely specific. Parts I and III consist of a number of radically subjective, stream-of-consciousness-like points of view of *different* characters. The focalizing perspective is strictly internal, but grammatically told in the third person. The transitions from one person's point of view to that of another person are completely unforeshadowed and abrupt – often the reader will have to re-read a passage several times to fully realize which character is actually carrying the point of view *now*.

These abrupt transitions between the individual, "personal" points of view in *vision-avec* of course contribute to emphasize the 'hidden', implied narrator (i.e. *l'enunciateur*) as an instance (the one who constructs these ruptures, chooses between the characters). Furthermore, this voice narrates more directly in the "authorial" central part, *Time Passes*, although points of view of characters and even of the house are being mimicked.

The implied narrator thus holds a privileged position in

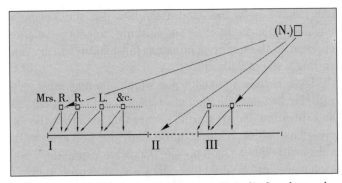

Fig. 2. The instance of the implicit narrator, N, is displaced towards the individual narrators' levels of insight which in their turn actually should be reproduced as being very close to the axis of the narrated time. Consequently, the structure of narration is 'flat'.

relation to distribution and to time (the perspective here being *vision-par-derrière*). But because the construction is radically and consistently being carried by subjectivity this instance is in a peculiar way definitely precluded from talking 'behind' the discourses of the single characters. These generally bear the form of a variety of associations and furthermore appear as rather disconnected (also as concerns time). Not only the preferred rhetorical tropes of the characters, but also the syntagmatic figures of their reflections thus individualize the characters. This applies to every single character, a fact which it will be far beyond our scope to demonstrate here. But for example merely at the level of man/woman-differentiation it is characteristic that men think in concrete, linear comparisons and, by the way, knock their heads against at the *same spot*, over and over again until they get through, lose their heads, or perhaps become distracted. Women, on the contrary, make

reflections within a symbol-carried metonymically directed register of tropes and furthermore think *circularly* in a construction of comparison which has almost the shape of a chain of signifiers (and thus differing from men's – arbitrarily, but radically – purpose-defined construction).

The narrative discourse, thus, is above all "personal". But in what you might call a multi-perspective form. Each and every point of view is radically subjective. But since they are different, they must necessarily modify and relativize each other. This mutual interplay, however, is not cast in the form of a well-calculated, thematically governed distribution of the single points of view by a sovereign, supreme (implicit or explicit) narrator. No, the subjectivity of the points of view, respectively, their taking into possession any dimension within the space of expression, is so radical that the instance 'behind' them, though indeed compelling proper admiration (and thus being objectified), does not after all appear as actually ruling or sovereign. The conspicuous lack of symmetry within the construction of the priority of points of view, and with the system of temporality, &c., also contribute to this fact, of course. All things considered, focalization is constantly moving; the whole construction of enunciation becomes emphatically unhierarchical and unsystematic, and consequently it appears as a heteromorphic parataxis made up of 'authentic', sovereign, subjective discourses – rather than as the segregation of one discourse (i.e. the implicit narrator's), which it of course is, in 'fact'. The inverted commas indicate that although physically the discourse certainly has one and only one source, nothing hinders a montage, which unfolds the demonstrated character of asymmetry and hetero-geneity[5].

The mode of function of the novel is, primarily, the creation of *distance* at various levels. Within each of the subjective points of view precisely this extreme subjectivity might possibly prepare for some sort of identification. This, however, is not the case, for the language and the syntax of the single discourses are so far from (the convention of) normality that already this fact calls for objectification. In addition to this, we have, as mentioned above, the shifts in point of view carriers. A typical example:

> ...they had gone up on to the bridge of the ship and were taking their bearings; the change from poetry to politics struck her like that; so Mr Bankes and Charles Tansley went off, while the others stood looking at Mrs Ramsay going upstairs in the lamp-light alone. Where, Lily wondered, was she going so quickly?
>
> Not that she did in fact run or hurry; she went indeed rather slowly. She felt rather inclined just for a moment to stand still after all that chatter, and pick out one particular thing; the thing that mattered; to detach it; separate it off; clean it of all the emotions and odds and ends of things, and so hold it before her, and bring it to the tribunal where, ranged about in conclave, sat the judges she had set up to decide these things. Is it good, is it bad, is it right or wrong? (104)

---

[5] Here it is almost impossible not to point out the parallel with non-figurative painting of the same period: the changes here can be regarded precisely and similarly as replacement of the one converging point of a traditional, conceptual recipient, by a number of parallel, heteromorphi-cally non-hierarchical positions. This is another version of the emphatic disruption of subject contiguity.

Only gradually does the reader realize that "she" after the first passage is no longer Lily Briscoe, but Mrs Ramsay. This technique of connecting of course slows down the reading and thus prevents a non-objectifying identification. But not only that. Also the tremendously underlined lability of the system of values actively opposes any accumulation of psychological identifications: each of the characters is ambiguous in terms of value – not in the sense of being positioned in between, but in the sense of being sometimes extremely captivating, and sometimes extremely disgusting in each others' views. As has been indicated, something like that can be said about the tri-polarized system of positions, as well: All values are exchangeable and there is no reliable stability in the relationship between characters and values.

Consequently, the novel has not only departed from any central, any one-point perspective; it actually exhibits and objectifies the receptional-aesthetical implications of central perspective by allowing itself to be made up of central-perspective fragments with mutually brutal transitions. Through its demonstratively polyvalent axiology and through its insistence on various, mutually clashing perspectives; through its superior renunciation of traditional, sequential, epic suspense, and through its stylistically and linguistically extremely difficult discourse; through its construction *To the Lighthouse* is doing almost everything possible – so one might be tempted to put it – in order to make itself visible as form, as construction, as artificiality, as impossibility... Or in other words: the novel is constructing its implicit reader in such a way that it objectifies itself to this reader as something with which *absolutely no* harmonical exchange can be established.

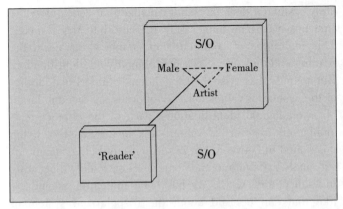

Fig. 3. The 'inaccessiblity' of the text to the reader qua its construction of narration and otherwise formal construction ('vertically') is isomorphous with the experience of the relationship with the surrounding world, which the characters of the level of action of the novel are expressed to have ('horizontally').

Aggregated: The "Saying" of the Text

Coherence and consistency (cf. fig. 3) thus characterize the relationship between the statements of the enunciation and the enunciated of the novel, respectively. The text agrees with itself on the fact that permanently balanced S/O-relations based upon and regulated by underlying supreme universal 'truths' are not elicitable: inasmuch as it demonstratively mounts non-coherence at both the vertical and the horizontal levels, the novel actually *is* coherent.

In a peculiar way coherence is also what characterizes the insight and knowledge of the novel at the two levels. Not only generally, but also particularly. This is due to the implicit narrator's positioning of itself at the same level as the "personal" points of view. No consciousness is privi-

leged in terms of insight compared to any other consciousness. They are all of them situated within a labile, ever-
changing universe in which there are now glimpses of sudden 'total insight' and now opacity, complete lack of
understanding of what is going on. These are the basic
conditions, and describing these conditions the novel itself
submits to them. The enunciation of the novel, consequently, *knows* no more than its *enuncié*. And, conversely, the
enuncié no more than the enunciation.

This is clearly emphasized by the novel's thematization
of *time*, horizontally as well as vertically. Thematically it is
demonstrated that subjective time is anything but coherent-
ly related to the great, to the factual, time[6]. What are
factually seconds may be as much as days. And conversely:
what factually are days or years may be only seconds in the
subjective time. Similarly a non-symmetric and incoherent,
apparently ungovernable relationship between the narrated
time and the time of the narration takes place at the vertical axis of the novel (as discussed above). Consequently,
the reader is not only confronted with the assertion that
time pulsates like that; she is being forced to go through a
sensuous experience of such a non-coherent, non-symmetri-
cal time also qua her proper reception.

All in all the novel demonstrates an absence of meaning,
of order, of presence, of direction, of "sense". Not, however,
by turning its own discourse into "non-sense". Nor is its
pointing out the absence of sense (not unambiguously,
anyway) intonated as tragical. Still the novel is greatly

---

[6] Cf. Ricoeur's, among others, distinction between the two times in
Temps et recit III, 1985. See also Ricoeur 1988, pp. 207-235.

serious, and it maintains the traditional aura of the work of art. It does so, among other things, by being constructed in such a way that it does not want to know more than it knows itself. And thematically it does so by focusing, as mentioned above, on the *specific* position of the artist as being outside normal exchange. Indeed, at one decisive point, the novel settles with the fundamental self-understanding within the framed field of art: the notion of the very *existence* of a privileged position of insight, and of art being in possession of that position. On the other hand, the point is that *art itself is aware of not being in possession of that position*. Art has at its disposal the truth that there is no such thing as a truth.

This raises the question of the "realism" of the novel – understood as its own apprehension of whether that which it incorporates *corresponds to*, truly represents what goes on in the real world.

No doubt the basic intention, indeed even the underlying incentive of the novel, is to demonstrate how the world *is*. It wants to acknowledge and incorporate the world, and its unfolding of the complex psychological mechanisms within the problematics of exchange, especially applying to the relationship man/woman, is serious. Deadly serious. Even the almost ostentatious artificiality of the form appears to be a function of this intention of honesty, truth, "realism" – for only in a shape like this is the text unable to escape the fate of becoming a denial of its own statement. A denial, both by mounting itself as a privileged, surveying view within a reality, claimed nonsurveyable – and by in that case, qua its function, itself being an example of a homogeneous and handy statement of the same kind as that whose existence it denies. The novel has to avoid any traditional epic suspense related to the sequence of events, indeed to avoid any outer plotting because plots are not found in real life, seen from the point of view 'down there' of real life itself; here the tensions are different, and "narrations" are always already secondary, i.e. non-authentic forms only possible to generate at a certain distance and within the frames of a certain illusion about order and surveying. If *To the Lighthouse* is exciting, it is so because of the intensity of the single passages, because of the possibility of recognition and cognition of the psychological life-and-death dramas performed within a level of action which is deprived of any outer events. In so doing, the novel of course reduces the number of its potential audience; not only by refusing to offer a universe of values, capable of structuring and perhaps thus compensating for the malaise of common experience of contingency. But also simply by not being capable of entertaining and concretely keeping the attention of the reader qua an introspection into *another* universe thus being experienced. Immediately, the universe and the problematics are the reader's own, though staged within its proper sophisticated register: as "art".

At this level of form a novel like *To the Lighthouse* departs from tradition: By exhibiting its *Kunstmittel*, its character of being a construction, by making itself hermetic, inaccessible – the work is emphasizing itself as something very special, truly mounted in reality, but which qua being what it is, is something different from the immediate appearance of this reality. This radical accentuation of the autonomy of art, its differenceness, its artificiality, makes it part of the intricate reality which it is presenting. And at the same level as this. This makes it decisively different from traditional prose, in its turn dissimulating its *Kunstmittel* and fundamentally being raised *above* the world by being able to structure it as different. By, so to speak, being able to be artificial in a natural way.

To the Lighthouse, then, in fact departs from a certain 'realistic' form and tradition. But, literally, it is far more realistic than the novelistic tradition from which it is so overtly trying to dissociate itself. Rather paradoxically, it is incorporating the consistent fulfilment of this tradition rather than being its counterpole. Virtually, the intentions of the whole project of *To the Lighthouse* are very similar to the one of *La Comédie Humaine*. Because it no longer wants to find or to establish order within the contingency, and instead presents it as precisely contingent, heterogeneous, a novel of this type indeed causes itself some costs in its relationship with its audience. And further ahead this has certain consequences for the whole framing of literature and art, for the construction of the institution. We shall return to this below. Substantially, *To the Lighthouse*, however, does not attack the institution, indeed in a certain sense it hardly manifests any exploration of its borderlines. On the contrary, through its consistent maintaining of the paradigms about truth, authenticity, honesty, it appears as a confirmation of, indeed almost as a tribute to, the most fundamental values within the self-understanding of this construction of framing.

Outlook

A careful fulfilment of the rules of the self-understanding of the field, however, does not generally guarantee an effect which secures maintenance of the function of the field.

A number of great novelists of world literature of the early twentieth century certainly act as immediate parallels to Virginia Woolf as perceived above. Proust, Joyce, Musil, and Faulkner are all *realists* in the sense that they thoroughly present the individual's relationship with the surrounding world just as it *is*. Present it with seriousness – and with truth as the guiding star. This, consequently, makes it a general feature that the traditional nineteenth-century novel, emphatically privileging the position from which it itself is narrating, can no longer, fundamentally, be used as a construction; the very order and coherence implied by this, no matter how much disintegration or disorder the presentations might contain respectively in quality of thematic focus or attitude – this order is indeed fundamentally *false*. False not only to the extent that it is unlikely whether viewpoints of that kind are even constructible. But false also because if the works in their vertical construction thus deny the disintegration which they otherwise claim to be universal, they would actually domesticate this disintegration. Make it surveyable and consequently harmless, turning it into a sort of travesty of its own status of being disastrous and irrevocable.

This fact has been *realized* by a whole generation of novelists at one and the same time. They certainly see the phenomenon in different ways, just as their suggestions for constructions of forms in which to work are highly differing. Kafka goes so far as to symbolically stage the individual's disintegration by locating it within universes and situations whose contexts and rules it will have no qualifications to understand, which will then seem absurd. The figure of thinking, however, is the same everywhere; alienation, disintegration, meaninglessness at the thematic level correspond to the mounting of an emphatic distance from the reader within the formal construction of the works, meaning a sort of obstacle or retardation of the immediate reception directed towards identification, which the bourgeois novel over its short but important flourishing unambiguously tended to give rise to. That mode of reception in turn was governed by and became governing within, the very mode of function of the field, the framing conditions by which production and reception of literature overall were regulated.

The question of the effect of these new works and thus also discussions on the issue of how and for what the audience of art is able to use art, however, are still kept in the background at this time. On the agenda is placed the *truthfulness* of literature, and consequently, inasmuch as receivers are included at all as having influence on the identity – the extent of *cognition* which literature represents and consequently will be able to give.

The gradual inaccessibilization, hermetization of literature which is going on is not, however, exclusively a sort of 'unintended' consequence of this different and more important effort (cognition): it can also itself be interpreted as an active part of this superior effort, in the sense that the more complex and inexpressible, contingent and incomprehensible the presented world was seen to be, the more the appearance of the work towards the reader, i.e. its formal construction, necessarily had to work out in a similar way. Anything else would appear as an immediate contradiction of the contents of cognition.

In der verwalteten Welt ist die adäquate Gestalt, in der Kunstwerke aufgenommen werden, die der Kommunikation des

First Development Section

Unkommunizierbaren, die Durchbrechung des verdinglichen Be-
wußtseins

is the wording by Th.W. Adorno,[7] one of the most perceptive and theoretically sophisticated standard-bearers of
exactly this modernism directed towards cognition.

It would, however, be wrong to claim that this modernism also, explicitly and generally, intended to break
down the very existence of the field in its quality of autonomy.[8] On the contrary: the very effort of preserving the
peculiar, the artificial, combined with the emphasis on the
position of the *artist* as being privileged with regard to
insight (= cognition) has rather been aiming at a consoli-
dation of the specific aura of art.

No, the objectification and partial decomposition of the
field which is the notorious effect of this tradition at least
at two different levels so to speak generates from the *inside*.
At one and the same time the "non-communicability"
causes a rendering visible of the field's very character of
being a construction – and a radical limitation of the
virtual and actual audience of art. But neither of these
consequences has actually been the main objective of art.
The incentive of art has been above all a fidelity to the
object, to the material, set by the basic paradigm of
cognition. Whether dodecaphonic music was to be enjoyed
by many or few or nobody at all was not the problem of the

---

[7] Adorno 1973, p. 292.

[8] As Bürger (Bürger, 1974) claims is the case with the socalled
historical movements of avantgarde. More about these and their position
and differentiation below. Cf. also note 1 above.

Darmstadt school: decisive was whether it was doing the *right* thing.

However, not all of the movements within what is rather vaguely conceptualized as "modernism" of art, had exactly this orientation towards cognition and truth. There were also examples showing that the frame itself, the very institutionalization of art, was attacked. As Peter Bürger rightly points out, this, among other things, applies to the so-called historical movements of avantgarde (i.e. futurists, dadaists, expressionists, surrealists, etc.). However, it is not correct when Bürger ascribes to all of these movements the basic intention of wishing to make "art return to the praxis of life" (which means out of the institutionalization as autonomous, liberated from the validity of – but consequently also precluded from influence upon – the fundamental rules of the rest of the world). Precise is the description of the dadaists, for instance, who, exorbitantly and directly play games with the horizon of expectation of the recipients, whereas the surrealists' notions of a more valid reality *behind* the appearances (a reality which could be evoked by disconnecting consciousness by means of "automatic writing") seem to be much more in line with the tradition of the search for substance and truth within the novel, which has been our above object of discussion.

The fact of different, co-existing orientations did not, by the way, cause greater problems, probably precisely because they were relatively easy to mix up within theoretical understanding. The paradigm of "cognition" from the truth-seeking 'mimetic' modernism was transferable into the primarily frame-elaborating art (which in its turn, was also to appear as 'incomprehensible', hermetic). Whereas the very incomprehensibility, the peculiarity, most militantly manifest within frame-breaking art, in an outer sense were absolutely applicable to the modernism seeking cognition – and thus at a superior level able to become a kind of common index of artistry.

Common to the currents however – with a certain generalization – is the fact that they both seem *inexplicably bound up with exactly that which they are so emphatically revolting against*. An art, both horizontally and vertically devoting all its energy to the demonstration of the constitutional impossibility of coherence is indeed a legitimate child of the phantasm about the coherence of everything. Exactly the way in which an art, having as its paramount project the objectification and the demolition of a certain type of framing, through this negation appears to be inseparably bound up with precisely those kinds of frame which it is trying to break.

Modernist art, consequently, is above all an art of *demolition*. A de-auratization, a breaking-up, de-automatization, are the watchwords of the critical theoreticians of aesthetics from Benjamin through Adorno to the Russian formalists being the pre-runners of later structuralists in Eastern and Western Europe. And the projects of demolition are sanctioned. However not by those who on the basis of another kind of criticism of society are building new societies, which in their views are alternatives to the existing ones. The zeal for demolition is characteristically bewailed by *Georg Lukács*, who in 1936 (while living in Moscow) with his important article *Erzählen oder Beschreiben* – and also in a number of other writings, among others the debate with Brecht – tries to produce an *objective* philosophical and aesthetic basis for coherence, in this case exactly the aesthetic construction of the novel.[9] This argumentation, it is worth noticing, debates against the background of the paradigms of truth and fidelity to reality, and it maintains the assertion that the precondition of truth is a privileged point of view making order. The subject, the historical subject. Balzac's position of narrating, for instance.

Lukács, however, was striving in vain. His argument was merely to become the matrix of the development of the literary politics of "socialist realism" in the so-called Eastern block. And here the invocation of truth was – rightly – even by those in power of the systems, at least unofficially, regarded as anything but precisely a search for truth. It is, however, rather interesting to regard the fact that Lukács is here extremely close to what was later to be conceptualized as recognition of the necessary *character of construction* of any aesthetic product.[10]

All that would have been necessary for him to do was to replace the invocation of the laws of objective truth by a (now overt) conative orientation against effect. But this, of course, would have meant a falling beyond both modernism and socialist realism; a falling into another kind of art which would hardly have been understandable within the

---

[9] Cf. – in another context – our discussion in ch. 1.1.2.

[10] Parts of Lukács' early work *Die Theorie des Romans* (Lukács 1920) point in the same direction. As to his later position it is probably exactly this structural parallel 'behind', which makes a modern theoretician like Fredric Jameson maintain the interest for Lukács in his interesting efforts to merge 'marxist' and 'postmodernist' positions. See for instance *The Political Unconscious. Narrative as a Socially Symbolic Act* (Jameson 1986), especially the chapter "Magical Narratives" (pp. 103ff).

First Development Section

(art-institutionally, respectively politically) utilized registers of clenched fists and dichotomies.

2.4

After Modernism:
The Possibility of the Impossible

Italo Calvino: *Se una notte d'inverno un viaggiatore*

Introduction

It seems evident that the above aesthetic construction of
"Modernism" could not be preserved in this form whether
you take an intensional or an extensional view of the
matter. The paradigm of constant disautomatization, of
constant expressive innovation would itself imply a steadily
increasing distance from conventional "meaning", would
itself terminate in emphatic non-communication. Accordingly, not only would the audience be limited almost
exclusively to professionals. The self-knowledge of art about
the paradigms of representation and truth would also
collapse, and silence would be the logical consequence. For
only the most field-domesticated experts on exegesis would
be able to argue that this non-sense was still privileged as
authentic and true. Indeed, this could even be argued about
silence itself. But, incidentally, classic Modernism was –
and still is – the occasion of philosophical readings: the
more hermetic and thus enigmatic the expressions, the
easier their application as suitable starting points for more
general reflexions on the nature of being – thus not specifically of aesthetic being. Consequently, this enigmatic art

First Development Section

has most conveniently given work to, and thus legitimation of, art sciences and criticism, forming the necessary intermediary between an incomprehensible art and an ignorant audience. But again this is a different matter although it has certainly not been without consequences for the structural development of the aesthetic field, cf. the discussions in chapter 1.1.

However, even though there are, also factually, many examples of the consequences outlined above for the con-tinued 'harmonious' development of modernism, in its emphatic form/content-congruency – this development was not the only one. Indeed, eventually it turned out to be a side-track. Modernism was indeed making discoveries, especially when compared to the previous ideal-typical bourgeois art, which had rendered possible the impossible. These discoveries were carried through, thus eventually calling for new constructions.

An art, discovering and demonstrating how its repre-sentation and truth are always, more than by anything else, determined by and within its reference to its own concrete expression, must find certain conclusions very obvious – at least as time passes. First of all, to generalize this acknow-ledgment as applicable not only to every piece of art, but into being true of the whole world: to acknowledge that any 'meaning' (including the one called "truth") only exists *eo ipso* its own expression, that is also *eo ipso* its own contextual field. Secondly, when this loss of an underlying reference or meaning *has been* properly demonstrated, pro-claimed, and staged as a tragical absence, then to transform this absence into another register, one which is no longer necessarily organized according to directedness by the vector of emptiness vs. fullness. Thus this vector as a whole can be conceived as being just one pole in yet another organization of meaning. And thus, thirdly, to discover not only that the buck is always passed, but also that any buck has a buck that is also passed. Or to use other imagery: that opposite traditional realism's understanding of the work-reality combination as a serial setup, and as a contrast to traditional modernism's emphasis of it as a parallel setup, one might imagine, or laboratorily develop, setups in terms of complex combinations of the serials and parallel principles of connection. Not in terms of a classic synthetic-mediating abolition of a contrast, but rather in terms of consciously taking seriously the impossible, the unrealistic features of both principles by implementing them in a field of unlimited heterogeneity. And then creating a position from which to contemplate the position from which to contemplate. Thus creating a position, and so on, and so on..., all in a chain infinitely jutting out into the nothing or the everything (according to position) formed by the rhizomatic labyrinth of meaning.

If on a Winter's Night a Traveller

In his works the Italian writer Italo Calvino (1923-1985) performs a transformation through and out of modernism like the one outlined above. This can also be seen in what he has done apart from writing (untraditional) traditional works. From 1973 he was a member of the international writers' association OuLiPo (= "Ouvroir de Littérature Potentielle")[1] which also includes a.o. Raymond Queneau

---

[1] See Oulipo: *La Biblioteque Oulipienne*, vol. I-II, Paris 1987 and Oulipo: *Atlas de littérature potentielle*, Paris 1981. OuLiPo, established

and Georges Perec. The experiments of OuLiPo and consequently a similar disrespectful-deconstructing attitude towards the grand aura of literature and art largely marks Calvino's voice everywhere. As mentioned, the development of Calvino's works and their reception might illustrate a number of modernism's processes of alteration, which we have outlined above. However, it is characteristic that Calvino's work extends in far too many directions, to permit a brief classification from above. Instead we shall turn to his late and undoubtedly best-known novel *Se una notte d'inverno un viaggiatore* (1979) in which Calvino's postmodernist poetics and technique are in full bloom.

The initial sentence of the novel is: "You are about to begin reading Italo Calvino's new novel, *If on a winter's night a traveller*".[2] And this *incipit* sets the tone of its highly peculiar construction. The novel has twenty-two chapters. Twelve of these – headlined chapters one to twelve – are written in the present tense and are explicitly directed towards "the reader" (who never gets a proper

---

in 1960, works in continuation of Queneau (one of the founders, with his basis in French surrealism) with literature as a laboratory in which different écritures can be produced, observing more or less arbitrary, formal rules. Quite openly, some of the members also carry through some of the principles in their 'ordinary' works, as for instance George Perec, who writes the famous novel *La Disparition* (1969) without using the letter "e". On Perec and OuLiPo cf. *Magazine Littéraire* No. 228 (le Dossier), Paris 1986. Calvino writes part of "Se una notte....." as an oulipoal construction, cf. Oulipo 1987, vol. II, pp. 25 ff. Further below.

[2] This and the following page numbers refer to the English translation (by William Weaver), the Picador Edition, London, 1982.

name) whose attempts to establish a coherent story for himself to read, and to conquer "the female reader" (called Ludmilla and outwardly focalized) are followed. The other ten chapters have all been given titles (for instance the first one is entitled "If on a winter's night a traveller") and they are presented as fictional fragments which the male and the female reader meet or find in their 'real' universes. These chapters are situated between the numerated chapters which in a traditional way always pass the ball to these in passages like the following:

> The last two desires are easily satisfied, and are not mutually exclusive. In the café, waiting for Ludmilla, you begin to read the book sent by Marana. [105, the crossing from chapter six to "In a network of lines that enlace"]

Together the titles of the 'fictional chapters' constitute a joint sentence/title which actually belongs in a metafictional register of commentary. It says "If on a winter's night a traveller/Outside the town of Malbork/Leaning from the steep slope/Without fear of wind or vertigo/Looks down in the gathering shadow/In a network of lines that enlace/In a network of lines that intersect/On the carpet of leaves illuminated by the moon/Around an empty grave/What story down there awaits its end?" But this is not revealed to the reader (the explicit as well as the implicit one) until the end of chapter eleven (204) – after which the novel is actually finished (205).

The "you" spoken to is *both* the one who is reading the book at the time in question – *and* a person acting at the primary fictional level of the novel. Thus the instance of the reader is being written into and out of the fiction at one and the same time; the implicit reader's reactions are multiplied and commented upon by the explicit reader's reactions. And the explicit reader even comments abundantly upon the implicit reader's reactions, thus making the narrative structure divide itself clearly into an 'ingoing' and an 'outgoing' direction. The reader, the one and the other, has to listen to both this and that instance at one and the same time. He has to let himself be absorbed by the tensions of the local, autonomous boxes in the system and to act as a kind of double-barrelled protagonist in the superior epic course and to stand completely outside a highly objectified, artificial and vertical construction.

The Enunciation of the Novel

Technically, this complex movement is brought about by means of a construction which at one and the same time spreads out the fictional levels in a self-repetitive, demonstratively vertical figure – and gathers them in a fictional level which remains in some sense one and the same.

The central level (which we shall call level II) is the world of the unnamed reader. In a way also the explicit reader belongs to this world (because of the consistent use of "you", but also because of the *Engführung* of the I-levels, e.g. p. 17). The level is pointing down 'into' the fiction and 'out of' it: formally the present tense is being used, but it works in two ways: as a historical present tense, i.e. telling *about* this "reader" as a third person, level II. But it works quite literally as well, being the present experienced by the proper reader of the novel ("you", or in fact me), which means addressing, appealing, thus setting a level I *in front of* the main fiction.

The gallery of characters at the central level (level II) includes, apart from the reader himself, "the female reader", Ludmilla, and her sister, the intellectual Lotaria, the swindling and constantly travelling Hermes Marana [!], Silas Flannery, the poet, the university professors, the publisher, &c. At first sight, the plot works as a con-secutivity of reading processes, of *beginnings*, being ceaselessly interrupted by *external* events. The reader buys a book, the continuation is missing, he finds it, but it turns out to be the wrong one, however this is a new exciting beginning of a novel, of which he now (also) looks for a continuation which also turns out to be wrong, but in itself is a new beginning, etc., etc. Similarly, the reader meets Ludmilla, the female reader to whom he is sexually at-tracted; a kind of love story develops, which also keeps the story going.

Calvino himself has explained 'the plotting' at this level as an Oulipo-project. Actually, he writes, he has been in-spired by Greimas' famous 'butterfly model' (cf. *Du sens* (1970), which is referred to in a note)[3]. The story plays through a certain model, in which the instances are shifted in accordance with a certain system to form a symmetrical figure. Figure 1 shows how Calvino sees this construction graphically.

According to Calvino this applies only to the 'reader chapters', i.e. the enumerated chapters. The third level, the 'fictional chapters'[4] differs from the first ones, but also

---

[3] Cf. *Comment j'ai écrit un de mes livres* (Calvino 1987), in Oulipo 1987, vol. 2. The note is on p. 44.

[4] Ibid., p. 4.

TABLES DE MATIERES

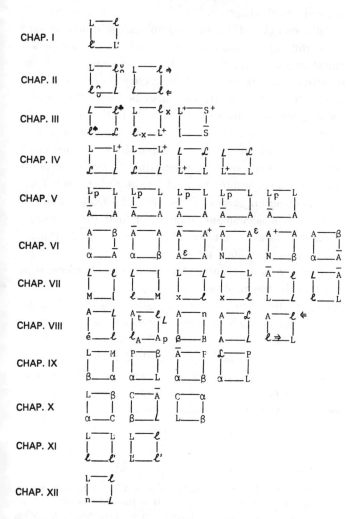

Fig. 1. Calvino's outline of his novel according to Greimas' system (reprinted from OuLiPo 1987, vol. II).

After Modernism: The Possibility of the Impossible 217

there an external, oulipo'ean principle of composition is utilized.[5] Each chapter takes place in a different universe, usually also in a different geographical location and even in a different historical time. Each is a first-person narrative and, as far as the fiction is concerned, told in the narrative preterite tense, but these chapters (claimed to be manuscripts at level II) may also begin in the present tense, addressing themselves directly to the 'you', to the reader (cf. 32-33). They are all exciting *beginnings*: they introduce a universe, they establish a plot – and then break off at the very point at which the dramatic suspense reaches a level where the model reader of the novel will have become engaged in it as well. The reader and "the reader" thus accompany each other, and the postulated "fictional" function (at level II) of the fragments towards level one is absolutely trustworthy.

In a way there is both coherence and incoherence: inasmuch as the fragments are "documents" in universe II they *belong* to this and thus do not affect the 'unity' of the fiction. But as each of them establishes its own fictional universe, being 'fictive' compared to the 'real' level II – and moreover claimed to be falsified fictions (!) – they break down this unity at the same time. Among other things this breaking down is caused by the very establishing of this 'genuine' interrelation between "the reader" (the

---

[5] This is asserted in the article, *Se una notte d'inverno un narratore* (in *Alfabeta*, No. 8, 1979) referred to (p. 44) in Marcel Benabou: *Si par un nuit d'hiver un oulipien*, in *Magazine Litteraire*, No. 274, 1990), discussing Calvino's relations to Oulipo from 1972 till his death. The issue in question of the Magazine Litteraire has Calvino as its *dossier*.

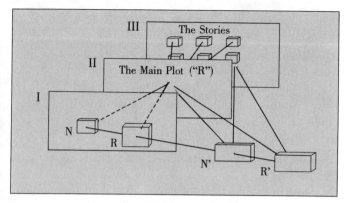

Fig. 2. The novel's structure of enunciation.

fictional person at level II), the conceptual reader and the actual reader.

Figure 2 attempts an illustration of the construction. As mentioned earlier, level III consists of *different* (obvious) fictions, each one, however, having the same 'status' in relation to level II. They do point into different directions, but they are linked (besides having the same status) by having to a certain extent the same themes (see below), and also by the fact that their titles are eventually joined into one story, which then actually makes them point forward to level I of the narrative structure, reflecting a kind of circle: At one and the same time this becomes partly a level for an independent negotiation between narrator(s) and reader(s), and becomes partly an integral function of the main fiction at level II.

It is important to note, especially concerning level I, that it produces a kind of self-repetitive effect outwards (forward, upward) along the vertical axis. Because the narrator's and the reader's instances are made 'independent', objective (the latter is even made into a kind of protagonist), *another* narrator's and reader's instance, narrating/reading the former ones, are becoming visible. This results in the outlining of another, and so on. It may also be put like this: the reader is never allowed 'just' to be reader: in this fiction his instance has always already been made explicit as an instance, and thus has been removed from itself over and over again; in a chain with no end. And likewise according to the narrator's instances. More on this below.

Constructed like this, the enunciation thematizes fundamental questions of the formation of fiction (concerning of course to a certain extent also the formation of meaning in general): what gives a status of "reality" to discourses, how are they made to function as referentially privileged statements – and how are they *read*?

Horizontally – The Statement of the Novel

Of course it is even rather a problem to separate out a horizontal level in the novel, cf. the above figure. It is not possible to locate what the novel is *about* at one definite horizontal level. Indeed, the very expression *about* can hardly be used. For the implicit idea of something 'under' the expression of the novel, supposed to be pointed out by this *about*, is exactly what this novel denies throughout its construction, indeed exposes to ridicule in a certain way. One therefore has to make do with noting that the novel *is*. Not *about* anything.

But of course a number of themes involved can be distilled off at the levels of the plot. Considering the construction it is small wonder that they are highly parallel to those of the enunciation.

On the face of it, the novel thus thematizes the very act of *reading*. This happens by means of the story about the "reader"'s experiences with the various fragments of fiction. And in the figures of the female reader and Irnerio, the "non-reader". The concern is how to invest oneself in what is read. But also, and far more important, how the *what* of the reading is to a certain extent completely subordinate. The *that* of the reading has priority. It is the very grasp and the being grasped. And this grasp, and this being grasped are fundamentally linked with the consecutivity of what is read, with the narration: with the very installation of another 'world' with another time which *If on a Winter's Night a Traveller* exhibits, places in quotation marks, and then after all *is* itself at the same time. Incidentally, the novel also takes the opportunity of mocking the ways in which grateful literature lets itself be used ("read"), having actually nothing to do with the characteristics of *that* literature itself (cf. the description of university students' way of reading, p. 63).

Altogether the novel emphasizes the character of *everything being construction*. Each action is here described as a product of its own circumstances, of time and chance. And by contrast, circumstances create potential "actions" in an endless series. The fictions are paratactic, unlimited in number, and their "meanings" depend on their circumstances, on their context. Thus *truth* is necessarily local, pragmatic. Truth *is* the very discourses – not what they in fact might refer to, but of course including pretended referentiality.

This may seem rather generalizing. However, everything

appears directly from what is 'happening' in the main plot (level II), i.e. to the protagonist/the reader. Furthermore, looking upon the concrete fragments of narratives one gets a quite similar statement. At all levels it is demonstrated how truth – also for fictional first-person narrators of the individual fragments – is constantly moving, indeed often changes into its apparent contrast as the context changes. Almost all the stories simply have as their major turning point such a change of or lability in fundamental values. From the traveller who gets himself domesticated with difficulty and yet is ordered away to an uncertain future ... across the Japanese student who desires the daughter and wants to set himself free from the power of the father/the teacher, and who is nevertheless seduced by the mother, thus being helplessly tied to that power ... to 'the Indian' looking for his roots, and after all finding only repetition.

To this can be added the achievements of the person carrying the name (comically waving, loaded with symbolism) Hermes Marana.[6] Constantly travelling through the world, creating guerilla movements for and against everything (yet all of them with connection to reading and literature), changing one act for the other, selling authors and books, changing truths as other people change their underwear – he becomes the one who, at one and the same time, as a *Spielverderber* is the constant reason for the fact that the protagonists' desire for fiction is never fulfilled, that nothing can be completed, form a whole, any genuine-

---

[6] The Greek god Hermes is the God of travellers and also the protector of thieves. Mara is the Buddhist God of Love who as an evil spirit holds human beings to earth, thus preventing them from reaching Nirvana, the beyond.

ness ... and as a *playmaker* makes the story in our novel continue by producing new diversions, new digressions, new lies. In short, he is completely out of hand, impossible to catch and constantly and without restraint he carries through his own subjective (but incomprehensible, 'hermetic' and thus unpredictable) truth. He is the actual dispatcher of the meaning of the novel – and he is so, not *in spite of*, but actually *because of* the fact that he exclusively *steals*. Though he is a person 'down there' in fiction, he actually never appears on stage in person, and he pulls the strings from somewhere else. All in all he is close to the instance of the implicit narrator of the novel – thus also pulling *this* into the space of fiction. Or conversely (which is the same thing), the fiction out of the hands of this instance.

Thus we do find convincing support for the general statements: Truth is subjective, truth is local, truth is contextual; truth 'is' construction. And, of course this makes truth 'smaller' than any universal, transcendental truth. But actually also very much bigger. Partly by *being* there. Most of all, however, by being *also* a lie.

The "Saying" of the Novel

This seeming paradox is embodied through the contest between Hermes Marana and (the female reader) Ludmilla, which turns out to be the prime external incentive for Marana's endless literary frauds and thus for the plot of the novel. Towards the end Marana's and Ludmilla's attitudes are revealed by the head of the secret police in a country to which the reader has been led in his search for the manuscripts:

> For this woman [...] reading means stripping herself of every purpose, every foregone conclusion, to be ready to catch a voice that makes itself heard when you least expect it, a voice that comes from an unknown source, from somewhere beyond the book, beyond the author, beyond the conventions of writing: from the unsaid, from what the world has not yet said of itself and does not yet have the words to say. As for him, he wanted, on the contrary, to show her that behind the written page is the void: the world exists only as artifice, pretence, mis-understanding, falsehood. [...] His trouble was not madness, perhaps only desperation; the bet with the woman had long been lost; she was the winner, it was her always curious, always insatiable reading that managed to uncover truths hidden in the most barefaced fake, and falsity with no attenuating circum-stances in words claiming to be the most truthful. [...] "I have understood my limitations," he said to me. "In reading, something happens over which I have no power." (188-89)

Throughout the novel Ludmilla herself characterizes her favourite literature in a number of demonstratively *differing* ways: a common feature is that they are attached to *reading* as an event. The very act of reading is conceptualized and maintained as singular, non-referring, irrevocable; thus as true in itself and not by virtue of this or that relationship with the registers of conventions on "truth". In contrast, by insisting on the world as "lie, shamming, fiction" – and thus the absence of any truth – Marana has focused on that truth precisely. Possible or impossible makes no difference in this case. Marana has had to realize that the very fic-tions he made in order to prove the impossibility of truth have become true in themselves through the act of reading. They have been able to become what could be called "pragmatic truth". The question of truth is thus moved to another register. And the discussion on dirigibility versus

First Development Section

the ungovernable, on subject versus object, also gets another framing.

This means that the S/O-relation at the statement level of the novel is scanned as being at one and the same time completely impossible and highly possible. It is impossible as a generally framed, normatively regulated relation; truly, it has, in different ways, the status of a sighting point or a superior referent to most of the fictional persons in the novel, but this status is unconvertible, unrealizable. As a phantasm, on the other hand, this image is definitely real, being the *framing* of the local, ideal-typical S/O-relations which are being actualized all the time (and thus being 'possible'). First of all in the reading, but also (within the more obscure thematics of level III) in the worlds of 'the double fictions'.

A similar marking is found in the enunciation structure of the novel. The reader's way into the text (almost mockingly multiplied in "the reader") is bound to take place within the difficult, frustrating, but inevitable absence of any superior external framing to secure the reception, thus having been able to supply the subject with authenticity and the object with existence. Everything is reduced to tentative pulls in a field which on one hand can be nothing but contingent. But which on the other hand is *aware*, though, of its own conditions of existence, knowing them supremely enough to exhibit them, put them into play, thus in this play establishing possible truths, possible subject/object-relations, consequently *both* being staged *and* authentic or valid *in* themselves. But – precisely – not beyond themselves.

What the novel says about the S/O-relation horizontally

and vertically is that it is both possible and impossible –
but not in the same register. So it is actually "impossible"
to establish a position from which it is possible in a
privileged, qualified way to say anything about the issue:
Such *sayings* have to be related to *doings*. As the novel
itself does it.

To a certain extent this means that the novel points
'only' towards itself in a circular movement. On the other
hand it does so emphatically by arguing that this is exactly
what can be done – nothing more, nothing less. The novel
utters itself as construction. In this way it succeeds in
getting both completely flat and unlimitedly deep (the
metaphors still refer to fig. 2 above): completely flat,
because by explicitating its vertical instances (reader,
narrator) and writing them together, making them converge
at one and the same level (II), it transforms them into
horizontal, i.e. thematic, instances – any movement 'out'
has always already been anticipated and inscribed, i.e.
written back, by the very discourse. On the other hand, the
text gets unlimitedly deep, because its consistent objectification of the vertical levels, their transformation into
issues of theme, establishes a self-repetitive multiplication
of them: a position is mounted from where the reader sees
the reader, which mounts a position from where the reader
sees, and so on.

Flat and deep – and as for the S/O-relation consistently
labile. Possible, but unstable, local: possible only in
concrete doings as for instance a reading. That is to say
'pragmatically possible'. Possible for instance *as art* – but
then only as art being "art" in each and every case, as
singularity; in unlimited dependence of the condition of
concrete, local framing.

In this light Calvino's proclamation of this novel as "lipophonie"[7] may be completely consistent. Because, by insisting on having been created in a play between rules/framings and signs, the former being completely arbitrary and (once chosen) definitely governing the meaning, it manoeuvres itself – to a certain extent – out of the position of survey and insight, it may be said to establish qua its self-repetitive circular construction. But of course only to a certain extent: the problem moves along, once again. And according to the statement of the novel there is no reason at all to conceal this fact.

Nor is there any reason to conceal that the construction of the novel naturally incurs what might traditionally be called certain "costs": the detailed, almost pedantically pedagogic deconstruction of the reader's expectations (at several levels), the many horizontal breaks, the almost frivolous self-reference (for instance the headings of the chapters). In a receptional aesthetic sense all these are elements creating distance, thus – emphatically – interrupting the reader's efforts to establish stable relations to the 'world' of the novel (as happens to the "reader" physically at the next level). The public success of the novel, however, demonstrates that readers do not seem to have been frightened by these elements of distance. Whether *this* is due to the fact that the traditional, narrative qualities of suspense in the plot (or in the fragments of plot), are so prevailing that they make the meta-fictional pointing fingers easier to 'forget' – or to the fact that the meta-fictional argumentation of the novel not

---

[7] "Lipophonie" is Oulipo's name for a piece of work produced according to OuLiPo prescriptions.

only sets premises for itself, but also fulfils them – well, to this the answer cannot be unambiguous, since current literature is a very heterogenous field. But there are signs in literature and its audience that might indicate, however, that a reorientation of not only the interest of literature but also the interest of reading is actually taking place.

Parallels: Outlook

A narrative construction like Calvino's is not unique in European/American fiction as a *type* in the latter part of the 20th century. However, it would hardly be possible to find anything similar, concretely.

Typological resemblances are to be found in the *renar-rativization*, in an emphatic difference from high modernism's repugnance against yielding time/space constructions to literature, which might absorb the reader into some progress of events. But, on the other hand also in the obvious *fragmentation*, in terms of a verticalization, a making visible the definite constructive nature of the structures of enunciation, which it actually more or less inherits from this modernism, implementing it into a new staging.

However, concrete means, messages, and techniques are different. From a *Milan Kundera*, whose humorously/philosophically small-talking explicit narrators (like the one we find in *The Unbearable Lightness of Being*) create a distance from the completely 'normal' people of the fiction, making them at one and the same time living human beings – and demonstratively incidental artefacts. Across, for instance, the Danish writer Svend Aage Madsen, arguing in his comprehensive prose work[8] in favour of the *narrative* in a kind of fantastic, allegorical "realism", thematically as well qua constructive enunciation. And to for instance an Umberto Eco: At the formal level his novels *Il nome della Rosa* (1980) and *Il pendolo di Foucault* (1988) maintain/return to more traditional narrative constructions. But into those, plots and thematics are implemented that play through basic theoretical problems of how meaning is engendered, like abduction, reception, and frame/sign interdependence – and thus the setting of meaning of the novels themselves.

These examples – and of course the ones mentioned are few out of many[9] – may illustrate some differences according to style and construction. From the point-of-view of the process of historical changes, which we have uncovered here, also the resemblances, however, are also very evident.

They can be described in various modes. It may be useful to start with the problem about the attitude towards "realism" in terms of a true *representation* of the 'real' world. The original bourgeois literature of a realistic type of style managed to create a space which to the immediate perception looks like – and thus genuinely represents – the real world. According to its self-knowledge this space (like

---

[8] Especially starting with *Tugt og utugt i mellemtiden* (1976) up to *At fortælle menneskene* (1989). Madsen definitely deserves international recognition through translations into world languages. In a Scandinavian context also the Norwegian writer Jan Kjærstad (the novels *Homo Falsus*, 1984, *Det store eventyret*, 1987, and *Rand*, 1990) is remarkable.

[9] See my chapter (14) in *Les Lettres Européennes*, in press, Paris 1992 on European literature 1968-91: Figures et Tendances Contemporaines.

the idea of the reality whose model it was) was without limits, and the stylistic construction above all was to hide the constructional character of the space, its limits, precisely in order to make it appear 'natural'. In some sense modernism had the same interest of moving towards representation and truth. But modernism had to a very high extent realized the constructional character of this constructed space, for instance by discovering that the real world 'itself' was contingent, heterogeneous, atomized and not at all divided into sensible, clear dichotomies in the form of manifest/latent, good/bad, true/false, *Wesen/Erscheinung*, etc. But in its recognition of this missing substance or lack of order, modernism remained tied to reiterating the exposure of this realization. In the concrete constructions this meant that precisely the *limits* of space had to be made clear, had to be objectified emphatically. And so they were. But of course – not at random – at the expense of the space as space.

Against this *If on a Winter's Night a Traveller* and similar novels apparently no longer find this challenge of the framing sufficient in itself. From original "space without limits", across "limits without space", a conception of the work realizing both the necessity of the space and the inevitability of the limits seems to be emerging. A space knowing its own limits: constantly reflecting, counting in its own dependence on framing. Of course no emphatic local space like that can 'represent' the unlimited contingence of the world. At most it acts as an allegory, standing at the side. And yet always already in the middle, because the framing dependence, the constructedness is a condition to which it itself is subject not only as a concrete single work, but also as species, as part of a field whose construction always already *has* regulated the meaning of the single work, also beyond its specific elaboration.

As for the construction of the novel, thus outlining itself, it seems that after modernism (and accordingly called post-modernism[10]) *cognition* as concern has simply changed its place. This can be put in a 'negative' way as art having "lost" its status of being cognitively "privileged". But it can also be put in a 'positive' way as art having escaped its duty (having hitherto radically confined its potentials) to communicate new acknowledgment – a duty whose consistent fulfilment already once has driven art into the literally absurd. In overcoming the regret for this 'loss', art can finally in its construction openly examine and reflect the conditions of possibility of meaning – and thus of cognition. It may seem to possess the qualities of doing so.

As for the novel's staging of the subject/object-relation, as we have seen it, the renunciation of any cognitive privilege naturally implies a decisive change.[11] The relation is being pulled out of the axis "possible/impossible" and consequently split up according to the character of the proper construction. The 'balanced' S/O-relation thus becomes (or remains) impossible in its status of universal fixed point of being, as Modernism already saw it. On the other hand the relation becomes *pragmatically possible* in local framings and it includes these: the latter is not just something which the work *says about* the world, it is some-

---

[10] Cf. Kyndrup 1986, and according to the novel especially Kyndrup 1987. The discussion of the term "postmodernism" is not very important right here, and we shall leave it. It will be touched on in ch. 5.3.

[11] Of course this applies to the entire idea of the "subject" on the outskirts of Modernity. This will be discussed below.

thing which the work *does within* the world in its capacity of construction. Something which takes place occasionally, transitorily, without claiming this 'place' to represent anything but itself, much less pretending to make a statement of any kind of universal validity.

Of course this renunciation of a pretension of universality in connection with the clear abandonment of cognitive priority (anyhow, as to the truth of the world 'out there') is what makes this literature seem "unserious", "superficial", "light" – all of them being words pejoratively loaded in the register of Modernity. Nothing is strange about this: any conceptualization has to unfold itself along the semiotic axes available at the time in question. New axes develop rather slowly. But of course there are good reasons to draw attention to the fact that for certain reasons the concepts in question cannot and are not supposed to be understood according to their traditional axes – and that in doing so and judging accordingly, analytic tasks may be taken too lightly (traditionally speaking). It is true that the 'impossible' S/O-relation has become possible. But only because it has split up, has been dismounted and transformed out of the frame of meaning which was the decisive condition of this impossibility. In other words, we are not talking about a problem which has arrived at its solution. At issue is that a problem can no longer be the same. So, if the impossible has become possible, the possible (:the impossibility) has become impossible as well.

2.5

First Development Section: Conclusion

The Change

The previous chapters have outlined the picture of a process of change. From the novels by Goethe and Balzac, across Woolf and up to Calvino three main types seem to be represented. Three kinds of literary construction, three conceptions of the relationship between art/literature and the world, three ideas of the preconditions and the position in the world picture of the subject/object-relation, and consequently three reconstructions of the subject.

The first type (cf. figure 1) is flat in its construction of enunciation. The literary work of art understands itself above all as a *picture* of the world. Consequently, it conceals as far as possible its own character of being an art construction, conceals its art-ificiality. This is done primarily by means of an introjection of the implicit reader into the world of the work, virtually subjectifying this world, making it the object of the reader subject's personal experience through identification. No matter whether the type pleads by its explicit thematics for the possibility, of the ideal-typical s/o-relationship, or the opposite, it is in fact, qua its construction, opting *pro* this possibility. By making itself an object, a 'world', to the reader subject's

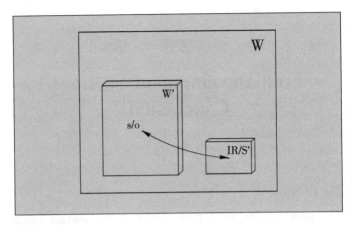

Fig. 1.

Einfühlung, it realizes, as a matter of fact, pragmatically, that very construction which it might deny or reject in its statement, at its enunciated level. This incongruity, or if you like, this initial self-deception is a common feature of this type. Actually, it is in accord with the discrepancy between, on the one hand the immediate self-presentation's intended character of being unconstructed, and on the other hand the extremely ingenious construction which in practice is necessary in order to construct such an apparent non-constructedness. Besides this ingenious construction we have, of course, the convention, the semiotic framing which makes it possible at all. If a picture is to 'resemble' perfectly, the original (the world) must be cognizable, conceptualizable. Picture and pictured are situated at the *same* level. Insisting on the possibility of the picture thus also implies insisting on the pictured after all being a "picture"; it implies the pictured to exist in such a state of order, of structure, of vectorizable organization of meaning, which such a 'resemblance' must presuppose. Consequently any experience of contingency is necessarily denied. This is one of the reasons why this art, originally stated by convention and by itself, as the most truthful, the most honest, fails with regard to its own criteria of value, as time proceeds. In other words, it is forced to realize that it is anything but "honest".

The second type (of which Woolf's novel is an example) consequently gives up the notion of anything immediate, natural, nature-like – precisely on behalf of the notion of verisimilitude. Just as the subject/object-relation of the 'real' world (seen through literature's optics) cannot possibly be mounted as a stable balance, neither can the work of art be mounted as an object of its reception. The result is an "honest" art, objectifying its own technical means of art, its *Kunstmittel*, its own character of being a construction. But, moreover, this art, by emphatically underlining its own character of being produced, being made up, is no longer able to regard itself as any kind of derivative picture of a more real world out there. Art itself is a "reality". No more and no less than the rest of the world is a reality. The very fact that this art at one and the same time maintains the pretensions of honesty, truth, and consequently, of cognition as the supreme motive of move-ment *and* as a consequence of this honesty is bound to become difficult of access, hermetical, all this make this type of literature a favourite object of philosophy. Its paradoxical, but inevitable, compoundedness of uncompro-mising search for lucidity on the one hand, and its (en-suing) necessary conventional opacity on the other, are almost roaring to be interpreted, expounded, deciphered. It is important to stress that even though this type indeed

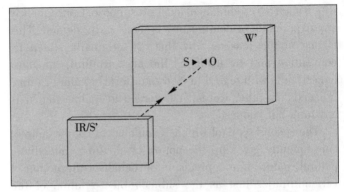

Fig. 2. The S/O-collision within W' is redoubled vertically.

emphatically accentuates the impossibility of the S/O-relationship, this relationship is more than ever still in the focus of attention. Now, not merely as a matter of thematics, but also as an insurmountable complication of the very communicative construction of the works. The work is positioning itself in the focus, so to speak matching, standing beside the world in a sort of parallel setup. Not just immediately because of that, but also qua its compact non-communicability this type consequently tends to abolish itself as "art", as something specially Other. In all circumstances a marginalization takes place. The utmost consequence of honesty becomes unlimited silence or undifferentiated noise. In neither case are potentials of expressive variability any longer available. And this makes the limitations of a development like that impossible to neglect.[1]

---

[1] This at least is a crude picture of the movement as sketched out within the microcosm of the laboratory. In historical reality the

First Development Section

The third type, actually, thus above all implements these limits in the construction itself. If the breakdown of the framing of art and thus the limits of art lead after all to a destruction of the ability of art even to unfold, to catch sight of and choose the opposite direction is near at hand then: instead of subordinating the construction to the truth you might subordinate the truth to the construction. This, of course, makes "truth" cease to be a truth in a universal sense. But was it ever able to be that? Was not truth in all circumstances to renounce everything but local pragmatic validity? Anyway, this question does not 'require' any genuine answer if the register has changed. This third type, having been called postmodern, in order to mark the difference also from *both* of the two previous types of 'Modern' problematics, in fact gives altogether another priority to truth as a problem. Just as the S/O-relation changes its status, by the way. Not so that the problem of truth or the problems of individual/ world-relationships are no longer dealt with thematically. Now they are simply dealt with within a framing which recognizes itself as "art" and precisely nothing but that. "Art" becomes "art" understood as an – acknowledged – frame condition, a specific space of uttering and construction, having of course its place "within" reality. But which cannot be said to resemble "reality", neither by being a valid, derivative picture of it, nor by matching it or even performing an intensified, or privileged manifestation of it. It is indeed *different* from (the rest of) it. And this is what makes its problems and the forces and

professional guardsmen of the field brought up a figure of assimilation making it possible to ensure the unfolding of the new art within the original premises – in spite of the immediate self-contradictions of this.

validities of its statements different both in terms of staging and in terms of status.

To the S/O-relation this means that it is no longer in the focus as a theme in the quality of being a *problem*, being something towards which the work necessarily must have a final attitude, exceeding the borderlines of the world of the work itself. Something to that effect becomes the case for the phenomenon/concept of "truth".

Concretely, the construction is characterized by overtly inscribing its immediate reader's subject as being a part of itself (the construction). This immediately mounts "inside" the work yet another reader position (S" in figure 3) surveying the relationship between the horizontal space of thematics (to the extent that such a space is segregatable at all) and the initial reader (S'). This very movement, however, automatically generates yet another position (S'''), generating yet another, and so on – to form a fundamentally endless chain through which the implicit reader at one and the same time regards the S/O-relations 'up from' the work, and is regarded by them, i.e. regards herself as a link in such a chain. The work as such, however, does not represent anything – not even other works or art as such. As part of a concrete game between certain – visible – conditions of framing and a certain construction of signs and meaning established as a fictive space (fictive in a referential, but of course not in a semiotic sense) the work obviously cannot avoid demonstrating, and respectively giving response to, exactly these possibilities of the process of formation of meaning, which it itself is presenting. Just as the presented spaces will of course be in a position to respond to problems elsewhere in the world, thus generating this or that concrete meaning. But because of

First Development Section

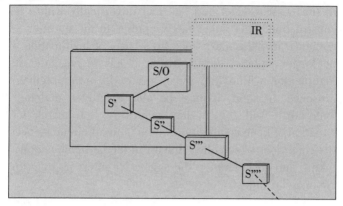

Fig. 3.

the overall construction, any pretension of *representing*
those circumstances is, however, out of the question. At
most a kind of allegorical proximity, a sort of virtual
metonymic *embroyance* may occur, more like some parallel
playing, than like Modernity's emphatic privilege to the
statement. This literature is, consequently, both dishonest
and honest at one and the same time. By presenting (the
unpresentable within) the very presentation,[2] and by
maintaining itself as not wanting and not being able to
be/do anything else, it has, as a matter of fact, to surrender
several of the privileges, which it as a discourse has been

---

[2] As J.F. Lyotard comments on an art which he would call postmodern
differing from that Modern one, which is linked with the notion of the
absent contents of substance. The difference pointed out by Lyotard is
whether the unpresentability is related to the substance (which is absent
understood as a loss) or – on the basis of this as accepted precondition
– is related to that very presentation which in its turn in some sense will
never be able to do 'anything' but reiterate its own relativity, cf. the
chain. See Lyotard, 1986, pp. 32-33.

in the possession of and has had intrinsically within its construction. This immediately applies to the question of audience in particular: since art's basis of legitimation is no longer situated outside itself, it has to engender its legitimation within and by means of its own pragmatic presence. In short, it must be able to attract, maintain, 'entertain'. And *this* in fact may very well match the situation of keen competition which is in all circumstances the conditions of so-called fine art in the late 20th century, taking into consideration the aggressive offerings from the commercial industry of entertainment.

History

The process of change outlined above is a change within *history*. We are not (only) dealing with different projections, different sets of optics during the analytic revelation of the constructions of the novels in question. The examinations demonstrate, one might say, that history exists objectively in the sense of mounting certain framings and conditions on/for the development of certain phenomena at certain ages. *In casu* of narrative constructions, fiction, "literature", "art". This does not imply that history lies 'under' phenomena, thus governing them. History *is* the sum of any phenomena, any institution, any discourse and paradigm existing at a certain moment as a play of complex mutual interdependence. Having demonstrated here how concrete constructions within the field of art have changed from the late 18th to the late 20th century we have not, of course, claimed that this process of change has happened by itself, independent of changes in society as a whole. On the contrary, it is a natural and unbreakable condition for the point of view chosen here that this alteration takes place precisely as part of a complex interplay, in which the realms are connected by means of non-coincidental constructions. This does not imply that assertions concerning supreme, transhistorical laws like "the ideological superstructure of society necessarily reflects the mode of production at its bases" are immediately verifiable. But on the other hand, there is hardly any doubt that economy governs politics more than politics govern economy. Empirical facts seem to confirm this.

The examination of these specific questions of dominance and influence within society as a whole is not the purpose of this book. We are even renouncing any further examination of how the change in constructions is specifically connected with the proper contexts. What we do wish to emphasize and thus have as one of the purposes of our examination is the fact that *actual historical change exists*. This is shown here as an alteration of certain concrete constructions and the conditions of their utilization implied by this alteration.

Concerning that item the first development section of the examination has demonstrated at least two important traits. First of all, within the crude three-phase model of change to which we have reduced history here, the examination has demonstrated that the first two phases ("realism" and "modernism") despite striking outward differences, seem mutually all in all to have more in common than either of them has with the third type. Both of them are, in construction as well as in thematic concentration, positively or negatively linked up with the problem of subject/object-relationship, of substance, and of truth within the framework of the notion of art as an autonomous field possessing certain privileges, but also certain delimitations because of this autonomy. In that way both of them – but each in its own way – are intrinsically linked up with "Modernity", in the basic concept of historical super-formation which a certain agreement from Lyotard to Habermas seems to have rendered possible. It seems equally clear that the third type at certain decisive points is *breaking out* of this unity within Modernity, that anyway it is placed in its periphery, pointing towards something other than the centre of Modernity. Perhaps it is just pointing out this periphery or dilution of Modernity which in the late 20th century is being characterized as "the postmodern condition", "the postindustrial", "the age of deconstruction", "the renaissance of Baroque", &c., &c. Of more specific art-historical interest in this, is the alteration of the overall context of legitimation and utilization of art which is thus suggested; an alteration which, if its visible tendencies are going to last, will inevitably change art and its role fundamentally, including also and not least the modes of condition of its production.

Secondly, this examination has demonstrated that this historical change – even once again including the reservation made unconditionally necessary by the crude phase model – is marked by a certain intrinsic coherence by the fact that the single phases *determine each other step by step*. This does not imply a denial of our emphasis on the complex relatedness to aggregate society. But the examination seems to have made it obvious that modernism is not recognizable outside its connection to that construction ("realism") which it is at one and the same time revolting against and is continuing. And, equally, the third, late, peripheric or postmodernist type is incomprehensible,

First Development Section

indeed perhaps even unthinkable without, above all, modernism's uncompromising revelation of the constructed-ness of the constructions of meaning: only this acknowledgement and the experience of its limitations make it possible to mount these, to some extent similar, constructions, but on a different stage, and thus radically altering their meaning. The realm is, consequently, coherent with itself: "History", understood as a *process* of change, also exists in this way.

Textual Analysis and the Field of Aesthetics

The discussion of the five novels in the first development section furthermore demonstrated some points about *textual analysis*. The detailed analyses of the enunciation of the works followed by discussions of the interrelation between what is said about enunciation and enunciated, respectively, have shown that any delimitation of the attention of the analyses into exclusively the *thematic* ("horizontal") levels would lead to drastically insufficient results. Insufficient, not only in a narrow sense as to the display of the works, respectively, but insufficient also as to the potentials of explanation of such analyses towards the art-historical processes of alteration. The way in which certain works expose themselves, expose their communicative construction, their *doing*, if you like, is such an important part of their features that analyses ignoring this dimension or giving it just a secondary position can hardly claim to be either critically or scientifically qualified.

We shall return to the problem of textual analysis below in chapter 5.1, and this whole problem shall be further illustrated through the second development section below.

It might, however, already be relevant to note one single point now, as it can be drawn out almost immediately from the revelation of the historical process of alteration. At issue is the tendency to exclude in particular the dimension of enunciation of literary works, an exclusion which has obviously been extremely predominant within the history of literary science/criticism as a professional subject. This exclusion is *also*, evidently, determined by other things, such as the context of utilization of literature as a topos of certain types of exchange of views within the bourgeois public system[3] partly as the central medium of formation within the educational system. But moreover, it is striking that part of the explanation of this exclusion seems to be inherent in the result of an analysis *without* this exclusion: the "first type" (Goethe/Balzac) analyzed here is trying to conceal precisely its character as a construction, and when the second type, modernism, exposes its *Kunstmittel*, objectifies the 'impossibility' of construction, this is still a *means* of maintaining the focus on the substance behind (*in casu*: the loss of substance). Against this background you might after all recognize parts of these exclusions as historically *understandable* (which does not make them more sensible or less reductive): they may be seen as expressive of the fact that art criticism/sciences accept the self-acknowledgement of art (and of the artists). Considering the third type, or the periphery of Modernity, it is evident, on the other hand, that *it* is investing so much force in the emphasis on its own relatedness as to signification to its character of being a construction that these works are not even recog-

---

[3] Cf. Habermas, 1976.

First Development Section

nizable without the understanding of and the inclusion of this relatedness. And, obviously, this is probably what makes us able to realize the exclusions in historical retrospect.

Finally a word on the *aesthetic* (*das Ästhetische*, to which we shall also return in the reprise section in 5.2 and 5.3). So far we have (implicitly) opted that apart from what the framing as "literary aesthetic" implies in itself for the specific meaning of phenomena, it appears that a certain multi-dimensional play between enunciated and enunciation, between what is done in the space and what the space itself does as a communicative construction – that a play like this appears under all circumstances to be a property of the aesthetic literary. Whether, and if this property is exclusive we shall not discuss for the moment. It is, however, indisputable, that the space of meaning, which is aesthetic/literary, is able not only to show pictures of subjects having different types of conflicts with their surroundings; it is also able to show how subjects see/acknowledge subjects/situations like these. It is, in other words, able to 'objectify', through this specific framing, a model of the formation of meaning – and thus of the formation of identity. Through – as mentioned – different stagings matching different conditions of different ages.

The State of Things

Our history thus seems to display the fact that the *aesthetic* and the *subject* both hold very specific, very peculiar positions within Modernity. And that this position – these constructions and especially their status within the hierarchy of the formation of meaning – is in the late twentieth century submitted fundamental alterations. We might here recall the fact that the merging of the two, concerning elicitation or dilution of status cannot in any way be regarded as incidental. In fact, from Romanticism onwards, the construction of the aesthetic is deeply and irreversibly infiltrated above all by (fantasms about) the problematics of the subject. Indeed, to an extent this even makes it possible from one point of view to characterize poetry as a *whole* from Romanticism until the present as "romanticism".[4] Even without including what has been shown in the previous chapters about the exclusive focusing on the issue of subjectivity within the literary work, thematically as well as in constructional communication, you may just recall the notions about the genius of art, the syndrome of originality, the entire metaphorics of ex-pression, including the general fixing of pre-lingual 'contents', substance &c., &c.

Without necessarily wanting to promote one particular direction of cause/effect it is, against the background of this entanglement, very near at hand to acknowledge the whole alteration of what the aesthetic is, is able to, and does, as closely related to changes in the construction and the status of the subject. The current intense discussions within philosophy about "the death" of the subject and the subject philosophy, respectively, seem in any case to indicate that something is going on[5]. Some even think the

---

[4] Which Harold Bloom is in fact doing.

[5] Cf. especially the French discussions of for instance Heidegger and the work of the German philosopher Manfred Frank who by means of a critical contrasting precisely of the German subject-philosophical tradition to French neo-structuralism – successfully – tries to objectify

First Development Section

position of the subject provides a model of historical phases according to which the subject within Modernity has held the position which *God* (within the whole construction of meaning) held in premodernity. Whereupon, within postmodernity, *language* seems to be taking over the position which was held by the subject within Modernity.[6] Furthermore, the interesting point is being made that every new phase necessarily has to be at the same time the discovery of the fact *that it must have been like that all the time.* And that is why it is − finally − possible to reject a so-called subject-criticism (among others from Nietzsche over Heidegger to Derrida *und zurück*) by referring to the fact that there is no reason for settling with the subject, as the subject is not what it has been supposed to be.[7] Because of the alteration of the framing, obviously, and implicitly: not any *more.*

The latter is also decisively important for the kind of influence between the alterations of the framings of art and the comprehension of the singular work of art. Evidently, *different* kinds of changes are taking place. A very common conception of the changes is that somehow they are pen-

---

the problematics into a position making it possible to rethink it, also through the optics of a 'history of constructions'. See for instance Frank 1984.

[6] As formulated among others by the Danish critic Hans Hauge in an essay characteristically entitled "Før, Under og Efter Subjektet", that is "Before, During and After the Subject" (Hauge 1990a). And if by language is understood something similar to what we have here been promoting and discussing as the construction and play between framing, sign and meaning, this point of view gets close to what has been elaborated through the concrete analyses so far.

[7] Hauge ibid. p. 59, p. 68.

dular in their structure, i.e. history is marked by repeated oscillations to extreme positions, being merely variations of each other and furthermore – along the axis – in relation to each other mutually positioned as kinds of opposition. This is probably due to the features of the model of conception, rather than to those of the changes; but, of course, processes of alteration being in some sense reversible, are imaginable. This, however, does not apply to the types of alterations which we are discussing here. These alterations are decisively *irreversible*. They are so, because if only once that position or that figure, towards which an overall construction of meaning is pointing, is deconstructed and thus 'decomposed' into its own character as a construction, then this whole construction necessarily alters its meaning irreversibly. Irreversibly because no comprehension once engendered can ever just be erased: inevitably it is bound to form part of the new framing of the sign. Consequently – if something like that was imaginable – even exactly the 'same' constellation of sign (i.e. constellation of concrete expressions) would get an irrevocably different meaning, if the framing was altered conclusively.[8]

This, of course, is the reason why "history" as well is alterable. Not only prospectively, but also in a way retrospectively. When, as we have shown, the framing of literature today seems to be changing decisively, in close connection with a similar alteration of the whole construction of the subject, this has consequences, and not only for future creation of literature. This alteration of the

---

[8] One might remember the short story by Borges *Pierre Menard, author of Don Quijote* (from *Ficciones*) which is a subtle *étude* on this basic theme within the change of meaning.

axes of the literary constructions themselves – exemplarily unfolded in Calvino above – is from now on going to be part of the game, no matter whether it is explicitly so or not. But it is also part of the game of what was already written before *this alteration was elicited itself* (or 'acknowledged', to remain within the metaphorics of the register of Enlightenment). The state of things necessarily forms the frame of understanding also for the reception of what has been: no effort of consciously abstracting from this fact will be able to alter it.

As a consequence this alteration of frame must thus *re*write history, indeed tendentially even 'deny' it as a process of gradual change. It can be demonstrated that what we have now once cognized (about art and the subject, the alteration) has anyhow always already implicitly been there as an insight (or a blindness, which is the same thing) in any of the works which before this insight of the altered frame conditions was acknowledged differently. Thus history, paradoxically, but necessarily, is abolishing "history" as a figure.

Second
Development Section

Rétrograde. Tu devrais ajouter un bouton à ton pardessus lui dit son ami. Je le rencontrai au milieu de la Cour de Rome, après l'avoir quitté se précipitant avec avidité vers une place assise. Il venait de protester contre la poussée d'un autre voyageur, qui, disait-il, le bousculait chaque fois qu'il descendait quelqu'un. Ce jeune homme décharné était porteur d'un chapeau ridicule. Cela se passa sur la plate-forme d'un S complet ce midi-là.

3.1

An Arbitrary Choice

Paul Auster: *The Locked Room*

Introduction

The Locked Room is the third and last part of *The New York
Trilogy* by Paul Auster, young American writer. It has now
already won almost cult fame. The first part, entitled *City
of Glass* was published in 1985; like *The Locked Room*, the
second part called *Ghosts*, was published in 1986. Since
then the three small novels have been collected and re-
published under this joint title.[1]

Seemingly, each of the three novels is telling its own
story. But, of course, the announcement of them as a "trilogy" entangles their universes of meaning. Thus, the first
two novels automatically form a frame of meaning for the
third one. As for this, it explicitly inscribes the first two
novels into its system of enunciation; the first-person
narrator states that:

> These three stories are finally the same story, but each one
> represents a different stage in my awareness of what it is about
> (294)

---

[1] All references will be to the joint English paperback edition (Faber
& Faber) 1989.

as the book has it. In a certain sense this makes *City of Glass* and *Ghosts* secondary compared to *The Locked Room*; here the 'real' story is revealed to and by the person who has written the 'fictions' of the first two stories. We shall return to this relationship. This is one of the reasons for focusing on *The Locked Room* and for discussing the other two novels less fully. The opposite procedure would not be equally pertinent.

The Construction

At one and the same time *The Locked Room* is completely straightforward and tremendously complicated. On the face of it, the construction itself is very simple. The novel plainly tells the story about something which is pretended to have happened to the person telling the story. Outwardly everything is credible and 'realistic'. We have a first-person narrator, and the perspective is *vision-par-derrière* with proper flash-backs and flash-forwards, told from a period (concretely stated as May 1984) some years later than the end of the narrated sequence of events. Furthermore, the narrator is even an author by profession. The other two parts of the trilogy (in themselves considerably more explicitly artificial in their constructions) are additionally connected to this universe as links in the narrative project of the third novel, according to the narrator.

So we are dealing with a report. To be sure, a report in which "literature" plays an important part. But we are not dealing with anything which directly exhibits or understands itself as "literature". On the face of it, the *Kunstmittel* are hidden, just as the implicit narrator behind the explicit one remains hidden. Nothing interrupts the impression of *vraisemblance,* not even the balance between narration and description.

The authentic story, so it seems, is about the dramatic life so far of the unnamed narrator. About how, one day, he (we shall call him A.) is contacted by the young and beautiful Sophie, the wife of Fanshawe, his closest childhood friend. Fanshawe has made an extensive literary production without ever having published anything; before he vanished into thin air he told Sophie to let A. (who is a man of letters) use his manuscripts at his discretion. Of course A. has to accept this. Like everything else of Fanshawe these manuscripts turn out to be excellent, and thus also a financial gain to A. Besides this A. falls deeply in (reciprocated) love with the not less excellent Sophie. In other words, he wins the princess and half the kingdom. He marries her and adopts her (and Fanshawe's) newborn son.

Aber: The long-lost Fanshawe writes a letter to A. A. is afraid of telling this to Sophie (which Fanshawe does not want him to do either), and in a long sequence in which he pretends to be writing Fanshawe's biography ('find the truth about Fanshawe'), but actually is trying to find Fanshawe himself, he ends as down and out, parted from Sophie, nearly killed. This is as far as the main story goes. Actually, we are told that later on he returns, regains Sophie, has another child by her, and lives on (but *without* Fanshawe's money) almost happily. And the report ends by a meeting arranged by Fanshawe on the day he has chosen for his death. A. does not continue the reporting up till his present (three years later), up to the time from which he tells the story. Thus, the insight, the position he has gained through his story, is claimed to be stable like the rest of his relations. In a sense he pretends to live happily ever

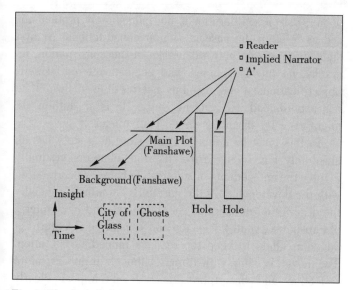

Fig. 1. The formal structure of narration in *The Locked Room*.

after. At first, he lived a grey, common life, then he won the great double prize in the lotto, but it turned out to have a reverse side which almost destroyed him. However, he changed his mind and is now able to enjoy the prize in due consideration of the downside of it.

Nothing is wrong with that plot, and furthermore it has a kind of happy ending. As to the mode of function there can be no discussion: the consistent, 'real' central perspective of the construction of enunciation sets the scene for an identification with the explicit narrator. And exactly because we are dealing with something like a torso of some *Bildungsroman*, or novel of formation, a story of acquiring knowledge about how to live, and told furthermore from a very high level of insight, because of all that the reliability of the first-person narrator is not immediately problematized as is often the case in similar constructions. At first sight there are no outward breaks in the construction, no cracks, no inconsistencies, and no meta-referential self-objectifications: a man recounts a series of events which he has experienced. He tells his story. He is an author. He might even be an author called Paul Auster...[2]

To this must be added that the story as a story has an absolutely convincing *drive*. Its nine chapters gradually involve the antecedents in a delicately balanced correlation with the development of the narrator's situation (especially the description in chapter 2 of childhood, and in chapter 7 of Fanshawe's youth). Also the above-mentioned features of adventure help to keep the reader's immediate attention. The novel is simply thrilling. Although it has a lot of reflection and description these levels appear clearly inferior to the story. In its style *The Locked Room* has a strong resemblance to the "hard-boiled" American detective story (Hammett, Chandler). The outward narrative construction is thoroughly adopted from here, which in itself adds a touch of the effect of this genre to the novel.

Straight

On the face of it, the thematics of the novel are not less straight than the construction. The thematics are developed from the transformation of the relationship between

---

[2] At that point the novel is almost overtly teasing (and thus also formally almost stepping outside itself). It is said about the younger son that "We named him Paul, in memory of Sophie's grandfather" (p. 300). The narrator himself is never named.

Fanshawe and the narrator, scanned as a concrete comparison. From the beginning – back to childhood, but also at the level of the primarily narrated time – the character of Fanshawe apparently represents perfection. He is empowered to establishing the ideal balance between on one hand being governed from inside oneself, being a subject, a ruler – and on the other hand being part of the surrounding world in such a way that this world (especially as represented by other subjects) gains body and legitimate existence. In short, Fanshawe appears to be a prize example of a supremely administered subject/object-relation. His superior position of power does not seem to be the result of a presumptuous will, it is apparently due to some natural, relaxed and indubitable ability, which so to speak *a priori* places him at a level different from anybody else's. Even as a child Fanshawe never felt personal uncertainty, or nervousness, or the pendulum swing between megalomania and feelings of inferiority which characterizes more 'normal' structures of characters, including that of the narrator. Fanshawe appears as an ideal, as the quintessence of potency, as someone to whom everybody must look up. Not only is he able to manage his self-relationship. But also all relations with fellow human beings are fully successful, cf. the respective episodes where, as a child and on behalf of a weaker friend, he takes upon himself to be the one who does not bring any birthday presents (210-12), or his self-sacrifice for a coloured friend on board the ship (280-81).

Fanshawe is much. But already at an early stage it is implied that he is *also too* much. That the perfection which he demands of himself and of the world (and of his relation to the world) cannot be honoured in the long run. The narrator's interpretation – and with that the explanation being offered to the reader at the immediate level – at first points out certain events in Fanshawe's story as crucial: the rough time when his father painfully died of cancer; in another phase the shock at his sister's nervous breakdown, which at least indirectly is suggested as having been caused by Fanshawe's superhuman position in relation to her, i.e. ultimately caused by his ambition for perfection. This again makes him break off, makes him leave his position as a promising student at the university, and take a dirty underdog job on an oil tanker. It is shown that in this way he tries to get rid of his own perfectionism, his own will and will to rule. He forces himself into a position as an object of coincidences, but (of course) he ends up by once again being the "subject", the centre, the ruler – because his deliberate disposal of his position is yet another powerfully positioned project in itself. For some years now, Fanshawe lives in France, ascetically, by trivial jobs, writing and writing, working hard on becoming an author. He refuses for instance a golden offer of a film career, and on the whole he renounces almost everything. Back again in New York he continues his life; he is apparently happily married to the lovely Sophie, and they have a baby – then he disappears into thin air. Disappears after having chosen A. as his successor with Sophie and with the baby. According to Fanshawe (later on) the publishing of his books was only a cover for the real purpose: to have someone providing for his wife and child. The success of the books takes him by surprise and makes him angry. What was meant to be a necessary *real* withdrawal turns out to become an exhibition of himself. Indeed without any concrete connection to his physical person, living incognito. But still

Second Development Section

as a painful making-an-object of his being a "subject". After another self-inflicted punishment of working as a sailor, he finally locks himself up in a house, and lives without any contact at all with the outside world; finally he takes his own life.

That is the story. What the narrator – and thus the reader – gradually realizes in this course of events is that above all, Fanshawe is locked up by his own ambition for perfection. To Fanshawe the demand for perfection, for an absolute truth concludes with a definite blocking up of the exchange with the surroundings, an exchange of course necessary for living, physically and mentally. But *any* such exchange also implies a compromise, a smear, an affection of the truth acting as an ideal beyond and above the field of concrete relationships. And as Fanshawe does not acknowledge this, he cannot live. Indeed, he realizes this. But he sees it as exactly his problem, his fate, as something which is the result of *his* way of being structured. "With me it's another story", as he writes in his letter to the narrator (238).

In his attempt to solve the mystery about Fanshawe (as time goes on becoming only an excuse), *and* by virtue of the pain of not telling the truth (about Fanshawe still being alive) to Sophie, A. is, eventually, placed in a situation parallel to that of Fanshawe. Or anyway resembling that of Fanshawe. According to the surroundings he even begins to look like Fanshawe. Therefore he is also about to perish, into the dilemma which does not and cannot have any solution. Not until he finally chooses an accidental person to be "Fanshawe", and afterwards is nearly killed by that person, i.e. realizes the reality effect also of deliberate arbitrariness, not until then does he – for this and for that reason – get rid of his identification with Fanshawe. It takes quite some time, but having got through that, the narrator simply turns out to have changed his mind. Not even after the reunion does he tell Sophie about Fanshawe's letter (or, later on, about his final meeting with him). *Truth* has got another status:

> That's why I never bothered to tell Sophie the truth – not because it frightened me, but because the truth was no longer important. (301)

From now on A. (and Sophie) refuse to be objects in Fanshawe's game; they even avoid spending the money from his books.

Hence everything is turned upside down in the end: Fanshawe has to lock himself up even more to avoid the exchange which he cannot stand. He cannot even stand being called by his name; even this merely verbal objectification of his person is unbearable to him (cf. p. 306:"'Not Fanshawe'! he shouted. 'Not Fanshawe – ever again!'"). His final conversation with A. takes place through a locked door. He is literally confined to disappearing into himself, as an unavoidable consequence of the norms and rules he has set up. He must perish because he did not want to enter any compromise. To him this is the truth, and it can be formulated as a truth, cf. the red notebook which he finally gives to A. But to A. the contents of the notebook are exactly nonsense, meaning that they elude any intelligible reasoning. As A. puts it:

> If I say nothing about what I found there, it is because I understood very little. All the words were familiar to me, and yet they seemed to have been put together strangely, as though

Second Development Section

Fanshawe	A.
cognitive truth	pragmatic truth
the special individual	the normal (average)
S/O-balance	lack of S/O-balance
strength	weakness
the author	the narrator
fiction	report
renunciation of: ambition	ambition
: material consumption	consumption, fulfillment of needs
: sexuality	fulfillment of sexual needs
Power:	Powerlessness:
Symbolically Giver	Symbolically Receiver
the perfect tense	the imperfect tense
death	life
+ → −	− → +

Fig. 2. A diagram of the system of values presenting what Fanshawe and A. stand for, respectively. As to values there is a transformation from the unambiguously positive positioning of Fanshawe in the beginning of the narrated time to a gradual inversion: Fanshawe's ideal characteristics are 'revealed' as being impossible, and instead, A.'s own 'pragmatic' truth takes the position of being a positive value in the novel. Actually perhaps not directly as an inversion of the values at the right side of the diagram, which are positioned by their respective contrasts at the left side; but rather as the 'mature' A. being pulled *out of* the level of the diagram, thus surveying the original construction of oppositions as impossible, as (pragmatically) untrue. It should be noted that only occasionally is A.'s 'new' position promoted as positive. Cf. also below the calling into the question of the immediate reading.

their final purpose was to cancel each other out. I can think of no other way to express it. Each sentence erased the sentence before it, each paragraph made the next paragraph impossible. It is odd, then, that the feeling that survives from this notebook is one of great lucidity. It is as if Fanshawe knew his final work had to subvert every expectation I had for it. These were not the words of a man who regretted anything. He had answered the question by asking another question, and therefore everything remained open, unfinished, to be started again. I lost my way after the first word, and from then on I could only grope ahead, faltering in the darkness, blinded by the book that had been written for me. And yet, underneath this confusion, I felt there was something too willed, something too perfect, as though in the end the only thing he had really wanted was to fail – even to the point of failing himself. I could be wrong however. (314)

The point is that A. does not swallow this last bait (either): he destroys the book, page by page, and there the story ends. A. is not going to solve any mystery, he is not going to meet any ideal requirement: he is going to live his own story with Sophie and the children, and that is all that matters (300). As it is said: "Beside it, the facts of my life are pure incidental" (ibid.). And they are allowed to stay that way. From having been originally the cringing witness of Fanshawe's incontrovertible superiority, over an identification of himself with him, also concretely (living with his wife and child, making love to his mother; he even *looks* like Fanshawe, more and more strikingly), A. and the novel reach a dissociation from Fanshawe's values, and by that also retrospectively from his seeming superiority. A. mediates the contrasts, realizing that this is the only thing to do: the alternative is death. Truth is death. Verbal "truth" is nonsense: real truth is choosing life, exchange, and its "delimitations", for instance in the shape of the smear of one's personal integrity. This is what A. chooses, and this becomes the new positive pole of the novel after the gradual and finally ultimate disassociation from Fanshawe's fanatic perfectionism (cf. fig. 2).

Straight?

The novel may be read like this. And yet it may not. The story comes right, and yet, obviously, it does not.

First of all, the whole construction of the novel (the trilogy), its narrative structure, is fundamentally at variance with what is said. Loose ends are fluttering at various levels: *The Locked Room* tells a story with "reality" as the object and referent of its story. It tells the truth about a sequence of events. It has as its *drive* the conflictuality of this truth. But at the same time it emphasizes thematically that a kind of truth like that cannot exist. Referring to the first two parts of the trilogy the author says:

> If words followed, it was only because I had no choice but to accept them, to take them upon myself and go where they wanted me to go. But that does not necessarily make the words important. I have been struggling to say goodbye to something for a long time now, and this struggle is all that really matters. *The story is not in the words; it's in the struggle* (294, italics added).

Yet, as we have seen, *The Locked Room* works out very well as a narrative. That is, it is important precisely where "importance" does not exist according to its own assertion. On the other hand it is more or less silent as to what it regards as important. Actually, it is uproariously silent: and the more you scrutinize it, the more it turns out to be strange and at variance with itself. The inclusion of *City of Glass* and *Ghosts* into the universe of fiction of *The Locked Room* is anyway one of the minor blockings. But there is a series of syncretism of names which nevertheless happens to look like a strange, mystifying laying out of tracks. Quinn, who is a p.i., and the protagonist in *City of Glass*, trails one Mr Stillman at the request of the latter's crazy son, Peter Stillman. Quinn goes to the dogs on the project, because he sticks to it steadily long after it is actually finished, and finally he disappears, leaving only a red notebook. And incidentally, Paul Auster, the author, plays a not very flattering subordinate part in this story. In *The Locked Room* Sophie then actually hires a private detective named Quinn to look for Fanshawe. Quinn disappears, but later on Fanshawe tells A. that Quinn has caused him a lot of trouble. So much so that he (Fanshawe) for a long time has seen no alternative but to tail Quinn in order not to be found by him – until he realizes that by this he himself is actually becoming attached to Quinn, and thus 'unfree'. This problem of who-is-following-whom is the whole theme of *Ghosts* which takes place forty years earlier. Here the characters have the names of colours (Blue, White, Green, etc.). In *The Locked Room* Fanshawe states having used the name of Dark. The person whom A. finally at random appoints to be Fanshawe, whom he attacks and by whom he is finally mutilated in Paris, is called Peter Stillman. And Fanshawe eventually gives A. – a red notebook. In this way the novels are united by a web of hints which are too significant to be overlooked, and hence weaving a level of intratextual self-references; on the other hand, however, they are too weak to be abducted just only fairly unambiguously.

Far more decisive, however, is the fact that the story about Fanshawe, which seems to constitute the novel's central point, *actually remains unrevealed*. Or even: gets more and more opaque, the more it is pretended to be cleared up. An example is Fanshawe's books: the enthusiasm for these books seems to be unanimous by A., the publisher, the critics, and the public (and for instance A.'s estimation of them is not stated as changing with his change of values). But we hear nothing about what their qualities really are. Apart from the fact that they are hard to shake off, as it is said. Why do these fictions never occur in the text? Because actually Fanshawe's own story also remains a mystery. What we get are in fact only the narrator's – often hesitating – interpretations. Only the axiological transformation of the interrelation between the narrator and Fanshawe induces the reader to think that qua identification the narrator lives through Fanshawe's problem, thus finally controlling, embracing it. But only apparently, and only in a certain vertical transformation. For behind this there is the locked room, incomprehensible and impregnable. The ending of the novel makes this completely clear: the reader actually never *sees* what Fanshawe has written to A., does not even get a hint. The reader consequently only knows the character of it from A.'s words (cf. the above quotation). A. does not understand it, or does not want to understand it; but he chooses to destroy it immediately. The reader can only rely on A.'s claim, and A. has proclaimed that truth is not what is interesting. What, then, is the truth about the story?

This does not imply another inversion of the statement of the novel as to attitude. It rather implies a roaring "perhaps", squeezing itself to being an outdistancing objectification of the axiological transformation and of the statements which the novel, at the immediate level, has claimed as its own (cf. fig. 2 above). Instead of stating that Fanshawe perishes in his own impossible perfection while A. survives ("happily") because of a hard-won acknowledgement of the necessity of pragmatics, one might just as well say that Fanshawe "wins"; once more, actually, A. does what he has been made to do. He really lives – silently – the life with Sophie which Fanshawe decided him to live. And Fanshawe 'admits' – once again perfectly surveying – that the first letter was a mistake, an affective act which he regrets; but still he is the one who has governed A. through the process which gave him (and the 'novel' qua the narrative construction) this new "comprehension". *Now* Fanshawe knows better: he knows enough to supply A. with a book which leaves precisely a block of darkness, of opaqueness. And which at the same time (cf. the quotation) leaves the feeling of something much too willed, much too perfect, i.e. something which has already anticipated, all the time, the objectification of itself, thus making itself immensely open or immensely closed and inaccessible, which somehow is the same thing. Perhaps making itself something which, on the face of it, takes care of letting itself be physically destroyed immediately, in order to be able to keep on living, sealing its own character of unexchangeable darkness?

What might appear to be a solution to a conflict, and at least to some extent acts as a solution to the narrative suspense of the story – in so far as it follows this track leading to a certain deictic satisfaction – is at the same time one immensely disappointing cadence. The scene is laid for a solution which never comes, which never will

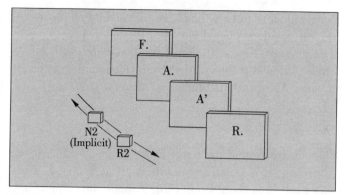

Fig. 3.

come, which, emphatically, *cannot* come, because there is
no room for it: the locked room is locked, and it stays
locked. Locked to A., locked to the reader, and especially
locked to Fanshawe, who is locked up inside it (or who has
locked us out of it). That is why the non-definiteness
characterizing the position of the narrating of the story is
very decisive: A. is leaving his own story, at the same time
as he destroys Fanshawe's red notebook. This is where the
story ends. The end of the story after that is not interesting,
or it is undecidable. Not even the continuation of time is
able to make the story end (cf. the block in fig. 1 above).
The narrative levels are like parallel blocks, interrelated,
but in such a way as to necessarily shade each other, no
matter what position ("point of view") is chosen by the implicit narrator or recipient (N2/R2 in fig. 3). The point is
that these positions have been set going, set sliding.
Various shades are being cast. Various points are being
dissimulated. Thus there will be no such thing as one
privileged point of insight. Insight cannot be acquired
except, maybe, owing to a movement, i.e. owing to some-

thing which, as to time, has been widened into a process of several positions placed one after the other. Like a narrative, actually, like a fiction. Like this novel with all its levels. There is nothing in-between. Outside (the stories) *is* outside. And inside *is* blindness, *tâches aveugles*.

The Text

The construction of the novel hence is open – wide open. Above all, it is pointing towards itself as a text; it deals with itself, it is about itself. Still, it should be emphasized, without abandoning the narrative, without abandoning the story which it forsakes, at the same time. Everything remains, in the potentials and the doings of the text as literature, connected with the very field of crossings between the fictitious, individual temporalities inside. Or, put in another way: connected to concretely measured loops within the great time outside, the time that has no past and no future.

But on closer examination, however, the text also points out, explicitly, its own "impossible" textuality at several levels. In one place A. refers to some "real" life stories and says:

> The point being that, in the end, each life is irreducible to anything other than itself. Which is as much as to say: lives make no sense. (253)

> These are true stories. They are also parables, perhaps, but they mean what they mean only because they are true. (254)

On the same occasion Fanshawe is referred to as having said about a story:

> For in this case it is the man himself who is the agent of his own destruction, and further, the instrument of that destruction is the very thing he needs to keep himself alive. (255)

These formulations can hardly be understood except as comments on the novel itself. Similarly Fanshawe's ultimate (but incomprehensible) text in the red notebook finally has to turn out as a kind of allegory of Paul Auster's trilogy. A block of lucidity – and a block of opacity. Enigmas within the great context can never be solved, because they only exist as concrete functions of certain point-of-view constructions. Any choice whatsoever might appear (or by a construction of enunciation be made to appear) to be necessary. But this will always be incidental. And still binding and yet fatal.

Therefore: specially tempered fictions, 'emplotments' converge into certain undecidabilities, into a sort of open closedness. It is impossible after all to decide on the one hand whether Fanshawe is the fanatic special case, being the basis for the narrator, the novel and the reader to posit themselves into the 'right' position, to the effect that 'righteousness' does not exist as a privileged position, but only as insights into the conditions of enunciation, the formation and intermediation of meaning. *Or* whether on the other hand it is actually Fanshawe who stages the narrator and, consequently, the reader, makes him and her the object of his own project, whose point remains hidden, locked up in the room. Or, in other words: Whether the implicit narrator of the novel is standing *behind* Fanshawe or *in front of* him (cf. figures 4 and 5). In a similar way the S/O-theme is fluctuating in an angle of about 180 degrees. The ideal balance is possible, personified by Fanshawe. It turns out to be impossible, also personified by Fanshawe:

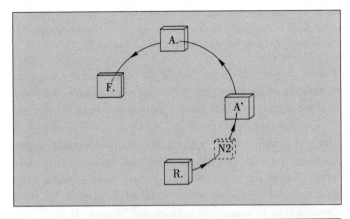

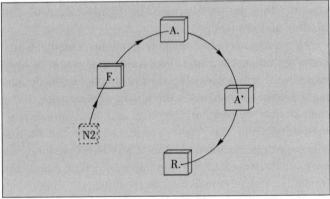

Figs. 4 and 5: The two possible "orbits" of the narrative construction. They reflect two differing, indecidable readers' attitudes, which in practice – impossibly – are redeemed at one and the same time. Fig. 4 shows an orbit which makes the reader a co-subject of the transformation process of cognition. Fig. 5 shows that which makes him a co-object of Fanshawe's/the implicit narrator's sovereign manipulations.

finally, he cannot stand either the world, or himself. Or can he? Is not the self-denying discourse, the emphatic illegibility which he leaves A. in the red notebook not just part of the game, an additional emphasis of his sovereignty? Is not Fanshawe the *really* supreme author who installs and governs the fiction which to A. and his family becomes the story of their life – and to the reader a 'real' story? Is there any substantial reason at all for believing that Fanshawe actually dies? Who is plotting whom, who is trailing whom, who is reading whom?

These are the questions of the text as a complex whole. Questions, asked not rhetorically shouting, but carefully constructed into a plot, which, as we have seen, also plots itself as a plot.

The Context

Thus *The New York Trilogy* knows itself in the highest degree, i.e. knows its own emphatic undecidability. "The solution" (if that is the word one wants to use) is formed by the construction itself. This might imply a disappointment, a fall, a trivialization, if seen from a certain traditional point of view (this construction being looked upon as less "real" qua its relative artificiality). But it also implies – as we have been discussing[3] – a radical change in the field of possibilities. A change which might be regarded as an enlargement or (within another well-known register) as a liberation.

---

[3] In chapter 2.5 above. Especially with the discussion in relation to the idea by Hauge (1990) about God being replaced by subject and later subject by language, as the centre.

But let us continue along the lines of the literary field's administration of this problem. The way in which Auster's text points at itself is different from the way in which Calvino's did it, cf. above. In Auster the emphatic stress on the paradox of the text itself as a construction of meaning is far more inherent to the text itself, cf. for instance the seeming continuation of narration. Put in another way, the dimension of the enunciation is less demonstratively emphasized here – without being less decisively present within the self-knowledge which the construction possesses (cf. the double movement). We are dealing with a series of cracks in a surface which is mainly unbroken, cracks, however, which turn out to lead to folds, which then – unfolded – radically change the whole structure of the surface, indeed change the entire orbit of the narrative hierarchy and hence the character of the reader's position. The enigma and thus the abductional energy of the implicit recipient is placed in a position different from the one in Calvino's construction. In Calvino the reader is being pushed *out of* his own explicit (self-repeating) picture. Here he is being pulled *into* a position, obviously dissipative and impossible to manage – at one and the same time unreservedly *inside* and self-evidently *besides* the construction (cf. the metaphorics in fig. 3 – or in fig. 4-5 where the pulsatory, labile, implicit reader-position necessarily delineates this helpless outside).

It is, by the way, interesting to notice how this problem of *abduction* is explicitly placed at the thematic centre everywhere in the great postmodernist narrative constructions. In Auster as a supreme characteristic in the detective plot of the story (but as the riddle which is not solved, and which can never be solved). In Calvino, as mentioned above, in the hunt for the originator and coherence in the universe of the plot, where the radical, horizontal discontinuity removes the question out into the self-relativizing problems of framing of the vertical dimension. In Umberto Eco's teasingly allegoric suggestions in *Il nome della rosa* in which he shows – also with clearly explicit allusions to the detective genre – an apparently real and proper abduction leading to a completely wrong conclusion. Or, ironically inverted, in his *Il pendolo di Foucault*, where the casual linking of a series of single signs into a certain inferential construction of abduction suddenly endows the arbitrariness of this with an effect of reality which becomes irreversible and fatal to the parties involved: the false or fictive abduction becomes the truth about the world, becomes a world. Or, finally, as in Milan Kundera, for instance in *Nesnesitelna lehkost byti* (1984, *The Unbearable Lightness of Being*) and *Nesmrtelnost* (1990, *L'Immortalité*), where the apparent absurdity of the singularities are carefully commented upon by a narrator, thus organizing through his *narrative* function the absurdities, while in his *thematizing* function he is maintaining at the same time the arbitrariness of the signs, the singularity of the singularities.

As to Auster's novel as well as to the other novels mentioned above: it would not have been possible to write them without the previous, gradual change ("development") of the novel as a construction and as a position. And, it would have been still less possible to understand them in their complex spreading of meaning without a "horizon of reception" containing this development and its individual stages, at least as residues of outdated framings.

In *The New York Trilogy* itself no residues as such are to be found. Here the story stands completely unfolded, densely compressed, illegibly maintained, invitingly inaccessible.

3.2

A Canny Construction

Max Frisch: *Homo Faber*

The Novel

Homo Faber, published in 1957 by the Swiss writer Max Frisch, is generally considered to be, uncontentiously, a major work – not only in German literature, but also in world literature in mid-20th-century. And rightly so. Of course, its success with the critics and the audience – it has been translated into many languages and has obtained good sales figures almost everywhere – is due to the fact that it addresses links between the actual problems of Western civilisation *and* experiences and conflicts of fundamental, even permanent influence on the lives of all human beings: man versus woman, parents versus children, age versus youth, memory versus repression, experience versus oblivion. But what the common reader, reading from inclination, may not always be aware of (but what is nevertheless an absolute precondition for the inclination to turn up like that) is that also in its construction of fiction, in its narrative architecture, *Homo Faber* is one of the most in-geniously and beautifully accomplished novels in the history of modern fiction. Relevant, beautiful, and canny – canny enough to include itself into the problems which it points out qua a rhetorical construction. However, this inclusion is not immediately obvious, which is typical of the novel's time.

The scene: World of the 1950s. The protagonist: Walter Faber (cf. Latin *faber* = blacksmith, i.e. a "maker", an organizer, a contractor; this allusion is emphasized by the title). Fifty-year old engineer, employed in an international organization, mounting turbines, mainly in the third world. Belongs to the kind of technical intelligence forcing through its own notion of the unlimited possibilities of technical-instrumental reason, without any thought or respect for other segments of existing value. Forcing through its own notion of language, technology, and calculation as being value-neutral instruments of the super-individual "progress" which is the very meaning of life, and of which the individual cannot, will not, and ought not be in the way. At one and the same time Walter Faber is an uncompromising representative of these values, and latently subject to a profound crisis because of them: continuously flying from himself, flying from his own biological ageing process, which to him appears as an outrageous insult to the ideology of constant innovation. Also, actually, flying from the physical condition of his own body, from his cancer of the stomach which symbolizes how his repressions live their own wild lives, in order finally to obtain power over calculation, definitively.

Faber is upset by some unforeseen events – for one thing the technology of a plane fails – and he happens to travel by sea to Europe instead of, as usual, by air. On board the ship he meets a young girl and falls in love with her, half against his will. He travels with her through Europe and becomes her lover. She turns out to be his natural daughter, but (maybe) he does not know that until later. His symbolic consumption of her/devouring her – in an attempt to adopt her youth, her future prospects – becomes literal, as, indirectly, he causes her death by accident. After yet another frightening travel through the new world, and later on through the third world, he chooses to return: to realize the limitations of technical rationality, to face cancer, and die in Athens, in the old world, close to Hannah, the love of his youth (which he has repressed until now), the mother of his daughter. He realizes, and he dies. Probably: at least this is where the novel ends.

The System of Values

The axiological structure of the novel appears to be rather simple. Not only do the axes of value in the novel follow some traditional contrasts in the common formation of meaning, they also do so with an extremely pronounced significant redundancy.

Thus we have, on the one hand, the set of values which is represented by Walter Faber in his basis and in his self-knowledge. Historically and geographically it is connected to the new Western culture of Western Europe and the US. It is based on the notion of a calculated reason, the belief in the unlimited possibilities of man (individually as well as the whole human kind) to control his surroundings – supposing, of course, that this human being realizes, acquires, and submits to the regulations and methods of objective reason. Thus *science* is the decisive tool of mankind, and consequently, its progress becomes almost a purpose in itself. Above all, this idea is prospective: the present, the actual moment, is seen as a function of what might come. The past, in every sense, is being repressed: this applies to history and tradition in general (symbolized, for instance, by Walter's conduct in relation to museums). But in the attitude towards the individual's life cycle the same mechanism prevails, which particularly means that death and the cycle of organic nature are repressed. Individual time is above all future, and that is why old age and physical decay are negative values. Altogether the position is linear, quantitative in its ideals of argumentation, and generally additive in its way of thinking. Nature and surroundings in general only exist as objects of control; all in all Walter's position appears to be un-natural, unauthentic, and, in the proper sense of the word, irresponsible, globally and individually. Even human relationships are seen as calculable contracts (cf. Walter's relationship to Ivy, his American girlfriend). Sexuality is menacing because it is based on exchange or even disposal of power; that is why autosexuality is practised in various ways (cf. Walter's clearly suggested, latent homosexuality, and respectively his sexual consumption of his own daughter through his relationship to Sabeth).

In figure 1 the axiological structure at this level is presented schematically. Opposite Walter's side, which by the individual story is clearly extrapolated to represent a male position, we have a female pole, above all personified by Hannah, and at the beginning by her daughter, Sabeth. Geographically and historically, this female pole is linked to the old civilization, to Antiquity (Italy, and especially Greece) and thus to the past, to tradition. It places feeling, sense, responsiveness and humbleness to fate above the idea of absolute control of the surrounding world, and consequently the orientation of human sciences towards

−	+
new culture	old culture, "nature"
repression	insight
reason	emotion
linearity	circularity
quantity, addition	quality
death absent	death present
inorganic	organic
future/present	past/present
unnatural, unauthentic	authenticity
autoerotics (homosex., incest)	developed sexuality (innocence/exchange)
natural sciences	human sciences, art
lack of responsibility S/O	responsibility
"man"	"woman"
Walter	Sabeth, Hannah

Fig.1. Schematical presentation of the linking of values by the supreme axis of values.

history and meaning above natural sciences' accumulation of laws to be utilized by the instrumental project of civilization. To this position our present is the product of a past and of a tradition from which nobody should or even could escape; equivalent to this, individual life means realizing also one's own changeability, including the reality of death. The repression of the past gives way to an interest in the exploration of the past; opposite Walter's job as a mounter of turbines for future production, Hannah is working as an archaeologist. Basically, this position is characterized by something which is circular, something which changes qualitatively, organically, something which is authentic, meaning that the individual rests in the realization of its own power and powerlessness, respectively, in its relation-ship to the surroundings. In this sense the position is characterized by global and individual responsibility. The relationships between human beings, and between human beings and the surrounding world are understood first of all as an exchange, as reversible processes in reappearing structures. Therefore, sexuality becomes a natural effect of this exchange. Also language is reversible; it is a pertinent system of chains representing paradigmatic choices. An example can be seen in Walter's and Sabeth's running "competition of allegories" towards the end (esp. pp. 150-152)[1]. Here Sabeth teaches Walter, to whom language, instrumentally and realistically (in a philosophical sense), has been supposed to cover as precisely as possible the objective state of realities, the way different metaphors may differ from each other *qualitatively* by being less "good" or "ingenious"; to Sabeth it is not the degree to which the sign coincides with the measurable attributes of the object that decides the quality or meaning of the expression. No, here the issue is the very play with the chainlike circling of the language around what might

---

[1] Page numbers here and in the following refer to Max Frisch: *Homo Faber. Ein Bericht.* Suhrkamp (st 354), Frankfurt am M. 1977.

finally not be or never be expressed after all. And also at that point Walter is willingly being taught:

> [...] wir fliegen hindurch. Gewölk in der Sonne vor uns: als müsse unsere Maschine daran zerschnellen, Gebirge aus Wasserdampf, aber prall und weiss wie griechischer Marmor, Körnig – [196]

as he puts it on his last trip back to Athens after Sabeth's death. At that point he is *very* far from the lapidary, fact-related narrative style, he was practising at the beginning of the novel. We shall return to the narrative structure, however.

As to the novel's attitude to the poles it is obvious that the male values of the left side are understood as negative, while the right side, defined as a female universe, is positive. First of all, it is clearly demonstrated that Walter's belief in technical rationality and in his own ability to set his own way, instrumentally, is constantly perforated. Walter's interpretations of the surrounding world simply do not work – neither do, actually, his planes, his turbines, even his friend's tobacco plantation. His stubborn repairing of superfluous shavers and cars looks grotesque, ridiculous, just like his fight against everything that is organic, even his own beard, looks pathologically neurotic. In the end he is actually eaten up by cancer, i.e. by that very untamed organic material, by nature, whose power he rejects so contemptuously and definitely. Thus the reader gradually realizes that Walter's rationality – though it claims to be just the opposite – is, first of all, retrospective, i.e. it is working as socalled subsequent rationalizations. In real situations – above all those immediately unforeseen – Walter Faber is always fickle, almost helpless. Not until afterwards is he able to provide his actions (which often almost unambiguously suggest quite different explanations) with a reason, acceptable to the ideology of his world view.

This is how the universe of the novel fundamentally looks. Through the novel Walter Faber is gradually being "moved" from right to left, in attitude. His revolt against the values on the left seems to have started already at the beginning of the narrated time, but it is not really working until Sabeth becomes his guide, so to speak, to the values on the right, when, physically as well, he is pulled back with her to the old world and its history. First by their journey back to Europe, and later on by their classical *Bildungsreise* from Paris through Southern France, Italy, and Rome and from there to Greece, the cradle of Western civilization. It can also be put like this: gradually, the protagonist obtains an attitude converging with the ('inner') one of the novel. Throughout the novel it becomes obvious that what is said to repel Walter Faber on the right side (for example women, feelings, death, responsibility, play, fate) as a matter of fact attracts him more and more openly. But the decisive condition for the movement to actually begin is, as mentioned earlier, his relationship with Sabeth which only becomes a relationship because they are mutually attracted to each other. And so only because Sabeth's mother, Hannah, in turn, conversely has repressed the left-side values, has withheld her father from her (literally, and of course, symbolically), has steered her round any male value and principle. In doing so she has made her amenable to fascination by the wonderfully (strangely) different ('male') self-delusion, which can then become her ultimate fate. The wise Hannah finally understands this, and even goes so far as to ask Walter's forgiveness. Thus emphasizing a connection *behind* Walter (who finally dissociates himself massively from his former attitudes) the novel suggests that behind or besides the apparently unambiguous system of values there is something else, something more.

The Structure of Enunciation

And indeed there is, as we shall see later on. However, first we shall look at the novel's narrative construction, being its most distinctive characteristic.

The novel is a strictly "personal" first-person narrative and is kept within the frames of absolute *vraisemblance*, also formally: a credible story which absolutely does not know any more than it is possible for it to know. So the subtitle of the novel, *Ein Bericht*. The narrated maintime is about three and a half months, from April 2 till July 21, and it includes flash-backs to the past, especially to the time of Walter's and Hannah's engagement and the assumed induced abortion in the thirties. The story has been written at two "stations" as they are called: the first from June 21 till July 8 in Caracas where Walter is ill in bed; the second from July 19 till July 21 in Athens where Walter is awaiting his final stomach operation (from which he is probably going to die). The narrating time of the first station is not explicitated until it expires (p. 160), and it is not pointed out in the text during the narration. As for narrated time, it goes on until Sabeth's death on May 28. At the second station, on the contrary, the situation of the point of narrating time is emphasized and it interweaves with the narration; typographically the passages describing the present are printed in italics. Finally the time of narration and the narrated time meet in the 'present/presence' which also means the end of the text:

08.05 Uhr
Sie kommen (203)

In fig. 2 the outward characteristics of the narrative construction are illustrated.

The first-person narrator, Walter Faber, is ostentatiously an *unreliable* narrator. This has certain effects, as he is at the same time the only focalizer, the only one carrying the point of view: everything experienced by the reader is – without exception – told by him. The "unreliability" is only gradually revealed to the reader. But as it happens, the attention of the reader is shifted, step by step, from what is told to what the narration hides or represses.

Faber's silence has two levels: one of those comprises his immediate repressions, that means where he happens to say directly in the text that actually he knows better. To this level can be assigned Walter's complete attempt to justify his relationship with Sabeth and especially the maintaining of this relationship during their journey to Greece, even after he *must* have realized that she is his daughter. Faber the engineer and mathematician miscalculates her age, for example (121)! Moreover, it is characteristic of Faber that he pours out a cloud of statistics, book references or superfluous hardcore information, exactly where things have come to a head for him – a pattern which of course the reader learns to decode.

This first "differentiation of insight" corresponds roughly to the distance between Faber's final level of knowledge (July 21) and his level in each of the narrated periods. But

284   *Second Development Section*

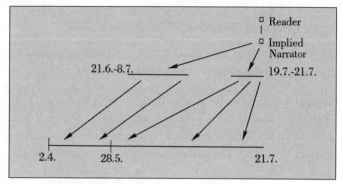

Fig. 2. Model of the narrative structure. Left-right marks the sequence of time, up-down the hierarchy of insight.

apart from this there is also a significant difference between the knowledge which *Faber* obtains – or is able to obtain, and that of the *novel*. We shall return to this. However, it is important already here to remark that of course the implicit reader is not simply being positioned into Faber's end point of convergence, of insight.

As mentioned, the reader gets used to the fact that reliable information about Faber's attitude is to be analyzed out of other discourses in which it may be apparently casual. An example would be Walter's story about his time in Paris after taking leave of Sabeth at the ship. He does *not* describe how, as it turns out to have happened, he went around the Louvre day after day hoping to meet Sabeth – since it is important to him to describe the meeting as coincidental. Yet the information appears later:

> Es war Frühling aber es schneite als wir in den Tuilerien saßen, Schneegestöber aus blauem Himmel; wir hatten uns fast eine Woche lang nicht gesehen, und sie war froh um unser Wiedersehen, schien mir, wegen der Zigaretten, sie war bankrott.

"Das habe ich Ihnen auch nie geglaubt", sagte sie, "dass Sie nie in den Louvre gehen – "

"Jedenfalls selten."

"Selten!" lachte sie. "Vorgestern schon habe ich Sie gesehen – unten bei den Antiken – und gestern auch." (100).

In this way the reader gradually gets used to questioning everything that is told. Very characteristic is the fact that, generally, Walter Faber the narrator in his chronological story at first skips the situations which are emotionally the most intense – in order to return to them later on. Consequently they are told with a kind of double *vision-par-derrière* (i.e. as the memory of a memory instead of just as a memory: with an extra distance). This applies to his last time with Sabeth (150-152) and to the accident itself (156-158). Of course, these delays serve to characterize Faber on the one hand. But they are also an important part of the narrative suspense, when the reader demonstratively "lacks" some kind of central event to which there are frequent references. One example is Walter's and Sabeth's sexual première in Avignon (p. 124-125). Another very significant example is a scene towards the end of the novel in which Faber sees, for the first time, all the films he has shot. They show him that even before he met Sabeth he was interested in things quite different from what he has reported (cf. his interest in for instance sunsets which is totally incomprehensible to him). But above all, they show that his report about his relationship to Sabeth on board the ship and later on the journey through Europe is completely beside the point (185-192). Here, towards the end of the novel, a reader who might not until then have doubted Faber's story sufficiently, will have this doubt established/strengthened, retrospectively. To Faber himself,

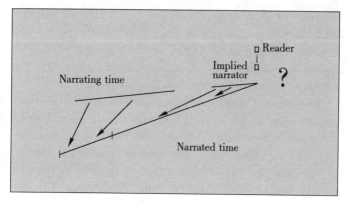

Fig. 3. Actually, the 'hierarchy' of fig. 2 above, graphically should also terminate in one point: the increase of insight takes place at the level of narrated time as well.

however, the scene makes him want to put out his own eyes (yet another heavy allusion to the Oedipus myth) – and finally makes him decide to go back to Athens. Eventually, Faber realizes that his deceit has been disclosed: we are close to the point.

And "the point" is the point of convergence at which the *vision-par-derrière* of the story becomes *vision-avec*, at which the narrator's fundamental unreliability finally turns into naked existence and by that becomes as much honesty as this person is able to show. One might say that the levels of the novel, and thus the novel as a whole, approaches itself by approaching the present which from then on will remain the "present" to any future reader. Although the reader all the time knows more than Faber, the narrator, and little by little gets used to comprehending the story as an iceberg of which only the smaller part is visible, and consequently has to be actively abductive, then the reader's immediate perspective is still merging with the hitherto differing levels at this final single point: just turning into a present "now" at the moment when it is bound to vanish. In fig. 3 we have tried to visualize the narrative structure moving towards this point.

In terms of functional structure the unreliable first-person narrator becomes the instance for a simultaneous ("vertical") complexity. On the one hand, the 'authentic' way of reporting, the first-person narrator's central perspective and the very structure of tragedy in the plot clearly initiate identification with, *Einfühlung* with the world of the text. Similarly Faber's movement inside the axiological system of the novel is undoubtedly contributing to the promotion of the reader's sympathy and identification: in the beginning Faber is unpleasant and wrong, but his rebellion is demonstratively clear (to everybody but to himself), and concretely he is also heading the right way throughout the novel. Thus he may be included in a Prodigal-Son syndrome. Besides that he is hit rather hard personally in losing not only his daughter but also his life: he never gets the chance to live out his new realization.

At the same time, however, the construction has some obvious features which create distance: above all, the narrator's unreliability initiates constant contemplative objectification in the reader's pattern of perception, thus slowing down or off-setting the identification. This pattern might communicate itself to the reader's attitude to the unambiguous value structure mentioned above. All in all the meeting with this unambiguity can hardly avoid raising questions about the construction as a whole. Any construction with a clearly unreliable first-person narrator always emphasizes the position held by the implicit narrator *behind* the plot-intrinsic part of the construction. Actually, this is the instance with which the reader argues when she is to decode Faber's explanations. And of course that is the instance which is the focus of interest when one is to discuss what the novel says as a whole.

Statement/"Saying"

On the face of it, *Homo Faber* is an obvious critique of the technical, instrumental rationality of modern man, and of the fact that he reduces his surroundings into the raw material of an unceasing, automatized, consciousless development. In other words, a critique of Modernity – or maybe rather a critique of civilization. But from where, on behalf of whom?

At the immediate level (cf. the above system of values, figure 1) the criticism of civilization proceeds on behalf of – civilization. It is true that the axis of values mimes a traditional dichotomy: culture versus nature. But characteristically, the positive, right, "natural" side represents "culture" as well, only in a more classical, traditional version. This means that actually just two different kinds of culture are confronted. At this level the novel is radical to an almost amazingly small degree. It is not even close to, for instance, classical modernisms' objectification of the apparent coherence of the horizon of reference as being a simulacrum, as a mere construction mounted somewhere within endless contingency. No, *Homo Faber* is rather, as it might be said, playing segments *inside* Modernity out against each other. What in fact the novel is warning a-gainst is de-auratization, de-romanization, which is bound to be the consequence of an infatuated, one-eyed realization of technological rationality. Above all the novel is arguing in favour of *moderation* inside the given horizon. This figure is further supported by a perspective of *mediation* which is the consequence of the emphasis on Hannah's recognition of *her* guilt: having, as a consequence of her own critique of the left-side male values, withheld from Sabeth the knowledge and experience of those values, Hannah has, unintentionally, made her vulnerable, made her accessible to its virtual attraction, in the very way that the fatal consequences are shown by the novel. At this immediate level the novel is not even opting for the classical cultural tradition of the right side, linked to the reversible logic of exchange of the female. No, even at this level clear consistency is bad: what is needed is stabilization, balance, mediation.

> Warum ich das gesagt habe? fragt sie jetzt immerzu. Damals: dein Kind, statt unser Kind (202)

as it is put at the end of the novel (and already earlier it has been pointed out that that very remark made Hannah give up her marriage with Walter then). This feeling of resentment in Hannah suggests that the whole tragedy, the whole blundering of their lives, the onesidedness in both sides, and finally the disaster – that everything could have been avoided had there been just a little less radicality in the very beginning.

Anyway, the statement of the novel can be turned in that direction. Still, however, at least two problems remain.

At the immediate thematic level, first of all, there is a whole cluster of values which do not really fit: the third world, death, fertility, and devouring, organic nature. It is true that all these values are in one sense linked with the right side, sometimes directly (the Frenchman Marcel explicitly links death, earth, and woman (p. 69)). But above all, this happens implicitly, negatively, as directed against Faber's left side. It contributes to the break-off of his centrifugal movement into sheer galloping ratio. The experience of jungle, vultures and death, of fertility and later on of sensuality (in Cuba); everything is fundamentally different from Walter's life up to now. But these values or perhaps even non-values also play a part different from the one they seem to be playing at the surface level. One could point out the impact of the jungle on Joachim, the friend, and later on Joachim's brother, Herbert. To them the braking has a quite different ultimate character than the nice cultural collecting-oneself, the reshaping course to which Walter seems subject. This is (precisely) *not* amplified explicitly in the novel. The attraction to the jumble of death and fertility, represented by the jungle and the absolute non-civilization, seems to be inescapable and unjustifiable. The position hints at a total, non-verbal negation of any value of civilization: which in Joachim is radically carried to the utmost as suicide; as to Herbert (even to a Walter, being very flexible at that time) already set forth as a completely incomprehensible, irreversible shift of attention and values over a very short period. Above all, Herbert loses every idea about future, about what he must and what he wants, about *where* to go. All of a sudden he is just going nowhere (pp. 166-169).

Although nothing "positive" is being formulated about this pole (geographically linked with the third world, the other two poles being linked with the old and the new world, respectively) it is obvious that it represents something different from what is represented by the thoroughly reasonable Hannah. More than anything else it appears as a position of no position, of non-sense, of non-life, of non-place: something which can be seen as in its own mode a joint rejection of any of the conflicting values in the surface structure. It represents something, seemingly threatening humanity at its very humanity: it represents bestiality, the real. And it is thus the place of boundless, unspeakable horror.

Less immediately obvious, but on second thoughts far more serious, is, however, the other problem: the one arising from the implicit narrator's position and competence, compared to the system of values of the novel's world. A thoroughly calculated, gradually expanded effect of the iceberg in the play of a first-person narrative structure on the narrator's narrative unreliability – a construction like this situates the implicit narrator in that very position of (narrative) projectual megalomania, which the novel explicitly wants to demonstrate as impossible (in its protagonist). Thus, by its ingenuity, its perfect calculation and structuration the novel becomes a kind of denial of its own immediate message. The implicit narrator simply resembles the rationalist Walter Faber, indeed more than that (because already at the beginning of the novel Faber is routed by his own explicit attitudes): it resembles the one Walter Faber would really *like* to be, the Homo Faber from whom the novel explicitly and clearly dissociates itself.

Knowledge?

Thus the novel ends by pointing out some positions outside its own immediate universe. Positions which can be understood on the one hand as noise, unnecessary or necessary, within an otherwise clearly and beautifully constructed signal. But which can also, on the other hand, be understood as a perspectivization, an elaboration, a more profound knowledge which the novel is unable to keep hidden though it might want to, at some level. In fig. 4 we have tried to schematize this movement of dissipation of the levels. The fact that there are *two* such movements may indicate, oddly enough, that either of them acts as a modification of the problem which the other one represents qua its relation of distance to the main structure. The presence, in relation to the 'heavy' opposition of right and wrong, of something unspeakable which is at one and the same time repulsive and attractive, anyhow implies a modification of the distinctness of the surface dichotomies and thus inflicts the projectual competence of the implicit narrator. Conversely, the self-referential inconsistency of the structure of enunciation gives more room to such a hole of non-sense which the third pole seems to be digging in a nice and perfectly arranged universe.

However, it is uncertain what the novel knows about its own knowledge at this level. This novel is not a self-relativating engine for producing new, always already deconstructed positions, shifting from subject to object, from supreme insight to subordinate link-in-the-chain the way we have seen it explicitly in Calvino (chapter 2.4). Nor does it point out – with leant-back, but uncasual subtlety – a space of non-sense which thus becomes the pledge of

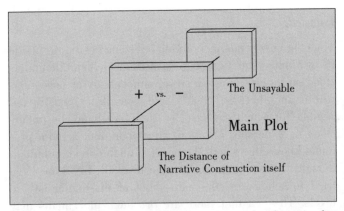

Fig. 4. Outline of the 'aberrant' positions compared to the main plot. One must imagine the distance of the narrative placed 'in front of' the main plot (relating to the reader), and the negating non-place 'behind' the main plot.

its own knowledge about the character of its structured meaning as we have seen in Paul Auster (chapter 3.1). No, in spite of the symmetry and in spite of the structure in some sense being paradoxical, this novel remains full of knowledge and sheerly ignorant at one and the same time. That is because it is what could be called isomorphous with its proper narrative construction of fiction. You might also say that it escapes its own possible knowledge *through* its own structure of fiction. It does so by committing itself to converging into a moment, a "now", which can never be repeated and which cannot be continued – or which can always be repeated and thus (in this very elaboration) is bound to go on and on, which happens to be the same thing. The decisive point is that this initial present cannot become past and thus object because nothing is following it. By virtue of the play of the first-person narrative construction at the empty spaces and thus at the implicit reader's inescapable undertaking of the formation of meaning, the problem of what the novel knows about itself is transmitted into becoming the reader's problem: the buck has already been passed. Whether the implicit narrator of the novel actually represses its knowledge through this construction, just as its "alter ego" Walter Faber is described in the fiction as constantly repressing *his* knowledge, is uncertain. It is a possibility. But this uncertainty may be understood as a result of a kind of knowledge which is not necessarily able to, or which does not want to, precalculate a homogeneous course in a heterogeneous field, thus positioning itself as privileged towards the field. We may be dealing with a knowledge which finds just a possible way out: the one that neither opens nor closes, the one next to both wisdom and stupidity, right and wrong; the one that makes the problem of enunciation terminate in itself by demonstrating that "knowledge" must be a figure overtaken by its own character of being a construction. That is why, having over-taken himself, Walter Faber must become silent. That is why the plot must freeze at the very point where it remains forever, thrown on and referring to its own temporal, spatial and epistemological structure: that point in which at one and the same time the novel can evade pragmatically and still hold the knowledge which, explicitly cognitive, it would be equally impossible to escape from or to phrase. Thus *Homo Faber* implicitly mounts an isomorphism between the self-deception of the novel and that of the subject. This implies certain perspectives when we consider the fact that in the point-of-view constructions of "real" lived life, points of convergence like the one in this novel are not constructible.

Homo Faber is not merely having it out with itself. It is a single shot and it is fragile. But having once been fired its fragility has forever become monumental and stable. Invulnerable and impenetrable in a certain sense. And embracing all the room for knowledge about its own complex character which we, not the novel, may possess.

3.3

Objective Relativity
of Absolute Authority

Isak Dinesen: *The Roads Round Pisa*

Introduction

Isak Dinesen's writings constitute a very special world of
their own within twentieth century fiction. And it is far
from coincidental that to readers as well as to critics they
appear as an illuminated island. One reason of course is
the indisputable mastery of her narrative constructions;
those in themselves will guarantee her a front-rank position.[1] But moreover it is perhaps the peculiar state of non-
contemporarity in Dinesen's work which is the main reason
for their ability still to appear as open, inviting, attractive
– and still mystically indefinite. This 'non-contemporarity'
is not only what characterizes the immediate relationship
between the very form of Dinesen's works and their time

---

[1] What is remarked here on Dinesen's writings as general is above all
related to her centre of gravity, qualitatively, the narratives. An example
of this "technical" mastery will be presented in the reading to follow.
See also my "Dinesen versus Postmodernism" (Kyndrup 1992), or
"Syndfloden og sandheden" (Kyndrup 1988). Both articles deal with *The
Deluge at Norderney*, and amongst other things, uncovers the narrative
construction.

(her contemporary world literature is signed with names such as Joyce, Proust, Virginia Woolf – and appeared *somewhat* different). No, the non-contemporarity, the clash between times (or the clash between discourses, to be semiotically more precise) is also inherent in the works. What we have in mind here is not the thematic transmission of the action into landscapes of the past, although this transmission indeed is an important feature of the constructions. No, the clash above all takes place between on the one hand the narrative construction which (seemingly) is in charge, and which even at the time of publication was emphatically *out-dated*, and on the other hand a theme which on a closer look is tremendously modern. Any reader of Dinesen's narratives, professional as *amateur* (or the rare combination of both), is thus simultaneously thrown in several different directions. Within one register she is thrown back into an almost pre-modern discourse not only because of the concrete rooms of action and the obviously oldfashioned olympic, narrative construction, but also qua the critique of the individuals' projectuality of controlling reality which, apparently rooted in a feudal-absolutist state of thinking, is emphatically and repeatedly exercised in the points of the intrigues as to attitudes. At the same time, however, behind the apparent "naturalness" of these narrative constructions, this critique is indeed surprisingly Modern. And, finally, is perhaps already (modally) "postmodern" qua its relaxed and virtually self-ironical *accepting* embodiment of the emphatically importunate undecidability of the problem of enunciation; this is remarkably different from the way contemporary modernism felt itself more or less involuntarily prisoned by a tragical feeling of loss of substance, evoked by the very same experience.

These clashes of discourse include and point out the problem of discoursive change in the works, and this is no doubt one reason why Dinesen's works are still able to fascinate. But these clashes also make the *reception* of Dinesen's works highly interesting because this, by virtue of these, demonstrates certain conventional blindnesses within different areas of the institution of literature. What we have in mind is of course primarily the totally unhampered concentration on the *author* as some kind of demonic subject,[2] a concentration which is rather misplaced judging from the works.

However, an explicit discussion of the Dinesen reception is unfortunately beyond the scope here. The following discussion of *The Roads Round Pisa* will in itself point out areas which such a criticism might take as its basis. For the moment let us just note Dinesen's success.

The Tale

The Roads Round Pisa has an important position in Isak Dinesen's first real work, *Seven Gothic Tales* of 1935: as the fourth of the seven tales it forms the centre of the book. In the Danish version of the following year, *Syv fantastiske fortællinger*, the tale was placed in the front, as the opening; this further emphasizes the importance of the fact that the protagonist in *The Roads Round Pisa* also acts as

---

[2] A clear example is Judith Thurman's famous mammoth biography which in fact itself became a *best-seller*. But also in Denmark the publishing of memoires in the form of auto- and Blixen-biographies has flourished, especially by writers who were then young, striving, talents hawked by the demonic, old lady – now dignified, aged poets and men of letters (Thorkild Bjørnvig, Ole Wivel, Aage Henriksen).

subordinate figure in the last tale of the collection, *The Poet*. We shall return to this later.[3]

The central position seems to be substantially well-founded in every way, for *The Roads Round Pisa* appears in thematical concentration as well as in narrative structure as virtually archetypal for the tales of the book.

The Roads Round Pisa is built as an ingenious hybrid between on the one hand a narration of a central perspective and on the other hand a cycle of narrations, thus marking a lot of different narrators' perspectives. As the focus of the one-point perspective we find the young Danish nobleman Augustus von Schimmelmann travelling in Italy in 1823. He is trying to run away from problems at home (problems concerning an extremely jealous wife), and he is above all searching for *truth*. Even from the start of the tale he seems to have a critical attitude towards truth as objective and absolute:

> How difficult it is to know the truth. I wonder if it is really possible to be absolutely truthful when you are alone. Truth, like time, is an idea arising from, and depending upon, human intercourse. What is the truth about a mountain in Africa that has no name and not even a footpath across it? The truth about this road is that it leads to Pisa, and the truth about Pisa can be found within books written and read by human beings. What is the truth about a man on a desert island? And I, I am like a man on a desert island. When I was a student my friend used to laugh at me because I was in the habit of looking at myself in the looking-glasses, and had my own rooms decorated with

---

[3] The English edition referred to here is the Vintage Books, NY 1972; it is a photographic reprint of the 1934 original edition. The Danish text used is Gyldendals Tranebøger 1985, photograph reprint of the 1950 edition.

mirrors. They attributed this to personal vanity. But it was not really so. I looked into the glasses to see what I was like. A glass tells you the truth about yourself. [165]

Augustus is in a state of contemplative searching, though rather passive. He becomes the witness of a series of violent incidents, which finally turn out to be different sequences of one and the same story, indeed even connected to his own life story.

At first Augustus witnesses a carriage accident; the passenger – Augustus thinks it is a man, but it turns out to be a (noble)woman – is severely injured. She confides to him the dramatic story of her relationship with her granddaughter and asks him to bring a message to this granddaughter in Pisa. The next day on his way to Pisa Augustus meets a young nobleman – who turns out to be a woman – with whom he converses and who hints at, but does not really reveal, a very mysterious story. After that Augustus witnesses how a travelling company, among others consisting of the Prince Potenziani who plays a leading role in the story of the old lady, develops into a challenge, on account of a certain *tale*. Augustus feels obliged to act as a second in the duel. In the meantime he watches a puppet show. The duel next morning is stopped by Agnese, the young girl, who goes in between, telling *her* part/version of the story which makes all the previous, isolated and up till then mysteriously disconnected parts join beautifully into a whole: the young Prince Nino actually did not let down the old Prince Potenziani, he just, without knowing it, deflowered a stand-in (Agnese) for Rosina, whom he was to have raped on behalf of the impotent Potenziani, thus making it possible for him to prove consummation of his marriage. The duel is off, and Nino's life is saved. But

Potenziani dies; the two young people could have had each other, but having been liberated from her secret the woman is no longer paralysed by the rape and must now (perhaps) be won; Rosina does not die in childbirth as predicted, and everything ends up with happiness and harmony. In gratitude Augustus gets a "smelling bottle" from the old noble lady which is the counterpart to the one he already has: thus (without knowing it herself) the old noblelady is identical with his grandmother's friend fifty years earlier. Augustus, however, keeps this knowledge to himself, feeling that

> ...in this decision of fate, [was] something which was meant for him only [216]

All rings are closed; the pattern filled in.

The Structure

On the face of it the structure thus seems complicated, yet not incalculable. Gerard Genette's distinction between *narrator* and *focalizer*[4] may be useful here: Augustus is the focalizer of the tale. The told universe is reflected through him. On both sides of this internal, personified instance of focalization (temporally acting in *vision-avec*) we find, however, a number of explicit instances (all working in *vision-par-derrière*): 'under' Augustus we find the "personal" narrators, giving Augustus and each other their versions, respectively, of the pattern, which only in the end appears

---

[4] See for instance Genette 1972; see also the clarifying explicitations in Rimmon-Kennan 1990, esp. pp. 71ff.

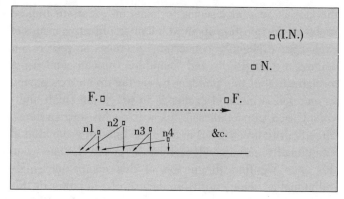

Fig. 1. The "personal" narrators n1, n2 &c. each tells their own version of the same events. The focalizer F moves in time.

to the perspective of Augustus[5] (the old lady, the young lady, Potenziani, Nino, etc.). 'Above' Augustus we find on the other hand an "authorial" narrator telling Augustus, and being explicit among other things qua the objectifying characterization of him: his melancholy, his corpulence, etc. This instance is very close to, but must necessarily, as a principle, be separated from, the supreme implicit narrator who takes care of distribution and linking of all these instances. In figure 1 there is a rough outline of the instances.

The Enunciated

The enunciated is also complicated, being formulated at a number of different levels of narration. Still the message of

---

[5] – and with that, fundamentally, to the perspective of the reader. But on this point we shall have to make certain qualifications, cf. below.

the stories generally seems to focus on a certain limited problem: the question about which intersubjective modes of exchange, especially concerning exercise of power and control, are possible – and desirable. You can condense a formalization of this problem by setting up an axis having as one pole a mode of exchange in which the single individual as a project thrusts his will on his surroundings, directly or indirectly, but in any case through some kind of intentionally anticipated exercise of power. Belonging to this pole we find the notion of this competent single individual as being *justified* in the exercise of power by this competence. This point of view has certain decisive implications: it emphasizes the fact that the regulation of being is *human* in all circumstances; in all cases the world, then, is recognizable as objects of value in front of a subject. Furthermore – as a consequence of the mutual clashes which these kinds of subjects will then necessarily experience – *hierarchical* differentiation of this field of human subjects is necessary. In the second pole of the axis we find another type of exchange which considers control to be mutual relations of obligation in which the subjects are able to change their positions in relation to each other, thus performing exactly a *mutual* exchange. This means that no single subject is able to act as a privileged regulator of character, direction, and content of the exercise of power; instead of this, qua the insight by the single subjects into the necessity of acting also as objects to other subjects' legal exercise of power, an alternation, regulated by the concrete interactions, between the position of being subject and the position of being object, between pride and humility, an alternation which may finally be recognized as an acceptance of some outer non-human supreme instance, an alternation of that kind takes place. God, fate, chance. Or, non-transcendentally staged pragmatically: just the acceptance of *what actually happens.*[6]

More than anything all the single stories converge in this thematic axis. According to *her* privileged conception of the world, Carlotta, the old lady, wants to force the young Rosina to marry against her will; Prince Potenziani sets up an intrigue (the rape) in order to make sure that the marriage will go ahead, thus getting the opportunity of "playing with" Rosina by depriving her of the possibility of a divorce on the plea of non-consummation of the marriage. These Great Subjects both *lose*: Carlotta by actually recognizing the limitation of her right of the subjective exercise of power, but Potenziani without such a recognition. On the contrary he is vexed because he has not been cunning enough to set up an even better intrigue, which would have enabled him to win. Potenziani then only sees the concrete, not the fundamental limitation of projectuality. Furthermore, Potenziani finds it quite natural to take advantage of the law of mutual obligation in the case of Nino, even when the purpose is to break this law in the case of somebody else (the intrigue). On the other hand the young ones respect this mutuality: Nino does what he has been ordered to do; contrary to all reason (not just because of the odds of it, but also because he has actually kept the promise he is being accused of having broken) he enters

---

[6] Congruent to this installation of values, the thematics of *truth* can also be mounted: truth as something transcendentally *behind* the exchanges versus truth pragmatically linked with them (in the first case the large subjects can then claim to *represent* truth through the projects; the other truth is not representable or monopolizable).

the duel; similarly the young girl plays her part as a stand-in and for a long time remains silent in spite of her unbearable dishonour. Still she is the one who in the very end through a higher bid saves Nino's life by telling the truth; in doing so, it turns out that she is also setting herself free. This is the type of exchange which is actually the "winner" in the tale: not because it beats the intriguers within their own register by thinking out even cannier plans (the way the – very symbolically – *impotent* Potenziani imagines), but by accepting chance, and thus worshipping mutual obligation and with that one's own integrity more than potential outer profit.

As should be evident from the course of events and from the very mounting of this axis in the tale, a positive evaluation of the pole of mutual exchange is made at the expense of the megalomaniac individual projectuality of the other side (as is thematically reiterated almost everywhere in Dinesen). This evaluation, however, takes place in a certain narrative structure. What is decisive is that the events happen removed from or 'outside' the Augustus experiencing them and through whom we are experiencing them. Everything, so to speak, is happening *in front of* him as though in a (puppet) theatre performance, in which he himself may be playing a very modest part, but which fundamentally has nothing concrete to do with his own problems. To him (and in the perspective of the reader through his focalization) it is this very distance that makes these events turn into a chain of allegories, carrying meaning and being attractive, and whose message is also made visible precisely because of their distance, their nature of otherness (cf. fig. 2). What Augustus is going through is a kind of formation process in a double-pole

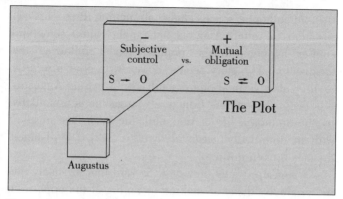

Fig. 2. Augustus' distance from the conflicts of the level of action makes the principal aspects of the conflicts visible to him – as in a theatre performance.

structure, in which he experiences, on the one hand, his own usual emptiness (and action-paralyzed melancholy) as opposed to the abundance of substance and *doing*, which is characteristic of the entire chain of events that he witnesses. But on the other hand he also seems to pick the attitude of the point of the sequence of events: there is a line from his initial rejection of truth as being privileged logos (cf. the above quotation), over the puppet comedy's playing with the (pragmatical) truth of lies in *Revenge of Truth*, and to his final renunciation of proclaiming the coincidence of the smelling bottles. Augustus' experience of events enables him to recognize his own indolence hitherto, and his (as is said to be generally characteristic of Northern people) constitutional distance from any kind of strong outburst of feeling. He sees his own decompressed space of melancholic depressiveness being confronted with a space which is chock-full of exchange, death, passion, risk: an authentic space. This confrontation throws his own situation in relief. And, as one might think, something similar happens to the implicit reader following this focalization. The story seems, however, to offer a *solution* to this also vertical north/south conflict qua Augustus' process of recognition. Concretely Augustus is assimilated by the authentic life of the south (he even has an affair with an, admittedly *Swedish* lady cf. p. 212). The distance, then, is broken down.

To sum up it may, however, be said that precisely qua the originally distance-making mounting of the opposition of values in construction, the text optimalizes its supreme critique of the calculating exercise of power by projectual reason – and thus, if you like, of the Modernity that has this reason as its primary property. But it should also be noted that at the same time the text mounts itself as a kind of contradiction of its own message: the nicely calculated and successful staging of the impossibility of staging made by the text itself seems to imply some sort of intrinsic denial. Or, in any case a problem of revocation for the sovereign, implicit narrator.

The Text

With this reading the text is placed as more or less in accordance with itself – or at least in accordance with its own discordance. It mounts a certain axiological taxonomy in a convenient, accessible position – and it indicates an access to the ostensive and intended process of formation (through Augustus' function of focalization). Because the scenario is removed in terms of time and space, a certain distance is marked, but probably this only makes the effect of exemplary objectification, which also allegorically points back to the time of the reader, even greater. Though Dinesen's text remains absolutely different from the texts written by her modernist contemporaries it can easily be conceptualized within the same historical context, perhaps as a parallel track in the process of historical transformation: the key words here might be the critique of Modernity, the individual thrown back onto itself, the problem of alienation (emphasized in Augustus' position, but also symbolically represented by the overall being *verrückt* of the story in space and time). Furthermore we have the rather high congruence between the text's statement and its structure of enunciation. Even according to the reading we have offered.

The question is, however, whether this reading is satisfactory and sufficient.

Above all the reading seems overtly to simplify the construction of enunciation by fixing its instances, placing them in firm positions, while they are actually labile, shaking, relative. In particular this applies to the position of Augustus, the focalizer. On the one hand it is technically correct that this position works as the reader's entrance to the story, and that qua the process it is also the carrier of the perspective. On the other hand there are so many demonstrative distances *inside* the enunciation of the text that the competence of the focalization is seriously affected. Augustus, in other words, is *unreliable* or in any case not directly reliable as a narrator/focalizer. He gets his observations *wrong*, for instance he twice mistakes women for men (and that is one mistake too many to be coincidental in the universe of the story). His part in the tale, also from an outside point of view, is that of the observer, and his mode of existence is that of reflexion, of pensiveness. On a closer look at the reflexions, which he actually makes, they turn out in practice to be rather trivial, or frankly banal, in spite of their solemn character. For instance in his conversation with the young woman concerning the relationship between men and women:

> [...] it has happened to me many times that a lady has told me that I was making her unhappy, and that she wished that she and I were dead, at a time when I have tried hardest to make her happy. It is so many years now since Adam and Eve" – he looked across the room to a picture of them – "were first together in the garden, that it seems a great pity that we have not learned better how to please one another" [184]

Indeed a profundity! But apart from the fact that this is the level of thinking which he stammers out, often with a lot of trouble and great solemnity, his acknowledgment of his own process is similarly miserable, apparently. In the case of the puppet comedy he manages to convince himself that if he himself has now entered a puppet comedy (i.e. the throbbing life of the south) then he wants to make sure that he does not get out of it again (199). But this point of view carries with it that very inside/outside-dualism which the "theatrical" symbolization intended to settle with. Augustus' immovability can, however, be seen even more clearly at the end of the story itself:

> Augustus took a small mirror from his pocket. Holding it in the flat of his hand, he looked thoughtfully into it [216]

Augustus' mania of looking at himself in a mirror has already earlier in the text been explained as something which he did as a young man in order to find *truth* (165, cf. the above quotation). It is decisively significant, thus, that he narcissistically regards himself in the final sequence in order to find the very truth which it has been the issue of the whole tale to show does *not* exist other than pragmatically, which means in concrete events, in concrete exchange. Or to put it briefly: Augustus has in fact learned nothing from what happened.

The reason for this is primarily that he is too slow, too heavy. Actually he is an almost ridiculous figure: he is pleasant and well-intentioned, but above all he is unable to realize his own limitations. This is perceptibly confirmed by the part he plays in the last tale of the collection, *The Poet*.[7]

This distance from Augustus cannot however be called unambiguous (though seemingly growing, whenever realized in the first place). This distance is above all a tendency, a

---

[7] It is of course a matter of discussion whether it is reasonable to infer from the characteristics of a person from another tale, though belonging to the same collection. In *The Poet*, however, Augustus is a character of no importance at all. And this makes the merging of names not just a coincidence (because we also have references to personal disposition, the wife's jealousy, &c.). Here (pp. 379ff) we meet Augustus as considerably older. Decisive in relation to the Pisa story is the establishing of the fact that as to Augustus there have been no changes whatsoever in the nature of acquiring more insight or *Gelassenheit*: Augustus is still bound to his Sisyphean labour of looking for authenticity, in this case pinned down to the point that he is only able to appreciate objects which other people are envious of. In other words he is still the rather ridiculous, contemplative person whom the smelling bottles in the Pisa story do not seem to have moved anywhere. In the introductory characteristic it is said about him: "He wanted to be very happy but he had no talent for happiness" (380). And the slightly ironical continuation – ironical if you have the Pisa story in mind – goes: "He had suffered during his youth".

shake, an irony, which establishes an ambiguity in the reader's relation to the figure. This ambiguity, however, has rather extensive consequences first for the structure of enunciation of the story, and later on also for its thematic statement.

The dissociation from Augustus is, precisely, an evaluation, an attitude. As it is not caused by the explicit narrator, apparently (who hides no sympathies), it singles out the implicit narrator as its sender. This links the explicit narrator *and* Augustus, the focalizer, at one level, while a connection between the implicit narrator and the first-person narrators "down" in the text is similarly established behind this level. The latter who is supposed to possess more insight than the former, or at least to be closer to the level of insight of "the tale", is, however, in its level of knowledge constitutionally handicapped by the fact that the first-person narrators *and* their stories are experienced by Augustus who is to some extent unreliable, or at least not specifically emphasized as a carrier of insight. Something potentially very full of insight is thus intermediated via a perspective constitutionally primitive – and which does not even know its own restrictions. The result of this is a high degree of uncertainty – which might be illustrated by an hourglass-shaped model of the topography of enunciation – *both* below (what is actually going on in the story) and above (what the narrator is actually trying to tell with this story).

This means above all that what seems at first glance to be an unambiguous linking of the story (and a linking of this to the story of Augustus) through the "disclosure" by the girl Agnese of the true inwardness of the case, in effect turns out to be anything but unambiguous. The messages of the single stories become ambiguous. It becomes uncertain what is actually happening: the exits (for instance for the young couple) are being covered up. But also the superior intention and meaning of the tale is now a matter of discussion, for what is the "meaning" of this lability in the narrative distribution? Why is the impotent Prince called "Potenziani" – is it just to jeer? Why is it exactly through "smelling bottles" (i.e. instruments of anaesthetics) that the supreme symbolic connection is established in Augustus' mind?

What is interesting in all these questions is not the answers there might be to them, but the fact that they can even be asked. Furthermore, at the level of the statement this entire 'labilization' of the instances in the structure of enunciation has as its consequence the fact that Augustus' problem is changing. On an immediate reading the polarizations of north/south, emptiness/fullness, appearance/authenticity seem to be an absolute and an existential

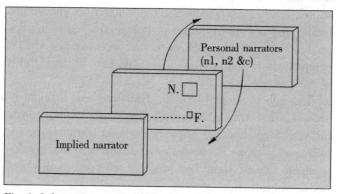

Fig. 3. It becomes uncertain whether the level of the focalizer F (= Augustus) is not, according to insight, behind (or 'beneath') the one of the personal narrators.

problem (to A., but with a general significance qua the reader's way of entrance). The dissociation of Augustus makes it appear rather as a structural problem of position, a relative problem more in the nature of a subjective projection than of an objective schism: Augustus' problem is an inherent part of his constitutional relationship to the world and thus it is bound to follow him in any circumstances whatsoever. What is at issue is Otherness as an intrinsic counterpicture. Augustus is being exposed and made ridiculous as tied up to his own miserable self-projections. But a part of this stultification hits the implicit reader – because Augustus is still the entrance, and the attitude towards the competence of his perspective is uncertain. The reader is left, without appeal, to make use of a perspective which may be unfit for use because it is incompetent; above that incompetence, then, we find the implicit narrator as a possible director. Relegated to a continuous pendling between on the one hand Augustus' flat, but serious perspective and on the other hand the supreme narrator's sovereign, but immensely inaccurate, labile and relaxedly ironical perspective, the implicit reader, then, is above all confronted with his own lack of competence in the tale, or rather: his lack of decidability of competence.

The tale is altogether open. Half-finished, it might be argued. This very nature of being existentially, constitutionally half-finished is precisely what Carlotta, the old lady, mentions as her experience of life *after* having dissociated herself from her ideology of projectuality and perfection hitherto:

"When I was a little girl", she said, "I was told never to show a fool a thing half finished. But what else does the Lord himself do to us during all our lives? [215]

This may be the text's metacomment on itself. To believe in the apparent sovereignty of a construction is a mistake: constructions are always only half finished; they move.

And most important is precisely the moving, the lability, the very existence of this simultaneous, incommensurable and undecidable ambiguity – which is not an either/or. Our original reading is *not contradicted* by the next one: the structure and statements of its values, Augustus' cautious process of formation, the outside/in-fascination – all these elements still exist as features of the text, as traces of a reading which are an inescapable part of its meaning. They are just framed by the possible presence of the others, like a picture being shaken. A picture which is supposed to show the immutability of Firmness. Which it still does. But it is being shaken.

The outcome is not one of mediation or denial. "The outcome" is the very moving, saturated by contrasts whose elements are located in different registers of discourse and thus unable to dissolve or to confirm each other. But for instance the problem of revocation in the text which we pointed out in the first reading, is reversed by the frame of the subsequent reading: the problems involved in sovereignly staging a demonstration of the limitations of staging thus seem to have been staged. But not in a register in which it is possible to characterize the staging as "sovereign". Or is it?

Conclusion

If "sovereignty" is the existence of a hierarchical system, within which a supreme arch-instance is able to act as a deciding resultant in a calculated system of levels of insight, then sovereignty is not the issue here. There is no such place here from which it is possible to survey the complexity of the text or to identify the position of the instances. But technically all this disorder of the enunciation is of course installed by a supreme implicit narrator. The text just does not contain any markers which make it possible to decide the plan or the direction of the construction – or rather, the text has lots of markers but they are pointing in different directions. It is this sort of (lack of) order which made us choose to read the text in two stages. Even though it would have been possible from the start to release all the undecidabilities in one and the same reading, this might have blurred the very special way in which complexity quite simply frames the quite simple.

To sum up: Technically the crucial reason for the complexity of the text is the lability of the authority of focalization (and with that of course to some extent the lability of the authority of the explicit, "olympic" narrator). This makes it impossible to decide what is up and down in the hierarchy of insight among the whole system of narrators in the text. If in fact the focalizer F is unable to understand the first-person narrators, n1, n2, etc., then their levels of fictionality change and the hierarchy of insight is altered. And it is not even a stable dilemma, but constant, virtual changes where the focalizer may at a given moment be precise and clearly recognizing, and the next helplessly misinterpreting, whether this is caused by concrete *tâches aveugles* or just by a common lack of acuteness.

What is decisive is of course that the implicit reader is partially pulled into this lability and into the ensuing uncertainty as to what is actually happening. This makes the reader one who both "understands" and "does not understand". Augustus' stupid perspective becomes an imperceptible part of his insight and consequently that of the reader's: With Augustus the implicit reader is simultaneously mounted in this conveniently objectivating "outside" *and* embarrassingly close to the centres of events, as their actual object. And consequently also both naively innocent, virginal – and accomplice of the ineluctability of the complications. Whether the "easy" mounting of the play is done deliberately or not.

The mode of function of the text is thus extremely complex. It is interesting to see how this complexity is clearly produced by the structure of the text itself, in this case. The mounting of the subject/object-relations in the various dimensions of the text has been done so as to make it impossible to fit them into one formula or just to make them correspond to each other at the same level. One will have to 'content oneself' with describing their proper developments phenomenologically and the system as a whole as "complex".[8] Compared to each other the single relations may most precisely be described as out of phase.

---

[8] "Complex system" here understood in the meaning it is being given by modern natural sciences. In the still unpublished PhD thesis *Realismens metode* (Aarhus Universitet, 1991), Frits Andersen applies this concept to realist literature regarding this as "complex" above all through its double and mutually incongruent determinateness by mimesis and "mathesis", i.e. narrative and *descriptive* elements of constitution.

They neither confirm, contradict, nor modify each other. They simply *are* there at the same time, in the same text, unable to communicate and still together making out the space of the text.

This space, consequently, is very simple and surveyable – and at the same time a labyrinth with no way out. Perhaps Dinesen's tale is not at all a side track in history (the way we suggested in the beginning). Perhaps it is rather a loop, necessarily outside at any time.

3.4

The Indeterminate Determinateness of Absence

Ernest Hemingway: *The Sun Also Rises*

Introduction

On the face of it the gap between Isak Dinesen's fictional space and the one unfolded in Ernest Hemingway's break-through novel, *The Sun Also Rises*, seems enormous. The two novels are truly almost contemporaries; Hemingway's novel is published in 1927. But who could imagine a dif-ference wider than this: from Dinesen's finely chased construction of frame-frame narratives under a cool, intensive, olympically omniscient narrator, operating inside a space historically and spiritually in a position of *marked* distance – and to Hemingway's hardboiled, 'simple' first-person report told by a narrator demonstratively anything but omniscient, and dealing with an absolutely recog-nizable, contemporary world described in a flood of apparently superfluous details?

The narrative constructions of course *are* widely different. However, according to their major thematical interests the two stories yet are parallel to an astonishing degree. And perhaps in the end they do even resemble each other in terms of their aesthetic construction – in spite of the striking differences in appearance.

The Text

The Sun Also Rises is full of action in the sense that it consists almost exclusively of descriptions of situations, i.e. actions and surroundings, including a huge quantity of speech lines reproduced as direct speech. A lot of things *happen*, but nevertheless almost nothing happens. Most of the events are totally undramatic and most of the descriptions do not contribute to the meaning of the narrative course: they include situations of eating and especially drinking, travelling routes, prices, &c., &c. The plot is not very compressed either as to external dramatic actions and their construction/sharpening.

Nor does the sequence of events imply any noticeable perspectives of change for the fictional persons involved: Jake, the predominant protagonist of the novel has a problem: during the war he was ostensibly wounded so that he is physically unable to make love. He is *impotent*. This does not prevent him from being in love with Brett. We now meet him in Paris where he is gadding about, with Brett (whom he cannot possess either in this or that way), and with Cohn, an acquaintance. Cohn and Brett go south together for some days without Jake's knowing and without Brett being specifically serious about it. Later on Jake goes fishing in Spain with Bill, another friend, and the events reach their climax when everybody meets at the Pamplona *fiesta*. Brett and her future husband, Mike, are violently annoyed by the very jealous Cohn. They all watch a bull-fight, and Brett runs off with a young bullfighter, however only after Cohn has thoroughly crushed him. Jake goes to San Sebastian alone to rest, but is called to Madrid by Brett in order to save her and bring her home because she has broken off her relationship with the young bullfighter. She ran out of money. And Jake does what she asks of him.

Nothing changes: Jake is still in love with Brett and still cannot possess her; Brett, it is hinted, returns to Mike and is bound to continue with her little affairs without really wanting them or being able to do anything about them. And so on, and so on. The only exception may be Cohn, who has made himself so emphatically impossible that at least he has to disappear out of the circle. But there is no indication that the events have changed him. In effect, nothing special happens: the result is given *a priori* as already suggested by the title of the novel.[1]

Jake is the narrator of the story, and this 'natural' form is strictly respected.[2] The story is told in the past tense by a first person; there is a sort a double focalization, in which, on one hand, the whole story, strictly speaking, is told from a position temporally placed after the whole sequence of events, i.e. through *vision-par-derrière*. This is among other things pointed out by a few cases of narrative prolepsis (for instance in the dramatic climax of the fiesta, pp. 165ff). On the other hand, though, no demonstratively manifest knowledge of the result of the events is being shown; actually the story is thus being told with a rather

---

[1] What we have in mind here is of course the original title, *The Sun Also Rises* and not *Fiesta* under which the novel was widely published later on. The edition used here is the Triad/Panther Book edition, Frogmore 1976, to which the following page numbers refer.

[2] Apart from one single little mistake, p. 183, where suddenly the conversation between the bullfighter Romero and his sword-handler, is being revealed though Jake has hardly been able to hear it. But of course he may just be imagining.

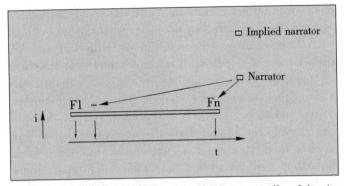

Fig. 1. The structure of focalization. The supreme teller, Jake, is watching himself experiencing the events.

simultaneous focalization, i.e. in *vision-avec*: Jake tells how Jake experiences the events in the situation.[3] Figure 1 outlines the simple construction.

Though the *form* of the personal narrative is strictly respected, it is demonstratively different from what one might immediately expect of this form with regard to the quantitative and qualitative weight of the socalled "interior sight", i.e. the internal focalization, in the perspective. Myriads of details about the nature of the phenomenal world *outside* Jake are reported. Above all the space is described by means of so many superfluous details as might often be found in for instance a holiday diary: names of restaurants, the quality of food and wine, the prices, the scenery, &c. Furthermore, page follows page of precisely reported remarks in direct speech, with only an absolute

---

[3] The construction of a 'double' first-person narrator like this has a considerable effect on the problem of reliability in the enunciation which we shall return to later.

minimum of staging remarks. When it comes to the protagonist's emotions and thoughts about the events, the flood
of details is usually radically reduced. With only a couple
of exceptions[4] the protagonist's self-experience at the
explicit level is either reduced to ultra-short, un-detailed
indications of the state of things or has even completely
vanished. This, however, does not imply that it has vanished from the consciousness of the novel, and thus from
that of the reader. By contrast: the immediate absence at
this level results in an enormous emphasis on it. The
groundwork is laid: a novel which is above all about that
which it does *not* say.

The Space

This does not at all mean that what it actually says is of no
importance. On the contrary this outlines the borders of the
meaning of that which is so emphatically not being said.

The central persons of the group, Jake, Brett, Bill, and
Mike share a special *modus vivendi* – and their existential
situations are also alike. They are all fundamentally dis-
illusioned about human relationships including love. Their
'style' now consists in accepting this miserable state of
things in the field of subject/object-interchange. Above all
it is important to seem *cool*, underplayed, unsentimentally
relaxed. Not that everybody is not conscious that they
themselves and the others are fundamentally unhappy: the

---

[4] Especially Jake's reflexions at night, pp. 28f in Paris and his wording
of his "philosophy of life", pp. 123f. But at least in the last case it is
highly uncertain whether we are dealing with a "report" or (perhaps
reported) psychological self-therapy, read: self-deception.

point is to accept the situation. Actually it becomes sort of an ideal to be as unhappy as possible and *at the same time* to act maximally carefree, stay cool.

This is one of the reasons why Jake also comes to hold a central position. He is the only one whose modal conflict has been caused from the outside (at least according to himself). The reason why Jake is unable to do what he wants to do is a physical problem which has arisen exogenously and which is apparently physically insoluble. All the others, it is argued, have totally similar modal conflicts, only these are apparently endogenous, i.e. consequences of intrinsic structures of character. This is above all the case with Brett, who is driven to necessarily possess the men she seems unable to get – and who consequently throws them away as soon as she has conquered them. The fact that she sometimes expresses her warm feelings for Jake – while at the same time exploiting him grossly – is above all connected to the fact that she is unable to get him. Already early on Jake mentions this explicitly:

> I suppose she only wanted what she couldn't have [29]

It is worth noticing that this also implies that Jake at least indirectly realizes that it would not have helped him in relation to Brett if he had not had this physical handicap. Because in that case he would not have been 'unattainable', quite the contrary. And in that case she would probably not have wanted him, except perhaps for a couple of days, cf. her affairs with Cohn and the bullfighter Romero.

It is told, though not in details, that with regard to human relations the desperados Bill and Mike act alike; the incredible and continuous consumption of alcohol is

Second Development Section

just one of the discrete hints. Any possibility of authentic togetherness and exchange is lost for good to all of them. The whole pattern of attitudes and actions, however, holds, in any case pragmatically, a positive pole consisting of parts of the world *outside* their own universe. Here *nature* as such is placed, but also the subject/object-exchanges taking place in a primordial-cultural, preferably 'primitive' modus, have this positive status. Bill and Jake's fishing trip, during which they sort of 'form part of' nature, is an example of such an authenticity. This is personified by the Englishman Harris whom they meet, and who in spite of his desire for being with them, after all rejects their invitation to accompany them to the fiesta: to him fishing is definitely more important than being together (pp. 106f). This "positive primitivity", moreover, is altogether the case with Spain compared to France, cf. Jake's reflexions after his return, on France's concentration on money (p. 194) – and next also France compared to the super-depraved USA. And above all it is the case with the bullfight: here exchange is primordial, regular and *aficionado* is something which you *are*, not something you can choose to be, cf. Jake's own wording:

> Somehow it was taken for granted that an American could not have aficion. He might simulate it or confuse it with excitement, but he could not really have it. When they saw that I had aficion, *and there was no password*, no set questions that could bring it out, rather it was a sort of oral spiritual examination ... [italics added]

After all, the course of events deny the 'objective' importance of these authentic values of exchange (cf. also the parallel thematics contained in Jake's conversion to

Catholicism): They are all clearly in the nature of being a compensation for the loss of authenticity, which the persons experience in their human interchanges. Jake and Bill do *not* choose to go on with their fishing when Brett calls, in spite of Harris' requests; without the slightest hesitation Jake sells/pawns his *aficion* by humouring Brett in her desire for the bullfighter, thus (mis)using his influence to make her spoil the young man. This whole field of authenticity above all seems to have a symbolic character, not least as a part of the persons' staged understanding of each other: the relationship to these values is something you 'have', which is raised above the constitutional miserableness of intersubjective relations. In return, it is something which might be sold without the slightest hesitation on any given occasion.

This code of behaviour and values is shared by the whole group, as mentioned. Furthermore, it is stable, since the events do not cause any changes, neither subjectively nor objectively. On the contrary they fundamentally confirm the state of things.

One person, however, falls through and breaks these rules of the game: Robert Cohn. The problem with his relationship to the group is not that he *is* substantially different from the others: the other men are also in love with Brett and everybody is more or less desperately searching for a feeling of reality. No, the problem about Cohn is that he is unable to accept misery and thus to stick to the cool *style*. Instead of realizing that he is unhappy and that his needs and dreams fundamentally cannot be fulfilled, he insists on trying to assert himself and his emotions. This makes him profoundly embarrassing, not just concretely in his relationship to Brett and her boy friend(s), but also as experienced by the others, because he somehow renders visible the miserabilities by making them public. And, probably, because his exposure of these miserabilities makes it distressingly visible that they are even miserable miserabilities. It seems rather awkward to feel understatedly miserable with reference to grandiose, unspoken miseries at the level of *Weltschmerz*, while somebody else feels definitely miserable, even for the same reason, and moreover allows himself overtly (but stupidly without knowing) to exhibit the sheer triviality of this reason. By making public what everybody else is hiding, Cohn involuntarily and without knowing happens to mock the others' patterns of behaviour, and in fact to make them trivial. It beats everything when he (subjectively speaking probably out of a blasé state of mind and a need for self-assertion) expresses his anxiety about *being bored* during the bullfight. That makes everybody, from the narrator to the last reader, curl their toes. We shall return to this below. But Cohn seems to be, as a *Spielverderber*, someone who everybody loves to hate. He is only halfheartedly defended (by Bill) when even Mike in his astronomic drunkenness is paying him back in his own coin, thus similarly breaking the code (p. 122). Cohn is thus technically also the one who – precisely by breaking them – renders visible these rules and this dominant/governing system of values.

All this appears if you take into consideration just the immediate unreliability of the construction of enunciation: generally speaking, the focalizer Jake never explicitly states these evaluations and patterns. Still they appear from what he is *not* telling – and of course from the events and situations he is recounting. There is even a tendency towards a more lapidary and narrative lack of information the more emotionally intense or disastrous the situation gets. An example of this is the situation when Jake is told that Brett has been with Cohn:

> Brett looked at me. 'I say,' she said, 'is Robert Cohn going on this trip?'
> 'Yes. Why?'
> 'Don't you think it will be a bit rough on him?'
> 'Why should it?'
> 'Who do you think I went down to San Sebastian with?'
> 'Congratulations', I said.
> We walked along.
> 'What did you say that for?'
> 'I don't know. What would you like me to say?'
> We walked along and turned a corner. [70]

The play between the huge emotional reaction which the reader, in the light of what is told, must expect, and the apparently total absence of this reaction captivates the attention for the absent, the un-spoken. Thus everything which is being said, for instance the 'naked' descriptions, become loaded with a potential symbolic character. Not only where this was obviously the intention (as for instance the description of the steers and the bulls, pp. 117f), but everywhere. The text itself becomes a sort of code, being almost complementary, compared to the uttered "statement": the suppressions are more significant than the utterances.

Despite (and at the same time also because of the complementary effect of the unreliability of the enunciation) the careful, intrinsic coherence and external referentiality of reality, the whole story at this level turns out to be a virtually decomposed, decompressed, incoherent universe. Certainly, an ideal of genuineness, authentic love, human interdependence, clearly exists (namely the one whose absence is the reason for the tragic character), but this is unobtainable, lost, at least to individuals from the (super)civilized, new world. Substantially nothing but emptiness is left behind. Parasitically one may supply oneself with a little authenticity by participating in somebody else's still not so depraved exchanges, but that does not solve the problem. The emptiness, the need, the longing are moving along: there is no such thing as a substance or a concealed/deeper content. Only the longing for one. The intersubjective exchange can only be maintained as a joint, unspoken consciousness that this is how it is and nothing can be done about it. Should anyone actually act as being able to do something about it, even this possibility would vanish.

The Space of the Space

To the focalizer Jake there is a well-defined difference as to values between what one *does*, the pragmatic state of things, on the one hand, and what one *is*, the being or essence of things on the other. At the level of doing we find doing and exchange within those registers valorized as positive, whereas the background, the deep feelings, substance, are nothing. At the level of substance, however, we find exactly the opposite state of things: all the hectic activities at the level of doing are shown in their real nature to be a compensation and are thus evaluated as negative, while the genuine feelings of authentic being in Cohn forms the positive pole. In fig. 2 this simple (and of course far too simple) reverse model is sketched out.

Since the course of the novel shows that the positive

pole of substance is unattainable (in the figure below to the left, thus the brackets) the overall statement, as mentioned, becomes an ascertainment of a tragic condition, of an unbearable and at its own level uncompensatable absence. This however depends on whether it is possible in the analysis of enunciation to equate Jake, the focalizer, on one hand and Jake, the narrator, *and* the implicit narrator on the other, at least as far as the fundamental taxonomy of values is concerned. Or, to use a spatial metaphor, whether these instances are situated at the same level.

When we understand it like this we are dealing with a 'horizontal' paratactic structure of enunciation (cf. fig. 3). It is certainly possible to understand the text like that: the silence of Jake, the focalizer, points out the absence; furthermore, the silence of Jake, the narrator, as to *his* situation from this point of view emphasizes this absence even more (because not even the distance in time and space from the events is able to break down the repressions

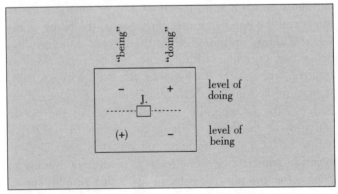

Fig. 2. At the level of doing, being and doing, respectively, are valorized as illustrated; at the level of being the state of things is reversed.

Second Development Section

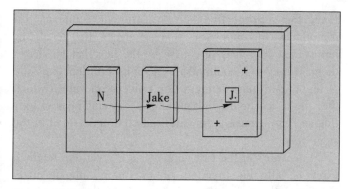

Fig. 3. The levels are placed at the same 'authentic' level as immediate realism.

and institute a difference). Finally the absence is thrown into relief even more emphatically by the supreme, implicit narrator's choice of this double authentic first-person narrative, i.e. of its own complete absence in the capacity of explicit instance. This paratactic chain of silent instances, therefore, only makes silence even more immense; the world of the text is immovable in its lay-out: it is made up of absence, of an emptiness which cannot even be described. It can only be framed and intermediated *as* an absence. It is unspeakable, and it is (because the important thing is what cannot be there) tragic.

The novel does not contradict this understanding. Nor, however, does it make this the only possible interpretation. For the novel can also be seen as primarily a *vertical* construction in which the instances of the enunciation mark precisely *different* levels of insight. This makes the silence – and thus the whole novel – change its meaning.

This happens if we move from what we have called the immediate unreliability to the mediate one. The reason why

Jake, the retrospective narrator, without comment just reproduces the emphatic repressions of the focalizing protagonist Jake may of course be the fact that he shares them. However, it could also be seen as a critical exposure of them, as a questioning of the universe of values which they perform. The implicit narrator's very staging of exactly this sort of unspokenness can finally be understood in the same way.

Many traits of the text support such a vertical reading. First of all the function of the unreliable focalizer automatically raises the question about the role of the unreliability in the construction as a whole: narrative unreliability always (also) points backwards to the instance which constructed it, alternatively accepted it (the implicit narrator, respectively the retrospective Jake). The reader not only has to find out *what* Jake is repressing, but is also confronted with the question of what the novel actually wants with such a conflict-evading consciousness as its entrance to the universe. The latter question in any circumstances objectifies the implicit 'will' of the text in a potential relation of difference towards the explicit (here: non-will).

Another point at which the text singles out a possible inherent inconsistency is Cohn's role and function in the universe of values. On one hand, it is Cohn who within the intrinsic universe of values breaks the rules by overtly trying to assert his own substantial will. But on the other hand his personal norms of value do not differ from those of the others. With this in mind it is striking *how* much (once again: unsaid) energy is being used to establish a distance to him, that is to say, demonstrate the distance of Jake, the focalizer in relation to him. The figure of Cohn –

which is actually the only external cause of the more dramatic parts of the intrigue – can therefore be seen as a way in which to emphasize – from the outside – the contradictions within the self-understanding of the intrinsic system of values.

Jake's state of *physically* caused impotence may be even more significant. While, as we have seen, Jake is just like the others by being involuntarily blocked in his capability, there is nevertheless a difference in the fact that Jake's problem is an undeserved and external one which *is unchangeable* because it is physical. At the level of description it is possible, the way we did above, to emphasize the similarity and the fact that it is made clear that Jake would not have been better off in his relationship to Brett, even without this calamity – and that qua the narrative construction it is impossible to decide whether Jake actually *did have* his vital parts shot off or whether he is just hiding a 'normal' impotence under this story. The point is that at this level that makes no difference. But in the vertical unfolding one might also choose to attach the greatest importance to the *difference* between Jake and the others. In that case, what irrevocably ("pragmatically") places Jake on a par with the others is also what radically ("substantially") separates him from them. *His* deceit is necessary in a sense unlike theirs – and therefore it can be comprehended as a double self-deceit: he is deceiving himself (and his immediate, implicit reader) into believing that his situation is similar to theirs; more particularly into believing that his deceit is identical to theirs. And so into believing that his affection for nature, bullfighting and swimming has the character of being a compensation compared to the 'essential' but unattainable authentic happiness. 'Reality' then might be that it is nothing but the ridiculous search for this underlying metaphysical authenticity which stands in the way of or at least disturbs the true authenticity (in the form of bullfighting, swimming and any other unpretentious, but serious exchange with the surroundings). Such a reading finds generous support in the novel, above all in the markings of the factual differences between Jake and the rest of them: *he* is the only genuine *aficionado*, and *he* is the one who provides the others with the goods of *his* world (from hotel rooms and tickets to privileged connections). On several occasions he also retires and goes to bed early, for instance; all in all he is the one among them who is able to – and wants to – be alone. No matter how much importance one might choose to attach to Jake's physical impotence within the fictional space there can be no doubt that it is emphasized clearly by the supreme instance of narration. The condition itself is so bizarre, so medically far-fetched and demonstrative in its *physical* staging of a problem which is otherwise – both directly and in a wider sense – extremely widespread as a *psychological* problem, so as to be recognized just as 'casual': in Jake's problem the narrator *singles out* this modal conflict as decisive, makes it a central symbol of the *whole* construction – quite irrespective of the concrete importance of the problem within the universe of fiction. But this of course implies a 'verticalization' of the reader's attention, just as the very undecidability of the actual status of the problem in the space of fiction has a similar effect. The somewhat comical implications of Jake's condition, standing out as rather far-fetched in an otherwise everyday-like universe at the fictional level, point in the same direction.

Finally, among these features contributing to elucidate

Second Development Section

the vertical dimension of the text we find the very marked *ruptures* with Jake's understatement, with his silence. Because so much has already been said qua the non-said, these ruptures imply a redundancy which is so distinctive that instead of emphasizing, these ruptures problematize and modify the significance and the placing of the motions described. This happens for instance the first time Jake in nocturnal solitude and unhappiness starts crying "... all of a sudden" [29] or even more explicitly at the end of the same chapter where Jake comments upon the whole problem of outside/inside:

> Then I thought of her walking up the street and stepping into the car, as I had last seen her, and of course in a little while I felt like hell again. It is awfully easy to be hard-boiled about everything in the daytime, but at night it is another thing. [32]

The final, crucial sentence may of course be seen as a special-school-teaching for some reader being slow of apprehension. In the general economy of the text this superfluous explanation, to put it mildly, however implies an objectification of Jake's self-knowledge and pulls it out of its status of being an implicitly approved basis. There is a similar effect when, later in the novel, Jake suddenly makes clear that for half a year he has been sleeping with the electric light on at night, because he had the idea that he would look at things differently when it was light (123). Or in the same place, when he, in one of his 'philosophical' reflexions, happens to interpret his unhappy love for Brett as if *he* was the one who was unable to pay his debt to her:

> Women made such swell friends. Awfully swell. In the first place, you had to be in love with a woman to have a basis of

> friendship. I had been having Brett for a friend. I had not been
> thinking about her side of it. I had been getting something for
> nothing. That only delayed the presentation of the bill. The bill
> always came. That was one of the swell things you could count
> on.
>
>   I thought I had paid for everything. [123]

He is however at once making it clear that probably the philosophy he is developing here will very soon seem "... just as silly as all the other fine philosophies I've had" (ibid.).

The situations supposed to show us the 'naked' Jake, alone and confronted with his tragic absence of substance are thus either close to toe-curling redundancy or overtly self-deceiving and/or primitive homespun philosophy. Thus the Jake of the fiction is exhibited in and by the enunciation. And when this highly problematic function of his at the level of substance, is compared to his imposing *puissance* at the pragmatic level, including his own undisguised satisfaction in this, we begin to see – still perceived in the vertical dimension of enunciation – a hint that the system of values at the level of statement is being reversed.

It should be evident that already the 'iceberg'-technique at the horizontal level generally initiates a vertical attention also as an effect of the lingual style which has won proper fame because of its short structure of lapidary main clauses. But the features pointed out above – and several others – directly prompt an experience of the system of enunciation of the text as manifesting *differences* at the level of insight (cf. fig. 4), i.e. as constructed as an operation of un-saidness, an 'iceberg' technique, also at the vertical level.

Regarded in this way the setting of values which we

have extracted from the horizontal level (fig. 1) is being changed. A double inversion is taking place: as is the case in the horizontal reading the immediate level of doing is positive and fascinating. But the authentic level of being behind this, which was then interpreted as the real (but tragically absent) content, and for which the hectic level of action as a whole served as a compensatory cover, is exhibited here as being really empty legitimation of the immediately hedonistic activity at the level of doing: thus it is Jake's, the focalizer's, understanding of the absent substance as being primary, which is here construed as negative, as superfluous. Instead the novel is declaring its solidarity above all with the cascades of unreflective easy-

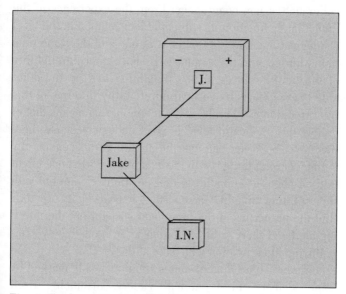

Fig. 4. To the vertical reading the competence of the instances elucidate and modify one another.

working doing, which it is describing. And funnily enough, its solidarity with its own inconceivable fascination for the elaborated descriptions of things, of surface – and thus its solidarity with the immediate reader's fascination at the same levels, sheerly in spite of, and thus mocking the notions of, any symbolic quality, any compensation, any superfluity, of these descriptions.

The Novel

The text, then, can be read in two ways. But the text – or the analysis – cannot privilege one over the other. The two meanings do not stand opposite each other as an either-or: they exist at the same time as a diversity of the text, a non-coherence, a non-congruency. From the experience of the immediately functioning subject/object-relation at the level of pragmatic action the reader is at one and the same time being hurled into the emphasis by horizontal unreliability of the untruthfulness of this fungibility *and* on the other side the emphasis by vertical unreliability in terms of this interpretation as (double) self-deception: this means that of course the pragmatic level is good enough because there has never been nor can ever be anything transcendentally "other" *beyond* things (with the exception of what one might oneself choose to appoint to that position). Congruent with this splitting up, this inconsistent heterogeneity we thus find the properties of the functional structure of the novel: on one hand there is an invitation to an immediately sympathizing identification with Jake at the level of action, and this identification thus becomes simultaneously marked by tragic defeat and euphorical victory, distancing itself respectively from the fixation of action as compensation for lost substance, and the fixation of substance as legitimation of the immediate, fascinating exchange. In so doing, the novel remains oddly folded into itself, apparently extremely dense and homogenous, but actually constantly collapsing in an unsurveyable and unceasable, but, *quod erat demonstrandum*, not undescribable – undecidability.

Qua this play between something immediately accessible and inviting on one side, and something totally opaque and non-integrated on the other, Hemingway's novel in fact looks like the Dinesen tale we were reading in the last chapter. But it is also interesting to compare Hemingway's novel with the contemporary 'classical' modernism like the one in Virginia Woolf.[5] For Woolf's careful consistency, regarding the relation between the emphatic blockings of exchange between the levels of the enunciated and the enunciation, respectively, to some extent finds its parallel here. In Hemingway the protagonist of the fictional space is living through an opaque, unsurveyable existence in a field, labile (as to values) of fast and slow, cold and hot, hard and soft exchanges. This existence is redoubled or reflected by the totally similar movement of the reader in the space of enunciation – or, if you like, the construction of fiction – featuring precisely the same labilities.[6] So in that sense a "congruency" is in common. But of course, at

---

[5] Indeed understood in the sense we did here (in the first development section, chapter 2.3).

[6] And this reader's space is of course also disturbed by Cohn's platitudes, his demythologizing of the conflict – while he is still, as a figure, maintained as a precondition for the construction of this space. Cohn, consequently, becomes a *Spielverderber* at more than one level – this is the source of the aggressive energy towards him.

the same time there is a difference, because where Woolf (and others with her) through the *open* structure of meaning links this meaning precisely to the limits of this constitutional openness, Hemingway's "closed" type of fiction[7] produces an infinite series of – symbolic and thus even fitted for further serial transmissions – meanings.

It is important to emphasize that once again it is the text itself which produces this complexity. And that this complexity does not hold the form of a canny, well-calculated, intellectual illustration of the problem from several angles: the complexity is a property of the construction itself. Silly, simple, incomprehensible, and as to values congenial with the modal basic conflict, which it is trying to thematize, in vain, but brilliantly, in the respective cases of Jake and the novel. "You'll lose it if you talk about it", is Jake's good advice to Brett in the closing scene (204). As a narrator Jake has indeed been talking ##and talking. And as a person of fiction he has kept silent, and kept silent. Kept talking, kept silent. Kept silent, kept talking. Just like the novel.

---

[7] The concepts of "open" and "closed" texts are here understood according to Umberto Eco's definition (following his revised reflections on these in Eco 1979, esp. pp. 7ff). Virginia Woolf, incidentally, in fact considered Hemingway's novel to be "not modern" (cf. Woolf 1980, p. 10).

Second Development Section

3.5

The Ignorance of Omniscience

Gustave Flaubert: *Madame Bovary*

Introduction. Flaubert Bovarisé?

"Madame Bovary, c'est moi". This is Gustave Flaubert's often quoted remark concerning what in the eyes of his audience and his critics is unquestionably his principal work, *Madame Bovary* of 1856.[1] It is evident that this – as it has been understood – explicit identification with the protagonist in one's own fictional universe by Flaubert is totally different from the way in which Hemingway tried to embody qualities of the heroes in his novels in his "real" life. Or desired/feared qualities of himself in his novels, if you like.

The connection between author and work has in the

---

[1] 1856 is the year of the original publication as a feuilleton in *Revue de Paris*, where a number of modifications of the text were made, partly against Flaubert's will. The first book edition is published in April, 1857. At any rate, Flaubert publishes revised editions in 1862, 1869, and 1873. In the following we refer to the Livre de Poche edition (which is based on the 1873 edition) *Madame Bovary. Moeurs de province*. Éd. établie, présentée, commentée et annotée par Béatrice Didier. Préface de Henry de Montherlant. Paris 1983. Among other things this edition contains surveys of the classic Bovary literature which we – as usual – shall not discuss here.

case of Flaubert-Bovary been analyzed and commented upon to an extremely high degree. The reason for this is – apart from the unquestionable success of the novel and consequently its place of honour as a *classic* in the institution of literature – above all the fact that the good Flaubert has made sure to leave immense quantities of material fit to illustrate this connection. It is a well-known fact that Flaubert was a tremendously slow worker, and with particular regard to *Madame Bovary* almost every tiny little move in the process of creation (and thus of the novel) has been commented upon in lots of letters and remarks by the author himself.[2] Furthermore, plans, drafts, and original manuscripts have been saved.[3]

But from a critical, historical point of view Flaubert's work itself is certainly interesting. It bridges the classic, bourgeois realism in Balzac on one hand, and such different types of novelistic art as Henry James' and Proust's on the other; this huge span between those who explicitly claim to be his successors is by no means a coincidence. Above all the relation to Balzac's realism has been widely analyzed and discussed. The alterations, especially according to the positioning of the enunciation by and within the enounced, between Balzac's and Flaubert's novelistic art, are indeed significant and highly appropriate to constitute

---

[2] See Gustave Flaubert: *Correspondance*, vol. I-IX, Paris 1926-1933; Supplément vol. I-IV, Paris 1954.

[3] See for instance Gustave Flaubert: *Madame Bovary*. Nouv. version précédée des scénarios inédits. Textes établis sur les manuscrits de Rouen avec une Introduction et des notes par Jean Pommier et Gabrielle Leley (Lib. José Corti), Paris 1949, in which the whole text from draft to final version is substantiated.

Second Development Section

"history". However, it is not the intention this time to construct that kind of relation; the historical "connection" is a different one here.

But still: Gustave Flaubert and Madame Bovary? The eccentric, intellectual mother's darling from Croisset, who hardly allowed himself to have any erotic life – as opposed to the banal, ignorant Emma Bovary, who is, partly as a consequence of an acute fit of having read too many novels, unable to make the stupidities of trivial reality come up even tolerably to her expectations from life – but who possesses (is being given), if nothing else, *désir* (cf. for instance p. 324)? What, in fact, does this story of dis-illusion about the incredibly stupid lives of ordinary country-people have in common with Gustave, spoiled son of *bourgeoisie*, who is making his career as a celebrated poet (and who was himself awarded and who accepted *la Legion d'Honneur*, cf. the chemist in *Madame Bovary*)? And why do we even ask this question in a context explicitly dealing with *the text*?

The analysis below will produce a kind of answer to both this and that – and so it will also give a sort of sub-stantial explanation of why it is that the author of *Madame Bovary* should absolutely deserve such an accumulation of biographical pipe-dreams as to make it almost impossible not to turn to spiteful remarks, perhaps as a kind of reversed defence of literary science.[4]

---

[4] Which for instance the English man of letters and writer Julian Barnes is doing in his *Flaubert's Parrot* (1985). This novel is from now on part of Flaubert's story.

The World of the Fiction

The world of *Madame Bovary* is an evil and a stupid one. A world of ignorance, self-righteousness, conventionality, lack of perspective, envy, non-understanding, non-love. A contemporary world: Northern France in the mid-nineteenth century. From the beginning we follow Charles Bovary. As a consequence of his mother's frustrated ambitions and despised love he is crammed into becoming a doctor notwithstanding his extremely modest mental faculties. He meets and marries Emma, a farmer's daughter, whom convent life and the reading of novels has furnished with a totally unrealistic level of expectations, about what life has got to offer, and from then on she is in the centre of the novel. We witness the gradual, inescapable process through which she realizes that the life she has been dreaming about cannot come true. At that point she has been cheated and deceived both mentally and materially, just as she herself has deceived the unsuspecting, imperturbably confiding Charles. She takes her own life. Charles becomes more or less crazy, and is, of course, ruined. He dies as well. Their daughter has to be sent off to do factory work. The extortioners, the money-grubbers, the agents of the system, however, do very well.

This might sound as if the novel acts out a clash between good, nice intentions on one hand, and the preposterous malice of the world on the other. But this is not the case. The distinction is at most a differentiation within the overwhelming stupidity which characterizes the world at all levels and all its representatives. Generally, it seems possible to distinguish between a *calculating* stupidity and a *spontaneous* stupidity. The coolly calculating, officious

Second Development Section

stupidity is connected with an insight in, and a submission to, the conventions of society at all levels; it is a restraining (in terms of needs), exploiting and in all respects disgusting stupidity which unambiguously leads to conventional success, as it is shown. The main representative is Homais, the chemist, and furthermore Lhereux, the money-lender, but also Emma's lovers in their 'reasonable' (:unpassionate) phases, and almost all the subordinate persons of the novel as a whole. Also linked with this side is natural science's (stupid) belief that everything can be explained, above all personified in the exorbitantly stupid (clever) chemist.

Opposite this (the right side of the table of recapitulation, fig. 1) we find naive, emotional, spontaneous stupidity. It is connected with art (above all post-romantic kitsch) and characterized by a total lack of insight (and interest) in the way in which earthly things are organized – although its unlimited necessity for satisfaction of all its needs certainly incorporates material goods. Emma is the only genuine representative of this pole; Charles may be close to it, but he is not characterized by the disastrous, intrinsic opposition between a (literarily mounted) ideal state of things and the possibilities of real life. Once and for all he has had it all come true: to Charles Emma represents the ideal which he – blind and deaf to what is going on – is above all extremely *satisfied* at having obtained, having made into his property through their marriage.

No doubt there is an obvious difference in the novel's evaluation of the poles. But this is a difference concerning the extent of the dissociation. The organized cheating and deception, the silly self-righteous repression of any non-everyday question (or transforming it into (pseudo)-scientific problems) of the left side appear massively unpleasant.

The oblivious, calculated, coolly calculating stupidity	The spontaneous, emotionally naive stupidity
Insight into the governing mechanisms of society	Lack of insight ...
Retention, repression of needs	Desire/ satisfaction of needs
Natural sciences secularization	Art/romanticism religion
Unpleasant, earthly success	Relatively pleasant, disaster
————	————
Homais Lhereux Rodolphe	Emma [Charles]
————	————
– –	–
[double negative attitude]	[negative attitude]

Fig. 1. The structure of values of the novel: Stupidity and stupidity.

The novel is intensively involved in its quarrels with these 'normal citizens' of society, like Homais. It is no coincidence that Homais is the one who gets the final kicks in the novel after Emma's death, cf. the description of his fight against a blind vagabond, who is finally captured and imprisoned for good (377) – nor that the very last words actually apply to him and his decoration (382). The values of the right side, however, are far from being described as positive, though Charles and Emma appear relatively more pleasant, also as a consequence of the way in which the (unpleasant) representatives of the left side exploit *their* stupidity recklessly, thus forcing them into disaster. Charles and especially Emma rather seem to be the *victims* of circumstances, Emma as a consequence of the twisted ideas she has been furnished with. On an isolated view Emma is for instance certainly not described as either pleasant or in any way worthy of imitation: she beats her child without reason, she is in all ways selfish and dull, and in her love affairs she constantly makes a complete fool of herself – but, rather out of habit and (twisted) standard ideas (cf. for instance p. 325) than out of genuine desire and emotion.

Thus the world of the novel does not contain *any* genuinely positive positions. We find two different degrees of lack of insight. One of these – according to the evaluation of the novel the one which is most dull and unpleasant – stifles the other. That is the only movement of the novel, and it is presented as inevitable. This certainly implies a thorough criticism of the society which the world of the novel claims to represent, indeed coincide with (cf. below). Above all a criticism of the boundless stupidity flourishing; secondly a criticism of the fact that the bad ones, the ones to whom human emotions are most strange, are the ones who are bound to win, at least in an outer sense. That is indeed a black picture.[5]

---

[5] The consequence of which, of course, is the trial against the novel for offending public morals (and religion). The extremely interesting (also in terms of the history of reception) speeches for the prosecution and for the defence from the trial and the sentence are printed in the

The question is, then, how this picture has been painted. Does it melt into its own blackness without any differences, or does it contrast other shades?

One of the significant features of the narrative construction is that it changes. The novel starts

Nous étions à l'Étude, quand le Proviseur entra, suivi d'un *nouveau* [...] (35)

This is how Charles Bovary enters the stage, which already, as a consequence of the pronoun "nous" holds the narrator of the text. A "personal" (i.e. internally focalized) narrative construction is thus prepared, and consequently Charles is seen from the outside at the following pages. But soon after his previous history is told in great detail and suddenly Charles is seen from the inside (42). The novel does not contain any other similarly unmistakable manifestation of the narrator's presence in the narrated space; at most small hints are given, especially in connection to visual observations, not-fixed to persons of the fiction, such as

On voyait alternativement passer [...] (166)

Enfin [...] parut un grand landau [...] (173)

Above all these manifestations thus serve to emphasize and confirm the novel's position within the mimetic *doxa*; the

---

edition of the novel referred to here (Flaubert 1983, cf. note 1 above).

Second Development Section

same function applies to the temporal anchorings of the narrator's perspective which is found for instance in the final merging of narrating time and narrated time:

Il vient de recevoir la croix d'honneur (382);

or in the description of Yonville in the "usual present tense" (103ff.), that is to say imperfect, terminating with the remark

Depuis les événements que l'on va raconter, rien, en effet, n'a changé à Yonville (106)

The reader, then, is demonstratively left in no doubt that both the narrator and the narrated are situated in the real world, in the reader's own world. The narration is in *vision-par-derrière* as if recounting of real events; a widespread use of *l'imparfait* emphasizes the authentic, but also the representativeness through the imperfectness of grammatical aspect.

Apart from the exceptions of personal internal focalizing, the narrator is also highly "authorial" and above all in every respect *omniscient*. True, we face sequentially changing focalizations through different persons of the fiction, but those are never 'clean' in the sense that the respective perspectives are reproduced as intentionally 'realistic'. On the contrary, the narrator is emphatically present in the presentation of the individual persons' thoughts and reflections. As mentioned the focalization is subject to variations, but Emma is quantitatively and qualitatively the prevailing focalizer. And not least here it is remarkable how the *narrator's* phraseology and entire linguistic world characterize the covert reproductions of inner monologues. An example

> A la ville, avec le bruit des rues, le bourdonnement des theâtres et les clartés du bal, elles avaient des existences où le coeur se dilate, où les sens s'épanouissent. Mais elle, sa vie était froide comme un grenier dont la lucarne est au nord, et l'ennui, araignée silencieuse, filait sa toile dans l'ombre à tous les coins de son coeur. Elle se rappelait les jours de distribution de prix...
> (78)

These metaphors, astonishingly expressive and accurate, evidently belong to the narrator and not to Emma. This is just one example among many others in the novel. Extremely vivid tropes primarily in the form of concrete allegories are a common feature of the narration; yet another example, in which the metaphorical register (the fire) is carried through the entire sequence:

> Dès lors, ce souvenir de Léon fut comme le centre de son ennui; il y pétillait plus fort que, dans une steppe de Russie, un feu de voyageurs abandonné sur la neige. Elle se précipitait vers lui, elle se blottissait contre, elle remuait délicatement ce foyer près de s'éteindre, elle allait cherchant tout autour d'elle ce qui pouvait l'aviver davantage; et les réminiscences les plus lointaines comme les plus immédiates occasions, ce qu'elle éprouvait avec ce qu'elle imaginait, ses envies de volupté qui se dispersaient, ses projets de bonheur qui craquaient au vent comme des branchages morts, sa vertu stérile, ses ésperances tombées, la litière domestique, elle ramassait tout, prenait tout, et faisait servir tout à réchauffer sa tristesse.
>
> Cependant les flammes s'apaisèrent soit que la provision d'elle-même, s'epuisât, ou que l'entassement fût trop considérable. L'amour, peu à peu, s'éteignit par l'absence, le regret

Second Development Section

s'étouffa sous l'habitude; et cette lueur d'incendie qui empour-
prait son ciel pâle se couvrit de plus d'ombre et s'effaça par
degrés. Dans l'assoupissement de sa conscience, elle prit même
les répugnances du mari pour des aspirations vers l'amant, les
brûlures de la haine pour des réchauffements de la tendresse;
mais, comme l'ouragan soufflait toujours, et que la passion se
consuma jusqu'aux cendres, et qu'aucun secours ne vint,
qu'aucun soleil ne parut, il fut de tous côtés nuit complète et
elle demeura perdue dans un froid horrible qui la traversait.
(158)

Though the protagonists are characterized also from the
inside, i.e. in their intrinsic contrasts, the result is still a
sort of marked *outside-in* perspective. The narrator's
instance somehow leans demonstratively over the persons
of the fiction, thus constantly and emphatically illustrating
the difference between itself (= the narrative instance) and
them.

The latter is important. It is evident that the purpose of
this almost importunate, constant correction of the figures'
"own" discourses is meant to obtain the greatest *precision*
possible in the thorough description of the persons. In one
sense, thus, this construction contributes to emphasizing
the events as *real* and the description of them as precisely
a *description* of something which exists; objective, true, and
accurate. Equally, a number of small narrative tricks
pretend that the narrated space somehow has its own life
compared to the narrative instance. For instance it is said
in connection with Emma's preparations for childbirth

Elle ne s'amusa donc pas à ces préparatifs où la tendresse des
mères se met en appétit, et son affection, dès l'origine, en fut
peut-être atténuée de quelque chose. (122, italics added)

Or similarly, concerning the first 'affair' with Léon

> Ce qui la retenait, *sans doute*, c'était la paresse ou l'épouvante,
> et la pudeur aussi. (142, italics added)

Furthermore, we have the above 'personalizations' of the narrative instance spatially and temporally, for instance in the beginning and the ending of the novel.

But also as to functional structure the high level of insight of the narrating instance may be said to strengthen the reality effect of the narrated space. This insight actually turns out to act as a much-needed counterpole to the imposing lack of insight which prevails within the narrated. Thus a sort of balance is created. The reader's perspective for realizing the stupidity and triviality of the life lived, becomes anything but stupid: the reader is transformed into the narrator's olympic competence, makes it her own, so to speak, through the vertical construction of the novel, which, as mentioned, emphatically underlines this competence. This constitutionally liberates the reader from the stupidity presented: for the presentation itself is made by an instance which is almost (in terms of insight) complementary to the level of the narrated world. Consequently, also in terms of values. If, by every means, the reader is to be touched to the quick, then it will always already be on behalf of somebody else. The narrator becomes the reader's actual point of identification. It is the distinct, thorough revelation of objective circumstances that turns out to constitute the main interest as regards aesthetics of reception.[6] Apart

---

[6] To this should be added the romantic 'misreading' which establishes, without difference, an identification with Emma, the victim: beyond any

from the attitude intermediated to the qualities of the presented world, the evident, epistemological implications of this construction are worth noticing: the world and its trivial calamities are visible, even highly visible. They can be recognized, understood, intermediated: objectively, accurately, insightfully.

The Impossibility of the Text

The text *may* be read like that – so we have seen for instance in Erich Auerbach,[7] who actually understands Flaubert's construction as a maximum of *absence* in narrative intervention. The narrator makes itself invisible and thus lets the reality presented talk 'for itself'. Fig. 2 sketches out how the principal relation seems to work directly between reader and the world presented.

---

doubt it has been common and has thus contributed to the public success of the novel. We shall return to this reading below. But in this context it is worth emphasizing that qua the construction also this reading must necessarily pass through a position of surveillance, which in turn then becomes a part of the victim's role as well, in an interestingly combined (voyeuristic-masochistic) role of the reader.

[7] Cf. chapter 1.1.1 above; Auerbach (Auerbach, 1946) writes among other things as follows: "Wir hören zwar den Schriftsteller sprechen; aber er äußert keine Meinung und kommentiert nicht. Seine Rolle beschränkt sich darauf, die Vorgänge auszuwählen und sie in Sprache umzusetzen; und zwar geschieht dies, in der Überzeugung, daß ein jeder Vorgang, wenn es gelingt, ihn rein und vollständig auszudrücken, sich selbst und die an ihm beteiligten Menschen vollkommen interpretiere; weit besser und vollständiger, als irgendeine noch dazugefügte Meinung oder Beurteilung es tun könnte. Auf dieser Überzeugung, also auf einem tiefen Vertrauen in die Wahrheit der verantwortungsvoll, redlich und sorgfältig verwendeten Sprache, beruht Flauberts Kunstübung." (432)

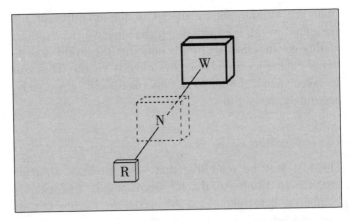

Fig. 2.

But on closer examination this relation is not quite that simple, not unambiguously, anyway. Actually, the narrator's extremely well-developed ability to reveal the state of the presented world is anything but discreet. Actually the narrator emphasizes himself tremendously as being something fundamentally different from the narrated. Not only because he himself possesses access to the insight which the rest of the world is deprived of. This in itself is a problem to which we shall return. No, the rendering visible is above all connected with the narrator's very pretension to be *omniscient*. This means that any person can be seen from the inside and from the outside. And actually are, one after the other, through different priorities. The narrator's constant (and necessary) change of focalization means that the 'lacking' positions of focalization, and thus some lacking information, are being emphasized more or less involuntarily. For instance this is often the case with Charles' perspective, and certainly Emma's when this is

Second Development Section

left. But, as a matter of fact, everything *cannot* be told at one and the same time – or at all. The narrator's shift of focalization demonstrates this in general, and in so doing, further exhibits the nature of these concrete shifts as being *choices*, priorities in an otherwise immense, endless continuum of potential information. But this again means that the whole nature of the narrative construction as an "objective" description of actual events collapses or is turned around: it becomes evident how, by contrast, this whole construction is extremely *subjective*. Not only qua the narrator's sovereign choice of cuts and focalization, but also qua its demonstrative self-positioning at all levels, even concerning stylistic details. The way in which the narrator (cf. the above discussion) leans over the persons, characterizing their experience of their surroundings in *his* words and tropes, instead of pretending to use theirs, supports this impression of something subjectively governed, presuppositionally conditioned, led by personal projections. Even the lauded lingual rhythm and ring of the discourse form a ground for this verticalization of interest, this objectifying exhibition of the narrator's instance, and consequently, then, the emphasis on its subjective character. The more objective and precise the narrator tries to be, the more he appears to be emphatically subjective. As this omniscience becomes evident as a construction further consequences arise for the entire world represented, for the entire character of the fictional space. Now the narrator's instance itself moves into the centre since it is the projections of this instance which create the space of fiction 'behind', anyway. Thus the figure/ground relation of the vertical construction is reversed (cf. fig. 3). And *that* inevitably leads to a problematization of the narrator's

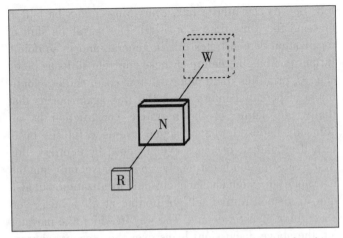

Fig. 3. The figure/ground-relation is reversed (cf. fig. 2 above).

statements about attitudes, or at least an exposure of the problem of revocation, the problem of self-referential incongruence of the axiological system as a whole. The narrator's instance acts (in both readings) as a (positively-loaded) counterpole, to the (in varying degrees) negative world in terms of insight and recognition: the narrator, in other words, possesses that very insight which the narrative so emphatically denies the world represented. This difference, however, is acceptable as long as the objectivity is credible. But as the radical unprejudiced objectivity is switched into a radical, prejudiced subjectivity things get different. The "fictional level" of the narrator's instance will then get closer to that of the fictional space. As a kind of ontological compatibility between the levels occurs, then, the result may be the appearance of a contradiction between the postulates of the possibility of precise and truthful insight (the narrative instance, N) and the irremediable stupidity of the world (the narrative, W), respectively. Put rigidly: if it is true that the world is stupid, then the narrator's insight is a lie – but then the statement about the world is not credible without further proof. Again, if W is true then N is not and then W (being a function of N) is not either. Conversely, if it is true that the narrator possesses insight, then the statement about the world is untrue – and then the narrator's insight is broken. This means that if N is credible, the statement on W is a lie – and then N is no longer credible.[8]

This logical wording of the problem is certainly a rigid simplification. Still it may illustrate the very special nature of the construction. This is not a synchronous contradiction, but rather what might be called a virtually pulsating inversion of the figure/ground-relation in the vertical construction.

This inversion opens up a vertiginous abyss of additions and corrections to the understanding of the statement of the novel as a whole. If for instance the narrator, as it is shown, is extremely *biased*, the 'truth' about the persons may very well be totally different. In any case, a third position enters the text, positioned *above* the importunate, explicit narrator: from this implicit narrator's discreet, non-localized position   possible alternative codings are regulated, such as the explicit narrator's self-irony, the

---

[8] It seems, then, that what we have here is a variant of Epimenides' classical Cretan liar's paradox. Christopher Prendergast (1986) points this out (181f.) and he is by the way – as opposed to the rest of the modern Flaubert discussions generally – conscious of the central status in Flaubert of this problem of revocation, of self-referential incongruence, which we have underlined here (cf. for instance ibid. 203f).

stupidity of the entire narrative and for instance the apparently involuntary violations of the redundancy of the explicit narrator's description of the events.

Decisive, however, is above all what happens to omniscience as a position, as a possibility. Omniscience, objectivity, truth are quite evidently the ambition in the text. But not less evidently this large-scaled – some might say megalomaniac – effort to satisfy this ambition implies an exposure of its impossibility: the closer and more precise this close description of anything or anybody, the more the discourse strikes back into the choices and cuts made by the narrator's instance, that is to say the more the whole reality effect of the fictional level – and thus the objectivity of it – is broken into bits and pieces. The construction implies its own collapse, not as an either-or, but as a both-and. The text glitters as a generous accumulation of penetrations, which after all in the very end just point out their own powerlessness, in the sense that they hit nothing but themselves. The world, for its part, is certainly a place of both insight and stupidity. But whether it is clever or stupid neither this nor any other description is able to say anything *objective* about, of course.

Flaubert, the Novel, and the Truth

This is where the novel is flickering. On one hand tremendously self-confident, convinced of its own infallible authority, it makes the *right* choices one after the other. And on the other hand, over and over again, it emphasizes the impossibility of its own ambition, and thus accentuates this as unrestrained and unsecured megalomania. That is because experience *is* individual, necessarily, and the laboriously established definite truth will never be anything but a construction made by the narrator's instance. In all its impressive cleverness, thus, the novel is at the same time almost incredibly stupid, being constructed with its *tâche aveugle* solidly pointed towards precisely that limitation of the possibility of its own insight which it spends its energy on showing as constitutively necessary in every other case.

Clever or stupid? No, clever *and* stupid. Does it know its stupidity, is it with or without its own will exposing the built-in short-circuit of this trans-subjective truthfulness? There is no answer to this; the discreet implicit narrator beyond the importunate explicit narrator is, as mentioned, not definitively locatable. Flaubert, of course being something different from his text, may sense the problem. This is perhaps the reason for his malaise about the enormous success of the novel. Of course he is aware of the high frequency among his readers of the above identification-oriented reading (cf. note 6). The very fact that it annoys him is not hard to understand, because to some extent it represents exactly that *stupid* use of literature in the romantic tradition from which he tries to dissociate himself with the very figure of Emma. On the other hand: "Madame Bovary, c'est moi" probably expresses the feeling of a kind of somehow sharing Emma's destiny. Above all, obviously, sharing the being torn apart between excessive dreams and excessive reality in the victim's role. But yet at some level also in *stupidity*: and there is perhaps the hint of a feeling that the narrator's cleverness in *Madame Bovary* among other things is nothing but a brutal repetition of the stupidity of the fictional characters.

Had Flaubert only been talking about the novel and not about the person of the novel the statement would have been exorbitantly precise: *"Madame Bovary*, c'est moi". Precise not only in the evident, genetical sense, but also in terms of substance, structure, function. Perhaps the way in which the novel stupidly looks over its own shoulder, completely impossibly denies itself sentence by sentence, involuntarily creates stupid, spontaneous identification while trying to establish reflective distance, unpleasantly arrogantly despises its own space of fiction, artificially is highly unsatisfying because of its overwhelming redundancy of construction and even thematics: perhaps all this after all makes it "realistic". Failed, in vain and ingenious.

In the writings of Flaubert, as is well-known, everything was later on to become even worse. But then, for instance in the insufferable *Bouvard et Pecouchet*, with a more steady consciousness of the necessity of distance and the impossibility of insight: here, in *Madame Bovary*, with hesitating blushes and pathetic grandeur is maintained, again and again, the very moment in which the mimetic *doxa* collapses and turns out to be an individual projection. Maintained through the text's way of being a text. Definitively pointing out its own impossibility, the unlimited stupidity of omniscience.

3.6

"Real Life" versus Superheated Fantasy

Jane Austen *Pride and Prejudice*
– and Denis Diderot *Jacques le Fataliste*

Introduction

In *Madame Bovary* we saw above all an unreserved *both-and*, an *everything-at-a-time*. A closeness, a depressing megalomaniac ambitiousness which yet, despite all its imposing convergence appears as a short-circuit committed to repeated self-reiteration – and which consequently ends up, maybe, in a dead-end as something forever roaringly advancing towards a point from which there is no way forward, and no way back. One can hardly imagine *Madame Bovary* surpassed as to passionless, accurate objectivity, and, at the same time, emphatically intrusive subjectivity. Neither before nor after; at least not within that quantitative standard which the novel itself sets up and thus insists on.

Instead we shall now enter a kind of intonation characterized rather by a figure of *either/or*. We shall end this second development section by reading the two novels *Pride and Prejudice* and *Jacques le Fataliste*, two radically different novels, on the face of it. The former appears, *qua* its construction and its patterns of themes and conflict-

functionality as the archetypal bourgeois novel which subsequent tradition develops, elaborates, repeats in different ways. Jane Austen's novel then *might* have been an adequate starting point for the first development section above. Diderot's novel, on the other hand, *was* the actual starting point, where it appeared as a type of construction which indeed, *qua* its overt, playful testing of the possibilities of genre, could be conceptualized as symptomatic of the novel in formation. But which, on the other hand, *qua* its immediate unserious openness and its hilariously obvious character as an experimental laboratory, as demonstrative fictivity, could not, for good reasons, emerge again as a literary type until now, at the opposite edge of Modernity, if regarded within the register of philosophy of history.

This mounting of the evident, but only implicit, *and* the unevident, but actual, starting point of the first development section as a common thematic end point of the present second development section is not undertaken merely for the sake of creating a tempting outward symmetry. Actually the intention is to examine whether the two novels are, after all, so widely different as they immediately appear. And, if so, whether this difference really does consist in what seems superficially to be the case. Clearly, the two novels are almost contemporary. It is true that *Pride and Prejudice* is not published until 1813, but there is every indication that the novel is a more or less revised version of a (considerably bigger and never published) novel entitled *First Impressions* which Jane Austen is said to have finished between 1796 and 1799 being only in her early twenties.[1] The two novels' stories of reception are, however, widely different: *Jacques le Fataliste* has probably never been read or appreciated but in narrow circles – and for a long period of time, as mentioned, was not appreciated at all – whereas *Pride and Prejudice*, from its very publication in 1813, became an enormous public success and the most beloved work of its author. The novel has continued to be appreciated by the reading public ever since; Jane Austen is still being read, and broadly read, i.e. not only by professional (wo)men of letters.

In the following we shall first read *Pride and Prejudice* the way it might be read: as a novel which knows and understands its own world, and which by employing simple, but extremely effective means, is able to lead its reader into this world. After that we shall – as in the previous chapters of the present development section – examine how this construction actually appears when regarded from the position into which history places us now. Not until then shall we turn to *Jacques le Fataliste* and through a re-reading examine the position of *that* novel seen through our present optics. Finally, we shall discuss the two novels, one against the other.

---

[1] See Chapman, 1964, p. Vff. The edition of Jane Austen's novel here utilized, by the way, is the Penguin Classics edition (Ed. and with an Introduction by Tony Tanner), Harmondsworth 1985, to which page numbers below refer. As to *Jacques le Fataliste* we shall, concerning factual information, utilized edition, and overall presentation and description refer to the analysis in chapter 2.1 above.

The novel is above all a love-story played within a universe in which woman's lot – especially if she is relatively impecunious – depends totally on whether she is able to make a good match (or even to marry). Here we meet the Bennet family in which the father and the two eldest daughters are fairly bright, while the mother and the three youngest daughters are almost stupid. The protagonist is the second daughter, Elizabeth. She may not be quite as pretty as the eldest one, Jane, but then she has got some brains: she is good at observing, analyzing, criticising her surroundings. Jane and a young man, Bingley (who is an extremely good catch), now fall in love with each other, while Bingley's friend Darcy almost repels Elizabeth, partly because of his rude, arrogant behaviour, partly because of some unpleasant stories told about him. Because of – as it is revealed later on – Darcy, Bingley suddenly withdraws from his relationship with Jane who becomes very unhappy (and her grief is due to serious feelings, not to the advantages of the match). Later on Darcy, who is very rich and an even better match than Bingley, unexpectedly proposes to Elizabeth who, however, (to his immense surprise) rejects him. She simply does not like him: partly because of the unpleasant stories about him, partly because of the very proposal in which he gives a detailed account of the enormous scruples he has had in making the proposal (primarily because of her family's social position and not least its rather invidious behaviour). After Elizabeth has demonstrated her sovereignty as to conventions and material matters, the story is inverted: the stories about Darcy's past turn out to be untrue. And as to the present, he changes his behaviour radically; even when Elizabeth's silly younger sister causes a regular scandal, Darcy actively and invaluably assists – and, significantly, in (intended) secrecy. He realizes that his behaviour up to now has been governed by *pride*; Elizabeth, in her turn, must realize that she has been afflicted by a hostile *prejudice* against Darcy. This and that swept away, Elizabeth and Darcy can finally be united. So can Jane and Bingley. Everything has a happy ending in a fourfold sense: the sisters have it *both ways*, emotionally and materially. The latter, however, is only of importance to their stupid mother. And to the reader, of course, to which we shall return later.

The most important attitudes of the novel clearly run along two different axes. One deals with *insight* versus ignorance or just lack of insight and reflection. This axis is very distinctive: Insight is emphasized as Elizabeth's primary, positive quality (reflected even in descriptions of her physical appearances which draw attention to her *eyes*, and thus metaphorically to her capacity for sight in moral terms, i.e. insight). But also Darcy, his counterpart Wickham, and to some extent the father are presented as being able to see through or at least to understand their surroundings. By contrast, the mother and the younger sisters are characterized as being uninhibitedly ignorant and dull. To add insult to injury, they even persist in their follies. The mother is simply embarrassing on any social occasion. She acts schemingly, not even realizing that this demonstrates her own striking stupidity. Stupid all the way to parody are also the clergyman, Mr. Collins. – Lady Catherine, to whom he so wheedlingly bows and scrapes, constantly praising her "condescension", does not either in any way stand out as exactly clever in her persistent behaviour. Since the axis of insight clearly ascribes positive value to a high level of insight, the presentation of Mr Collins and his mistress furthermore implies a dissociation from the implicit emphasis on social hierarchy, represented by these figures altogether. Among the important characters, finally the eldest sister, Jane and her beloved Bingley are provided with a certain, but definitely not extravagant insight. Both of them are easy to fool and to rule. Jane, above all, is marked by *positive* prejudices towards everybody and everything. This is lovable, but not very clever – or for that matter practical, which Elizabeth demonstrates over and over again.

Independent of the axis of insight there is another axis, dealing with moral constitution: it segregates the characters into being *good* or not. Good are, above all, Elizabeth, her sister Jane, and Bingley. Darcy also turns out to be good. Neither the silly young sisters nor even the stupid Mr Collins are presented as particularly bad persons: they just hardly know what they are doing. Conversely, Mrs Bennet is situated at the bad side because she, apart from being stupid is also heavily selfish and unpleasant, so too the condescending Lady Catherine. Furthermore – as it turns out – Wickham and also, at least to some extent, the father, Mr Bennet, who for mere convenience fails in his responsibility to bring up the young daughters. Schematically, the two axes can be said to divide the universe of characters into four fields as sketched out in figure 1.

Throughout the novel, in fact, there are only few changes of the positions of the characters within the universe of values. Wickham, who appeared to be good, turns out to be bad; correspondingly, Darcy, on the other hand, turns out to be fundamentally good, and he even gets

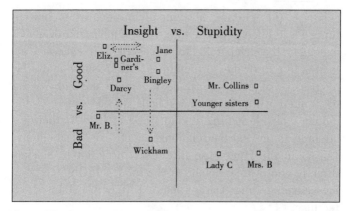

Fig. 1. The basic position of the persons is constant. Elizabeth has just *experienced* the 'reversal' of Darcy and Wickham by the intrigue.

better and better. By means of his relationship to Elizabeth he realizes that pride, personal and social, is a *bad* quality. Elizabeth makes a similar movement at the other axis: She becomes aware that her prejudice has governed her understanding and made her blind (and thus deprived her of insight). The defects of the protagonists, respectively, Darcy's pride, and Elizabeth's prejudice, correspond to their respective main axes; the defects are repaired, and the protagonists can finally be united, representing at one and the same time the highest insight and the highest goodness: neither pride nor prejudice.

The alterations and the positions of this rather simple and unambiguous universe of values mark a number of statements as to attitude which we shall discuss briefly. Above all, *balance* within the subject/object-relation is generally promoted. This balance is founded partly on insight (including insight about one's own effects), partly on goodness (i.e. certain, absolute limitations as to how to bring these effects into action). It is emphasized over and over again through parallel examples that both excessive attempts to govern the surroundings, officiousness and a far too passive, object-like attitude, indolence, are bad. We are confronted with officiousness both in the shape of the mother's match-making attempts and in Lady Catherine's attempts to prevent the relationship between Elizabeth and Darcy. In the latter case the effect turns out to become directly contra-intentional, as the aunt actually acts as a messenger telling Darcy about Elizabeth's thawed-out feelings.

Scheming are also Mr Collins, Wickham and Bingley's sister who all in different ways become losers, not least as a consequence of their scheming. One should never act excessively; only fools and people with bad motives do so. But also passivity can be exaggerated. We see that with Mr Bennet, whose house gets more or less disorganized and scandalized for that reason; furthermore, with Jane and Bingley, both unsuspecting and insecure. They obediently accept both being separated and brought together. Especially Jane's ever passive, receiving, almost comically automatic, positive attitude to any event of the world, throws Elizabeth's critical empathy into relief. The ideal seems to be balance, mediation, the golden mean. Indeed, a balance like that is *possible*, obtainable: you just need a fair moral and open eyes, and in case you do not have that, you may get it (cf. the markings in the end of how one of the youngest sisters improves herself under a new and better influence). Particularly *women* should not accept the position of mere object, and thus should reject any social constraint which determines their intimate lives, through arranged marriages. You should marry out of "better feeling" (166; Elizabeth's wording as her friend gives her consent to the fool Collins), and higher position, materially or socially, does not at all imply any automatic privileges: privileges, if any, are to be deserved in virtue of one's *own* qualities. Consequently, we are altogether dealing with a concept of the individual about to break away from regulation by preconditioned, supreme rules, and about to get close to governing and developing itself within a rational, i.e. reasoned and reasonable, consensus. The system of attitudes of the novel as a whole argues polemically against this historically evaporating system of norms, which had up to then predetermined the status and the lives of individuals, independent of their personal qualities and dispositions. And above all these polemics are directed against the image of woman upheld by these norms.

The novel's construction of enunciation is substantially flat. The narrative voice is authorial and as a principle omniscient; with respect to time the perspective is also olympic with inserted prolepses and for instance a final panorama of the persons' continued lives. In practice most of the story, however, is told in *vision-avec*. There are shifts between direct comments and observations made by the narrator, and the use of focalizers among the persons of the fiction. Elizabeth, the protagonist, is the primary focalizer. It is through and by her that the actual central perspective is unfolded. It is also, largely, her level of insight, including her misinterpretations, which is followed by the text through the sequence of events and consequently followed by the reader. The revelation of Wickham's true nature, which the narrator, *qua* its omniscience would have been able to undertake right from the start, (except this

would have deprived the intrigue of its phase of complications and furthermore would have ruined the consecutive
transformation of Darcy and Elizabeth) is for example
ingeniously withheld by means of varied focalization. This
happens when Elizabeth gets Wickham's untruthful version
of the controversy with Darcy, and where the reader must
with her believe it (pp. 121ff). The ingeniousness develops
almost to untrustworthiness on a later occasion when
Wickham acts as what might euphemistically be called
"incomplete focalizer":

> The farewell between herself and Mr Wickham was perfectly
> friendly; on his side even more. His present pursuit could not
> make him forget that Elizabeth had been the first to excite and
> to deserve his attention, the first to listen and to pity, the first
> to be admired; ... [187]

This of course happens on behalf of the suspense of the
narrative. The suspense, by the way, increases distinctly
towards the end of the novel where the story about Jane's
engagement to Bingley is stretched over a long sequence,
without Elizabeth's story with Darcy – although this is the
focus of the reader's interest – being developed any further
(pp. 344-375). But the instance of the narrator is above all
unstriking. Except for one single place with an overt reference to the character of construction of the novel,[2] the
narrated world appears to be at the same level as the 'real'
world of the narrator. This, of course, is due to the level of
fictionality and to the common *vraisemblance* in the

---

[2] "It is not the object of this work to give a description of Derbyshire"
(265).

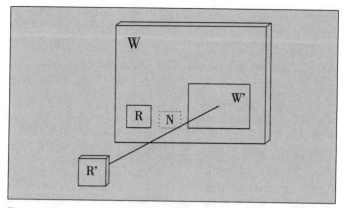

Fig. 2. W' becomes a picture of W within the same level. The narrator N and the model reader R are seemingly placed outside W', but still inside W.

sequence of events and space, but also to a number of narrative choices which make the narrated world independent of its narrator by claiming them to be at the same level. As for instance, when the narrator suddenly pretendingly lowers its level of insight compared to its protagonist:

> ...but Elizabeth, less clear-sighted *perhaps* in his case than in Charlotte's [italics added; 186]

or towards the end, when it/she writes about the hopeless Mrs Bennet:

> I wish I could say, for the sake of her family, that the accomplishment of her earnest desire in the establishment of so many of her children, produced so happy an effect as to make her a sensible, amiable, well-informed woman for the rest of her life [393]

Implicitly: but I, the narrator, am unable to change "reality" no matter how much I should like to.

Altogether, a mainly 'flat' narrative structure is established, as mentioned. The world W' of the novel is part of the real world W (cf. fig. 2); though the uninsistent instance of narrating may in principle possess unlimited insight, in practice it possesses no other insight but the one with which its own position within the same world provides it. Also the model reader R is situated in the same world; this "identity of worlds" is altogether the fundamental condition by which this construction of fiction operates. As to mode of function the novel unambiguously works with *identification*, i.e. it tries to lead the reader into the narrated space by turning it into her (own) experience of the world; the primary identification here applies to the protagonist, the predominant focalizer, Elizabeth. Very seldom a male focalizer is brought into action; the universe, is thus, above all, seen through female eyes: technically, substantially and thematically.

With the exception of a little stylistic clumsiness here and there no clear breaks appear within the construction of the novel: it performs a clear and unambiguous statement of a certain world which it simultaneously elicits. This world cannot be comprehended as symbolic, and its story does not sketch out an allegory on anything different from itself; it is merely *descriptive*, it describes the world the way the world is, regarded objectively. Secondarily (though not less important) the novel itself constitutes a world of experience, an experience which it, in total accordance with its own statement about the real world, makes accessible to its reader in order to make her turn this world into her own (world of experience). There are, consequently, no cracks or incongruities between the worlds of the novel, or, if you like, between the novel's mimetic-referential and its phatic relationships to world 'contexts', respectively. The novel wants to do what it actually does, and it is doing what it actually wants to do. It is, just like the ideal of the individual it presents, governed from the inside; it is reasonable and coherent. It emphasizes truth and honesty. Above all it believes in *development*, in happy endings. Of course intrigues and misunderstandings may occur in any sequence of events. Sensibility and justice, however, will win in the end. And justice, among other things, means that if there are, as here, in a whole universe two persons, distinctively different from everybody else in that they possess the right qualities – then of course they will be united and live happily together. The world is indeed good enough. And furthermore: it is good enough because we made it good enough.

... or legitimizing Projection?

This is how the world *is* which *Pride and Prejudice* unfolds on behalf of real life. Or, at least so is the picture into which the reader is drawn and within which she might be able to act emotionally. Only, however, with her eyes half screwed up, deliberately indulging in the novel's own illusion about itself. That is why an observation, just a little bit keener, not only makes the contours of the picture shake and the colours of it merge more or less uncontrollably: it threatens the picture with quick and total decomposition. And thus threatens to deprive it totally of that character of being a model or a representation which it claims to have – in order perhaps to make it representative in a way quite different from the one intended.

Most immediately evident is perhaps the double standard of morality and the almost directly self-contradictory character of the value system of the novel. As mentioned, the novel repudiates the tradition which compels women to marry socially 'upwards': its dissociation is both objective in the sense that the conventional system which invokes this compulsion is ridiculed (for instance in the person of Lady Catherine and her oily Mr Collins), and also subjective in the sense that women, who overtly "invite" for it or who are even fixated by it, are presented as stupid (the mother, the younger sisters) and/or ridiculous (Miss Bingley's vain attempt to catch Darcy, especially pp. 92ff). Evaluated as positive, on the contrary, are Elizabeth's refusals, first of Mr Collins' proposal (which is relatively profitable), and later on of Darcy's (which is extremely profitable). It is positive to renounce this kind of material wealth and social ascent. But apparently this does not imply that these goods in themselves are valorized as negative within the universe of values of the novel, because Elizabeth's reward for her renunciation – which clearly *is* a happy ending – actually consists in obtaining the very goods which she renounced. In other words: the bad things apparently are good enough when it comes to convincing the reader of the fact that good is good. Or put in another way: the novel has not eliminated substantially the pandering to social ascent which it pretends to reject. And as a matter of fact the novel presupposes a similar double standard of morality in the reader, when supposing that what was convincing as a reward is identical with what was placed as unimportant, or at least not decisive. As to this context it is symptomatic that Elizabeth's change of attitude towards Darcy actually happens precisely while she is visiting Pemberley, and is confronted with the earthly pleasures. Not that this connection is explicitly interpreted as a connection: this change is of course due to the fact that Darcy all of a sudden behaves himself. But as part of the novel's double entry there is no doubt that the material superabundance prepares the ground for moral re-evaluation (by Elizabeth *and* the reader). The idea is even overtly entertained previous to the relationship between Elizabeth and Darcy is taken up again. Soon after Elizabeth's (and the reader's) introduction to the estate in all its splendour, Elizabeth thinks:

> 'And of this place [...] I might have been mistress! With these rooms I might now have been familiarly acquainted! Instead of viewing them as a stranger, I might have rejoiced in them as my own, and welcomed to them as visitors my uncle and aunt. – But no,' – recollecting herself, – 'that could never be: my uncle and aunt would have been lost to me: I should not have been allowed to invite them.'
>
> This was a lucky recollection – it saved her from something like regret. [268; note the exclamation marks]

Shortly after that Darcy behaves astonishingly kindly and courteously to the uncle and the aunt. And Elizabeth's regret ...?

The real (double) moral is then that what matters is to renounce from overtly *wanting*, i.e. omitting to *show* that one is interested in social ascent. Elizabeth words it directly during the great scene of mutual explanation with Darcy:

> The fact is, that you were sick of civility, of deference, of
> officious attention. You were disgusted with the women who
> were always speaking and looking, and thinking for *your*
> approbation alone. I roused, and interested you, because I was
> so unlike *them*.

And, Elizabeth adds, if anyone should still be unaware of
the fact that "love" is thus linked with *exchange* rather
than with any particular, metaphysical 'community of
substance':

> To be sure, you knew no actual good of me – but nobody thinks
> of *that* when they fall in love.' [388]

This remark is of course meant as a joke – but Elizabeth
does represent perspicacity and insight among the characters of the fiction. And evidently, with reference to the
universe of the novel, she is right.

The consequence of this whole double entry accounting
of attitude is a manifestation and an emphasis of the
instance of enunciation at the expense of the presented
space of fiction. Obviously, the implicit narrator is the one
who, *qua* its governing of the sequence of events of the
fiction, decides that Elizabeth's "brave" choice, brave
because it has its price, actually turns out after all not to
cost anything, but on the contrary wins her the great
jackpot. This observation does not make her choice lose its
aspect of bravery: because as a matter of fact Elizabeth
could not possibly *know* how it would turn out, when she
made this choice. Or could she?

But the narrator could, anyway. Indeed, not only could
the narrator "know": the narrator actually made it up like
that. The double standard of morality is consequently part

Second Development Section

of the construction, which thus begins to look so smartly arranged that it loses any immediate "naturalness". This for instance applies to the above description of Wickham (the novel p. 187), in which the truth about Wickham's fraud is being suppressed by means of inner focalization: the narrator here has to manipulate its own construction of point of view, and thus the reader's, in order to convey its message, which argues amongst other things that active manipulation ought to be restricted. Something similar can be observed within the mode of focalizing in the case of Darcy, where the omniscient narrator may blithely use inner focalization when dealing with the underlining of the authenticity of Darcy's distance in the beginning (pp. 104-105), but where Elizabeth, after the 'conversion' towards the end, must remain a focalizer, in order to maintain the suspense of the narration, though Darcy's distance at that time turns out to be (have become) a misunderstanding. The character of artificial *setup* becomes more and more intrusive. Above all, however, the excessive redundancy of the narrative begins to collapse. Comprehended into a universe which a narrator tries to elaborate, in order to knit together, two sets of mutually incongruent values, to make it possible by means of nice self-acknowledgement to score the (stated) dirty gains, this solid, repeated emphasis on examples of contrasts turns out to appear suspicious: is not, for instance, the roaring stupidity of Mrs Bennet, the youngest sisters or Mr Collins precisely so urgent for the narrator in order to emphasize Elizabeth's relative "sensibility"? Otherwise, this "sensibility" would hardly be convincing. And is not their almost pathologically hysterical fixation with "the good match" not just a way of disguising that the 'nice' sisters Elizabeth and Jane are factually led by similar motives, but only within a different self-interpretation? Or in other words: if these subordinate characters appear comical, don't they rather throw more or less unintentional comic light upon the whole attempt of the narrative to unfold a trustworthy world? As the reader's identification with the central figure begins to fail like this, another relationship becomes more and more insistently clear: the one between the narrative's instance and Elizabeth. The figure of Elizabeth, in fact, is the only main character from whom enunciation does not establish any distance of attitude at all, other than the temporal difference of insight, necessary for the story to emerge at all. This axis of identification, however, changes the status of Elizabeth's wordings of her understanding of the sequence of events. This not only applies to passages as the one quoted above, in which she explains to her wondering fiancé what actually did happen. Altered light is also thrown upon her manifesto-like claims to control her own behaviour:

> 'But it is fortunate,' thought she, 'that I have something to wish for. Were the whole arrangement complete, my disappointment would be certain. But here, by carrying with me one ceaseless source of regret in my sister's absence, I may reasonably hope to have all my expectations of pleasure realized. A scheme of which every part promises delight, can never be successful; and general disappointment is only warded off by the defence of some little peculiar vexation.' [263]

Apart from the almost comic self-objectification of this fustian, it conveys, as thrown back onto the narrator and thus the narrative, something about the overall *setup* of the construction. The narrator's and Elizabeth's asserted

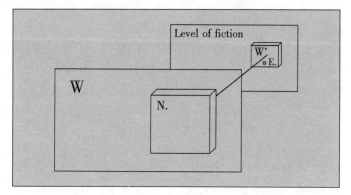

Fig. 3. W' and N are falling apart: N is being drawn out in W, while W' (and Elizabeth) are clearly being displaced to a level of fiction only connected with W via N in its capacity of being a construction.

shrewdness, assumed to keep both of them mutually air-borne, on the contrary thus threatens to crash them both simultaneously. The construction as a whole suddenly seems to have the character of a clumsily creaking projection: the intrigue and its entanglements are staged in order to put Elizabeth in a position in which she by attitude can suspend the project of "man/social ascent", thereby making herself deserve exactly that. In other words, the whole matter seems to be the mounting of a construction able to *legitimate* the trivial state of things, a machine, making it possible to have it both ways by disguising the sallow deliberation of the wish for a rich husband.

As a consequence of its inadvertent display of its own awkwardness the novel thus once again becomes 'realistic', but now in another sense. What the reader is confronted with is the narrator N (cf. fig. 3), who demonstrates that if you want to get out of the morass you must set up an intrigue, build up an excuse, implement a morality. Or, in other words, write a novel. If that novel succeeds, it makes it possible at least to dream about the wonderful things which (unfortunately, but reasonably) must be banned. And, we may add, if the novel fails it exposes the acknowledgment that this is how things are.

Pride and Prejudice is probably doing both. As a horizontal world it offers a functionable experience of a mediation of the contrast between the right attitude and the right destiny. As a vertical construction it inadvertently demonstrates the impossibility of a project like that. The unfolded world will always already be a projection of that very subjectivity and, consequently, of that very problematics of the subject, the purpose of which the novel was to constitute a machine for finishing. If not even the "alternative attitude" is anything but an adjusting facelift of the subject's mode of action in relation to the otherwise constant jackpot, then this construction can, at the most, sketch out the problem, but not offer any solution to it.

The novel, consequently, falls apart into an either/or. For the construction does not articulate any knowledge about this falling apart. Or put in another way: it does not itself point out a position from which virtual reader's positions matching the two readings can both be seen at one and the same time.

In this it differs, as mentioned above, from *Madame Bovary*, the latter in one and the same point switching between two different extreme positions, thus paradoxically merging. And which know that they are doing so, while the novel, step by step, persistently, laboriously and mercilessly still maintains the mimetic construction of the room.

Second Development Section

Obviously it also differs from *Jacques le Fataliste*, which in its turn overtly mocks the mimetic *doxa*.

Jacques le Fataliste

We shall return to this comparison. But first a little about how *Jacques le Fataliste* differs from itself.

In chapter 2.1.1 above (to which we generally refer) we analyzed Diderot's novel, noticing that it is extremely vertical. It constantly breaks off its horizontal coherence in order to demonstrate its own character as a construction. By means of that it above all wants – and actually manages – to emphasize the explicit narrator's sovereign position and ability in relation to the reader: both as a brutal *Spielverderber* and as a constructive *playmaker*. We regarded the novel, considering its position on the threshold of Modernity, as above all an homage to the subject, as the triumph of subjectivity. *Jacques le Fataliste* makes the possibility of freedom palpable: explicitly not the freedom of every individual subject to establish projects, through which the courses of its own and its fellow subjects are pre-fixed, turning the fellow subjects (and somehow also the project maker itself) into objects. Projects of that sort are bound to fail, because they take it for granted that freedom can be suspended. As the developments of subjective liberty cannot be pre-calculated with certainty in any concrete cases, one might as well leave it. And consequently, like the protagonist Jacques, choose to adopt the attitude of true freedom, being on the one hand conscious of one's subjecthood under the reign of the partly incalculable influence of circumstances – and being on the other hand ready to make the most of the chance of playing a part, and thus in concrete situations able to influence the circumstances in question. Real freedom then means insight in the conditions and restrictions of determination, which the novel thematizes horizontally as well as vertically. Horizontally through the allegoric stories, through Jacques' entire problematics of fatality; vertically through the narrator's fiction-producing demonstration of potence, still, however, constantly collapsing, going out of control, overrunning. As demonstrated, a congruence seems to exist between the ways by which the enunciation and the statement scan the subject/object-relation. Whereas the novel explicitly renounces mimesis in relation to presented worlds, it does, as a matter of fact, make a point of being "mimetic" in its construction. Altogether, consequently, it opts for the existence of a sensible *balance* of the S/O-relationship, and not least it proves this possibility in virtue of its own unfolding.

As it has now become obvious, however, *Jacques le Fataliste* has one decisive problem concerning its own notion of the well-balanced renunciation of unrestricted project-realization: itself. The novel itself is a problem in the sense that the cheerfully fabulating, explicit narrator of the novel's construction, in his entire and sovereignly realized riot against projectuality, is actually himself staged by and thus makes visible an underlying implicit instance of narrating, which to a great extent has as its pre-calculated project the formulation of exactly this concrete riot against overcalculated projects as well as against passive conformity towards supreme force by systems. It opts in favour of balance. This first of all elicits a classical problem of revocation, of self-referential inconsistency; in its rhetorical construction the novel itself does exactly that which it horizontally and at the explicit vertical level intends to demonstrate as impossible. This problem alone may not be crucial; it is relatively easy to argue against. You may for instance claim that the characteristics of the explicit narrator necessarily influence the underlying implicit narrator; using the temporary merging of the levels of fiction as supportive examples it is also possible to argue that the implicit narrator to some extent is mixed with and forced into a parallel with the explicit one. If the former seems to want what the latter actually does, some kind of order within the disorder is, however, to be found. It is true that in some sense this only displaces the instances and consequently the state of the problem, but it may be argued that it states a sort of seriality and thus relativity about competence between the instances. This modifies the problem of revocation. Far more crucial to the original reading is the second problem, not least emphasized by the possibility of the sketched-out arguments against the problematics of revocation. That problem is that the novel, the indeterminability of all its horizontal and vertical instances taken into consideration, might, in fact, just as well be said to opt for the total decomposition of the subject. All instances relativise each other: from the elegant manipulation of the explicit narrator to the ingenious stupidity of the figures of the fiction – nowhere is any anchorage established which demonstrates any attitude or even supports any density of values, latently or overtly. The very fact that the novel mocks any mimesis, because it does not have and does not want to have any stable "room", means that the self-reiterating movement of relativisation is only actually frameable from the outside, contextually. The text 'itself' is helplessly tied up with the problem of constructedness which it itself has chosen to focus upon at every single level, visible as well as invisible. As the text, consequently, so to speak, performs a *following of itself*, is the yesman of itself, it becomes deprived of any element of constancy, which might have made it cease, turn upside down, or even be misread. Or: it cannot do anything else, which in this connection is the same.

The "either/or" of the novel, consequently, is not connected to any particular point: even the text's own knowledge about its own uncertainty and indeterminability is uncertain and indeterminable. *Jacques le Fataliste* is able to project itself out into the whole scale of tones as a *continuum* of different meanings. If you were to offer examples, just to make an ironical point, within certain registers of philosophy of history, you might say that *Jacques le Fataliste* would have no trouble in acting as an early-modern critique of pre-modern determination of individual, as high-modern critique of the ideal-typical principle of projectuality of Modernity, as modernist playing through the individual's loss of substance of identity, or as postmodern critique of the modern construction of the subject as a whole.[3] And so on, and so on: the only thing which the novel is *not* able to do is to mount a 'stable' structure of function in the sense of positioning one model reader: neither a single one switching in one point, nor a double one, mutually ignorant of each other.

---

[3] Just by the way: the second of the four positions would – because of the relative contemporaneity – obviously be the most difficult to understand and to accept as well; this might be the reason for the rather low status of the novel within the ideal-typical literary (and philosophical) canon of Modernity. Cf. the discussions of this in 2.1.

Second Development Section

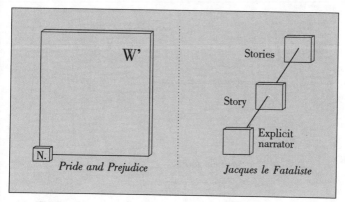

Fig. 4. The constructions of the two novels respectively within their own registers

That the novel thus works with a continuum of virtual model readers does not imply that it means anything. However, it does imply something about *the way* in which it as a consequence of its construction is able to significate – within contexts being in this or that way always already determined, anyhow, and thus implying meaning.

Pride, Prejudice – and Endless Fatality

We shall of course return to this – in the conclusion of the second development section of the next chapter, and in the cross-breeding of the first and second development sections in the *Stretta* section as well. For the moment let us discuss once again *Pride and Prejudice* as opposed to *Jacques le Fataliste*.

To the initial question of whether the novels actually are different, we shall, evidently, have to answer yes. Not only are they different in the obvious, immediate sense which

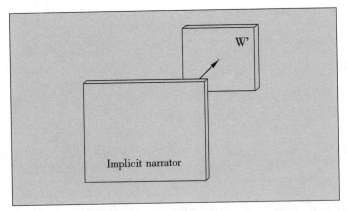

Fig. 5. The position of the implicit narrator in *Pride and Prejudice* (cf. also fig. 3 above)

analyses within the register of philosophy of history of the first development section would lay bare, already because of the fundamental constructions of the texts, including among other things functional structure (cf. the sketches at figure 4). The two novels are also different in this context: where *Jacques le Fataliste* still exclusively refers to the construction itself, to the constructedness itself, if you like, attention in *Pride and Prejudice* is shifted to the relation between the space and the construction, as we have argued above.

Further examination of the differences will reveal a level at which the texts actually, peculiarly enough, resemble one another. In fact both of them, more or less *wider Willen*, happen to emphasize, indeed even thematize their implicit narrator. *Pride and Prejudice* intends primarily to say something about (its) world, W', but happens to emphasize that very instance which is presented as *not* being privileged compared to this narrated, 'real' world: the implicit narrator

Second Development Section

(see fig. 5). In *Jacques le Fataliste* the priority is intentionally linked with the overt, vertical dimension as a whole, i.e. primarily with the explicit narrator, controlling the excesses towards the reader. Here as well, however, a shift towards an objectification of the dissimulated, underlying governing control is taking place. That is, the implicit narrator is objectified (see fig. 6).

The resemblance, however, is merely a sort of structural merging at this special point; concretely the constructions are still widely different. But these differences have several consequences and perspectives which are rather interesting for the question about the overall contextual determinateness of reading and interpretation.

Pride and Prejudice is, you might say, inadvertently fixed by something which it cannot manage (the fulfilment of its own intention to be without contradiction): it is bound to express emphatically this very contradiction, but it does so by means of references which are so concrete (the presented world's different 'living' attributes, the redundant

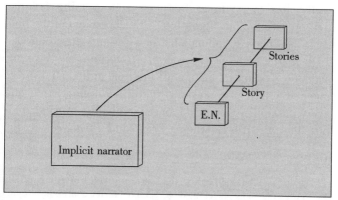

Fig. 6. The implicit narrator in *Jacques le Fataliste*.

unambiguity of the system of values) that it, so to speak, remains within its themes, concretely tied up with these – and consequently tied to what these themes will be able to represent semiotically. The either/or of the novel concerns the concrete 'own' character of the text, and this either/or is to some extent coherent in its concrete contradiction. The projections of the narrator are actually isomorphous with the ones of the protagonist Elizabeth. Consequently, the 'closed nature' of meaning of *Pride and Prejudice* is stable – and as such in a certain sense semiotically open.[4]

Conversely *Jacques le Fataliste* is not on the face of it marked by the inability to do what it intends. It seems to be in a state of happy accordance with its own interests. It is, however, you might say, in a state of such thorough but autonomous accordance with itself that it becomes impossible to differentiate. It remains fixed to its own problematics as a construction. Its either/or thus redoubles itself in a virtually endless series of differing semiotic framings, precisely because it is linked with (exclusively) the construction. Consequently *Jacques le Fataliste* is perfectly close to anything; it is open as to meaning, but also tied up with the pre-figurating by this openness of the field as being "open". And as such in a certain sense closed.

It is true that *Jacques le Fataliste* escapes any supreme semiotic fixation by having all the time anticipated it and made it relative; it plays, virtually performing each and every possibility. The text, consequently, fits everywhere – but thus also fits nowhere. *Pride and Prejudice*, on the

---

[4] "Open" and "closed" still in the sense in which Umberto Eco (Eco 1979) uses the concepts, cf. also ch. 1.4, note 8. We shall return to this question below.

Second Development Section

contrary, does not escape: it lets itself be caught, developing a certain space. It only performs one possibility, and even misses that, according to its self-understanding. The text fits only there – but exactly for that reason it can also be brought into a position of fitting everywhere. "We have a sign-function when something can be used in order to lie", is Eco's reformulation of Peirce.[5] In this sense an ability of representation may be ascribed to *Pride and Prejudice*: it may within different framings – in its "closed" wholeness – be understood as for example referring, symbolically or allegorically, to a meaning *different* from itself. And *that* spectrum of possibilities will obviously be legion.

Consequently not only *Jacques le Fataliste* – as is immediately evident – might be said to formulate a critique of the construction of *Pride and Prejudice*. The latter may also within its own premises be said to pinpoint the omnipotent incompetence of *Jacques le Fataliste*. The unlimited virtuality of *Jacques le Fataliste* turns out to resemble the trivial endlessness of "real life". Whereas the flat, accurate beautifications of *Pride and Prejudice* of what was assumed to be real life conversely become the perfect starting point of excessively unrealistic fantasies.

All of this obviously appears only from the proper constructions of the texts.

---

[5] In his essay "Peirce and the Semiotic Foundations of Openness", in Eco, 1979, quoted here p. 179.

3.7

Second Development Section: Conclusion

And that brings us to the end of the road of the Second Development Section. Before compressing the movements of the two development sections into the following *stretta* we shall briefly summarize what has been the issue here.

We have read and analyzed seven extensive epic texts whose times of emergence embrace the period between 1986 and 1774. In Auster's *The Locked Room* we saw above all how the text sharply points out its own opacity: it stages its construction of enunciation as an undecidable choice between two orbits, each of them having a decisive and mutually inconvertible consequence for the meaning of the text. But neither of which ever becomes a key to the locked room, which stays locked. Frisch's *Homo Faber* turned out to be isomorphous with its own construction of fiction in such a way as to enable it to escape the unbearable knowledge which it holds, exposes without wanting to know; the vanishing trick from the carefully constructed, completely unrealistic point of convergence becomes at one and the same time an ominous evasion of the problem and a subtle definitive exposure of it. Dinesen's *The Roads Round Pisa* turned out to set off, in a more supreme sense, the problem of *insight* and authority *qua* its construction of narrating. It is at once masterfully authoritative and endlessly self-relativating. Authority, competence, olympicity are here all *morcelées* into its point-of-view-dependent ambivalence between hierarchical order and labyrinthine opacity. In virtue of this ambivalence the instances appear closely coherent, mutually dependent, but out of phase as part of a self(re)generating, and insoluble problem of revocation. In Hemingway's *The Sun Also Rises* we saw that the iceberg construction of the enunciation of the novel makes it possible at one and the same time to hold two different readings in the form of a diversity within the text on the subject problematics. By means of its *silence* the novel stages the fragile uncertainty of powerful potency as a loop, as a bated breath, which by never letting itself go never gains any direction, but which emphatically maintains both possibility and impossibility. Also in Flaubert's *Madame Bovary* the issues are knowledge and insight, but here directly pointed out in the unbearable and megalomaniac self-presentation of the construction. We saw here that the naked, precise, truth-seeking objectivity turns out mercilessly to terminate in precisely the disguised *bêtise*, in the clear, dull subjectivism which it is the immediate intention of the whole project to reveal and to repudiate. Not as an either/or, but as a both/and, in which wisdom and stupidity, omniscience and ignorance stand side by side, each one in sublime isolation presented, respectively, by the mutually incommensurable axes of the construction of fiction. Finally we demonstrated that the redundantly in-order universe of Jane Austen's *Pride and Prejudice* contains a contrary double game, through enunciation, in which both explicit values and inner norms of behaviour generate a highly complicated relationship to the norms of the immediately incorporated world. The result is here an either/or which not even the novel itself is capable of surveying. Finally we returned to Diderot's *Jacques le Fataliste* and saw that the noisy self-thematization of the construction is not, after all, capable of making itself heard above the silence of the lacuna of enunciation, which emphatically denies the critique of subject-projectuality constituting the thematic centre. The novel locks up its own openness, and precisely by renouncing any reference, towards which it might act as an interpretant, it remains bound to reiterate its own openness, everywhere and nowhere. This makes it almost the contrast of *Pride and Prejudice* which, in spite of its incompatible self-contradictions has a semiotic character of representation, and consequently functions as a potential object or medium of transmission.

What, then, are the consequences of these analyses? Well, on the face of it three recurrent features may be noticed:

First of all the works *differ radically from themselves*. They all skid into some kind of impossibility or the other, actually disintegrate, in the sense that at one or several levels of their total saying they send out contradictory signals, deny themselves, undermine themselves, or destroy themselves. To use one of the by now rather insipid fashionable concepts, it might be said that the works in one way or other *deconstruct* themselves, that they stage and make visible the impossibility of their own (rhetorical) construction. And thus: show the possibility of this construction in terms of its being determined by its nature of construction. The explicit knowledge of the works themselves about their respective skids apparently differs:

with some of them it is an obviously conscientious, and cunning part of the construction (e.g. Auster, Dinesen), with others self-knowledge seems to be present but apparently carefully and painfully restrained (e.g. Flaubert), whereas with others again it seems to stand out only involuntarily and unacknowledged (e.g. Frisch, Austen).

This leads us to the second supreme statement which can be made: *the works differ radically from each other.* Obviously not the *same* skid happens in each and every work. As we have seen there may be a concrete self-referential inconsistency in the form of self-contradiction at the level of statement, or of mutual clashes between the vertical and the horizontal within the text; the construction as a whole may prepare for something which it neither can nor wants to fulfil; almost every conceivable type and combination of functional mode seems to be working within the works; their knowledge above all about themselves, but also in general, is obviously widely differing. That is: the fact that each of these works is radically different from themselves does not imply as a consequence that they are all concretely identical. They are different; each of them in its own individual, irrevocable way performs this difference from itself.

But thirdly we shall, however, reconsidering the first statement, maintain that *the works are extremely alike in their way of being different from themselves.* This applies not only to the fact that they differ from themselves, that is, but also, as a matter of fact, to the way in which they do so. The similarity is not one of precise position of the difference within the construction. As stated above we have seen that the skid may take place, the impossibility may emerge or appear, anywhere – and that it may take widely differing shapes. Still there is an astonishing similarity in the fact that the differing, apparently everywhere, deals with the relationship between what is said and the "saidness" of what is said, i.e. in different ways, it has something to do with the system of narration and the construction of the works' enunciation. The very existence of this diversity as to the construction of the works may be expressed in the way that each of them – but consequently all of them – is characterized by such an extent of "openness" within their construction, that they contain a position of interpretant which is capable of making visible this diversity. Whether this position of interpretant is explicit (i.e. 'conscious' as part of the overt knowledge of the work itself) or not, is of less importance in this context. It is present, and in one way or the other it *surveys* certain apparently basic characteristics of the rhetorical construction of the works, which it itself is at the same time a part of. And by means of which the works are "alike", since it is part of each of them.

To conclude, we have demonstrated that all these works are characterized by a *certain uncertainty*. This means that on the one hand each of them skids into boundless diversity thus emphasizing its constructedness, its rhetoricity. But that on the other hand this boundlessness is framed by and thus most concretely linked up with certain properties of this very construction. Through this the texts have appeared as *singularities*, that is as singular, irrevocable phenomena, not *representing* anything different from themselves. They have not – despite the two-hundred-year span in their respective times of creation – been regarded as historically representative of the period in which they properly emerge.

As should be obvious this makes the *modus operandi* decisively different from what was in the first development section practiced in relation to a series of works from the same historical period. There different intrinsic contradictions or diversities, the "incongruities" of the sayings of the works were also revealed, seen especially as based on the intrinsic relation between their various treatment of the subject/object-relation, vertically and horizontally. But these differences were then conceptualized as *representative*, *in casu* of certain historical phases of the development of epic literature of and around Modernity. The difference was then regarded as systemic, general, typical: the works chosen might 'act' historically in a supreme typological sense, as adequate representations of other works. The difference between, and intrinsically inside, the works chosen here, in the second development section, does not claim to represent any (development-)historical differentiation or any other systemic typology for that matter. Each of the differences is an item of the concrete construction of the single work.

We are, consequently, dealing with *different* differences in the two development sections, respectively.

Stretta

Synchyses. Ridicule jeune homme, que je me
trouvai un jour sur un autobus de la ligne S
bondé par traction peut-être cou allongé, au
chapeau la cordelière, je remarquai un.
Arrogant et larmoyant d'un ton, qui se trouve
à côté de lui, contre ce monsieur, proteste-t-il.
Car il se pousserait, fois chaque que des gens
il descend. Libre il s'assoit et se précipite vers
une place, cela dit. Rome (Cour de) je le
rencontre plus tard deux heures à son pardessus un bouton d'ajouter un ami lui
conseille.

4.1
One, Two – Three?

On the one hand: The first development section has demonstrated that novels originating in different historical moments, within the period which we are examining, are different, but still alike in the sense that they do contribute to one history, to one course of development, by means of which for instance the novel gradually becomes what it is today. It is a characteristic feature of this consecutivity that every step is a precondition for the next. This means especially that the present state of things, i.e. what the novel is able to, what it is, and what it does today, is a *product* of what happened previously. Concretely, the *insight* into its own character as said construction, which is perhaps what the novel of today implies above all, is consequently a definite historically produced possibility exactly at this moment. The respective insights, perspectives and constructions of the novels are altogether unaccidental. Not in the sense that 'the development' takes definite, deterministically predictable directions. But it seems to imply that it is possible, from a certain historical point, to reconstruct the process which led up to this point. It should be noted that we are not talking of massaging interpretations of the works' 'statements' into definite rooms of understanding, *a priori* ranged and arranged, into a register of philosophy of history; we are talking about analyses of above all the texts' ways of being texts, of their knowledge about themselves, of the construction of their 'said-ness' *as* construction. Of, in short, how the works "are".

On the other hand: The second development section, however, has demonstrated that a series of novels with different moments of emergence within the same historical period truly are concretely different, but still basically alike in the sense that each in its very construction seems to skid in a certain way. That is, these works appear as historically parallel, standing side by side, to the extent that they all of them possess the acknowledgment, the insight or the skid which in the first development section was shown to form the result of the total development (so far). And it is worth noticing that we are not talking about the mere interpretative transformation which is necessarily a consequence of any so-called recontextualization (because lingual codes, including the meaning of idioms and metaphors do indeed change), i.e. at issue is not that the text should 'have' an intrinsic, definite construction which then from a certain viewpoint is *construed* differently. As we have stated in every single case we are dealing with properties, features of the constructions themselves. It is not a matter of the works being "readable" like that, but of the works "being" like that. Altogether the second development section contains the statement that the narrating literature of this period *is* in one way or another subject to an insoluble conflict with its own knowledge.

Thus we have two differing statements about the 'same' object which appear to be mutually contradictory. Or, put differently, which as regards the same realm of objects offer two different registers of understanding, registers which applied on concrete works seem to make these works look different, actually *be* different – but in such a way, it is worth noticing, that the readings in both registers cannot possibly, it seems, be simultaneously "true" concerning the same work.

This may be called a contradiction, and it is a contradiction in the sense that if the statement of the first development section about this type of text is "true", then the statement of the second development section apparently cannot be "true" as well at the same time. And, conversely, if the statement of the second development section is true then the one of the first development section cannot be so as well.

This, however, is a "contradiction" only if you insist on being able to read one 'resulting' force out of these two registers – and of course, given a certain definition of "truth". You might in fact formulate the problematics alternatively: the literary works, i.e. texts acknowledged in the field of "literature", have here been demonstrated as subject to *different* forces. These forces apparently work simultaneously, but mutually heterogeneously, so that they at one and the same time draw the text into different directions, indeed are even able to make them different from themselves. The statements might then also be read as follows: every text is *at one and the same time* part of a 'historical' process in which it inherits and changes something present, thus sending it on as a source or a condition of possibility for a new change – *and* necessarily itself the virtual object of a reading within that understanding of whose genealogy it itself is a part. In a certain sense the mutual connection between the development sections is very simple. The course of the first reading constitutes the condition of possibility for the other, in fact it produces the situation which in turn determines the outlook of the second reading. The first reading, consequently, *results* in the second, but without simultaneously abolishing or 'denying' its own validity.

The movement may be illustrated using the subject/object-relation as an example. The first development section demonstrates a gradual development within both the thematical elaboration of the s/o-relation by the novels and the way in which they as texts stage this and themselves in the capacity of a function of this relationship. This development 'results' in a situation in which the impossibility of the relation in its classical Modern scanning, as a realizable ideal of the world emerges to view. No longer 'merely' said, but *done*. The relation consequently appears in its character as a *picture*, a construction, a fantasm, a model, a metaphor. The readings of the second development section, consequently, are bound to demonstrate this impossibility, i.e. this 'pictorial' character. This, however, does not in itself alter anything about the importance which the subject/object-construction has in fact had historically. What happens, however, is a fixation, a 'bringing along' of a certain historical point: a certain, historically produced view is projected into texts whose historical rooms of emergence are different. On the one hand it may consequently be stated that the readings reiterate themselves backwards (without, as stated above, analyses for that reason showing the 'same' – indeed the texts are singularly different). But they do not simply repeat themselves; they do also in turn constantly accumulate – both insight and blindness. They are mutually connected in a course which step by step determines itself causally all the way through. This is also the matter in the zone of crossing between the first and second development sections. The reading of *The Locked Room* must necessarily, after the reading of *Se una notte d'inverno un viaggiatore* be the way it is. Similarly all the readings respectively bridge each other in a definite succession. Still the reading of *Madame Bovary* is not immediately connected with the reading of *Le Père Goriot* – and the readings of *Jacques le Fataliste* are not connected with each other. How then, may readings seem connected one by one in one long succession and still not be connected mutually crosswise?

Obviously this must be the consequence of changes of the positions from which the readings are made. On the face of it, one might be tempted to generalize and suggest that the difference consists in the historical, contextual readings of the first development section being "contemporary" (each of their own time), whereas the ones of the second development section seemingly might be laid down as "present". This distinction, however, is not tenable, because on a closer look it must be clear that also the position of philosophy of history necessarily is "present". Consequently, we are dealing with different present positions. Another obvious idea might then be to regard the differentiation as caused by the way in which the development sections privilege different levels of the proper texts. In the first development section a main priority might be given to the thematics (of the presented world's space), whereas the second conversely emphasizes rhetoric/enunciation, and furthermore one might imagine that the enounced and the enunciation were respectively subject to different historical inertias. The enunciation might then, qua its framing of the enounced, which in fact makes it work as a more immediate link of transition to the reader, be thought generally to represent a higher degree of 'presence' (i.e. relative contemporariness as to readers) compared to the thematic level's natural, higher degree of being linked with its historical context of emergence. This distinction, however, cannot be sustained on a closer look either. Since the levels of the text are in practice mounted into one and the same construction, their contextual sensitivity as to time must in principle apply to the whole. A different thing is that against the background of the development sections it is evident that the respective positions of analysis do indeed have diverging *priorities* between the statements about the levels of the texts, and consequently enunciation plays a different role in the second development section from the role it played in the first development section. But, as has also been demonstrated: this alteration is one of the consequences produced by the described development itself (first development section).

Thus it does not seem possible to implement any common, supreme distinction either in the historical context or in the intrinsic constructions of the texts, a distinction which would be isomorphous with the respective positions of examinations of the development sections. Or put in another way: it does not seem possible to construct one unambiguous third position able to hold, contain or survey the two (types of) positions which the first and the second development sections present respectively. It seems as if the two positions of analysis, each of them *both* in their mutual (gradual), 'causal' connection *and* in their mutual heterogeneity, must be maintained as "valid" or "true" in the field – and, consequently, that the readings of which they are the occasion, must similarly be maintained like that, collision or not.[1]

Now, does the fact that *different* views upon, and consequently statements about, the given object are apparently true at the same time, then imply that *any* statement may be true? Or, to put it another way: would this not actually remove the criteria of relevance and truth from the material, and thus approximate these criteria to the regarding point of view, the consequence of which is that *anything goes*, i.e. that the analysis fades into subjective voluntarism, into a completely closed, hermeneutic circle?

We shall return to the concept of truth in 4.2 below. But it can immediately be stated that it is no necessary consequence of *several* views being possible, that *all* views would become so. Because the existence of several different 'valid' views does not automatically imply an abandonment of a demand that these views, in every single case, should be able to motivate themselves in empirically existing positions and processes, should be able to link themselves to existing problems or parts of the material itself, which in this case is the field we are situated in. The fact that *several* views or modes of access are possible according to these criteria only implicates that the field must be heterogeneous; not that it is 'all-embracing'. In our case the notion of philosophy of history is solidly anchored in the field (i.e. in "literature"), just as the subject/object-problem and the different stagings of this indeed are. But also the

---

[1] *That* statement of course itself constitutes a 'third position' of that kind, although different from the one that one supreme, 'organizing' point of view would be. We shall return to the problem below in 4.3 and concludingly in 6.

self-confronting dissipation, the skid of the intrinsic coherence of the texts themselves, the revelation of the rhetorical construction of the text, including its respective
attempts to take into possession, and to lose any power over
the very room it intends to represent: also this position
itself is above all, because it is a *result* of the development
which the above modes of thinking include, equally
existing, well-founded and – *qvod erat demonstrandum* –
well-foundable.

Metaphorically the issue may be expressed as a matter
of point-of-view, quite literally. In his discussions of the
question about whether it is the implicit consequence of the
notion of "unlimited semiosis" that any analysis goes,
Umberto Eco touches a similar problem, among other things
in the distinction between "indefinite" and "infinite".[2] For
example he construes Peirce like this

> for Peirce semiosis is potentially unlimited from the point of
> view of the system but is not unlimited from the point of view
> of the process [28]

where "the process" is the concrete semiotic process. This
point of view might be transposed into our context by
stating that from the point of view of the respective
positions themselves, their statements (concerning the texts
in question) do indeed contradict each other and consequently become "impossible". But from the point of view of
the system as a whole, here the point of view of the "field",

---

[2] Umberto Eco *The Limits of Interpretation*, Bloomington 1990, which
is Eco's settlement with at least parts of so-called deconstructionist
criticism. We shall return to the viewpoints of this book in chapter 5.1.

the existence of mutually differing statements is neither the expression of a self-contradiction, nor even strange in itself; this state of things truly implies statements *about* the field which (the way any act of signifying does) indeed *changes* it. But still this does not make the field all-embracing (and consequently semiotically empty). If you follow up on these metaphors of point of view, you might say that from the point of view of the single positions the co-existence of several, contradicting positions truly imply that *any* position is potentially "true" (or false; just as true or just as false as any other position). Conversely, however, from the point of view of the field it is in no way an evident consequence of the existence of diverging positions that any imaginable position should be equally "true", or even pertinent. In order to be so it should, seen from the point of view of the field, be groundable *in* the field. The fact that the field is changing, and changeable, however, does not automatically make anything good at any time. It would only do this if, for instance, the position "anything" were itself present within the field.

This we shall illustrate further in our discussion of field and truth below. For the moment just briefly concerning the text-readings of the first and second development sections above: they cannot be concluded into one converging resultant. What these sequences of readings have in fact *proved* cannot briefly be concluded. Their statements are linked with the course they unfold. *Proving* is not at issue here: what goes on is that a certain series of mutually connected positions and consequently movements within the field *are shown*. But that process too is obviously taking place within the field. Taking its place. At first it was there. Then it was there. And now it is here.

4.2

Field and Truth

Two different courses have been completed, two different tracks have been left in the 'same' realm of objects. Our results are 'true', but they are different. They are not the only true ones: other positions are able to, have been able to, and will be able to cause yet other truths. This, however, does not imply that any statement in or around the field, is true.

What is "truth"? Obviously we shall not here be able to reconsider a discussion which has kept philosophy busy for several thousand years. But we shall allow ourselves to comply with a distinction between "the claim that the *world* is out there and the claim that the *truth* is out there".[1] If there is a "truth", which is supposed to be an "intrinsic" property of the world, this is not the one which we discuss here; only descriptions of the world can be true or false.

---

[1] The wording is Richard Rorty's (Rorty 1988, pp. 4-5). This of course does not imply that we agree with Rorty in everything – or for that matter that the reference as such supplies this point of view with any authority. It is, however, adequate in general to give a reference to the extensive critical dialogue which Rorty – from a position, whose fundamental ideas are not far from the ones exposed here – makes with the philosophical tradition.

Truth is, thus, 'a property of linguistic entities, of sentences'.[2]

"Truth", consequently, always refers to the rules of certain language games, i.e. to certain instituted semiotic codes. Like for instance "art", "literature" – or "science".

Art, here literature, first. In his discussion of what "literature" is, Gérard Genette distinguishes between what he calls constitutivist (or essentialist) conceptions on the one hand and conditionalist conceptions on the other hand.[3] As constitutivist he characterizes the conceptions, which ascribe to "art" stable, intrinsic properties in the tradition from Aristotle and on. So far so good. To conditionalist conceptions he, conversely, counts only those which ground their definition of art upon changing, *subjective* judgments of taste:

> Je considère comme littéraire tout texte qui provoque chez moi une satisfaction esthétique

goes the type example.[4] Genette, thus, apparently seems to think that conditionality implies subjectivity. This means that in his systematization he overlooks the possibility of precisely the type of determination of art which we shall opt for here: one, which is *objective* and simultaneously *conditional*.

---

[2] Still in Rorty's wording, op.cit. p. 7.

[3] See Gérard Genette: *Fiction et Diction*, Paris 1991.

[4] Op.cit. pp. 26-27. Genette's purpose with this discussion is different from ours. It is, however, difficult to see that his further distinctions on this occasion (fiction/diction; thématique/rhématique) are particularly productive, if even tenable.

By "objective and conditional" we here understand something which is on the one hand completely conditional: it is a semiotic convention which makes certain objects belong to "art". Above all twentieth-century art has strikingly pointed this out through the continuously assimilated "anti-art" from Guy Débord's sheer nothing to Piero Manzoni's canned personal faeces. Furthermore, it is obvious that convention changes and has changed historically; not only have objects continuously been respectively excluded and included. Besides that, axiological re-classifications within convention constantly take place. Following this, it is evident that this convention is – or at any rate at different times may be – compound, complex, heterogenous. What is decisive, however, is the fact that this convention, on the other hand, is simultaneously *objective* (in a philosophical sense): in actual fact it *exists* as a language game 'out there', and it does so in certain shapes at certain times and in certain situations. The convention is not a part of the world outside language (although the objects, with which convention deals, of course are); *the convention* is, however, part of the world of language, and consequently of the world of signification. The convention is objective and conditional in the same way as language systems are: they *exist* objectively; otherwise communication, including for instance translation, would be impossible (and discourses like the present would be senseless). But they are not *finally decidable* because – as a consequence of their concrete conditionality in any spatially and temporally defined point – they cannot possibly have a mode of existence of pragmatic independence, or for that matter just outside history. Language systems are always active as precisely implicit codes, which can only be made explicit by means of other, similar codes. *Semiosis* is un-limited. Furthermore, any act of signification within the system is in principle performative; it alters the system, perhaps to an immensely small extent, perhaps to a rather great extent. Still neither changeability nor non-objectiv-ability cause language to be subjectively coincidental. A person may obviously choose her own language: but this would be an alternative, so to speak parallel, system, and the price to pay will be that no-one understands her. Similarly a person may choose her very own definition of "art": this may then be included in the convention by means of the community of concepts within the language system. But its 'meaning' and importance will depend upon how much weight it turns out to *get* pragmatically – not upon the accordance with intrinsic properties of given objects, which it may probably already *possess*.

Consequently: art *is* there – but it is precisely what it is. Literature, in particular, is made out of 'frozen sentences', i.e. sentences which at a given time, by being put down in writing, have been removed 'out' of the language – and thus permanently have become a part of it by being linked with exactly this irrevocable outer form. A literary text plays along in the objective and conditional systems of both language system and "literature". Works of other art forms are, by the way, also double-determined by their conven-tional sign systems *and* by art respectively. These cases are only often easier to distinguish, since no identity of semiotic medium is the case.[5]

---

[5] On the face of it the analysis within art forms other than literature may appear more difficult, because verbal language, by means of which the analysis is to be worded, belongs to a sign system other than the one

The "objective" and "conditional" imply that a work of art, including a literary text, *has its own ontology* which then must be respected,[6] i.e. must *always* be taken into consideration when the signification of a given work is analyzed. The discussion about "finding" versus "making" of textual analysis is, therefore, not solvable as an either/or. It is a matter of "making" – but within, and related to, what is to be found.[7]

What is to be found is *the field* of literature, as we call it here. Any field, for instance a magnetic field, is influenced by forces which are not immediately visible, but which still sovereignly lay down premises for movements within the field. Precisely like the pattern of the iron filings on the paper which are governed by the invisible magnets, as they showed us in our childhood physics lessons. Only the "field" in question here is not following the laws of classical mechanics within the paradigm of scientific modernism. A field like that may be "complicated", i.e. influenced by different forces, but so that those, according

---

about which the analysis is supposed to speak. There is of course no reason for minimizing this problem of transformation; the merging of sign systems, however, has often made literary-scientific analysis perform a sort of semiotic act of displacement by *mixing up* the two registers. And *that* mistake is difficult to correct, because very soon it becomes unclear which signs belong to which register.

[6] As for instance expressed by Eco, op.cit., 1990, p. 72.

[7] The finding/making-discussion is above all, for purposes concerning primarily theory of science, performed by Richard Rorty who even designates "two kinds of textualism", a "weak" and a "strong textualism" respectively according to these modalities (Rorty, 1982). Eco discusses Rorty's distinctions (Eco, 1990, p. 56f). See also below in the discussion of the analysis, ch. 5.1.

to certain formulas of the theory and experimentally in practice, may be proved to terminate in a *resulting* force. What we must imagine here, on the contrary, is a *complex* field in the sense of the so-called new scientific paradigm.[8] In this complex field every single point will be influenced by several different types and levels of force, each of them independently "resulting", i.e. not projectable into each other, but standing side by side. In this field these mutually non-congruent forces are not surveyable from any privileged point, neither inside nor outside the system: only from positions which always already themselves are under the influence of the forces, and *which consequently move*, is the system acknowledgeable and describable. The description, consequently, must always also incorporate this very movement and thus itself be tied with, be a function of its own course. And it must respect the character of these forces whose effects are not deterministically precalculable, but which have to be discussed in categories like "possibility" and "probability".

"Field" is a metaphor, a metaphor here in something which understands itself as a science about art. A metaphoric redescription, which pleads in favour of "objective conditionality", tries to supersede an old, here predominantly essentialist one. Developing work by Mary

---

[8] Cf. for instance the discussions in David Bohm and F. David Peat: *Science, Order and Creativity*, 1987, and for instance in Henri Atlan and William Paulson, see Frits Andersen, 1991, espec. pp. 96ff. See also the (as concerns the perspective of parallelism) interesting discussions of the properties of the modes of function of complex systems within biology, in Robert Rosen 1985.

Hesse,[9] Richard Rorty regards the history of art and science altogether as a chain of "metaphoric redescriptions" of nature rather than insights into the intrinsic nature of nature. These metaphoric redescriptions (and Hesse's statement is based primarily on natural sciences) are not necessarily thought of as getting into any 'closer' or 'more complete' relationship with what they describe; they create a framing which is different and which, consequently, performatively implies different possibilities – which may then perhaps be designated "progress", if *that* is ideologically pertinent within the institution of science in question.

Science about art is itself immediately included as part of the semiotic institution of "art", is becoming a power of the field which it attempts to map.[10] Conversely, the "knowledge" of the works not only constitutes the substantial condition of possibility of their metaphoric redescription in the register of "science"; this "knowledge" is often even the outer emphatical occasion of this redescription. What has been shown here is, among other things, that literature through its development over the last two hundred years has gradually and systematically *as literature* undermined any essentialist understanding of what "literature" is. So far, literature has 'resulted' in constructions which *show* (and not just *say*) that the

---

[9] Op.cit., 1988, p. 16. He quotes from "The Explanatory Function of Metaphor" in Hesse, *Revolutions and Reconstructions in the Philosophy of Science*, Bloomington, 1980.

[10] This may be one of the reasons why the Anglo-Saxon part of the world usually does not even use the designation of "science" in this context, i.e. keeps on using the term "criticism" instead.

question of true or untrue evades any absolute, olympically privileged answer: that is because it will always already have been asked. And that means: said.

4.3

Stretta

And that means: said. Said, just as what we say here is said: and which, by means of its saying, has intended to show that the course of this saidness is not reducible into one privileged position either. That is, intended to show that this *knowledge* about this literature cannot and shall not escape *its* proper form if it is to be able to talk about that which it wants to talk about. This, on the one hand, in no way makes the fields of discourse's "knowledge about literature" and "literature" identical. But, on the other hand, it is hardly a coincidence that an aesthetically inspired construction may be assumed to be adequate to the formulating of this knowledge.

What we have done may be described as a double, self-causing movement of recontextualization. Double, because it has included both on the one hand a recontextualization of the works, primarily expressed in the inter-relation between the two development sections. And on the other hand a recontextualization of the positions of knowledge – i.e. the repeated recontextualization of the position of knowledge by itself – through the alteration, which their gradual acquisition of the texts' knowledge might bring about as regards their knowledge about the texts. The movement has been self-causing in the sense that it has demonstrated that knowledge and texts *themselves* in their mutual positions constantly alter themselves and each other (whereas the supreme frames of alteration obviously are part of and determined through a totality of meaning related to society as a whole).

The double, self-causing movement of recontextualization, which we have made, is *not coincidental.* Nor is it just tentative, made in order to demonstrate the interpretational effects of "recontextualization". As has been remarked extensive parts of so-called deconstructive criticism apparently regard it as their purpose to demonstrate the fact *that* recontextualization alters the meaning of a text.[11] In itself this very statement is of course tedious – especially tedious to make again and again. What is interesting, on the contrary, is to examine the way in which concrete, in different ways "naturally" (within the objective, conditional field) occurring recontextualizations *factually* influence the results and basic conditions of unfolding of interpretation. This applies to 'naturally' occurring recontextualizations, but may for instance also apply to experimentally set-up

---

[11] Remarked for example by Richard Rorty, who in his discussion of Derrida among other things writes: "Deconstruction is not a novel procedure made possible by a recent philosophical discovery. Recontextualization in general, and inverting hierarchies in particular has been going on for a long time. Socrates recontextualized Homer [...]" (Rorty, 1988, p. 134). It may be worth noticing that the critique here is directed against the activities and pretensions of the literary deconstructive criticism. Rorty regards Derrida as above this tediousness; in his own recontextualizations (for example in *La Carte Postale*) Derrida achieves a *doing* in which the concrete effects of the clashes become decisive, for instance through irony, their formation of new types of discourse, &c. This "doing" Derrida repeats (in order never to repeat himself) – but without turning it into a method, even less referring to it as a such, Rorty thinks.

recontextualizations, as has by now become possible, cf. for instance the activities of the OuLiPo-group.[12]

The movement here, in the two development sections, is a result of a series of choices. The works, their succession, the whole *set-up* of the construction might have been different. However it is not: everything is exactly the way it is. If the works of the first development section had appeared in the second and *vice versa*, the single readings would have turned out differently. Truly, we do assert that the supreme track of meaning, made by the movement of the book, might grossly have remained the same. But within the framing of the present form this must necessarily remain an assertion.

The world does not change by itself in accordance with some intrinsic nature towards a certain *telos*. Everything is a product of time and chance.[13] But at issue will always be a *concrete* time and a *concrete* chance. And consequently a "product" which is a state *within* the world. A coincidentally and subjectively chosen point of view does not have the same ontological status as supreme semiotic codes which govern our exchange of meaning and its differentiation.

Thus: If the analysis demonstrates that the texts are quivering, bound to repeat their own endless distance from themselves, then this is because the field just then concretely makes possible, evokes, makes necessary precisely this fact. If everything is a product of time and chance,

---

[12] OuLiPo is further commented on in connection with the analysis of Calvino's novel in ch. 2.4 above.

[13] Once again Rorty's wording, cf. Rorty, 1988; 22.

every essentialist definition of art is a lie. It is a lie, but it may be – and definitions of that kind indeed have been throughout history – a reality. It is then "true". The same perspective applies to the notions and approaches which we in section 1 above have systematically criticized for being reductive, out of touch, &c. The critique of the positions is certainly correct, because it is well-founded in its own pertinent understanding of the field. But it is wrong because it criticizes *realities* which are themselves performative forces of the field, and consequently somehow constitute it. Existing, often languid, semiotic formations of meaning are criticized as if they were just arbitrarily chosen points of view. Because of that art *is* epistemologically privileged, and it is so in capacity of ontological determinateness (as differing from its semiotic determinateness); because of that the existential message *is* primary, compared to the artificial elaboration of the literary form, which *is* merely a "form" opposing a "content"; because of that, intrinsic coherence *is* a decisive, presuppositioned criterion of quality to all art. These properties *are* art, because art is understood like that. And art is unable to be like that because we have proved here that it is not.

There is no such thing as a privileged metavocabulary. And what has here been unfolded *is* a privileged metavocabulary. Not even to mention the position which is able to say *"There is no such thing as a privileged metavocabulary"*.

This is the condition of any attempt to produce another meaning on the basis of existing meaning. The positions do condition and reproduce and mirror each other infinitely. But "infinity" is not the same as "undecidability". Infinity is definable, focusable, positionable; is perhaps even elucidatable from positions which simultaneously elucidate their own necessary movement the way we have attempted to do it here. Perhaps elucidate by means of a metaphoric redescription, which then immediately already is on its way down to the other dead metaphors, which constitute meaning in general, in order to perhaps end as "truth". Truth, conversely, is not a function of construction, no more than construction is a function of truth. Truth *is* construction. Doing, time, chance: concretely, completely existing and approachable. And transcendentally, completely incomprehensible.

Consequently, as applying to the joint saying of the development sections: It is tied to exactly this course, to exactly this, its own construction of uttering, which among other things maintains it as a *course*. It is completely singular, but in no way for that reason "subjective"; its construction and its development correspond to constructions and developments within the field. It is true, because it demonstrates the movement of its own truths and their "said-ness". And in a little while it is going to choose, a bit abruptly, but necessarily, to let its voice die away, setting up a parallel motion, performed by a substituting voice. Subsequently, at this level, agreed silence must rule.

Precisely folded into itself, simple and inaccessible, at one and the same time an impossible construction and completely tediously coherent, Milan Kundera's novel *L'Immortalité* (1990) is for the time being a monumental embodiment, within "literature", of this incomprehensible clash. Here the levels of fiction are in an unlimited and technically 'impossible' sense entangled with each other. Here enunciation and enounced, "fiction" and "reality", play and fatality, are finally completely *morcelées* and still ultimatively massaged into each other. It is no longer "literature" – and it is only what it is because it is "literature". And it knows that. It *is* an *Engführung* of the recent two hundred years of European novel, and that is why we now give it the last words here.[14] The voice, it should be noticed, belongs to the fictional person Milan Kundera, novelist, Czech exile, living in Paris. This Kundera has a little *rendez-vous* with a couple of the characters of the novel, which he just concluded, in order to celebrate that he just concluded. The novel, by the way, was to have been entitled "The Unbearable Lightness of Being" – but that title he had, unfortunately, already used once for his preceding novel, it is said:

Une étrange emotion s'empara de moi: "Tu étais prêt à te faire arrêter comme violeur uniquement pour ne pas trahir le jeu..."

Et soudain, je compris Avenarius: si nous refusons d'accorder de l'importance à un monde qui se croit important, et si nous ne trouvons en ce monde aucun écho à notre rire, il ne nous reste qu'une solution: prendre le monde en bloc et en faire un objet pour notre jeu; en faire un jouet. Avenarius joue et le jeu est la seule chose qui lui importe dans un monde sans importance. Mais ce jeu ne fera rire personne et il le sait. Quand il avait exposé ses projets aux écologistes, ce n'etait pas pour les amuser. C'etait pour son propre amusement.

Je lui dis: "Tu joues avec le monde comme un enfant mélancolique qui n'a pas de petit frère."

Voilà! Voilà la métaphore que je cherche depuis toujours pour Avenarius! Enfin!

---

[14] The quotation is from *L'Immortalité*. Roman. Traduit du tcheque par Eva Bloch, Paris 1991, pp. 410-11. The French edition is authorized by the author as original.

Avenarius souriait comme un enfant mélancolique. Puis, il dit: "Je n'ai pas de petit frère mais je t'ai, toi."

Reprise

Gastronomique. Après une attente gratinée sous un soleil au beurre noir, je finis par monter dans un autobus pistache où grouillaient les clients comme asticots dans un fromage trop fait. Parmi ce tas de nouilles, je remarquai une grande allumette avec un cou long comme un jour sans pain et une galette sur la tête qu'entourait une sorte de fil à couper le beurre. Ce veau se mit à bouillir parce qu'une sorte de croquant (qui en fut baba) lui assaisonnait les pieds poulette. Mais il cessa rapidement de discuter le bout de gras pour se couler dans un moule devenu libre.

J'étais en train de digérer dans l'autobus de retour lorsque devant le buffet de la gare Saint-Lazare, je revis mon type tarte avec un croûton qui lui donnait des conseils à la flan, à propos de la façon dont il était dressé. L'autre en était chocolat.

5.1

Textual Analysis.
Literature, Philosophy,
and Criticism

0. "Reprise". "The statement" of the two development sections above shall not be summarized, nor shall we attempt to repeat it: the statement is constituted by its own movement, its own development, is folded into this movement and consequently cannot be extracted from it without decisive alteration. This also implies that the "assertions" of the exposition section shall not be claimed as "proven" or "unproven"; these assertions *and* the developments together constitute the very statement. To the supreme staging of *history* as inscribed in a movement like that we thus have nothing to add. The movement cannot and shall not be frozen, and it is not compressible or translatable into something, which for instance from one point is able to survey with privilege movements of that kind. What the movement is able to and is bound to, is to let itself be repeated and continued.

However, certain aspects of the movement we have made, are empirical parts of a number of theoretical discussions and considerations within the general debate of literary theory, as also suggested in the exposition section above. The purpose of this "reprise" will then be to point out certain perspectives, which the movement of this book seems to mark out in these discussions and considerations in selected realms.

These realms are at first in the present chapter *textual analysis* and in that connection the ever-hot discussion about the borderlines between literature, philosophy and criticism/literary science. Then, in the following chapter, we shall sketch out certain perspectives on the theory of the *novel*. The present book deals with the novel, and yet it does not. The novel is at one and the same time 'merely' an example, and because of the singular way in which the movement carries itself, it is posited in more than just an ordinary thematic centre. In a subsequent chapter we shall similarly discuss the implications which the considerations of the book have for the status and the role of the *aesthetic*, in particular regarded in its historically changing mode of function. The last chapter, finally becomes both *reprise* and *excursus*: through an outline of an analysis of Bernardo Bertolucci's film *La Tragedia di un Uomo Ridicolo* we shall demonstrate an application to another art form of the analytical and theoretical developments. First, however, in this chapter, textual analysis.

1. The field. Decisive to the developments of textual analysis has first of all been the definition of literature as a *field*, i.e. the assertion that the meaning of any literary single work is immediately connected to its semiotic framing *as* literature. This basic notion about a semiotic instance of framing, about a *code*, which is specific to concrete genres of discourse is not particularly new, either in application to the language system in general, or to the discussion of the aesthetic/literature. One may just recall Peirce's "habit", Saussure's "milieu", Nelson Goodman's "system of representation standard", Jauss' "Erwartungshorizont", Bürger's "Institution Kunst", Fish's "interpretative community", Weber's "instituted/instituting", Paulson's "artificial autonomous system", or Bennett's "reading formation". Within different registers theoretical notions like these, all of them, express the conception that the meaning of singular signs/singular works is necessarily always regulated by codes or conventions, and that these conventions are *specific* in terms of genres of discourse and consequently in terms of any concrete "situation of signification", but at the same time changeable.

Whereas this, on the one hand, at least to several traditions, is indeed evident, it has, on the other hand, hardly ever to any decisive extent, analytically been taken seriously, *inter alia* in the important sense that the notion has also been extended to apply factually to the position of the analysis itself.

The definition here of the field as *objective* and *conditional*, and the double, self-exposing movement of the analysis, may act as an example and consequently as a contribution to such a binding inclusion of the role of the institutionalized/institutionalizing context into the signification – and consequently into analysis. This inclusion establishes the possibility of certain decisive, fruitful differentiations. By means of the literal register of the field metaphorics itself it becomes possible to include gradations of the *strength* of the field, also concerning its limits and edges. Furthermore, the objective *historical* dependence of meaning is reflectable without necessarily ending up in either the deterministic straitjacket of philosophy of history, or in the obvious ignorance of anti-historicism. Above all the distinction between work and field may be the occasion of a fruitful literary historical figure of mounting, for the interrelation between works of the past, their contemporary position back then in the field (and consequently 'meaning'), and their history of position up to the 'present' state of problems, that means what they actually mean (in terms of "science"...). This model finally establishes an immediate possibility of experimentally *setting up* works in foreign fields, for example in order to examine field strength and/or meaning. But it also presents an effective argument against what this possibility of recontextualization has produced in terms of theoretical assertions within certain traditions, for instance in Stanley Fish and parts of deconstructive criticism, concerning the *total context-dependence* of meaning. Texts may be brought to signify differently within differently institutionalized contexts, and as a part of this it is of course possible to construct 'subjective' codes and so conduct meanings in an unlimited way. But as long as we work with the *objective* fields (and, as stated above, the language system as such bears the same character) *anything goes* is not at issue: the meaning of singular signs is, to a certain extent determined by conventions of the field, and if the concrete construction of these singular signs is stable, so is "meaning". It is true that because of the character of the systems as infinite patterns of relations, meaning is not ultimately *decidable*, exhaustively, and cannot even be formulated if not by means of another language system which in turn raises a series of new questions (cf. below). In practice, however, meanings may easily be isolated as a realm of possibilities, by means of this model, and above all it is possible to exclude variations of signification for which no support can be found in the semiotic construction in question.

The notions that anything in principle means or uncomplicatedly may be brought to mean anything, apparently has its basis in some fundamental confusions of especially *infinity's* position and character within the language system. The language system as such is infinite in the sense that it is inexhaustible or un-finalizable; any sign is described by other signs and is linked to these "encyclopedically".[1] Every sign/referent-relation itself contains a position of interpretant which in turn as a new sign makes itself the object of yet another position of interpretant, &c., &c., cf. already Peirce's chains of signification. The language system is thus constituted by an *infinity* of relations, defined for instance by closeness, distance, opposition, similarity, difference, contiguity, &c. Everything is linked with everything in a figure which very precisely meta-phorically has been described by the mathematic type of labyrinth, *the rhizome*.[2] Although the *formation* of signi-fication, or the *semiosis* thus is infinite this is not the same as stating that everything may mean anything: *semiotically* the infinity does not imply that the relations of meaning are also indeterminable, or at least not isolatable by excluding a series of alternative inadequate possibilities. Concretely, to lingual signs as well as to for instance literary texts, any "meaning" is related to an immediately conventionalized level of code which is historically specific, and objectively existing *precisely* (only) *in capacity of convention*. This level of code – and consequently the concrete meaning – is

---

[1] Cf. the interesting distinction between conceptions of language system organized as 'dictionary' and 'encyclopedia' respectively, for instance in Eco, 1984, pp. 44-86.

[2] See Deleuze/Guattari, 1977.

describable and accessible insofar as transmission of meaning is possible at all.

Although the field will often in practice be treated as relatively stable within perhaps considerable periods of time, particularly in examinations of the distant past, it is worth noticing the fact that the historical changeability of the field in principle is quite literal in the sense that the field will at no moment be identical to what it was at the previous moment. This of course is above all due to the fact that any act of signification within the field necessarily alters the field. In fact the field is subject to an everlasting movement of transformation, which may be advantageously conceptualized, as Samuel Weber argues,[3] in the relation between something "instituted" and something "instituting" (the latter consequently also covering the negative, the excluding parallel movement).

Descriptions and examinations of the field, which are *essentialist* (in Genette's sense), may actually in one way be both possible and desirable, whether in the shape of for instance Nelson Goodman's considerations of how the aesthetic is characterized by certain densities or redoublements[4] within signification, or Roman Jakobson's notions about the literary as the dominance of an especially directed stratum within the lingual expression.[5] Whether this "essentialism" is relative, i.e. nominalist and conditional in the sense referred to here (like Nelson

---

[3] In his book *Institution and Interpretation* (Weber, 1987), *inter alia* in continuation of René Lourau: *L'Analyse institutionelle*, Paris 1970.

[4] Cf. for instance *Languages of Art*, Goodman, 1969, pp. 252ff.

[5] Cf. the above-mentioned stratum-model, Jakobson, 1960.

Goodman's) or genuinely essentialist (i.e. also philosophically realist, the way Jakobson is, anyhow to some extent) is not decisive, regarded pragmatically; it is the quality of the arguing compared to the field in question which decides the concrete usability.

This applies to the concrete statements, but obviously not automatically to the pertinence of self-understanding. Having in mind the most recent discussions and movements within literary theory we might state that the current tendencies, both in works of art (in one way) and in a series of theories (in another), to point out exactly the staged infinity as basic precondition must be acknowledged as precisely a *feature of the field* – just as we have also here examined and demonstrated the gradual historical emergence and retrospective unfolding of this point by means of the two development sections. In *that* sense this "acknowledgment" is inevitable, "true", and in that sense it is only natural to project it backwards into the literature of the past as a whole, indeed to a certain extent it is even unavoidable. Consider, however, a conceptualization of the condition of infinity in a 'genuinely' essentialist way, i.e. with the status of an achieved acknowledgment of a quality of the world "out there" (as differing from: of the acknowledgment of the world), which in turn subsequently transposes this endless relativity into any register of meaning, with the status of being preconditional to any activity of interpretation, thus positioning this feature *outside* the object in which it operates, and without making visible the character as *movement* precisely of this transposition; even though a conceptualization like that, as a plain statement about singular works, may be pertinent to the stage of development of the field (theoretically coincidental, but historically uncoincidental), then a conceptualization like that in capacity of structure and consequently statement, would in principle be completely congruent with any traditional, essentialist notion about the specific properties of art as an intrinsic quality of the object itself.

The notion that textual analysis necessarily should discuss meaning compared to the semiotic *field*, and consequently, that everything is not identical with anything, is probably what Richard Rorty would call "weak textualism"[6] and thus contemptuously accuse of being 'just one more victim of realism, of the "metaphysics of presence"'.[7] To Rorty, the great thing at this time – unless you are just a half-hearted pragmatist – is to be a strong misreader, with the expression of Bloom; one who is "...in it for what he can get out of it, not for the satisfaction of getting something right" (ibid.).

Rorty's distinction appears far too crude. Strong textualism more or less corresponds to what we have implicitly argued against in the above discussion of infinity, whereas Rorty's version of weak textualism rather corresponds to traditional conceptions of the New Criticism type, which becomes clear not least from the epistemological ambitions, which he ascribes to it as a general feature. Or put in

---

[6] Rorty, 1982, especially the essay "Nineteenth-Century Idealism and Twentieth-Century Textualism" (pp. 139-159). In his later books (Rorty, 1989, Rorty, 1990) Rorty distinguishes between the "strong textualism" praised here (for instance Bloom), and deconstructive criticism in general towards which he, in the meantime, becomes strongly critical. More about this below.

[7] Op.cit., p. 152.

another way: there does not seem to be sufficient support for ascribing to any (not exclusively *making*) textualism the besetting sins of traditional literary criticism.

Perhaps, though, the distinction is above all caused by the heat of the discussion. For at the same place Rorty remarks that all (privileged) vocabularies are temporary historical resting-places. In saying so he makes two statements at the same time: one is that these vocabularies *are* there. And the other is that they change. But if they are there, do they not then necessarily form part of the formation of meaning, *that* formation of meaning? And would not then any analysis of any meaning (if an analysis is even of interest, but we still allow ourselves to take that for granted) if occasion should arise, take these metavocabularies respectively into consideration?

This, anyway, is precisely what is implied by our notion about *the field* and the analysis. Weak or strong, textualism or not. The movement of interpretation *is* potentially infinite, but it is neither mysterious nor indefinite: something is to be *found* within which the *making* takes place, insofar as we are dealing with a textual analysis which tries to get hold of the semiotic makings of the text. Semiotic infight, obviously, is possible. But most often it will be impertinent to a textual analysis of that kind.

2. Enunciation. Another important point in relation to textual analysis of this book is the positioning of the *enunciation* of the texts, still strictly speaking their "enounced enunciation", their rhetoric, the construction of their uttering. Or: the specific way in which they, as texts, make themselves accessible to their implicit reader. Their communicative construction.

This dimension is, we shall assert, decisive within any

Reprise

type of communication, including of course especially such which are *mediate* in the sense that they are to 'freeze' their own rhetorical act and thus make visible the redoubling in a conceptual, 'enounced' enunciation on one side and a 'real' enunciation on the other (the former thus becoming a part of the object of the latter). This, consequently, applies to other literary genres and other art forms as well. It is, however, particularly clear in the novel[8]. Especially as regards the novel, however, the repression of the position of enunciation within meaning has – for several 'good' historical reasons – been absolutely predominant. This "referential-emotive fallacy" (which it might be called in the terminology of Jakobson) has been a stable part of the comprehension of especially novels, both within criticism's more or less 'scientific' textual analysis and in the common reader. It has, in other words, held a central position in the field, and consequently it has influenced the whole development of the novel, obviously through the production side as well.

In the development sections above we have argued in favour of the existence of virtual tensions between the horizontal and vertical 'worlds', respectively, of the novel construction; we have exposed the fact that the knowledge of the texts concerning their own rhetoric may vary, and that it may in different ways converge with or diverge from the statement of the emulated world at the image level of the novels. Choosing as a metaphoric matrix a certain figure – a generalized version of the "subject/object-

---

[8] In 5.2 below we shall, as stated, outline implications of the present to the reflection of the abilities of the *novel*. In 5.4 we shall hint at an implementation of this approach to the discussion of another art form.

relation" of subject philosophy – we were able to show how certain 'contradictions' or 'incongruencies' between enunciation and enunciated might even cast off potentials of explanation, which applies both to the development story, scanned by philosophy of history, and to the 'presence-projecting' abolishment of this philosophy of history. It may be worth emphasizing once more: the demonstration of these 'contradictions' or differences between the rhetorical levels of the texts, did not intend to postulate some eternal, constitutional discrepancy between these levels. The discrepancy or the difference is a *possibility*, necessarily always historically 'concrete', i.e. embedded into the historical double-determination of field strength, which we have demonstrated.

As regards both history and history of theory, it is interesting to see how the concern with enunciation, in the pragmatic aspect of reading, in "aesthetics of reception" has increased gradually over the last thirty years. This has happened in parallel and simultaneously within widely different theoretical traditions, at least following two different main tracks, a structuralist-semiotical one (Barthes, Todorov, Genette, Lotman, Eco) and a more hermeneutic-philosophical one (Ingarden, Gadamer, Jauss, Iser) – with certain common points of departure both in American prose theory (from Henry James, over Lubbock and to not least Wayne C. Booth) and in early Russian/Czech structuralism (Jakobson, Mukařovskij).[9] This emergence obviously is no coincidence: it is in accordance with certain alterations within the field of "literature" which – as we have seen –

---

[9] In his essay "*Intentio Lectoris*: The State of the Art" (in Eco, 1991), Eco briefly outlines this "archaeology".

are traceable in the construction of the literary works. It is symptomatic that the theory and the analysis which reflect enunciation, at first were regarded (and to some extent regarded themselves) as a more or less exotic special discipline: *"Rezeptionsästhetik"*, "audience-oriented criticism", "reader-response criticism" &c. These disciplines were introduced, special anthologies were produced, and all in all an "orientation", almost a "camp" within literary criticism/*Literaturwissenschaft* was at issue. This was based on a fundamental distinction: on the one hand there was the (representational) ontology of the literary works, primarily scanned in an epistemological register, what the works *were* (representing) and what they *stated*, a concern related only with the production of texts. This was the real, *hard-core* dealing with literature, then naturally closely related with philosophy, indeed from time to time regarding itself as superior to this, exactly by virtue of literature's claimed epistemological privileges. On the other hand, then, there was the question about the pragmatical discussion of the works, oriented towards their effect, their *"doing"* as a function of their concrete constructions. That which is eventually becoming evident – and that, of which at any rate this book thinks to have contributed to a demonstration – is the fact that *this distinction is (no longer) maintainable.* The issue of the "pragmatics" of the texts, their aesthetics of reception, their communicative construction can*not* be detached either from their ontological status or from their epistemological substance. Or put differently: the "ontology", the mode of being of the texts, and the question about their content of acknowledgment, their cognitivity, are necessarily entangled with their "doing" as texts: their "statements" detached from their "enunciation" is a metaphysical abstract. The texts must therefore be comprehended as possessing both dimensions, which we have attempted to show here, by tentatively calling this the "saying" of the texts. "The aesthetics of reception" is, one might say, dead as a separate discipline. Killed above all by the texts' still more importunate emphasis on exactly *enunciation*: the pragmatical discussion of the texts then no longer is comprehensible as something merely applied to their (epistemologically scanned) ontology. *That* of course alters the understanding of literature as outlined. It also sets the scene for some decisive alterations within the interrelation between literature, philosophy and criticism. We shall return to these in the end of the chapter.

The alteration of the comprehension of literature implies, predictably, another retrograde skid: tradition's separation of ontology and "pragmatics" appears at least immediately to be analytically incomprehensible. And the new analyses of the old works produce new results, which now appear *more truthful* and more *complete*. So they are, but – once again – they are so as related to that position of the field they express. Only in that sense is it possible to talk about the *adequatio intellectus et rei* of analysis. The works, the analyses or the worlds as such are, of course, in themselves neither more nor less true.

3. Partial perspectives. But they *are* there, present. In that connection the question of the opportuneness of partial perspectives within textual analysis might be raised, cf. the critiques, which we made in section one of a series of different textual analytical approaches.

Towards 1960, when the dealing with literature, most clearly on the continent, experienced an increasing need to acknowledge itself as "scientific" (which was expressed, among other things, in a *re-baptizing* of the literature disciplines), this, rather symptomatically, resulted at first in precisely a "balkanization", a splitting up of these "scientific" literary interests of acknowledgment into different relations and realms of the literary work.[10]

A consequence of the above remarks on both field and enunciation is that any textual analysis should be performed within the *notion* about a totality of dimensions and relations. A totality like that does "exist" within the formation of meaning, "objectively" in the same way as the meaning-giving code of the field is objective; and conditionally in the same way as this. Concretely this implies that a series of basic dimensions and relations are to be reflected in their capacity as existing and co-determining the meaning, although in practice their concrete statements will be infinite and inexhaustible. They are, however, indeed concretely isolatable. Within this notion about a wholeness there is, on the other hand, no problem in carrying out partial investigations of certain areas. They just cannot, the way it actually has been the besetting sin, rightly pretend one by one to *exhaust* the purpose of analysis. Or put in another way: any concrete, critical, semiotic analysis must take place consciously regarding and respecting that specific *semiosis*, which, in terms of production and reception as well, gives meaning to the expression in question, here "literature". And this brings us back to the inclusion of the field.

---

[10] See Arne Melberg, 1991.

4. Analysis as a Laboratory. This, in turn, implies – not surprisingly either – that also the point of view of the analysis itself must necessarily be taken into consideration as positioned within the field. For some reason, when finally they aimed at being 'scientific', the humanities have repeatedly searched for ideals and support in conventions and paradigms of *Wissenschaftlichkeit*, which have long ago been given up by advanced thinking within these hard-core sciences (i.e. the natural sciences), which humanities aimed to resemble. Something similar has, unfortunately, been the case with the social sciences. The fact that the position of the analysis is not only always a part of, but also influences the state of the object, and consequently the result of the analysis, since Einstein is not even new within natural sciences. Here it has also been figured out that systems often are, perhaps always will be, "complex", i.e. intrinsically incongruent, un-describable in the categories of "resultants", and 'only' comprehensible by means of figures such as probability, dependence, movement and contiguity. Quite parallel to these observations literary textual analysis must incorporate its own doing, must so to speak institute its own field within the field in such a way that the influence, which the analysis' point of view and movement have upon what is analyzed, and consequently upon the result of the analysis, is made visible as a part of this "result" (which itself very well may *consist of* a movement like that, *qvod erat demonstrandum*). By means of this another position is obviously objectified, whose influence must be made visible, &c., &c. *ad infinito*. These influences are not finally determinable from any privileged point. Therefore, the analysis must hold or constitute a sort of machine for the projection of positions of analysis in a way which makes visible their movements and field-dependencies respectively. In this sense the analysis may advantageously be comprehended and employed as a "laboratory", in which certain experimental set ups (i.e. conventionalized texts) are subjected to certain selected influences (i.e. positions of analysis) of varying doses and types. The different responses of the materials examined, i.e. of the texts, to different stimuli, i.e. positions of analysis, will then give information about their construction of both texts and contexts.

In this strategy of laboratorial test of certain effects of certain stimuli within limited areas, one may, obviously, find elements which recall what art itself in fact does. Thus pertinent strategies of analysis may resemble fruitful creative strategies, or vice versa. There is nothing surprising about this. Often analysis may even profit from pretendingly imitating art thus mimicking aesthetic constructions, or conversely, art may mimic the cognitive interest of acknowledgment of analysis.[11] But the fact that the developments and strategies of analysis may resemble the ones of literature and *vice versa*, does not make textual analysis and literature one and the same thing.

---

[11] Quite immediate examples might be Umberto Eco's well-turned "essay" *On Truth. A Fiction* in Eco, 1991, which is, precisely what the title says it is. Or the other way round Milan Kundera's discussions of the great predecessors, for instance Goethe, in *L'immortalité* (Kundera, 1990). This parallel motion of course is the reason why inclusion into the teaching of literature of *creative writing/animation littéraire* may be exceedingly profitable especially according to *text-analytical* competence. See about this Andersen 1985, and Kyndrup 1986, pp. 191-201.

5. Literature, Philosophy, Literary Criticism/Science. Some people seem to think that the borderlines between literature, philosophy and literary criticism are about to be wiped out. Everything is becoming literature, it is argued, by some with regret, by others in triumph.[12] It is even proclaimed, triumphantly, that literary criticism is the literature of our time.

These statements of course in themselves have performative effects. On a phenomenological view it is indeed not very difficult to find support for a certain movement of convergence between the discoursive genres. At issue here is above all the self-referential objectification, the "verticalization", which as stated is apparent within literature, and which, as we have argued, must necessarily be included into any analysis of literature. But also the "post-metaphysical" philosophy (post-Derrida, who is post-Heidegger who is post-Nietzsche, who is post-the whole German philosophy...), and no matter whether this philosophy is revisiting Kant, Aquinas or Plato: since it is thrown upon regarding meaning as linked with at any rate relatively local language games, which are constantly moving, also philosophy must necessarily again and again point out its own movement, and that even by unceasingly changing its movements in order to prevent the invocation (i.e. of the necessity of that movement) itself to become a sort of new transcendental referent. Is not then in fact philosophy becoming "literature" just as parts of literature always have wanted to become philosophy by claiming certain epistemological privileges?

---

[12] Cf. Rorty, 1991, pp. 85ff.

The existence of outer points of resemblance is incontestable. And it is indeed impossible to prophesy the future of the semiotic landscape. In principle one might imagine these three fields merged into one and the same. That is, however, not very probable. Why should these fields merge into one, when they take care of different tasks within the exchange of meaning, tasks which are precisely dependent on their mutual distinctness? On the face of it, one might point out the fact that in case no distinction of discoursive genres was to be found between literature and literary criticism, that making visible the analytical movement which we above compared to an experimental laboratory, would be impossible. Because in that movement it is precisely the clashes between movements within and inventories of *different* registers, which engender meaning and consequently insight, here into the construction of the analyzed literature.

Let us for a moment regard the distinction between the fields, regard what each of the genres of discourse is able to, does, is. The field of *art* is still above all characterized by its relative autonomy, by its relative independence of that kind of rationality of purposiveness which supremely governs the acts of signification in our world. Furthermore, the field of art is not merely a passive, stable damming of signification and phenomena. Art is above all a process, an ever-changing active transformation, a research, if you like, of what exists and what signifies, but certainly, according to the rules and strengths of its own field. Art is an institut*ing* (... or field*ing*), as Weber has pointed out.[13]

---

[13] Cf. Weber op.cit.

Phenomena are constantly, surprisingly, included in and excluded from art, are situated in it, perhaps partly sort of crabwise, or even in a pre-future sense. This establishes a series of certain movements and clashes within the continuous transformation of what "art" is, and for what it may be utilized.[14]

Obviously the pretension about the creation of universality through transcendence of contingency, which *philosophy* has traditionally regarded as its purpose,[15] is not maintainable if the conceptual realism and any (other) notion about something 'beyond' contingency are to be given up. It has become evident that also philosophy in its capacity of philosophy must include and focus upon the role and meaning of its own enunciation within/to what it says. Besides that, philosophy will above all be needed in the shape of history of ideas (and extensive areas of philosophy have in fact, reasonably, been history of ideas for a long time). History of ideas, among other things, deals with what happens to philosophy as a field throughout history, but also with the way in which ideas and thinking altogether have crossed between the fields, including the field of art, have unfolded inside fields, which have framed thinking and being. This discipline holds an obvious central importance to any discussion of knowledge and is indispensable within any humanist formation. It is not, however, as far as we can see, merging either into what art does and is able to on the one hand, or into what art criticism/art science is able to and does on the other hand.

---

[14] We shall, as noted, return to these, especially in chapt. 5.3 below.

[15] As Rorty words it, for instance in Rorty, 1988, p. 25.

The fact that a history of ideas, when dealing with for example "history", necessarily must work with and within double-determinations similar to the ones of art science, and not least with a necessary including of enunciation, of the uttering itself and its objects, corresponding to those of art sciences, does not in itself indicate any merging or any potential identity. Object, methods and purposes are still different.

Criticism, art science/sciences, it seems, is thus able to become 'itself', able to constitute its own genre of discourse, its own justification. In practice criticism has often slid and taken to imitating either its object, the art, on the one hand, or its partial ideal, philosophy, on the other hand. Both, it seems, are reductions of the proper purpose of criticism. Criticism, or art science, must have as its purpose the studying of art as a field, through the study of the singular works, historically and currently, in the relation between the works' determinateness and unfolding, and the field's frame conditions – obviously including the question of the position and function of that field within the overall formation of meaning. But in the centre should be the question of what art *does*, what art *is able to* (and has been able to and will be able to and would have been able to do). Although, as stated, certain methods, which might resemble the ones of art, may be fruitful in that connection, criticism consequently is clearly *cognitive* in its purpose. And already that makes it different from art, which is also so many other things. Art science establishes a field of knowledge about what art is, is able to and does – and it imparts that knowledge. Among other things it imparts art and art's abilities aiming at an audience's utilization of art. Within the proper premises of art itself – or within quite different premises. Literary criticism's traditional condensing of the cognitive substance of literature, i.e. the fixation of the central general values and attitudes, which literature might be carrying, is historically linked with the position of the teaching of literature as a central subject of formation within the educational system, a position in which its duty was to be the carrier and the intermediator of exactly these values. Of course the literature of a society will always carry society's central values in some sense. But it will also, the way it is framed, be and be able to do many other things. As stated above, it seems as if literature itself, in the present edge of Modernity, is about to change its character, and above all is beginning to point out its own abilities and doings *in capacity of signification*. In any case abilities within the game of signification are given priority above 'neutral' intermediation of general values by literature itself at this moment. And, consequently, necessarily also by criticism, and respectively by the teaching of literature. But, peculiarly: precisely frames and conditions of the formation of signification, in production and in reception, theoretically and practically, as the reality of fiction and the fictionality of reality; all this precisely appears as a flagrant "central discipline of formation" of a time in which already the qualitative extent (but not only that, cf. 5.3) of the exchange of information seems to make desirable, indeed make necessary, an elaboration of above all the "optics" of comprehension.

Philosophy does not resemble literature, and literature does not resemble literary criticism. And literary criticism does not resemble philosophy. Purposes, starting points, traditions are different, and it is difficult to imagine exactly a uniforming attempt which might be able to take a central intrinsic position in any of those fields. At any rate not within the field of dealing with literature. The interest of that must be to sharpen, to give profile to, and to maintain that autonomy, which frames and consequently is a part of making possible this specific "doing" of art – and consequently in turn makes possible the art sciences. There is no reason to confuse the completely unaccidental merging of characteristics of development (the emphasis on enunciation, on the infinity of the staged infinity) of the genres of discourse with a merging of *semiosical* identity and/or of potential tasks in the system of signification.

5.2

The Novel: 'Pragmatics' and Abilities

0. About the novel it has been said that in late twentieth century it is no longer able to do anything except to mock itself as a genre, as a form. If by "novel" is understood precisely that specific construction which particularly during the nineteenth century appeared as the literary archeform corresponding to the unfolded *Moderne* – then of course this assertion may be sufficiently motivated. But just as "the subject" has not disappeared, although the genetic and functional context, which engendered it in its Modern form, has changed, so also "the novel" has continued to develop itself in a changing context, with changing purposes and potentials as well.

1. The Theory of the Novel. At issue here is the European novel and its history within Modernity. And still at issue is perhaps just as much signification, history, art and interpretation, the employing of the novel only being an example. But in all circumstances: a series of novels have been at the centre of the individual analyses and thus of the reflections. And by means of this, certain contributions to a notion about what the novel actually is, does and is able to, have appeared. In this chapter we shall briefly summarize these contributions and put them in perspective.

We shall, conversely, *not* attempt to discuss these contributions in relation to the existing tradition of theory of the novel, nor shall we take an explicit position on this. Elements of traditional novel theory have been mentioned along the road, and obviously we realize that the reflections of this book are, voluntarily or involuntarily, variously indebted to this tradition as a whole. The reason why we shall not elucidate this debt through a systematic dialogue with this tradition is − apart from necessary priorities of space − that the physiognomy of the tradition of the theory of the novel appears thoroughly isomorphous with that of the tradition of the novel; in other words that the very movement within the relationship between history and understanding, which we have made here, and which we have argued is indispensable, if so, at any rate should also be made the basis of a systematic discussion of the theory of the novel. Or, worded more rigidly: no novel-theoretical contributions within the tradition (as known to us) are 'up' to the reflections on the possibilities of the novel here: i.e. only the present state of the novel's development (or folding, bending, if you like) also make possible the under-standing of its historically originally *un*honoured potentials (seen from this point). The theories then are, for good reasons, limited by and to what they know.

An example to support this could be found in the funda-mental schism of the theory of novel which tradition shows in general. On the one side is the (long) tradition, which above all deals with the novel as a *statement* about the world, as a *model world*, as a suggestion for a solution to the world's problems; and which deals with what the novel *is* in that context. On the other side, distinguished from that, are positioned the considerations of the novel's narrative *technique* and 'outer' construction, which especially during this century have become more and more marked. In general this schism, however, has not explicitly by the theories themselves been considered to be a schism. Still, of course, one may today find an idea of this schism more or less clearly inherently included also in the older theories. For instance in Georg Lukács' early work *Die Theorie des Romans*, which in all circumstances is to be mentioned here, because it, despite its peculiarities, is the most pregnantly precise wording of the construction (as regards content) of the archetypal novel of Modernity.

The peculiarities, also in their relations to Lukács' later works, we shall leave here.[16] But his fundamental definition of the novel as working within the relation between contingent world and problematic individual is immediately highly adequate for the material he deals with. One of his pregnant wordings of the intrinsic splitting of the problematic subject-relation in the novel is this:

Die Selbsterkenntnis und damit die Selbstaufhebung der Subjektivität wurde von den ersten Theoretikern des Romans, den Ästhetikern der Frühromantik, Ironie genannt. Sie bedeutet, als formelles Konstituens der Romanform, eine innere Spaltung

---

[16] In his essay on *Die Theorie des Romans* in *Blindness and Insight* (de Man, 1983) Paul de Man has exposed the relation between what is called "pre-Hegelian terminology" and "post-Nietzschean rhetoric" in Lukács – and furthermore exposed the whole notion about temporality which, also later on in Lukács works, 'saves' the organic nature of the novel, but at the same time (in de Man's opinion) ruins the traces of a "genuine hermeneutic" of the novel, which were in fact the consequence of the underlining of *irony* as the figure through which the novel links "homogenous and organic stability" with "heterogeneous and contingent discontinuity".

des normativ dichterischen Subjekts in eine Subjektivität als Innerlichkeit, die fremden Machtkomplexen gegenübersteht und der fremden Welt die Inhalte ihrer Sehnsucht aufzuprägen bestrebt ist, und in eine Subjektivität, die die Abstraktheit und mithin die Beschränktheit der einander fremden Subjekts- und Objektswelten durchschaut, diese in ihren, als Notwendigkeiten und Bedingungen ihrer Existenz begriffenen, Grenzen versteht und durch dieses Durchschauen die Zweiheit der Welt zwar bestehen lässt, aber zugleich in der wechselseitigen Bedingtheit der einander wesensfremden Elemente eine einheitliche Welt erblickt und gestaltet. Diese Einheit ist jedoch eine rein formale; ... [Lukács 1920, 67-68]

It is easy to see that this description of the subject's simultaneously 'inward' splitting and 'outward' ("formal") unity as the *intrinsic* mode (of being) of the novel is in some sense isomorphous with the also immanent "incongruency" which we in a crude metaphorical figure have demonstrated above in the same literature, but here as incorporated in relationships between the reader-relation of enunciation and the world-statement of the enounced (i.e. in fact "within" the formal unity).

The fact that Lukács does not feel called upon, to a higher extent, to reflect this splitting into also the *outer* constructions of the text, their rhetoric as a whole, obviously has good reasons. For instance, at this time he does not *know* the art of the novel of the twentieth century, which is soon to force exactly this question into the agenda, by, as mentioned above, first making the split total through a perfectly consistent fulfilment of the claim for truth; through a presentation of contingency as contingency. And later again: as presented contingency. It is suggestive, however, that here the very notion is inherent in the young Lukács. Later, as may be well-known, he was to interpret its unfolding in the practice of literature in a completely contrary manner.

The alteration of emphasis, the inversion, if you like, during the twentieth century from focusing on ontology and epistemological substance as lying *under* the phenomenological movement, to the concept of being, doing and abilities as lying *in* that movement itself, in the pragmatical unfolding, seems indisputable, as regards the novel and as regards the subject – the former making the latter clear, because the subject needs precisely a construction of movement in order to 'do' itself (and that raised – and raises – certain problems for traditional philosophy). The old approaches and focusings, however, are tenacious. A good example might be that Milan Kundera, who, if any, as a current novelist works precisely and eminently within the *'doing'* of the novel, but whose reflections about the novel (in *L'art du Roman*) are in no way on the same level as his own art of the novel. For example he states (following Hermann Broch) as follows:

> Decouvrir ce que seul un roman peut decouvrir, c'est la seule raison d'être d'un roman. Le roman qui ne découvre pas une portion jusqu'alors inconnue de l'existence est immoral. La connaisance est la seule morale du roman [20]

Here linear projectuality and cognitive substantialism are completely intact. As opposed to, fortunately, Kundera's novels, which do not believe in things like that.

2. The Ability of the Novel. What the novel is able to, and what is made visible by the readings of novels here, is to *contain and expose its own "said-ness"*. This is not a historically produced ability (although it has changed throughout the history of the novel and consequently not least has been made visible): this is an intrinsic ability of the genre (which in turn, obviously is historically 'produced').

The world, the space, which a novel presents or unfolds will necessarily always have to be 'seen' from some point. This of course is actually also in the life lived, indeed the subject's general condition when facing the contingency of the world of phenomena; phenomena are always 'seen' from somewhere, and consequently selection and giving priority are indispensable. Contingency in itself 'signifies' nothing. In the novel these processes of structuration must necessarily be undertaken far more distinctively. For in the novel a fictive world is to be presented linearly, as a course – literally, which should be noticed, because of the sign-after-sign-character of the lingual construction. This implicates a series of transmissions and condensations, especially as regards *temporality*: bridges, paths, capable of functioning between the narrated world's (fictive) time, reading's concrete time and (the notion about) the real world's time. Additionally the fictive world must also in a plain physical sense necessarily be 'regarded' from some point (or some points) in order to even become a "space"; it cannot just be seen from everywhere or from nowhere. In that way different, concrete narrative time/space-constructions, chronotopes,[17] emerge, which in themselves contain

---

[17] With Bakhtin's expression. Bakhtin has discussed the types of chronotope systematically, *inter alia* in continuation of his own typologizations of the folk tales. See for instance Mikhaïl Bakhtine *Esthétique et théorie du roman* (Bakhtine, 1978). As regards the very problem of the transformation of temporality in the narrative there is good reason for once again recalling Paul Ricoeur's interesting

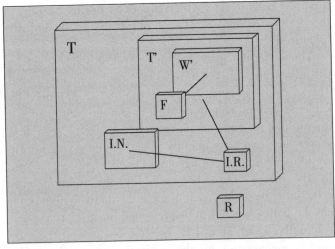

Fig. 1. The basic form of narrative enunciation.

and put into perspective their own mode of construction. Illustrated in the simplest version imaginable (cf. fig. 1): the world of fiction W' in front of itself distinguishes at least one time/space-organizing instance (which may be called a sort of focalizer, which it is not, however, in a strictly narratological sense – called F in the figure). This focalizing instance's relation to W', which then at the primary level unfolds the text 'itself' (T'), now appears as a construction mounted by the implicit narrator (I.N.). *This* constructedness, in turn, appears to the implicit recipient (I.R.) as a diversity within the text, as its *choice* of construction. Facing the real recipient R, then, the 'whole' text T, including T' with W' and F, and I.N. and I.R.

considerations in *Temps et Recit*, see for instance Ricoeur 1988 or Ricoeur 1991.

appears; appears as the carrier of this entire system of vertical distinctions (besides, obviously, and in different ways connected to, whatever system of horizontal differentiations, W' itself may be presented as carrying); appears as a potentiality, above all concretized as the reader's immediately confronting relation to the "model of reception", the *Rezeptionsvorlage*, to the implicit recipient. This sketches out, as already discussed, the "real" reader, in a possible new implicit reader's position, which consequently in turn sketches out another, and so on in an infinite chain, in an always already displaced trace, which may be explicitly marked by the text. This basic system of instances may altogether be complicated almost endlessly, just as we have seen the novels read do so in differing ways. But in no circumstances can they be reduced more than to what is outlined here as their crude basic form.

What does that imply? It implies that the novel, when saying something always simultaneously implies its own 'saying'. Or, that in the novel one never just sees a world, one always sees somebody seeing a world. Or, that the novel always performs the S/O-relation (in a general sense) in several dimensions at one and the same time; the novel is obviously ultimately 'said' by someone (its author), but it creates a space, which may be seen through someone else or through several others; the novel, consequently, gives reality to, *incorporates, performs*, in fact the very dilemma between the great infinite space and the limited perspective which is indeed the basic condition of any individual. On the one hand the subject actually possesses only its own perspective, concrete and restricted through the concreteness of time and space; on the other hand, in order to be able to think, to become a human being, to become something different from contingency within contingency, the subject must exceed this restricted perspective, must become 'more' than itself: must become able to see itself seeing.

This very said "said-ness", this enounced enunciation, uttered uttering, is in principle inherently included in any communicative act of signification. It is manifestly co-signifying within communicative artefacts, i.e. 'frozen' statements which, holding a stable structure of signifiers, are accessible to repeatedly realized acts of communication. This among other things includes any kind of art.[18] But it is especially clear and emphasized in literature, because literature is of verbal language, i.e. operates in that sign system which we usually utilize also for 'general' communication; that in which we "say". And within literature, finally, it is to an eminent degree the novel, the narrating prose, which makes visible, which exposes, which demonstrates this issue, exactly because the novel, according to identity of genre, emulates both course of time and space (as differing from for instance poetry).

What the novel performs, makes clear, points out,

---

[18] But obviously with important differences between for instance performing (e.g. music, theatre) and non-performing (e.g. literature, visual art) art forms. But also another interesting distinction may be made: between *autographic* and *allographic* art forms/expressions. This distinction is due to Nelson Goodman (see for instance Goodman, 1972, pp. 95ff) and aims at discussing whether the work in question in its identity is dependent on the demonstration of its own concrete history of creation, i.e. 'the distinction between original and forgery of it is significant' (as for instance pictorial art), or whether it is exclusively made up of conventional signs and thus in principle not altering its signification from version to version (e.g. literature). We shall touch on these distinctions again below in ch. 5.4.

consequently, is 'general' states of things within and conditions to the exchange. Art, here the novel, thus indeed points beyond art itself, becomes "transaesthetic". But it does not become transaesthetic through the cognition or insight it might explicitly formulate or thematize: it does so *as a form*, actually irrespective of what it is 'about', of the acts it presents. It *acts* in any circumstances.

In order to sum it up: what the novel *does* is to include the reader into a time/space-construction, in which it is possible for her to see her own point of view at the same time as seeing; the reader sees herself seeing. This is the novel's *ability*: to make visible the world's, i.e. the world of significations', character of being said, of being seen, of mounted constructions of points of view – and this ability is due to precisely the fact that it is thrown upon the emphatic emulating of its own 'world' just like that. *Within* this construction, of course, it may then put any "problem" of the world to discussion, i.e. see itself seeing those problems.

This is what the novel *is*: a "said-ness" like that. Or a said world. The being or the substance of the novel cannot be comprehended without including this "said-ness", not any more. This is the point to which the novel has brought the state of things.

3. The Novel. Consequently, there may obviously, curiously enough, be argued in favour of the statement that the novel is still a privileged place for discussing the subject/object-relation. "Subject/object", however, not in terms of the splitting, dejectedly megalomaniac subject facing a frightening contingent world, but in terms of a series of framed games with the infinite potentialities of an evident contingency. And "discussion" in terms of a *doing*: as a concrete performance of some of these potentialities in their character as constructions, fictions, said-nesses.

The novel of today then, does not constitute a parody of itself as a genre, in a pejorative sense: it seems far more obvious to regard the novel's ability of today as a kind of making visible, an elaboration of, a potential, which it has possessed all the time. Should one dare, using cautious inverted commas, to speak about a *'substantial'* potential? This may be especially tempting when considering the sparkling forms of the eighteenth century, considering Fielding, Sterne, Diderot, who then no longer appear to be primitive or dead-ends, and whom a Milan Kundera today emphasizes as the best ones, which is in no way coincidental. One might say, with reference to the young Lukács' register, that the novel seems to have unfolded that irony, which it in its central-bourgeois form contracted into a sort of hermetisizing infight, unfolded it into a kind of exhibitionist clarification, at one and the same time grimacing and jubilant, pointing out also the irony of irony. And so on. Whether *this* is a decline, obviously depends on point of view and orientation. But – in fact quite a number of novels are being written 'about' this problem. And this problem indeed is not just the novel's problem.

5.3

Field of the Aesthetics: Historical Change of Function

1. The Situation. Phenomena and appearances designated "aesthetic", towards the end of twentieth century – and we are still discussing exclusively our own part of the world – constitute an exorbitantly peculiar, inhomogeneous field. First, it seems as if the attitudes, which are active both in production and in reception, are generated by the most different segments of historical genealogy; and thus it also seems as if attitudes, which seemed historically outdated, are now being revived. We do face both classical 'organic' art, renewed efforts of avantgarde, and an unserious, quoting ecclecticist art. Secondly, a series of apparently mutually opposed tendencies are on stage, which still seem to flourish brilliantly at one and the same time. It appears on the one hand as if a thorough *democratization* of the access to the aesthetic in terms of both production and reception, is taking place. But at the same time at certain levels also a sharpening, a distinctly delimiting hermetization goes on, which points out art and the aesthetic as above all a business for a highly specialized *elite*. Furthermore, an overall spreading of the aesthetic is taking place, again both in terms of production and experience, into more and more areas. Different fields and realms 'borrow' from art's status and aura in order to use it within other rationalities of purpose. This applies, for instance, in particular to the field of publicity in general, but in certain cases in such a way as to make the border-line between art and commercials vague. For instance in the video clip. Furthermore, however, this takes place supremely as a sort of *aesthetization* of more and more realms in terms of an increasing conscious and unconscious inclusion of aesthetically related criteria, also when dealing with phenomena and activities which have nothing to do with the traditional area of "art". From gastronomy to jetliners, from politics to sexuality.

These alterations are being comprehended and inter-preted in widely different ways. From some quarters they are regretfully regarded as one enormous making-kitsch, as a decline, as a thorough vulgarisation of all values in general, and of those of art in particular, everything as a consequence of the destruction of art's traditional autonomous status as free of purpose, a destruction engendered by the possibility of positioning art and the aesthetic as servants of anything. From other quarters, however, these alterations are welcomed with different degrees of enthusiasm and with different motivations: some talk about a setting *free*, a liberation of the aesthetic as a mode, and perspectives of development of art hitherto unthought-of are heralded.

Among the major concepts which have been used about this condition of apparently thorough alterations, are *the postmodern*, and about the art corresponding to this, *post-modernism*. The attitudes towards and just the definitions of this "condition" and an art like that, have been enor-mously different, corresponding to the heterogeneity of both the characteristics of development and the attitudes in general. Consequently a series of discussions have flourished about the "postmodern", discussions showing astonishingly strong emotions, and, often concentrating on the very *term*, have to some extent hindered the reflections of the very phenomena which this concept was supposed to label.

Because of that we shall not discuss the term here, but merely in these discussions about the postmodern point out a peculiarity which may have certain symptomatical implications. At issue is the fact that a series of the thinkers, who in different ways have been deeply involved in the description and the analysis of this "postmodern condition", later on have declared that they *regret* ever having utilized this concept, this term. This applies to both a Jean-François Lyotard and a Richard Rorty,[1] but also further 'below' in the theoretical ranks this is a common attitude. Now why this distaste for a major concept of this type? Well, the malaise may of course be immediately motivated by for instance an unfruitful debate, or merely by the fact that the concept has become overloaded, has collected too much signification, too many aggressions, to much (negative) fashionability into itself. But the distaste might also have some more substantial grounds; it might be connected with the feeling of something instantaneously far too overwhelmingly evident about the concept and its characterization of its time. *That*, in turn, might be due to the fact (and consequently suggest) that the alterations which the concept attempts to label *are* precisely changes of rather supreme codes and not just 'common' changes of phenomena within relatively stable codings. Precisely skids

---

[1] Lyotard in several interviews, Rorty for instance in 1991;1.

of supreme codes evidently have so instantaneously performative consequences that the very skid will become almost invisible even before it is 'over': now in fact it constitutes another framing of phenomena, which in turn consequently *are* just what they are now. And furthermore are so, as we have seen it through the readings of novels in this book, also in a certain sense in historical reverse. The characterizing of this totality by means of a major concept may consequently very well be experienced as pragmatically importunate and theoretically stupid: and that perhaps makes it incomprehensible that you did it yourself yesterday.

Whether, however, this distaste for a labelling concept of that type should in fact indicate a certain character of the processes of change, must obviously remain an assumption, a guess, a possibility. The fact *that* clear, violent changes are in play at the level of phenomena is on the other hand completely indubitable.

2. The Aesthetic. Before discussing these alterations we shall, however, make a little detour across the construction itself. Once again: we do comprehend "the aesthetic" as a "field", a "framing" within the formation of signification, *objectively* existing and *conditional* in the sense that it is not based on certain, intrinsic properties of objects or experiences, but is exclusively based on engendered conventions which in themselves have implicated this 'specificity', which is then (have become) a characteristic of the aesthetic.

The notion that the construction looks like that, and that for instance constitutivist definitions of the aesthetic are completely untenable (but evidently in the capacity of positions *within* the aesthetic field indeed form a part of it) we are unable to prove. To try to make it obvious has been one of the main purposes of this book. Especially the movements in twentieth century within and around art appear as one long making-this-construction-probable. This applies to the constant checking out of the borderlines, where non-art has been turned into art just by means of demonstrative movings into the institutional frames of the convention. This applies to the sheer nothing of anti-art, for instance in the shape of serious happenings in which audience's proper reactions were supposed to constitute "art". It applies to the double-ironical points which have appeared from the fact that objects and projects, provocative to the institution at first, actually were assimilated *as* sheer provocations, only to become at the next turn, within their own self-acknowledgment (i.e. their predecessors'), "art" in precisely that sense against which they initially revolted.

We shall not continue to repeat these stories. We shall notice, however, that if "the aesthetic" has this character of being an objective and conditional "field" within the formation of meaning, then it possesses a peculiar, compound set of properties. First, as a consequence of the conditionality it is self-carrying and self-depending, because in a certain sense always obliged to 'live on' its own performativity (including for instance – and probably rooted from those, one might think – the inexterminable phantasms about precisely the *non-conditionality* of art). The field, consequently, is *fragile*. Secondly, however, the field shows off a completely unique, strong and continued history, theoretically and practically, which hitherto always has been plastically rearrangeable so as to appear an unshakeable support of the momentous manifestations of tradition, positively or negatively. Thus the field is also *solid*. Finally, it is not difficult to realize that the field factually is changing, has changed, and probably will change. In fact, at the level of details, in rather fast cadences as shown already by the art history of the twentieth century. So the field, thirdly, is *movable*.

3. The Change. Fragile, solid, movable. Which change is concretely taking place?

With all the usual proviso as regards the ambiguity of the movements and the simplification of this generalization: what is taking place is a transformation of the aesthetic field from being and acting primarily as something *ontologically specific* into being and acting as something *optically specific*. That is, from having been something which appeared as properties of objects, consequently making them something special, into being something which seems to be a property of points of view, of comprehensions. Comprehensions *of* objects and phenomena, of course: the aesthetic is a factor of a concrete (perhaps institutionalized) exchange within which the optics just no longer, in the capacity of quality of species, appear to be submitted the determinateness of the object. This may also be described as a transformation of the *comprehension* of "the field" from being defined and delimited essentialistically into being precisely conventional, that is conditional. In our register this is a transformation *within* the objective conditionality towards a recognition of itself as that. The movement is thus able to substantiate its own self-acknowledgment, *inter alia* the way it is expressed here, cf. also the discussed (ch. 5.1 above) general "shift" into reader-response-oriented criticism. But in principle we are of course here already deeply involved in self-grounding inferences. So let us return to the description of phenomena, to the change.

This change may be expressed by means of several different metaphorical registers. As regards the double-conceptualization "instituted/instituting"[2] it may be comprehended as a displacement *from* "instituted", that is the authorized, the domesticated, *into* "instituting", that is towards a greater priority of the movement of assimilation itself, i.e. from a being-aesthetic to a making-aesthetic. Also in an overall sense we are dealing with a movement from "being" to "making" and "doing", from ontology of identity to ontology of pragmaticality ('pragmatics') when defining the aesthetic and thus art. This movement implies that the zone of differentiation has moved, and this makes the whole problematics of delimitation change its character. Topologically comprehended and horizontally regarded a de-differentiation is taking place: the phenomena within contingency can no longer 'objectively', i.e. qua assumed intrinsic properties, be classified as for example "art". This de-differentiation in some sense makes contingency more evidently contingent, as every classification is more and more clearly linked to above all the classifying instance. "Being" becomes, so to speak, infinitely 'flat', infinitely alike, or illimitably unlike, which is the same thing. Simultaneously with this topographical de-differentiation a new *differentiation* however takes place within the optical, the vertical dimension. Distance, position, point of view, "doing", use, usefulness: "the seen-ness" distinguishes itself in the capacity of being the zone of differentiation,

---

[2] Cf. Sam Weber 1987, see also above, ch. 5.1.

and in the place of the topographical variability a series of possibilities of varying perspectives and depth of focus *in the relation to* the contingent landscape emerge. To remain with this imagery: from having been related to one project of mapping 'down there' in the landscape, exploring this, the encircling of the aesthetic becomes more and more a question of outlining and performing *different modes* of mapping, different grids, different formations of perspectives, seen-nesses and said-nesses.

On the face of it, all this implies something which may look like a kind of de-stabilization of the field. First of all it sends a certain type of ripple historically *backwards* through the aesthetic field. None of the existing, carefully elaborated maps will any longer have the same status. They appear to become maps of maps; this recontextualization turns them, as we have tried to demonstrate, paradoxically but inevitably into becoming kinds of loop, made up by and making up their own genealogy simultaneously. Secondly this transformation implies an open *intractability* as regards classification, an uncontrollable wobble or multi-perspectivity within perception. That is if "the aesthetic" may be potentially present anywhere, may be implied anywhere, is able to change position to different times and contexts as a property of the same phenomena; does then in fact the field *exist* any longer? Are we not, then, dealing exclusively with temporary interpretative communities' arbitrary subjective projections which are at the most the agony of the final and total de-differentiation, the agony of the fact that each and every sign becomes objectively without any difference and consequently indifferent, which is the inevitable, final consequence of (the fantasm of) identity-ontological de-differentiation?

4. Some Consequences. Perhaps. This is difficult to say, and for good reasons we are unable to predict what is going to happen. But on the face of, it appears as a misinterpretation to claim that what is taking place points in that direction. There *are* however, as stated, certain apparently immediately contradictory tendencies within the field. But it seems as if a change of the comprehension of the aesthetic, such as the one outlined here, may explain some of these tendencies, also as regards their mutual contradiction.

Among the distinctive traits is an increased interest of art to be immediately attractive, fascinating, to keep the recipient involved. Or even to be *entertaining*. This has manifested itself as a *'return'*, in the novel to narration, in pictures to the figurative, in music to classical forms and figures, in architecture to ornament, &c. The emphatic non-entertaining-ness of high modernism and avantgarde seems to be a closed chapter. This tendency may obviously be explained as a *necessity* caused by the still more 'equal' situation of competition with other offers, in which art is placed, as it is no longer as a field just like that *a priori* privileged as valuable. But also the way in which much art now shamelessly and explicitly puts itself out to please, plays at its own elements of fascination, is probably altogether only possible *within* art, because the pragmatic, the doing, has been moved into the centre: not only as an accepted, but as a decisive axis of unfolding, given high priority. In the capacity of a point of convergence as regards interest, and also as regards theme.

Now, however, could not this shameless hunting for effect, for audience, together with this return to outdated, perhaps partly worn-out forms – could this not be one enormous making kitsch out of art, one huge platitudinizing, a reduction of art to commercials, to obligation-free surface aesthetics? And consequently the destruction of a field which, if any, has been able to preserve itself as a protected area of *substantiality*, *Wesenlichkeit*, in the all-embracing process of rationalisation of Modern society?

One may obviously think so. From a traditional Modern point of view it is in fact hardly possible to think anything else; from that point any recycling, any transformation of interest of acknowledgment into interest of effect must necessarily appear as kitsch in a pejorative sense. But perhaps the issue is that "kitsch" is about to change its value, or at any rate about to differentiate itself into several different forms. In all circumstances this is a rather near consequence of the verticalization's (self)objectifying of enunciation (and obviously not only within literature) that *several model readers* are installed beneath each other.[3] But this potentially makes the kitsch change its character into becoming itself a sign within the work's play with the model recipient; a sign which may itself be 'flat' and still form part of a subtle and complex game.

The formation of a 'column' of model recipients like that may consequently serve as a possible explanation of the apparent contradiction between clear tendencies towards *democratization*, a broadening out, a popularization, both in

---

[3] In his essay *Intentio Lectoris: The State of the Art* Eco (Eco, 1991) touches on something similar; among other things he states that: "... I am in fact implying that many texts aim at producing *two* Model Readers, a first level, or a naive one, supposed to understand semantically what the text says, and a second level, or critical one, supposed to appreciate the way in which the text says so" (p.55).

production and reception of aesthetic expressions on the one hand – and the not less clear tendencies towards an exclusivization, an *elitarization* appearing on the other hand.

These two tendencies *may* of course be oriented in opposite directions, may turn out each to represent their own interest, 'fighting' against each other. But actually they may also be comprehended as consequences, both of them, and simultaneously, of a transformation of the aesthetic as discussed here. This does not prevent the fact that we are dealing with two *different* effects. But thus an understanding of these effects as being not mutually at variance is established.[4]

Democratization appears as a consistent consequence at several levels. First of all a fulfilment of the call for fasci-nation by the competitive situation of competition results in a greater audience. But the moving of, if you like, the subtlety or the complexity, to the vertical level, furthermore makes it possible to count on "accessibility" in several dif-ferent stages, perhaps even as a precalculated differentia-tion.[5] Conversely the emphasis on the "optical" character of the aesthetic has the consequence that also the monopoly of production is modified concurrently with the thus neces-sary dissolution of Romanticism's role of the artist. If the artist becomes an *entrepreneur*, or playmaker, rather than an Inspired Creator of Substance, it is obvious that the

---

[4] Which of course turns the comprehensions of "democracy/popularity" and "elite" respectively into some specific ones, cf. below.

[5] Which is in fact very clearly traceable in practice, so this point of view is not purely speculative (either). One might point out the readings of the novels above – but also certain developments within recent film.

access to "create by oneself", to also invent rules of the game, is subjectively experienced as being extended.[6]

Also the elitarization, the sharpening of the field of aesthetics, productively and receptively, however, appears consistent. If "the aesthetic" is acknowledged to be an optical factor, then ambitious art has to be extraordinarily uncompromising to operate and to set through a different-ness which is now both infinitely limited (that is, as to a certain perspective) and infinitely illimited (as it is no longer relatable to a certain topos, to certain properties of species). Consequently specific optics, capable of creating insight into the insight of this opticity, are to be constructed, and already technically the establishing of a vertical hierarchy of model recipients like that makes heavy demands on art.

Consequently we do face well-founded tendencies towards both sharpening, self-willed-ness, exclusivization – and a broadening out, accessibilization, democratization. This would in fact be odd or even contradictory in a 'topographical' comprehension of the aesthetic *realm*. But in a comprehension of the aesthetic as predominantly optical, as linked with the point of view on objects, to the relation between objects and the regarding of them, these two tendencies in fact may at one and the same time be pertinent; obviously as a differentiation of the field. But also this differentiation is vertical. That is, not just constituting forces which neither abolish nor even fight each other 'within' the same level.

---

[6] Which is by no means the same as saying that everything that comes out of this is equally "good". But that is another story.

5. Liberation? It is only a few of the tendencies within the possible process of verticalization which we have been able to touch on here. A series of further semiotic analyses are ahead, for example of the conglomerations of the aesthetic with other realms, and altogether of the development of the institutional form or of partial fields of our system of signification. As regards the political as a field, and culture in a broader sense, several problems are immediately urgent, and comparative examinations applying to the transformation of the aesthetic are immediately at hand. This, however, has to be left open here.

In all circumstances, the tendency towards a verticalization, if it is tenable as an alteration of the framing, implies that the field, in quite a different way than ever before, becomes unsurveyable, labile, unpredictable. If the aesthetic may be included, perhaps and perhaps not, as an element of and into any type of act of signification, the discourses may become exceedingly difficult to control, i.e. to maintain as segregated and serious in their respective traces, by means of "discursive police forces". This holds some perspectives which, if added to the claimed tendency of democratization, might be very far-reaching.

It is still too soon to say anything especially well-documented about these items. Or it may perhaps already be too late. Some apparently regard the 'detachment' of the signs and the verticalization of the ascription of meaning as a kind of *liberation* from the tyranny of Modernity, and consequently as a sort of end point of history, in which – and on and after which – the number of possibilities have all of a sudden become *legion*. A notion like that is obviously sheer nonsense. The fact that the sign/reference-linkings, and the architecture of the fields of signification and other densities seem to be taking on another form which, compared to the preceding constructions, may metaphorically be described as 'more free', does not in itself imply that the present situation should herald quite different deep-structures of the formation of signification. And *that one* at any rate is of course neither more nor less "free": the processes of alteration, guesses and temporarities, sketched out here, aim to characterize *states of things in the field: as the field seems to see itself.* This or these states of things are constructions themselves, just like the ones they replace, and just like the ones they will be replaced by themselves. It is impossible to state anything qualified about whether the transformation towards the optical, which today is perceptible (and thus provable) both within art and within the understanding of art, whether this state of things or this stipulated construction constitutes the beginning of perhaps a stable state of things of this (unstable) type. Or whether we are dealing with a short, transitory bridge, a (new)baroque passage, between more stable, also as regards mode of being, systems of signification, especially regarding the aesthetic. So far, the most supreme thing to say for sure about the field is still that through all its turbulence it yet, in a peculiar way, appears as stable. And yet fragile. And evidently changeable. Which means: unchangeably in change. A change of which any act of signification within the field forms a part. Including this one.

5.4
Film:
Another Kind of Reprise

Bernardo Bertolucci: *La Tragedia di un Uomo Ridicolo*

1. Why Film? According to a common notion film as art form is to the twentieth century what the novel was to the nineteenth. In other words it is above all the film which in our time is capable of *gestalting* the individual in the world, using bold epic brush strokes. No doubt, this point of view is at certain levels adequate; many facts even suggest that the film within its short history in fact does repeat the developmental stages of the novel in a condensed form. It would lead us too far to take a closer look at the history of film here; at any rate today's film unfolds a series of different forms, also including a number of broadly epical ones, which also sociologically-quantitatively constitute a major part of what might be called the consumption of fiction.

It is a common, 'popular' attitude of reception (and against the background of this it is not surprising) that film is a specifically un-conditional art form: it is supposed to represent *factually* that or those spaces 'of' which it clearly enough shows pictures. Consequently, it is supposed to be directly perceivable, so to speak across cultural, social and historical code-dependencies. What is more surprising, however, is the fact that these kinds of notion, which thus deny the film any allographic[1] character, placing it almost beyond the autographic (as immediate, un-elaborated) do actually thrive in contexts of a more theoretical outlook as well.

In all circumstances these notions are very close to what have explicitly or implicitly been common ideas as regards narrating literature – and whose untenability it has been one of the main purposes of this book to demonstrate.

This is one good reason for taking up film in an excursus like this: in the outline of an analysis of this film we shall demonstrate that also film as an art form is, in its signification, linked with its – objective and conditional – semiotic conventionality; that concretely, as regards meaning, it is dependent on its *enunciation*, on its narrative construction, on its 'language'. And in that connection we shall suggest that also film is a "product" of history in at least two different ways.

But besides that we have chosen precisely *this* film, because both as regards theme and construction, it is able to say something about this book, which we want it to say. This excursus, consequently, also forms part of a self-exposure of our own uttering, and in that capacity it forms part of a quite different *reprise*, along a quite different track, which among other things work on finishing this long-winded speech.

2. Reconstruction. *La Tragedia di un Uomo Ridicolo* was released in 1981, and qua its advanced narrative construction it is more closely related with earlier Bertolucci films like *Il Conformista* (1970) than with broad

---

[1] Cf. Nelson Goodman's distinctions; see above in ch. 5.2.

story-narrating ones such as the megawork *1900* (1976). This film is extremely difficult to summarize, because opacity – as shall appear – is its basic thematic and constructional principle. Since the film may be not immediately physically accessible to everybody, we shall, however, try a crude reconstruction as the background of our analysis.

The space of the film is Italy of the 1970s, the vicinity of Parma. The protagonist of the film, *Primo*, is a rich, self-made owner of a big farming industry called the dairy. At the beginning of the film he is celebrating his birthday, and among other things he receives a pair of binoculars as a present from his son, Giovanni. Through these binoculars he now sees his son being kidnapped by unknown men. Later on, at the scene of the crime, we meet both the police, Primo's wife, Barbara, and the son's – alleged – girlfriend, Laura. She is a student, but works at the dairy. The parents never knew she was their son's girlfriend. Now Primo and Barbara (on Barbara's insistent initiative) count up all their valuables in order to procure a ransom, if demanded. Primo gives notice to the workers that he will have to sell the company, which will then be closed down. Laura visits their home, and in connection with her visit a letter is found demanding a ransom of two billion. She behaves mysteriously towards Primo, as if she wants him to understand something (he thinks). Primo is now contacted by another worker/student, Adelfo, who says that Laura sent him. He suggests that he knows something about the kidnapping, but he does not really want to reveal what it is. However, he makes an appointment to meet Primo again. In the meantime another letter is received, in which the demanded ransom is halved. Adelfo's/Laura's potential connection to the kidnapping is further emphasized. The police urge for information, but are kept out of it. Behind Barbara's back Primo sets out for the meeting with Adelfo, but is received by Laura, who, among other things, in an ambiguous situation tries to seduce him. Then Adelfo arrives and claims that Giovanni is dead, killed by his kidnappers during an attempted escape. Laura beats Adelfo. Then she tells Primo that Giovanni often intended to kidnap him, in order to get money for his friends (i.e. left-wing activists). Primo faints. Laura and Adelfo take him home. Here Barbara is throwing a great party in order to collect money for the ransom. Primo is unable to make himself tell Barbara that Giovanni is dead. He makes love to her. When the next day he is finally close to telling her, the police burst in and search the house. The chief of police clearly emphasises his understanding that the kidnapping is a fraud, a fake. Barbara hinders further investigation by fainting. Primo now makes a plan: in order to save the dairy from ruin he will keep Giovanni's death hidden and pretend to pay the ransom (the ransom is apparently collected 'privately'); the ransom is then supposed to secure the working of the dairy. Laura and Adelfo seemingly countenance the plan. Together Primo and Laura now make a false letter about the deliverance of the ransom. Laura once again attempts to seduce Primo. Barbara and Primo are now supposed to deliver the ransom. Primo tries to swop the suitcases so that he only has to deliver a copy, filled with old newspapers, but Barbara discovers the trick, and threatens him with a pistol into delivering the 'right' suitcase with the money. She thinks he cares more for the money (and the dairy) than for his son. At last then, at the castle-like residence, Barbara is expecting the liberation of Giovanni. The strain is too much for Primo and finally he tells Barbara that their son is dead. But she does not believe him, and calls it only wishful thinking. Laura and Adelfo arrive and propose to Primo that he gives away the dairy to the workers; they do not want to run the risk that he just takes the billion for himself – and for the moment they are the ones who are in possession of the money. Primo considers this irresolutely. But then all of sudden Giovanni is there, free. Primo runs for champagne, and the film is finished.

3. The Narrative Construction. It is, however, most uncertain whether even these outward 'factual' events in fact are 'real' or right in the presented 'world' of the film. It is true that these are the ones actually shown. But the events are narrated with Primo in the capacity of carrier of point of view and this even in a double sense. The whole course of events is *narrated* by Primo from a position placed after the finishing of the action, but not further fixed (Pe at fig. 1). It may all be just a dream. The narrating voice cuts in on selected occasions, giving comments, asking questions, showing doubt. But this explicit instance of narrator is only there as sound (coming from an undefined future) across the pictures. These, then, pretend to picture what is told. But also here Primo seems to be the focalizer, i.e. we see what he is able to see, quantitatively and qualitatively, sequence by sequence (P1-Pn) – not through subjective camera, but (mostly, cf. below) in a so-called standard film language (cuts on movements, following directions of the gazes &c.). The construction, consequently, is doubly "personal". What is intermediated is what Primo, from a much later, unidentified time (or from quite another world) is able to and/or wants to remember of how he saw certain

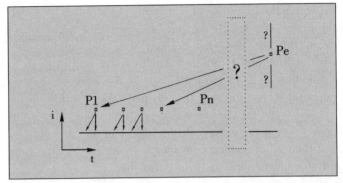

Fig. 1. Primo in the capacity of explicit narrator (Pe) regards himself experiencing the singular sequences (P1 ... Pn). Within these sequences he is (perhaps) in his own self-acknowledgment surveying, i.e. is 'above' the events. This he also pretends to be in the explicit perspective of narration. But in fact it is impossible to decide whether he 'objectively' is above or below his level of the singular episodes. Furthermore, the indefinite distance as to time and space (the punctuated bloc at the figure) makes it impossible to objectify Pe compared to the events.

events (or how he *thinks* that something which he was unable to see has taken place). To make this uncertainty complete Primo is both in the capacity of focalizer and in the capacity of narrator explicitly unreliable. Unreliable, firstly, in an immediate traditional sense; he leaves the stage with a final remark directly to the audience saying, "The truth you must find out yourselves – I prefer not to know it". By this he throws backwards through the whole report an explicit intention of *not* having aimed at truth: how then should one's attitude be towards what he claims to be true? But the unreliability is, secondly, redoubled through Primo's own explicit, but highly ambiguous claiming of his own status as "ridiculous" (which he found out when he was five years old, he remarks in the very beginning). *Is* he ridiculous, and in what sense? A fool, being fooled by the others? Or, on the contrary, one who cunningly fools the others, among other things by pretending to be "ridiculous"? Is it, consequently, the cunning project of the whole narration (of the explicit narrator, i.e. Primo) to *conceal* a certain, i.e. "existing" truth – or does it just dutifully present the obvious facts only without itself abducting these, because it dare not do so? The point of this construction is that these questions are unanswerable. And the several possible answers thus constitute *that* very twilight in which the model recipient is obliged to regard the space of the film, horizontally as well as vertically. And consequently that twilight, which the implicit narrator apparently has chosen to throw upon the space of the film.

4. The Film. This is the plain construction and story of the ridiculous man's tragedy. If you go into details, it is in fact even worse, i.e. the opacity is even greater. This is above all due to opacity concerning the question about to what extent the implicit narrator 'respects' the claimed 'personal' construction. Or asked in another way: what is actually the model recipient supposed to do with the vertical differentiation of the construction? *The pictures* originate (in an intermediated form, cf. below) in the level of the course of events (W' at fig. 2), but also there they are claimed as being seen by Primo. Are the pictures then to be acknowledged as representing Primo's *projections* (both in capacity of Pf, i.e. focalizer, and Pe), i.e. as qua their choice of cut, being meaning-bearing representatives of Primo's (assumed twisted) comprehension? Or are the pictures themselves to be understood as "real" in the sense

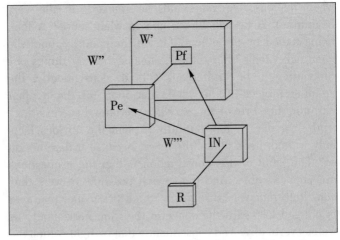

Fig. 2. An outline of the instances in the utterance of the film.

that they, truly, do accompany Primo's (Pe's) report, but still in the scenario of the implicit narrator are supposed to act as a contrasting *correction* of Primo's verbal interpretations? This question is impossible to decide, because the construction supports both interpretations. On the one hand there are scenes, in which the narrator, Pe, overtly admits "imagining" events which he has not witnessed at all (i.e. Laura's and Adelfo's discussion as "terrorists"; Primo (Pe) even states that 'they do not think I regard them'). This at any rate *is* a projection. But in other situations the pictures immediately contradict Primo's interpretation of them. An example is the situation when the mad chief of police stumbles; Barbara smiles, and Pe states (i.e. explicitly in retrospect) that at least he had made Barbara laugh (although in fact it was not him). Or when Adelfo tells Laura and Primo about Giovanni's death, in such a way as to make it possible for himself, in answering Laura's questioning response, to shake his head negatively at her (and the camera), but invisible to Primo who stands behind a partition wall. Is this Primo's imagination or reality's correction? That question remains open. The result, of course, is in all circumstances a sharpening of the reader's vertical attention – but in several different, simultaneous directions of decoding.

Furthermore, the implicit narrator manifests itself also directly and emphatically. The camera, in capacity of camera, is made demonstratively clear in several places. When Adelfo 'pursues' Primo in the loudspeaker van the loudspeakers are utilized as 'eyes' from a position on top of the van, consequently 'seeing' Primo (instead of the opposite which would be more natural considering that Primo is the focalizer); correspondingly, while biking Primo is later on pursued, in snowfall, by a camera *inside* a car – with windscreen wipers in function; when, towards the end, Primo closes the door to the dance hall, the sound is deadened (as if the camera actually was 'placed' outside, which in fact it is); on a certain occasion Barbara – emphasized – plays the leitmotif of the background music as incidental music on the piano; and finally we have the ending itself where Primo is encircled and frozen as the only thing left of the total picture, while he gives his statement about non-truth. He is pointed out.

It might be said then that Primo's double point of view is redoubled once more through the implicit narrator's demonstrative markings.[2] The result is a complete blocking

---

[2] Which, strictly speaking, tendentially makes this instance explicit and consequently makes room for another instance 'behind' these manifestations, and governing them. As this differentiation has no

of the possibility of any stable decoding at the level of theme. What did *factually* happen in W'? Did Giovanni kidnap himself, helped by his comrades, did he think better of it, and consequently give up, when the dairy seemed to be closed down – but did he then undeservedly get an extra chance through Primo's great (and also ridiculous) plan, to get both the billion and the control? Or was he in fact kidnapped, and did Laura and Adelfo indeed spend – as Primo (ridiculously) asserts in the end – the billion to have him liberated? Or is it in fact Barbara, the mother (playing a mysterious role, at one and the same time an action-paralyzed victim and a cool organizer all the way through) who stages it all behind (the ridiculous) Primo's back? Is Primo's own intervention and 'plan' a cause of success or failure? Are his worries about the dairy, i.e. the world and the work, ridiculous or incomprehensible, or both? Does he in fact love the dairy more than he loves his son, does he even hate his son? Has the ridiculous Primo perhaps staged the whole thing, including the kidnapping, in order to save the dairy? Or are they all conspiring against Primo (as suggested by the final picture of the ridiculously embarrassed Primo facing the others, standing in one row – but whose picture is that?), not only in this present intrigue, but altogether? The world versus the ridiculous Primo? Primo, who is ridiculous and tragic because he does not know? Just as the film because of that, does not know? Just as the recipient because of that, does not know? Is *this* Primo's dream?

All these abductions (and several others) may find

---

decisive consequences to the construction in this connection, we shall leave it here.

reasonable support in the film. And at this point we are even only dealing with the condition of W'. Furthermore we have the question of the W" (the implicit narrator's relation to Pe's projecting relation to his own story) and W'" (the model recipient's relation to the implicit narrator's staging of this horizontally and vertically undecidable construction). And so on. The worlds metastasize themselves outwards and upwards; there is always someone else in the space, regarding the first one, i.e. regarding himself regarding; a ridiculous man who does not know whether he does not *want* to know or is not *able* to know the truth. A man forced to take into consideration all these possibilities, each and every one of them unbearable to himself. That is the "tragedy". And a man who qua this still knows everything worth knowing: the fact that he himself creates these truths. That is the "ridiculous" thing.

Consequently, what the film above all draws attention to is the undecidability of its worlds, and, not least, the constructedness of this undecidability. The ridiculous man's tragedy is one of *knowledge*, but it deals with knowledge by repeatedly pointing out its own non-knowledge in a series of (well-calculated) modulations. Exactly there, outside the camera, or in another camera angle may no doubt be found the pieces missing in the puzzle of "truth". *Inside* the point of view the missing things are the ones most pointed out: still, however, there *is* no story outside this cut, outside this enunciation.

But it is apparently possible to *stage* this state of things. "The tragedy of a ridiculous man" is dishearteningly hermetic, because in a many-doubled sense it is limited to the perspective of one person. You cannot get *out*, you cannot get beyond the perspectivelessness of this perspective, beyond its self-confinement. But the tragedy of a ridiculous man is also dishearteningly open because it spreads out a vertiguous number of possibilities of variations of isotopies, abductions, truths – because it is so emphatically *undecidable* at any level, from the most trivial to the most subtle one. Finally it is, what may not yet have been be emphasized appropriately, immediately extremely attractive; with its beautifully elaborated pictures of landscapes, cities, tableaus, and human beings, with its fascinating central figures, especially the ridiculous Primo and the demonic stager Laura, and with Ennio Morricone's leitmotifical, simultaneously melancholic-monumental and cabaret-like lightfooted music in minor key. Stiflingly hermetic, vertiguously illimitable, and both sensuously and identification-psychologically attractive. Completely, in fact both importunately megalomaniac and unreasonably humble, absorbed by its own concrete construction which constantly teasingly points out what is beside, in front of, or behind the present cut of the camera. Which, in its turn, consequently is never let out of sight: the cut's character of being a cut. Wrong, ridiculous, or precise: but still a cut. In film it is impossible to turn around and see what cannot be seen. This is demonstrated by this ridiculous man's present tragedy.

5. And the Film. Film *does* indeed in one sense have a more direct character of representation of or reference to something 'behind' the level of appearance of the film. Any picture actually is a picture *of* something, which consequently must have 'been' there. Must have been set up exactly like that, must have been made projectable into a two-dimensional pictorial level by means of a photographic lens exactly like that. In that sense this 'motif' is singularily present *before* the film's representation of it, and in that sense it is autographically irrevocable (as opposed to for instance the 'world' of the novel, which does not in any sense 'exist' outside the signs' conventional emulation of it).

On the other hand: the motif is always set up for exactly this, and this set up does in fact precalculate the very reduction or superposition of the two-dimensionality. At any rate it is necessarily a *cut*, whose borderlines once and for all are frozen by the position of the camera in question. And although this cut, truly, always refers to what is outside itself (sometimes emphatically, as we see it with the ridiculous man above), then this outside 'is' not there. It does not exist (in the same way as the motif) 'physically' as a part of the world of the film. Although the selectivity of the cut itself also is an autographic feature it seems to a high extent to point beyond itself by also forming part of a conventional code function.

And on such conventional code functions film is finally completely dependent in its *linking* of the single pictures. The course of a film is created by cuts, by leaps, which in themselves are 'unnatural' (in "reality" points of view are always moved continuously). The film's way of creating epic course and emulating certain constructions of focalization, the so-called standard film language cutting on movements, directions of gazes &c., is a completely conventionalized semiotic code system. A code system which in practice has become able to make itself invisible as a 'language' (which is in fact its intention, cf. the nineteenth-century novel), but whose artificiality may easily be proved experimentally for example through commutation tests. Also so-called "faction" (news reports &c.) are grossly cut according to this code, which despite all its artificiality consequently

Film: Another Kind of Reprise

'guarantees' the 'verisimilitude' without having anything especially reality-like about itself. To this should finally, obviously, be added the specific conventions which govern the perception of the two-dimensional picture (the transformation from three- to two-dimensionality and 'back again').[3] What the film sees, in other words, it is seen to be seeing. It sees itself seeing. The film might in fact be claimed to be code-governed to such an overwhelming degree that this allographic character completely superimposes the singular character connected with the proper motif. And at least to a degree which decisively contradicts the naive notions about an immediate, 'natural' perception of film. The medium, the pictures *themselves* do in no way, as demonstrated here, diminish the ambiguity as to levels of "reality", which might be employed.

The language of film, its relations to the "real" both in terms of production and reception, are highly complex. The tragedy of the ridiculous man makes visible, by overtly staging the concealedness through a whole series of functionally connected levels of fiction, *both* the extreme closeness to reality (through what is always not seen) *and* the extraordinary abilities of this form-conventionality to create 'artificial' *Gestaltung* (being perhaps the most 'real' altogether).

6. The Parallels. It is not difficult to see the points of similitude between this basic construction and what we

---

[3] See for instance Nelson Goodman's discussions of the conventionality of perspective through the simple example concerning the fact that vertical lines do not converge the way they 'should', whereas horizontal lines (in the picture) do. For instance Goodman 1969, pp. 10-19. See also Gombrich's polemic (Gombrich, 1972).

have made probable as regards literature. Concretely, of course, we are dealing with differing kinds of semiotic fields respectively, of "institutions" (although they also have a point of convergence as "art"): film has, especially because of the autographic traits mentioned, on the face of it a higher extent of historical links with context and thus a smaller potential of actualisability (consequently an 'old' film of for instance thirty years ago often immediately seems considerably more old-fashioned, 'out-dated', than for instance a novel or a poem of a hundred years ago). To this should be added a series of 'technical' differences of the very dimensions of unfolding: in film *temporality* (like in music) is an immediately structuring device, also for the act of perception; furthermore, it has as its disposal a sound-level for contrapuntal co-production of signification. Film also, in a special way, mixes the performing and the non-performing (just like for instance recordings of music). Obviously we cannot discuss all this in detail here. What however appears indisputable is that the *type* of construction is basically the same: as regards the organization of signification through an objective and conditional formation of code, a field. This field historically, both prospectively and retrospectively, instantaneously regulates the signification also of the singular concrete constellations of signs. Which consequently necessarily are to be comprehended through these their concrete constructednesses, through the way in which they actually through their 'said-ness' manage to say what they say, exactly there.

This we have demonstrated in at least two ways through the analysis of *La Tragedia di un Uomo Ridicolo*. As regards the parallels between the respective constructions of this film and this book, that will do.

Coda

Surprises. Ce que nous étions serrés sur cette plate-forme d'autobus! Et ce que ce garçon pouvait avoir l'air bête et ridicule! Et que fait-il? Ne le voilà-t-il pas qui se met à vouloir se quereller avec un bonhomme qui – prétendait-il! ce damoiseau! – le bousculait! Et ensuite il ne trouve rien de mieux à faire que d'aller vite occuper une place laissée libre! Au lieu de la laisser à une dame!

Deux heures après, devinez qui je rencontre devant le gare Saint-Lazare? Le même godelureau! En train de se faire donner des conseils vestimentaires! Par un camarade!

A ne pas croire!

6

Interpretation, Culture, and Interpretation

1. Interpretation, Cultural Studies, Culture. It is no coincidence that we have consistently utilized the term "analysis" about our approach to literary texts in this book. With this somehow technically and clinically resounding term we have attempted to establish a distance from the (more or less etymologically well-founded) elements of *translation*, which are inherent to the more common designations of the dealing with texts. Above all *interpretation*, but also exegesis, *Auslegung* and similar terms. All of those, so to speak a priori, determine the purpose of dealing with texts, as carrying a given meaning *out of* its system and into another; that is, they aim to find "meaning" as a sort of significative substrate of the project of signification in question.

In these terms and in the praxis which they traditionally have labelled is held a series of more or less unexpressed presuppositions about the whole formation of meaning and the purpose of dealing with it. These are, as stated above, historically well-founded. And in certain contexts they may probably also continue to serve purposes which might be regarded as "sensible", that is, as parts of education &c. On the other hand, we have here argued that regarded against a pretension to meet scientific standards of careful description or revelation of *in casu* the meaning of literary artefacts, these acts of translation are in many cases highly reductive and thus problematic. What a given construction *says*, we have demonstrated, is necessarily also entangled with its significative *'doing'* as a whole, its 'pragmatics', which *inter alia* includes its enounced enunciation and its specific relation also with its own framing, constituted by for instance conventions of discursive genres, here called "fields". An inclusion of *totality* in this sense, consequently, must be a precondition of any adequate "interpretation". Not that "interpretation" is unable to, or perhaps should not actually, with regard to purpose and context, go far beyond what we have here designated "analysis", especially concerning contexts of basis and function. We just claim that in any case this "analysis" must be an indispensable part of the approach, wherever you want to go.

In the previous chapter we tried by means of an example to make plausible that what we have here played through, in the case of the novel, may with similar justification be applied to another art form, the film. The constructions of meaning of all art forms may at a certain level be claimed to be structurally isomorphous, and the demand for interpretation's inclusion of totality, enunciation and field-dependence consequently moves along from one art form to the other. This of course does not imply that the material is "alike" or even equally accessible. Above all "enunciation", and consequently the whole "model reception", the *Rezeptionsvorlage*, has highly varying shapes in each art form respectively, which must thus be comprehended completely specifically. In most art forms the theoretical and analytical description of the dimension of enunciation – as was the case with literature – is furthermore still rather undeveloped. The need for more or less extensive projects of development, however, does not in itself change the justification of these fundamental demands on the interpretation of works of art.

We shall now proceed one step further and assert that similar demands may be and should be made as regards interpretations of *culture* as a whole. On the face of it, this notion is obviously rather opaque, since already the extension and the reach of the conception of culture is so. "Culture" includes phenomena, embracing in the most narrow sense certain produced "artefacts", in the broadest sense a given civilization as a whole. The duplicity or compoundedness of the conception of culture is, by the way, not accidental.[1] "Cultural studies", consequently, include a spectre embracing the most supreme social-anthropological 'megahistorical' discourses, and concrete analyses of produced objects such as art. But even notwithstanding this conceptual diversity we do indeed assert that the considerations of the demands concerning interpretation, which we in this book have made as regards the novel, could also fertilize cultural analysis in a wider sense.

Why is that? Above all because culture is also something "done". No matter whether it takes the shape of

---

[1] The constitution and the history of the conception of culture have been discussed extensively in a series of publications from the "Center for Kulturforskning", Aarhus University, see for instance *Kulturbegrebets Kulturhistorie*, 1988. Especially as regards the intrinsic interrelation between the 'broad' and the 'narrow' conception of culture, see in this Johan Fjord Jensen: *Det dobbelte kulturbegreb – den dobbelte bevidsthed*. Besides that, the compoundedness of the concept may also be substantiated in the semiotic sign/field-model utilized here (each 'pole' corresponding to its proper level).

'frozen' artefacts, or governing rules of exchange or supreme differentiations of discourse, we are dealing with structures "being done", 'pragmatic' structures, or more precisely, structures which *are* "pragmaticalities". And that in turn means: which can be comprehended as communicative structures, i.e. as utterances, which are consequently being uttered, i.e. as utterings. With reference to what we have discussed here, this implies, first, that this utterance's uttering, the enunciation, obviously should be included in cultural analysis. And secondly, that utterance and uttering should be interpreted with specific regard to that kind of intermediating level of the semiotic code, that kind of "relay" of the formation of signification which we have here designated "the field". And finally, thirdly, that any inter-pretation of that kind should reflect and make visible its own position and movement within and in relation to the realm within which it operates.

2. Interpretation, Interpretation, Culture. This may appear far-fetched. "The "being-said" of culture"? "The uttering" of culture? "Enunciation"? In all circumstances: interpretation of culture, too, should acknowledge itself as an independent discourse, which deals with concrete constructions, islands, fields, utterances, their doings and abilities. It is a co-creator of these, and it is a part of their re-creation. But it does not merge with them, and any interpretation is itself, as a singularity and as a part of its own field of discourse, part of the greater meaning-establishing play within and among phenomena, fields, saying and doing.

At any rate, also in cultural analysis the interrelation between what is seen, the sight, and what the sight sees, is extremely complicated, because the instances seem to be infinitely entangled with each other in their incessant, mutual conditionality. This among other things implies that conceptualisations such as "proofs" and "order" in an absolute sense are hardly pertinent. Also here one must operate with categories such as probability, movement, trace and relative order. But once again it may be relevant to refer to the fact that advanced natural sciences operate with completely similar categories in the interrelation between regarding and object. *Order* or *ordering* is not subjective or objective there either: it is relative, context-dependent, and – *existing*,[2] i.e. always already a part of the game, a co-player.

Culture *is* interpretation. Above all "culture" utters and differentiates itself by its way of regarding phenomena and structures, by its mode of perception, its uttering, its instituting.

But interpretation *is* culture as well, is always that very culture, which as a context elicits its horizon, its position, its ability.

Interpretation is, in other words, interpretation. Interpretation interprets itself, terminates into itself. This may on the face of it seem poor, may perhaps look like an anaemic, implosive figure of movement, thrown upon living from what it itself engenders, like some galloping tautologic cannibalism. As we have shown above, this is, however, not the case just like that. Because what interpretation is part of, and what it continuously creates and re-creates, actually *is* there, is present in the capacity of codes and rules, which frame signification, changing and temporarily, but

---

[2] See for instance the discussion of this in Bohm and Peat, 1989, pp. 119-125.

Coda

outside, and/or submitted to cadences of movement other than the concrete interpretation itself.

Interpretation is a movement within something which moves. Truth, Nietzsche writes with a spectacular wording, is a mobile army of metaphors. This may of course be understood, and indeed has widely been understood, to mean that there is no reason to deal with "truth", since it may be declined *ad libitum* anyhow. This statement might, however, also be read more literally, as a kind of exposition of the basic conditions and purposes of interpretation. At first that truth *is*, i.e. exists as convention, as phantasm, as figure. Then that it is *mobile*, changeable, and that as an *army* it may be utilized, and is utilized, for different purposes, and at different levels. And finally that it is constituted by *metaphors*, by exactly rewritings of, or representatives of, something which then is its underlying "truth" – which then in turn (according to the statement itself) is an army of metaphors representing, and so on. The purposes of interpretation, then, would be to decide the positions and activities of these armies, their masters, their purposes and their semiotic-referential status (as "metaphors"), at concretely fixed times, in concretely fixed contexts.

In doing so it is not impossible that these interpretations would be able to sketch out maps of the mutual positions of the armies, of how fields, discourses, phenomena were also linked with or not linked with each other. A map like that, or for instance the claiming here of its possibility, has, however, no other status than that of what is mapped. A map like that would not constitute any privileged position for the establishing of a general order, allowing the transgression of the conditionality of the conditionalities, allowing, finally, the surveillance of the movement of the movements. Such a thing as a "mastery-free communication" (with polemical *hommage* to Habermas), this non-hierarchical, locally organized contingency is unable to offer. But it may be able to reflect the masteries of the respective communications including their incongruencies and 'impossible' clashes, their *différends* (Lyotard), for instance through a movement which in turn is able to make them the object of another, a different communicative movement. Not that this movement then, or ever, by doing so succeeds in escaping its own problem of revocation, its own self-referential inconsistency. It may, however, be able to make it transparent by turning it into an explicit part of its own very movement.

This is all there is. Tautological it is not, since the self-referentiality is not circular and self-confirming, but centrifugal, infinite, self-relativating. The material incessantly changes its position and character, unpredictably but unaccidentally. For the material *is* there, in the same mode and in the same sense as the world is there.

The concrete examination of this book has been directed towards a certain literary genre, the novel, of a certain period of time. The examination has performed a certain movement, which in itself constitutes its central statement. On the basis of the observation of the physiognomy and course of *this* movement we have then, moreover, extrapolated, so to speak induced, a series of more general statements, not just concerning the analysis of other art forms, but also concerning cultural analysis and even certain basic conditions of history, interpretation and exchange of meaning. This movement of generalization may have been pushed too far. But *if* it is appropriate to do what we have done, then at least two factors have contributed to this. First of all the fact that the movement went in the direction it did. It should be an evident consequence of what has been stated here about the formation of meaning that it is impossible in the same way to make inferences from an examination of the general conditions of meaning to the doings and abilities of the novel. Secondly because – to emphasize it one last time – these inferences are made not just on the basis of what has been *said* here. The *dictum* even contradicts itself at certain points. No, the 'result' of this examination is constituted by its proper movement, by its *doing*, at this moment on the verge of becoming something *done*. This movement (and this book) is bound to end where it departed from: in that very position – in yet another position; as a departure.

Select Bibliography

Adorno, Theodor W.: *Ästhetische Theorie*. Hrsg. von Gretel Adorno und Rolf Tiedemann. Frankfurt am M. 1973.

Adorno, Theodor W.: *Noten zur Literatur*. Hrsg. von Rolf Tiedemann. Frankfurt am M. 1981.

Aiken, Susan Hardy: *Isak Dinesen and the Engendering of Narrative*. Chicago 1990.

Andersen, Frits: *Litterær animation*, SILAU/C 10, Aarhus 1985.

Andersen, Frits: Realisme som repetition. In *Passage*, nr. 7, Aarhus 1989.

Andersen, Frits: *Realismens metode*. [unpublished Ph.D. thesis, Aarhus University 1991].

Auerbach, Erich: *Mimesis. Dargestellte Wirklichkeit in der abendländischen Literatur*. Bern 1946.

Austen, Jane: *Pride and Prejudice*. With an Introduction by R.W. Chapman. Lnd. 1964.

Austen, Jane: *Pride and Prejudice*. Ed. with an Introduction by Tony Tanner. Harmondsworth 1985.

Auster, Paul: *The New York Trilogy. City of Glass. Ghosts. The Locked Room*. Lnd. 1988.

Bakhtine, Mikhaïl: *Esthétique et théorie du roman*. Traduit du Russe par Daria Olivier. Préface de Michel Aucouturier. Paris 1978.

Balzac, Honoré de: *Le Père Goriot*. [La Biblioteque précieuse]. Paris 1935.

Barnes, Julian: *Flaubert's Parrot*. Lnd. 1985.

Barthes, Roland: From Work to Text, in Roland Barthes, *Image*

Music Text. Essays selected and translated by Stephen Heath. Lnd. 1977.

Barthes, Roland: *S/Z.* Paris 1970.

Barthes, Roland: *Le plaisir du texte.* Paris 1973.

Barthes, Roland: *Image Music Text.* Essays selected and translated by Stephen Heath. Lnd. 1977.

Baudrillard, Jean: *L'échange symbolique et la mort.* Paris 1976.

Bennett, Tony: Texts in History: the Determinations of Readings and their Texts, in *Post-structuralism and the Question of History,* 1987.

Blixen, Karen: see also Dinesen, Isak

Blixen, Karen: *Syv fantastiske fortællinger.* København 1985.

Blonski, Marshall: Introduction. The Agony of Semiotics: Reassessing the Discipline. In *On Signs,* 1985.

Bohm, David and Peat, F. David: *Science, Order & Creativity.* London 1989.

Bonnet, Jean-Claude: Mille Nuits et une. In *Magazine Littéraire,* no. 204, Paris 1984.

Booth, Wayne C.: *The Rhetoric of Fiction.* Chicago 1961.

Booth, Wayne C.: *Critical Understanding. The Powers and Limits of Pluralism.* Chicago 1979.

Booth, Wayne: Rhetorical Critics Old and New: The Case of Gérard Genette, in *Reconstructing Literature,* 1983.

Borum, Poul: Thinking and Painting. In *Poesien og romanen,* 1989.

Bradbrook, Frank A.: Virginia Woolf: The Theory and Practice of Fiction, in *The Modern Age* (ed. Boris Ford), Harmondsworth 1976.

Bratt Østergaard, Claus: *Romanens tid.* Om køn og civilisation i det 18. og det 19. århundredes fiktion. København 1987.

Brombert, Victor: *The Hidden Reader. Stendhal, Balzac, Hugo, Baudelaire, Flaubert.* Cambridge 1988.

Brooks, Cleanth: *A Shaping Joy. Studies in the Writer's Craft.* Lnd. 1971(a).

Brooks, Cleanth: *The Well Wrought Urn. Studies in the Structure of Poetry.* Lnd. 1971(b).

Bürger, Peter: *Theorie der Avantgarde*. Frankfurt am M. (es 727) 1974.

Bürger, Peter: *Vermittlung – Rezeption – Funktion*. Ästhetische Theorie und Methodologie der Literaturwissenschaft. Frankfurt am M. (stw 288) 1979.

Bürger, Peter: *Zur Kritik der idealistischen Ästhetik*. Frankfurt am M. 1983.

Calvino, Italo: *If on a Winter's Night a Traveller*. Translated from the Italian by William Weaver. Lnd. 1982.

Calvino, Italo: *Hvis en vinternat en rejsende*. Overs. af Lene Waage Petersen. København 1984.

Calvino, Italo: Comment j'ai écrit un de mes livres. Biblioteque Oulipienne No. 20. In *Oulipo* 1987.

Chapman, R.W., 1964, see Jane Austen 1964

Culler, Jonathan: *On Deconstruction*. Theory and Criticism after Structuralism. Lnd. 1983.

Culler, Jonathan: *Framing the Sign*. Criticism and Its Institutions. Oxford 1988.

de Duve, Thierry: *Au nom de l'art. Pour une archéologie de la Modernité*. Paris 1989.

de Man, Paul: Semiology and Rhetoric. In *Textual Strategies*, 1980.

de Man, Paul: *Blindness and Insight*. Essays in the Rhetoric of Contemporary Criticism. 2nd. ed., revised. Introduction by Wlad Godzich. Lnd. 1986.

de Man, Paul: *The Resistance to Theory*. Foreword by Wlad Godzich. Manchester 1986.

Dehs, Jørgen: Subjektet og begyndelsen. En romantisk introduktion til det ikke-absolutte jeg. In *Subjektets status*, 1990.

Deutschsprachige Literatur im Überblick. [Verfasserkoll. Hans-Georg Werner, Werner Feudel ...]. Lpz. 1973.

Diderot, Denis: Éloge de Richardson [opr. in *Journal Etranger*, janvier 1762]. Her fra Diderot, 1968.

Diderot, Denis: *Œuvres esthétiques*. Ed. P. Vernière. Paris 1968.

Diderot, Denis: *Jacques der Fatalist und sein Herr*. Übersetzung und Nachwort von Ernst Sander. Stuttgart 1972(a).

Diderot, Denis: *Jacques le Fataliste et son Maître*. Postface de Jacques Proust. Paris [Livre de Poche 403] 1972(b).

Diderot, Denis: *Fatalisten Jacques og hans herre*. Oversat af Marck Kalckar. Genève [n.d.]

Dinesen, Isak: *Seven Gothic Tales*, N.Y. 1972.

Eco, Umberto: *A Theory of Semiotics*. Bloomington 1976.

Eco, Umberto: *The Role of the Reader*. Explorations in the semiotics of texts. Lnd. 1979.

Eco, Umberto: *Semiotics and the Philosophy of Language*. Lnd. 1984.

Eco, Umberto: *The Limits of Interpretation*. Bloomington 1990.

Erlich, Victor: *Russian Formalism*. History – Doctrine. 3rd. ed. New Haven 1981.

Fish, Stanley: *Is There a Text in This Class?* Cambridge, Mass. 1980.

Fjord Jensen, Johan: Det dobbelte kulturbegreb – den dobbelte bevidsthed, in *Kulturbegrebets kulturhistorie*, 1988.

Flaubert, Gustave: *Correspondance*, vol. I-IX. Paris 1926-33. Supplément vol. I-IV, Paris 1954.

Flaubert, Gustave: *Madame Bovary*. Nouvelle version précédée des scenarios inédits. Textes établis sur les manuscrits de Rouen avec une Introduction et des notes par Jean Pommier et Gabrielle Leley. Paris 1949.

Flaubert, Gustave: *Madame Bovary. Moeurs de Province*. Éd. établie, présentée, commentée et annotée par Béatrice Didier. Préface de Henri de Montherlant. Paris 1983.

Frank, Manfred: *Was ist Neostrukturalismus?* Frankfurt am M. 1984.

Frisch, Max: *Homo Faber. Ein Bericht*. Frankfurt am M. 1977.

Genette, Gérard: *Figures III*. Paris 1972.

Genette, Gérard: *Nouveau Discours du Récit*. Paris 1983.

Genette, Gérard: *Fiction et diction*. Paris 1991.

Goethe, Johann Wolfgang: *Die Leiden des jungen Werthers*. Mit einem Nachwort von Ernst Beutler. Stuttgart [RUB 67 [2]] 1984.

Goethe, Johann Wolfgang: *Den unge Werthers lidelser*. Oversættelse og efterskrift af Alex Garff. [Translated from the orig. ed., Lpz. 1774]. København [n.d.]

Goldmann, Lucien: [Über die "Theorie des Romans"], in *Lehrstück Lukács*, 1974.

Gombrich, E.H.: The "What" and the "How": Perspective Representation and the Phenomenal World. In *Logic & Art*. Essays in Honor of Nelson Goodman. Eds. Richard Rudner and Israel Scheffler. New York 1972.

Goodman, Nelson: *Languages of Art. An Approach to a Theory of Symbols*. London 1969.

Goodman, Nelson: *Problems and Projects*. Indianapolis 1972.

Goodman, Nelson and Elgin, Catherine Z.: *Reconceptions in Philosophy and Other Arts and Sciences*. Lnd. 1988.

Greimas, A.J.: The Love-Life of the Hippopotamus: A Seminar with A.J. Greimas. In *On Signs*, 1985.

Gunder Hansen, Nils: Vesterlandets misère som fabel – introduktion til Baudrillard I-II, in *Semiotik* 3, 1981 [and] 4, 1982, København 1981-82.

Habermas, Jürgen: *Borgerlig offentlighet – dens framvekst og forfall*. Henimot en teori om det borgerlige samfunn. København 1976 [transl. after the German 5th. ed, 1968].

Haken, H.: Operational Approaches to Complex Systems, in *Complex Systems – Operational Approaches in Neurobiology, Physics and Computers*. Ed. H. Haken. Berlin 1985.

Handbuch der Literaturwissenschaft, Hrsg. Oskar Walzel. Die Romanischen Literaturen von der Renaissance bis zur französischen Revolution. Potsdam 1924-26.

Hauge, Hans: Hvad var det ny og det kritiske ved den ny kritik? In *Nyt 17*, Center for Kulturforskning, Aarhus Universitet, Aarhus 1989(a).

Hauge, Hans: R. Rom, romance, roman, romantik. In *Passage*, nr. 6, Aarhus 1989(b).

Hauge, Hans: Før Under og Efter Subjektet. In *Subjektets status*, Aarhus 1990(a).

Hauge, Hans: Historiens vendinger, in *Findes historien – virkelig? Den jyske historiker 50*. Aarhus 1990(b).

Hauser, Arnold: *Kunstens og litteraturens socialhistorie I-II*. Red. Mihail Larsen. København [n.d.]

Hemingway. Hrsg. von Horst Weber (Wege der Forschung, Band 146), Darmstadt 1980.

Hemingway, Ernest: *The Sun Also Rises.* Frogmore 1976.

Hvad er metafysik? Hvad er moderne? Red. af Hans Hauge. Aarhus 1990.

L'Interprétation des textes par Jean Molino, Roger Chartier, Christian Jouhaud, Claude Reichler, Marie-Jeanne Borel, Nicole Loraux, Jean-Michel Adam. Sous la direction de Claude Reichler. Paris 1989.

Ivanov, V.: *Idejno-estetičeskie principy sovetskoj literatury*, Izd. 2, Moskva 1975.

Jakobson, Roman: Linguistics and Poetics, in *Style in Language*, 1960.

Jakobson, Roman: *Elementer, funktioner og strukturer i sproget.* Udvalgte artikler om sprogvidenskab og semiotik. Med indl. af Eli Fischer-Jørgensen. København 1979.

Jameson, Fredric: Postmodernism, or the Cultural Logic of Late Capitalism, in *New Left Review* 146, 1984.

Jameson, Fredric: *The Political Unconscious.* Narrative as a Socially Symbolic Act. Cambridge 1986.

Jameson, Fredric: Afterword – Marxism and Postmodernism, in *Postmodernism Jameson Critique*, 1989.

Jauss, Hans Robert: Literaturgeschichte als Provokation der Literaturwissenschaft, in *Rezeptionsästhetik*, 1975.

Jauss, Hans Robert: *Ästhetische Erfahrung und literarische Hermeneutik.* Band I: Versuche im Feld der ästhetischen Erfahrung. München 1977.

Kant, Immanuel: *Kritik der Urteilskraft.* Hrsg. von Wilhelm Weischedel. [Werkausgabe X]. Frankfurt am M. 1974.

Kellner, Douglas: Jameson, Marxism, and Postmodernism, in *Postmodernism Jameson Critique*, 1989.

Kittang, Atle: Estetikk og poetikk: Supplerande kommentarer. In *EST I, Grunnlagsproblemer i estetisk forskning*, Oslo 1991.

Kjørup, Søren: *Æstetiske Problemer.* En indføring i kunstens filosofi. København 1971.

Kripke, Saul A.: Naming and Necessity, in *Semiotics of Natural*

Language, ed. by Donald Davidson and Gilbert Harman. Dordrecht 1972.

Kulturbegrebets kulturhistorie. Red. af Hans Hauge og Henrik Horstbøll. Aarhus 1988.

Kundera, Milan: *Jacques og hans herre*. Hyldest til Denis Diderot i tre akter. Overs. af Inge og Klaus Rifbjerg. Aarhus 1984.

Kundera, Milan: *L'art du roman*. Essai. Paris 1986(a).

Kundera, Milan: *Romankunsten*. Essay. På dansk ved Eva Andersen og Marie-May Mio Nielsen. København 1986(b).

Kundera, Milan: *L'Immortalité*. Roman. Traduit du tchèque par Eva Bloch. Paris 1990.

Kyndrup, Morten: *Dansk socialistisk litteratur i 70'erne*. København 1980(a).

Kyndrup, Morten: Funktionsanalyse. In *Meddelelser fra Dansklærerforeningen*, 2/1980. København 1980(b).

Kyndrup, Morten: *Æstetik og litteratur*. Aarhus 1982.

Kyndrup, Morten: *Det postmoderne – om betydningens forandring i kunst, litteratur, samfund*. København 1986.

Kyndrup, Morten: Det venstre æg sidder mellem stolene med blottede tænder; det smiler – postmodernisme i litteraturen. In *Vinduet* nr. 2, Oslo 1987.

Kyndrup, Morten: Hvad kan epikken? Den narrative fiktions udfoldelsespotentialer, deres litteraturhistoriske transformationer – og teoriens nøjsomhed. In *Poesien og Romanen*, 1989.

Kyndrup, Morten: Dinesen versus Postmodernism, in *Isak Dinesen. A Reassesment of her Work for the 1990's*, ed. G. Woods. Ottawa 1992.

Kyndrup, Morten and Stæhr, Claus Pico: *Realismebegrebet i den moderne litteraturteoretiske debat I-III*, København 1982.

Lanser, Susan Sniader: *The Narrative Act. Point of View in Prose Fiction*. Princeton 1981.

Lehrstück Lukács. Hrsg. von Jutta Matzner. Beiträge von Cesare Cases, Lucien Goldmann, Alberto Asor Rosa, Agnes Heller, Werner Mittenzwei, Bertolt Brecht, Anna Seghers, Theodor W. Adorno, Gerhard Fehn, Lothar Baier. Frankfurt am M. 1974.

Link, Hannelore: *Rezeptionsforschung*. Eine Einführung in Methoden und Probleme. Stuttgart 1976.

Lukács, Georg: *Die Theorie des Romans. Ein geschichtsphilosophischer Versuch über die Formen der großen Epik*. Berlin 1920.

Lukács, Georg: Erzählen oder Beschreiben, in *Essays über Realismus*, Probleme des Realismus I, Werke Bd. 4, Berlin 1971.

Lukács, Georg: *Essays om realisme* – med modindlæg fra Bloch, Brecht, Eisler, Gotsche, Ottwalt. Red. Henrik Reinvaldt. Bd. 1-2. København 1978.

Lyotard, Jean-François: *Le Différend*. Paris 1983.

Lyotard, Jean-François: *Le Postmoderne expliqué aux enfants*. Paris 1986.

Melberg, Arne: Poetik och estetik. In *EST I, Grunnlagsproblemer i estetisk forskning*, Oslo 1991.

Molino, Jean: Interpréter, in *L'Interprétation des Textes*, 1989.

Neubert, Fritz: Frankreich. In *Handbuch der Literaturwissenschaft*, 1924-26.

Norris, Christopher: *Deconstruction: Theory and Practice*. Lnd. 1982.

Nøjgaard, Morten: Romanens meddelelsessituation. Nogle grundproblemer i romananalyse. In *Romanteori og Romananalyse* 1977.

On Signs. Ed. by Marshall Blonski. Oxford 1985.

Oulipo: *Atlas de littérature potentielle*. Paris 1981.

Oulipo: *La Biblioteque Oulipienne*, vol. I: Preface de Noël Arnaud, vol. II: précédé des Deux Manifestes de Francois le Lionnais. Paris 1987.

Pedersen, John: Georges Perec, den skrivende puslespiller, in *Poesien og romanen*, 1989.

Poesien og Romanen. Akterne fra kollokviet 11. & 12. november 1988 Romansk Institut. Poesien og romanen – former og erkendelsesformer. Teksten og tanken: hvordan er den kunstneriske tekst en tanke vendt mod verden? Udg. af Maryse Lafitte. Københavns Universitet, København 1989.

Postmoderne. Zeichen eines kulturellen Wandels. Andreas Huyssen [and] Klaus R. Scherpe (Hg.). Hamburg 1986.

Postmodernism Jameson Critique. Ed. by Douglas Kellner. Washington, D.C. 1989.

Post-structuralism and the Question of History, ed. by Derek Attridge, Geoff Bennington and Robert Young. Cambridge 1987.

Queneau, Raymond: *Exercises de style*. Paris 1947.

Prendergast, Christopher: *The Order of Mimesis. Balzac, Stendhal, Nerval, Flaubert*. Cambridge 1986.

Reading de Man Reading. Ed. by Lindsay Waters and Wlad Godzich. Minneapolis 1989.

Reconstructing Literature. Ed. by Laurence Lerner. Oxford 1983.

Rezeptionsästhetik. Theorie und Praxis. Hrsg. Rainer Warning. München 1975.

Ricoeur, Paul: *Från text till handling*. En antologi om hermeneutik redigerad av Peter Kemp och Bent Kristensson. Sthm. 1988.

Ricoeur, Paul: Narrated Time, in *A Ricoeur Reader: Reflection and Imagination*. Ed. by Mario J. Valdés. N.Y. 1991.

Riegert, Guy: *Le Père Goriot. Balzac. Analyse critique*. Paris 1973.

Rimmon-Kennan, Shlomith: *Narrative Fiction: Contemporary Poetics*. London 1990.

Romanteori og romananalyse. Red. af Merete Gerlach-Nielsen, Hans Hertel, Morten Nøjgaard. Odense 1977.

Rorty, Richard: *Consequences of Pragmatism*. (Essays: 1972-1980). Brighton 1982.

Rorty, Richard: *Contingency, Irony, and Solidarity*. Cambridge 1989.

Rorty, Richard: *Essays on Heidegger and Others*. Philosophical Papers vol. 2. Cambridge 1991.

Rosen, Robert: Organisms as Causal Systems Which Are Not Mechanisms: An Essay into the Nature of Complexity. In *Theoretical Biology and Complexity*. Three Essays on the Natural Philosophy of Complex Systems. Ed. by Robert Rosen. Orlando 1985.

Rothmann, Kurt: *Erläuterungen und Dokumente. Johann Wolfgang Goethe Die Leiden des jungen Werthers*. Hrsg. von Kurt Rothmann. Rev. Ausg. [RUB 8113 [2]]. Stuttgart 1987.

Russell, Bertrand: *Vestens Filosofi og dens sammenhæng med politi-*

ske og sociale forhold fra før Sokrates til vore dage. Bd. I-II. København 1962.

Sander, Ernst: Nachwort. In Diderot, 1972.

Sanders, Hans: *Institution Literatur und Roman*. Zur Rekonstruktion der Literatursoziologie. Frankfurt am M. 1981.

Schanz, Hans-Jørgen: Det uerfarbares erfaring, in *Th. W. Adorno – og det æstetisk moderne*, 1985.

Schanz, Hans-Jørgen: Pragmatik og tendenser i det 20. århundrede, in *Tendenser – omkring pragmatik, kunst og modernitet*. Aarhus 1988.

Schanz, Hans-Jørgen: Hvad er metafysik? Hvad er moderne?, in *Hvad er metafysik? Hvad er moderne?*, 1990.

Schmidt, Lars-Henrik: *Den sociale excorsisme*. Konstruktion af det sociale hos Rousseau og Nietzsche. Aarhus 1987.

Scholes, Robert: *Semiotics and Interpretation*. New Haven 1982.

Scholes, Robert: *Textual Power*. Literary Theory and the Teaching of English. New Haven 1985.

Scholes, Robert: Les modes de la fiction, in *Théorie des genres* (G. Genette, H.R. Jauss, J.-M. Schaeffer, R. Scholes, W.D. Stempel, K. Viëtor). Paris 1986.

Semiotics of Natural Language, ed. by Donald Davidson and Gilbert Harman. Dordrecht 1972.

Šklovskij, Viktor: *Theorie der Prosa*. Hrsg. und aus dem Russischen übersetzt von Gisela Drohla. Frankfurt am M. 1966.

Šklovskij, Viktor: Konsten som grepp, in *Form och struktur*. Texter till en metodologisk tradition inom litteraturvetenskapen valda av Kurt Aspelin och Bengt A. Lundberg. Sthm. 1971.

Style in Language, ed. T. Sebeok, Cambridge 1960.

Subjektets status. Om subjektfilosofi, metafysik og modernitet. Red. af Hans Hauge. Aarhus 1990.

Sørensen, Peer E.: *Håb og erindring*. Johannes Ewald i Oplysningen. København 1989.

Sučkov, Boris: *Istoričeskie sud'bu realizma*, Izd. 3, dopoln., Moskva 1973

Suhamy, Henri: *La Poétique*. Paris 1986.

Tekst og trope. Dekonstruktion i Amerika. Red. af Lars Erslev Andersen [and] Hans Hauge. Aarhus 1988.

Textual Strategies. Perspectives in Post-Structuralist Criticism. Ed. and with an Introduction by Josué V. Harari. London 1980.

Th. W. Adorno og det æstetisk moderne. Red. af Hans-Jørgen Schanz og Hans Jørgen Thomsen. Aarhus 1985.

'*Theorie der Avantgarde*'. Antworten auf Peter Bürgers Bestimmung von Kunst und bürgerlicher Gesellschaft. Hrsg. von W.Martin Lüdke. Frankfurt am M. 1976.

Todorov, Tzvetan: *La notion de littérature et autres essais*. Paris 1983.

Tygstrup, Frederik: *Erfaringens fiktion*. Essay om romanens form. København 1992.

Ungari, Enzo: *Bertolucci*. Offenburg/Baden 1984.

Warning, Rainer: Opposition und Kasus – zur Leserrolle in Diderots "Jacques le Fataliste et son Maître". In *Rezeptionsästhetik*, 1975.

Watt, Ian: *The Rise of the Novel*. Studies in Defoe, Richardson and Fielding. Harmondsworth 1985 (1957).

Vattimo, Gianni: *Das Ende der Moderne*. Aus dem Italienischen übersetzt und hrsg. von Rafael Capurro. Stuttgart 1990.

Weber, Samuel: *Institution and Interpretation*. Afterword by Wlad Godzich. Minneapolis 1987.

Wellmer, Albrecht: *Zur Dialektik von Moderne und Postmoderne*. Vernunftkritik nach Adorno. Frankfurt am M. 1985.

White, Hayden: *Tropics of Discourse*. Essays in Cultural Criticism. 2nd.pr., Baltimore 1982.

White, Hayden: *The Content of the Form*. Narrative Discourse and Historical Representation. Baltimore 1987.

Woolf, Virginia: An Essay in Criticism, in *Hemingway*, 1980.

Woolf, Virginia: *To the Lighthouse*. London 1988.

Index